Leadership and Cultural Change

Contemporary confluences of leadership decision-making and citizenship behavior often unintentionally contribute to the depletion of the world's resources—escalating health, education, and social crises, as well as community, societal, and cultural struggles—to adapt to emerging global shifts. Leadership and management practices in this context affect the well-being of organizational members (e.g., their safety, health, financial security, etc.) but also entail positive or negative impacts on consumer practices and collective community well-being (e.g., education, obesity, cancer, safe or green driving, energy conservation, diversity based health care, etc.).

Decision-making in most businesses and organizations is largely responsive to demands for short-term profit or cost minimization. On the consumer side, both cultural values and the corporate marketing practices that sustain them encourage high levels of consumption necessary to sustain corporate practices. In exploring the emerging applications of behavior science to these challenges, this book showcases emerging work by internationally recognized scholars on leadership and cultural change. The book will aid organizations and leaders in creating new models of stewardship, and will open opportunities for innovation while adapting and responding to growing social upheaval, technological advances, and environmental concerns, as well as crises in the global economy, health, education, and environment.

This book was originally published in three special issues of the *Journal of Organizational Behavior Management*.

Ramona A. Houmanfar is an Associate Professor and Director of the Behavior Analysis Program at the University of Nevada, Reno, USA. She is the author or co-editor of two books and over sixty other publications; and the editor of the *Journal of Organizational Behavior Management*. Her recent scholarly interests have focused on behavioral systems analysis, rule governance, leadership communication in organizations, and cultural behavior analysis.

Mark A. Mattaini is an Associate Professor Emeritus at Jane Addams College of Social Work, University of Illinois at Chicago, USA, and the President of the Association for Behavior Analysis: International. He is the author or co-editor of eleven books and over ninety other publications. He is the editor of the interdisciplinary journal *Behavior and Social Issues*. His recent scholarship has focused on nonviolent social action supporting peace and justice.

Leadership and Cultural Change

Managing Future Well-Being

Edited by
**Ramona A. Houmanfar and
Mark A. Mattaini**

Routledge
Taylor & Francis Group

LONDON AND NEW YORK

First published 2018 by Routledge

2 Park Square, Milton Park, Abingdon, Oxfordshire OX14 4RN
52 Vanderbilt Avenue, New York, NY 10017

Routledge is an imprint of the Taylor & Francis Group, an informa business

First issued in paperback 2019

British Library Cataloguing in Publication Data
A catalogue record for this book is available from the British Library

ISBN 13: 978-1-138-56061-1 (hbk)
ISBN 13: 978-0-367-89219-7 (pbk)

Typeset in Garamond Light
by RefineCatch Limited, Bungay, Suffolk

Publisher's Note
The publisher accepts responsibility for any inconsistencies that may have
arisen during the conversion of this book from journal articles to book chapters,
namely the possible inclusion of journal terminology.

Disclaimer
Every effort has been made to contact copyright holders for their permission to
reprint material in this book. The publishers would be grateful to hear from any
copyright holder who is not here acknowledged and will undertake to rectify
any errors or omissions in future editions of this book.

Contents

CONTENTS

Citation Information

The following chapters were originally published in various special issues of the *Journal of Organizational Behavior Management*. When citing this material, please use the original page numbering for each article, as follows:

Editorial
Leadership and Cultural Change
Ramona A. Houmanfar and Mark A. Mattaini
Journal of Organizational Behavior Management, volume 35, issue 1–3
(January 2015), pp. 1–3

Chapter 1
Functions of Organizational Leaders in Cultural Change: Financial and Social Well-Being
Ramona A. Houmanfar, Mark P. Alavosius, Zachary H. Morford,
Scott A. Herbst and Daniel Reimer
Journal of Organizational Behavior Management, volume 35, issue 1–3
(January 2015), pp. 4–27

Chapter 2
Leadership and Culture
Jon E. Krapfl and Blina Kruja
Journal of Organizational Behavior Management, volume 35, issue 1–3
(January 2015), pp. 28–43

Chapter 3
Collective Leadership and Circles: Not Invented Here
Mark Mattaini and Casey Holtschneider
Journal of Organizational Behavior Management, volume 37, issue 2
(April 2017), pp. 126–141

Chapter 4
Integrating Organizational-Cultural Values With Performance Management
Carl Binder
Journal of Organizational Behavior Management, volume 36, issue 2–3
(April 2016), pp. 185–201

Chapter 5
Selection of Business Practices in the Midst of Evolving Complexity
Maria E. Malott
Journal of Organizational Behavior Management, volume 36, issue 2–3
(April 2016), pp. 103–122

Chapter 6
*Consumer Behavior Analysis and the Marketing Firm: Bilateral Contingency
in the Context of Environmental Concern*
Gordon R. Foxall
Journal of Organizational Behavior Management, volume 35, issue 1–3
(January 2015), pp. 44–69

Chapter 7
Job Satisfaction: The Management Tool and Leadership Responsibility
Donald A. Hantula
Journal of Organizational Behavior Management, volume 35, issue 1–3
(January 2015), pp. 81–94

Chapter 8
*Seven Life Lessons From Humanistic Behaviorism: How to Bring the
Best Out of Yourself and Others*
E. Scott Geller
Journal of Organizational Behavior Management, volume 35, issue 1–3
(January 2015), pp. 151–170

Chapter 9
*An Industry's Call to Understand the Contingencies Involved in
Process Safety: Normalization of Deviance*
Kevin Bogard, Timothy D. Ludwig, Chris Staats and Danielle Kretschmer
Journal of Organizational Behavior Management, volume 35, issue 1–3
(January 2015), pp. 70–80

Chapter 10
*Leadership and Crew Resource Management in High-Reliability Organizations:
A Competency Framework for Measuring Behaviors*
Mark P. Alavosius, Ramona A. Houmanfar, Steven J. Anbro, Kenneth Burleigh
and Christopher Hebein
Journal of Organizational Behavior Management, volume 37, issue 2
(April 2017), pp. 142–170

Chapter 11
Behavioral Education in the 21st Century
Kent Johnson
Journal of Organizational Behavior Management, volume 35,
issue 1–3 (January 2015), pp. 135–150

For any permission-related enquiries please visit:
http://www.tandfonline.com/page/help/permissions

Notes on Contributors

Mark P. Alavosius is the President and CEO of Praxis[2], and a Graduate Faculty in the Behavior Analysis Program at the University of Nevada, Reno, USA.

Steven J. Anbro is a doctoral student at the University of Nevada, Reno, USA. His general area of interest is the application of the principles of behavior science to professional groups, particularly large organizations.

Timothy Baker is Associate Professor in the Department of Internal Medicine and Associate Dean for Medical Education at the University of Nevada, Reno School of Medicine, USA.

Carl Binder is Co-Founder of The Performance Thinking Network, USA.

Kevin Bogard is Refining Operations Manager at Marathon Petroleum Company.

Kenneth Burleigh is a doctoral student at the University of Nevada, Reno, USA. His research interests include change management, rule-governed behavior relating to bureaucratic improvement, Performance Management, and behavioral safety.

Gordon R. Foxall is Distinguished Research Professor at Cardiff Business School, Cardiff University, UK, where he is responsible for research in Consumer Behavior Analysis and the Marketing Firm. He is also Visiting Professor of Economic Psychology at the University of Durham, UK.

E. Scott Geller is Alumni Distinguished Professor at Virginia Tech, USA, and Director of the Center for Applied Behavior Systems in the Department of Psychology.

R. Kevin Grigsby is Senior Director of Leadership and Talent Development at the Association of American Medical Colleges, USA.

Jennifer Hagen is the Associate Dean for Faculty Development and Professor of Internal Medicine at the University of Nevada, Reno School of Medicine, USA.

Donald A. Hantula directs the Decision Making laboratory at Temple University, USA. He specializes in organizational behavior and evolutionary behavioral economics. His work combines behavior analytic, economic, and evolutionary theories to explore the ways in which we adapt to a complex and uncertain world.

Christopher Hebein is a doctoral student at the University of Nevada, Reno, USA. His research interests include leadership, human performance, consulting, and organizational behavior management.

Scott A. Herbst is the lead consultant and Founder of SixFlex Training and Consulting. He earned his PhD in Psychology at the University of Nevada, Reno, USA, with a focus on Behavior Analysis.

Casey Holtschneider is an Assistant Professor at the Social Work faculty of NEIU, USA and Executive Director, the LYTE Collective, Chicago, USA. Her areas of expertise include youth homelessness, youth development, clinical practice with youth who have experienced trauma, and qualitative research methods.

Ramona A. Houmanfar is an Associate Professor and Director of the Behavior Analysis Program at the University of Nevada, Reno, USA. She is also the editor of the *Journal of Organizational Behavior Management*.

Nicole Jacobs is a Clinical Psychologist, Associate Professor in the Department of Psychiatry and Behavioral Sciences, and Associate Dean of Diversity and Inclusion at University of Nevada, Reno School of Medicine, USA.

Kent Johnson founded Morningside Academy, USA, and currently serves as its Executive Director. He has published many seminal papers and books about research-based curriculum and teaching methods.

Jon E. Krapfl was Associate Dean and Chief Operating Officer of the Mason School of Business at the College of William & Mary, USA, before he retired in 2012. His primary interests have been in business strategy, business cultures, leadership, and instruction in higher education.

Danielle Kretschmer works at Marathon Petroleum Corporation after completing the Industrial-Organizational Psychology and Human Resource Management program at Appalachian State University, USA.

Judith L. Komaki is Professor of Psychology at City University of New York, USA.

Blina Kruja is a M.Sc. candidate in Life Science Economics and Policy at the Technical University of Munich, Germany.

Timothy D. Ludwig is a Professor at the Department of Psychology, Appalachian State University, USA. He is currently serving as editor of the *Journal of Organizational Behavior Management*.

Maria E. Malott is CEO of the Association for Behavior Analysis. She has experience in consulting and has consulted in areas of advertising, restaurants, retail, manufacturing, hotels, banking, government, and other institutions.

Mark A. Mattaini is an Associate Professor Emeritus at Jane Addams College of Social Work, University of Illinois at Chicago, USA, and the President of the Association for Behavior Analysis: International. He is also the editor of the journal *Behavior and Social Issues*.

Michelle L. R. Minnich earned her PhD in Industrial/Organisational Psychology at City University of New York, USA.

Zachary H. Morford is a teacher at Koan School, USA. He earned his PhD in Psychology from the University of Nevada, Reno, USA in 2015.

Martha Pelaez is a Frost Professor at the College of Education, Florida International University, USA. Research interests include adult intelligence and derived relational responding, behavioral systems approach to child development and morality and rule-governed behavior.

Melissa Piasecki is the Executive Associate Dean, Senior Associate Dean for Academic Affairs, and Professor of Psychiatry at University of Nevada, Reno School of Medicine, USA.

Daniel Reimer earned his PhD in Psychology at the University of Nevada, Reno, USA, with a focus on Behavior Analysis.

Douglas L. Robertson is Dean of Undergraduate Education and Professor of Higher Education, Florida International University, USA.

Thomas Schwenk is Dean of the University of Nevada, Reno School of Medicine, USA, and Vice-President of the Division of Health Sciences.

Gwen Shonkwiler is the Director of Evaluation and Assessment in the Office of Medical Education at the University of Nevada, Reno School of Medicine, USA.

Gregory S. Smith is the Research Program Coordinator in the Office of Academic Affairs at University of Nevada, Reno School of Medicine, USA. He earned his PhD in Psychology at the University of Nevada, Reno, USA, with a focus on Behavior Analysis.

Chris Staats is ES&S Manager at Marathon Petroleum Corporation.

INTRODUCTION

Leadership and Cultural Change

Last May, the Association for Behavior Analysis International hosted the Seminar on Leadership and Culture Change. This special selection of presentations, beginning the day before the 40th annual convention and continuing as an organized set of talks during the Saturday and Sunday sessions, was intended to help leaders promote socially significant practices in their organizations and to encourage additional behavioral research in this area.

Focusing on how behavior analysis finds common ground with other sciences by investigating the behavior of leaders—as well as the potential for collaborative research among academic groups, businesses, and communities—this seminar was divided into three subject-specific modules: organizations and the private sector, educational settings, and leadership and cultural change efforts in the field of behavior analysis. Due to the popularity of the program content, articles based on the seminar presentations were invited for publication in the *Journal of Organizational Behavior Management* and *The Behavior Analyst*.

We thank program committee co-chairs, Mark Alavosius and Timothy Ludwig, for their outstanding leadership and contribution to the planning and implementation of the seminar. In addition, the leadership seminar program committee worked with coordinators for the Community Interventions, Social and Ethical Issues, and Organizational Behavior Management program tracks, who provided support, dissemination, and funding to assist in integrating the seminar with the annual convention. Special thanks to the Organizational Behavior Management Network for providing additional support. Finally, we are also grateful for the assistance and hard work of the Association for Behavior Analysis International team, both on site and in the office.

Seminar speakers demonstrated how behavior analysis offers a powerful technology for shaping the world; social leaders were shown how a science of behavior can enhance the safety, ethicality, and effectiveness of organizations and institutions; and behavior analysts were challenged to adapt to an ever-shifting cultural landscape and to turn their knowledge and skills into actions that could influence and improve social institutions.

Social responsibility served as a unifying theme throughout the presentations and the articles selected for this special issue of the *Journal of Organizational Behavior Management*. Social outcomes loom as key features of leadership decision making and citizenship behavior as the world's resources are depleted, health and education crises increase, and communities, societies, and cultures adapt to a new context. Social significance in this context not only relates to leadership and management practices that affect the well-being of organizational members (e.g., their safety, health, financial security) but also has a positive or negative impact on consumer practices and community well-being (e.g., education, obesity, cancer, safe or green driving, energy conservation, diversity-based health care). Leadership decisions within organizations that are oriented toward local outcomes also in many cases may have a profound impact at larger scales. Corporate decisions, for example, have often been made without adequate attention to externalities—the costs of those decisions that are paid by others. The struggles associated with the imminent need to reduce carbon emissions to a level that will prevent runaway global warming is one good example. Decision making in the businesses involved is largely responsive to the demand for short-term profit; externalities like carbon emissions that do not contribute to profit are often not among the immediate contingencies that shape those decisions. On the consumer side, both cultural values and the corporate marketing practices that sustain them encourage the high levels of consumption necessary to sustain corporate practices. On neither side, therefore, are values associated with sustainability, and ultimately cultural and human survival, integrated adequately into the associated decisions and practices. There is a genuine dilemma present here; networks of interlocking behavioral contingencies shaping and sustaining the actions of organizational leaders (whether in the for-profit or other sectors) support present systemic arrangements. Leaders can no more step outside contingency arrangements than can anyone else; as a result it appears that different contingencies, including some arranged by systems outside of existing sets of interlocking behavioral contingencies, are likely to be required to shift leadership practices. Behavioral systems are open systems, however; this is where the hope lies. Behavior analysis in collaboration with other concerned disciplines and groups may have the potential to contribute to the design of new repertoires and contingency arrangements consistent with survival and nurturing values.

Similar analyses can be made regarding highly probable impending crises regarding water resources, failing justice and corrections system, dangerous income and asset disparities, human rights violations, and global violence. As the noted activist physician Paul Farmer notes, although many of these issues have the potential to affect everyone over time, many are already resulting in excess mortality, disease, and basic rights violations for those in the most disadvantaged areas in the world, including what have been called the "sacrifice zones" in the United States. These effects, externalities of existing structural arrangements that often offer short-term advantages to others, thereby constitute "structural violence" (Farmer, 2013, p. 150). When the challenges faced are of this scope, and current cultural systems are so poorly prepared to deal with them, advancing behavioral systems science supporting values of survival, justice, and caring seems worth a considerable investment. Given the limited work in these areas thus far, a shift toward priorities guided by such values will also require different kind of leadership practices within the behavior analysis discipline itself.

In order to explore the emerging applications of behavior science to these challenges (and to serve as an establishing operation for the expansion of such efforts), forthcoming special issues of the *Journal of Organizational Behavior Management* will showcase current scholarly work on leadership and cultural change. The selected articles will aid organizations and leaders in creating new models of stewardship and open up opportunities for innovation while adjusting to growing social upheaval, technological advances, and environmental concerns, as well as crises in the global economy, health, education, and environment. They will also address the potential of how collaborative research among academic groups, businesses, and communities can affect the well-being of populations and forestall crises. The limited current extent of such collaboration in areas of social significance, and the narrowness of focus that has often been present in work that has been done, clearly needs to be shifted. The promise of making a genuine impact on the world that initially brings so many young people to the field is now an urgent need, and one that we cannot meet alone. Leadership repertoires that support extensive and effective collaboration, establish marketing efforts for practices directed toward survival values, and encourage expansion of behavioral systems research directed toward our most pressing challenges are critical priorities for the global community, and for behavior analysis, over the next several decades. We need to be at the table, or supporting those who are. The present set of articles offers an encouraging start.

Ramona A. Houmanfar
Mark A. Mattaini

REFERENCE

Farmer, P. (2013). *Repairing the world*. Berkeley: University of California Press.

Functions of Organizational Leaders in Cultural Change: Financial and Social Well-Being

RAMONA A. HOUMANFAR

MARK P. ALAVOSIUS

ZACHARY H. MORFORD

SCOTT A. HERBST

DANIEL REIMER

Social responsibility looms as a key feature of leadership decision making and citizenship behavior as the world's resources are depleted, health and education crises increase, and communities, societies, and cultures adapt to a new context shaped by emerging technologies, political upheavals, global warming, and other drivers of behavior change. In this article we call for future work in behavior analysis, emphasizing the importance of organizational leaders' decision-making behaviors in establishing organizational practices that support prosocial behavior and eliminate aversive conditions within cultural systems. The discussion expands on recent behavior analytic literature on cultural change and leadership behavior by first providing a summary of popular definitions of human well-being and relating this concept to prosocial behavior. By drawing upon these definitions, we then summarize the behavior analytic concepts of metacontingencies and macrocontingencies as a framework from which behavior analysts can continue work to promote prosocial behavior and human well-being writ large.

A plethora of books and articles describe the potential for a science of behavior to resolve larger societal issues. Skinner's accounts of behavior in *The Behavior of Organisms* (1938) and *Walden Two* (1948) are notable, as these lay out the conceptual groundwork for cultural analyses and provide a description of a utopian community designed to promote and sustain residents' well-being. *Walden Two* is a novel describing how the science of behavior could be applied to the design of communities and culture and reveals much about Skinner's conception of a good life. Before the start of either of the first two journals in behavior analysis, the *Journal of the Experimental Analysis of Behavior* and the *Journal of Applied Behavior Analysis,* Skinner imagined the grander possibilities of this science. Skinner continued to write on this subject throughout his career, reiterating with a profound steadfastness the global outcomes to which this science can contribute (Skinner, 1948, 1953/1965, 1987, 1971/1990).

As a number of scholars in behavior analysis suggest (Alavosius & Mattaini, 2011; Alavosius, Newsome, Houmanfar, & Biglan, in press; Biglan, 2009; Biglan & Glenn, 2013; Glenn, 1988; Glenn & Malott, 2004; Houmanfar, Rodrigues, & Ward, 2010; Malott & Glenn, 2006; Mattaini, 2013), the science of behavior has reached a point where we can contribute to cultural change by supporting social actions by individuals in positions of power and creating behavioral technologies that promote human well-being. Socially significant leadership in this context not only relates to leaders' actions and management practices that affect the well-being of organizational members (e.g., their safety, health, financial security) but also has a positive or negative impact on consumer practices and community well-being (e.g., education, obesity, cancer, safe or green driving, energy conservation, diversity-based health care). Social responsibility is not new ground for behavior analysts to consider. Wolf (1978) and Hawkins (1991) explore social validity and functional assessment of the societal importance of the goals, technologies, procedures, and impacts achieved by applications of behavior analysis. Their analyses consider the social validity of interventions applied to help special needs populations and provide a framework to consider the impact of behavior science on larger social issues. Many published research reports of applied behavior analysis across settings and populations include consideration of social validity. It has been a defining dimension of applied behavior analysis (Baer, Wolf, & Risley, 1968) since the start.

In this article we expand on recent behavior analytic literature on cultural change and leadership behavior by first providing a summary of popular definitions of human well-being and relating this concept to Biglan and Glenn's (2013) notion of prosocial behavior. We then summarize the behavior analytic concepts of metacontingencies and macrocontingencies within the context of the obesity epidemic as a framework from which behavior analysts can continue work to promote prosocial behavior and human well-being writ large. We chose obesity as an example as the problem is global, involves consumptive behavior influenced by corporate actions, and is illustrative of problems requiring cultural change. Lastly, we call for future work in behavior analysis, emphasizing the importance of organizational leaders' decision-making behaviors in establishing organizational practices that support prosocial behavior and eliminate aversive conditions within cultural systems.

WELL-BEING: A DEFINITION

Human well-being is admittedly a nebulous concept and relates to other words (e.g., *happiness* and *prosperity*) describing positive aspects of human existence. For example, *Merriam-Webster's Dictionary* (n.d.) defines *well-being* as "the state of being happy, healthy, or prosperous." A number of national and international reports attempt to measure human well-being. Helliwell, Layard, and Sachs (2013) edited the most recent publication of the *World Happiness Report,* in which they summarize national happiness data from 156 countries, describe the benefits of well-being, and suggest the most significant detractors from human well-being (to which we refer later). Similarly, a Gallup (2014) report evaluates the well-being of all 50 U.S. states based on six criteria—life evaluation, emotional health, work environment, physical health, healthy behaviors, and basic access. All six categories are measured via self-report. For example, life evaluation is measured by comparing one's current life circumstances to what one expects to occur in 5 years, and emotional health is measured by asking questions regarding the quality of one's daily experiences. The Organisation for Economic Co-operation and Development (OECD; 2013) describes guidelines for measuring *subjective well-being,* which is defined as "good mental states, including all of the various evaluations, positive and negative, that people make of their lives, and the affective reactions of people to their experiences" (p. 29). Although this definition initially appears extremely vague, it can be broken down into behavior analytic concepts. The OECD goes on to clarify that the three defining elements of subjective well-being are life evaluation, affect, and eudaimonia. The first element, life evaluation, refers to both the term *subjective* and the reference to evaluations in the official definition.

According to the OECD, life evaluations "capture a reflective assessment on a person's life or some specific aspect of it" (p. 30). That is, they refer to one's verbal behavior describing one's experiences. A number of approaches in behavior analysis have focused on one's evaluative life statements and how these might assess well-being. Wolf (1978) somewhat reluctantly includes self-evaluation in his discussion of social validity and acknowledges that these data are admittedly suspect but nevertheless important to evaluating behavior change efforts. Hawkins (1991) encourages more functional assessments by including the perspectives of significant others (family members, organizational members, community members, etc.) in determining whether behavior change is socially meaningful. Hawkins's discussion expands Wolf's perspective to invite input from important members of the client's community and set the stage for even broader vantage points on measuring the benefits and costs of behavior change efforts.

Verbal reports of well-being are to be interpreted with caution, as perceptions of subjective experiences are difficult to anchor to objective measures of social benefit. Besides the difficulty in interpreting verbal reports as indicators of social well-being, language complicates behavior change efforts that might be used to advance cultural changes. The language we use to describe our behavior, goals, values, and more alters the motivating effects of consequences we might encounter. We do not respond to the contingencies alone; we also respond to the rules we use to describe those contingencies. Acceptance and commitment therapy (ACT) is a behavior clinical treatment rooted in behavior analysis for situations in which one's developed verbal repertoire prevents one from contacting, or interferes with, direct contingencies operating in the environment (Hayes, Luoma, Bond, Masuda, & Lillis, 2006; Hayes, Strosahl, & Wilson, 1999). The primary focus of ACT is to eliminate the stimulus control of one's verbal behavior over one's nonverbal behavior such that one's nonverbal behavior can interact directly, and effectively, with naturally occurring contingencies.

ACT studies specific to organizational settings have come about in the past decade and tend to be referred to as ACTraining because of differing populations and techniques (Bond, Hayes, & Barnes-Holmes, 2006; Hayes, Bunting, Herbst, Bond, & Barnes-Holmes, 2006). Research with ACTraining demonstrated the effectiveness of exercises that target values clarification, mindfulness, cognitive flexibility, and perspective taking. So these address behaviors important to more than a business's bottom line by focusing on socially important behavioral events that when improved also aid the business. To date, ACTraining studies have improved mental health and innovation (Bond & Bunce, 2000); reduced stigma, stress, and burnout (Brinkborg, Michanek, Hesser, & Berglund, 2011; Hayes, Masuda, Bissett, & Guerrero, 2004); reduced absenteeism (Bond, Flaxman, & Bunce, 2008); and improved college performance (Chase et al., 2013).

The second element of subjective well-being, affect, is defined by the OECD as a person's feelings, and as it contributes to human well-being, the OECD considers both positive and negative affect. Although this is a vague definition, feelings have been subjected to behavior analytic theoretical analyses. Layng (2006) distinguishes between emotions and emotional behavior. He discusses emotions as private events that indicate the operation of particular contingency arrangements. For example, the underlying contingency of one's description of fear and anger is similar—distancing oneself from an event or object (Layng, 2006). The distinction between fear and anger then resides in the behavior that functions to produce that greater distance, even though the underlying contingency remains the same. Similarly, Layng (2006) argues that "basic 'positive' emotions may . . . be described as contingencies involving nearing relations . . . achieved by either bringing oneself closer to an event or object, or by bringing the event or object closer to the individual" (p. 158). Thus, if we consider affect from a behavior analytic perspective, we can define it as a private event indicative of particular sets of contingencies operating at any given point in time.

Eudaimonia, the last element of well-being, is defined as "a sense of meaning and purpose in life, or good psychological functioning" (Helliwell et al., 2013, p. 113). The OECD (2013) states that eudaimonia implies maximizing an individual's potential while also admitting that eudaimonia is conceptually vague. Although even less clear than the other two concepts, eudaimonia might be thought of in two possible ways from a behavior analytic perspective: the relative absence of coercion and optimal freedom to choose. Behavior analysts have long written about the prevalence of coercive cultural systems and how they detract from human well-being (see Sidman, 1989; Skinner, 1987). As Sidman (1989) states, "Coercion is not the root of all evil, but until we adopt other than coercive ways to control each other's conduct, no method of physically improving our species will keep our survival timer from running out" (p. ix). Choice, behavior analytically speaking, simply refers to situations in which organisms may allocate responding to one of multiple possible options (Fisher & Mazur, 1997). A limited number of behavior analytic studies have demonstrated that animals and humans prefer situations in which more options are available to those situations in which fewer options are available (Catania, 1975; Karsina, Thompson, & Rodriguez, 2011; Ono, 2000, 2004; Suzuki, 1997, 2000). However, others have shown that the presence of too many options tends to be less preferable (Schwartz, 2004) and that people tend to take longer to make decisions, or fail to make them at all, given too many options from which to choose. Thus, we argue that eudaimonia is related to optimal freedom to choose—that is, the point at which preference for a particular number of options is determined in relation to fewer options while response rate and response latency are not significantly impacted. In conclusion then, we can define boundaries that depict the level of human well-being in terms of the following:

1. One's verbal behavior with respect to one's other behavior and environment
2. The sets of direct acting contingencies operating in one's environment
3. The level of coercive control in one's environment
4. The degree to which individuals have an optimal level of choice

PROSOCIAL BEHAVIOR

Biglan and Glenn (2013) provide a definition of *prosocial behavior* as "any belief, attitude, or behavior that contributes positively to others and/or to society as a whole" (p. 7). Very briefly, we can consider *beliefs* and *attitudes* as words describing, respectively, one's verbal behavior or general behavioral characteristics (i.e., *attitude* seems to encompass more than verbal behavior). Thus, this definition can simplify to mean any behavior, verbal or nonverbal, that contributes to the well-being of others and/or to society as a whole. Thus, prosocial behavior would include any behavior that

1. Operates in the context of positive reinforcement contingencies for others
2. Minimizes aversive or coercive conditions and the contingencies of others while not explicitly operating as *part* of those conditions or contingencies
3. Aids others in identifying or achieving optimal levels of choice

INCREASING HUMAN WELL-BEING: A BEHAVIORAL SYSTEMS PERSPECTIVE

Biglan and Glenn (2013) offer a number of utilitarian suggestions for improving human well-being, including reducing toxic and aversive conditions, reinforcing prosocial behavior, teaching and promoting prosocial norms and values, setting limits on opportunities for problem behavior, and promoting psychological flexibility. Each of these suggestions rests on changing the behavior of individuals such that change leads to measurable improvements for others. However, larger scale applications are needed if behavior analysts are to help achieve the larger outcomes required to address problems confronting humanity in today's world. One example of health-related practices that directly relates to individuals' well-being is obesity. The economy of the United States has already experienced the overwhelming costs associated with obesity, with predictions that more and more money will be spent on dealing with the direct and indirect outcomes of being overweight and obese in the future.

An analysis of the burden of obesity internationally estimated that around 1 to 7% of the total health care costs of a country is spent treating the direct or indirect outcomes of obesity (Finkelstein, Fiebelkorn, & Wang,

2009; Withrow & Alter, 2011). Estimates for the United States specifically are approximated from a 12% increase, or $51.6 billion annually (Forman, Butryn, Hoffman, & Herbert, 2009), to $66 billion (Wang, McPherson, Marsh, Gortmaker, & Brown, 2011) to as high as $75 billion annually (Finkelstein et al., 2009) attributable to direct costs of obesity. The cost is mostly attributed to increased medical expenses from comorbidities such as heart disease and diabetes, though it is difficult to accurately calculate because of the many mediating factors (Wang et al., 2011). These estimates are only in terms of direct costs of obesity. There are also indirect costs that have been calculated for the effect of overweight and obesity on society. For example, costs associated with a loss in work productivity are estimated to be as high as $580 billion annually (Finkelstein, DiBonaventura, Burgess, & Hale, 2010). Similarly, Wang et al. (2011) utilized estimates of incremental workdays lost, the cost of absenteeism, and the cost of presenteeism for individuals with a high body mass index, which they based off the 2008 National Health and Wellness Survey, and determined that the loss of productivity in the United States due to obesity was between $390 and $580 billion.

Decline in childhood obesity rates in recent years and the large-scale initiatives that brought about the decline demonstrate the powerful impact of large-scale interventions. Specifically, among children ages 2–5, 14% were obese in 2004. That had dropped to 8% by 2013 (Ogdon, Caroll, Kit, & Flegal, 2014). These data are based on a report from the Centers for Disease Control and Prevention. According to Ogdon et al. (2014), likely factors contributing to this important drop included general heightened awareness, changes in Supplemental Nutrition Assistance Program (food stamp) regulations, and high-profile individuals (New York mayor Michael Bloomberg and Michelle Obama) lending their status to the cause.

Behavioral interventions have offered pragmatic solutions to weight loss and weight control as related to personal health and well-being, quality of life, wellness, and longevity. The following sections provide an overview of the behavior analytic literature focusing on behavioral as well as cultural interventions associated with weight loss.

Behavioral Interventions

The initial behavioral study on weight loss (Ferster, Nurnberger, & Levitt, 1962), as well as seminal publications immediately following it (Foreyt & Goodrick, 1993; Stuart, 1971; Stunkard, 1975), attributed overweight and obesity to an excess in behavior, namely, eating. This behavior was believed to be controlled by certain environmental cues. Thus, behavioral interventions were based on reducing the stimulus control on overeating behavior. There are a number of strategies typically utilized in behaviorally based weight loss interventions: self-monitoring, stimulus control, contingency management, and changing behavior parameters (Foreyt & Goodrick, 1993).

For example, in a recent study conducted by Hausman, Borrero, Fisher, and Kahng (2014) a group of nine undergraduate students were taught to accurately discriminate portion sizes correctly using stimulus equivalence training. The results suggested that accurate portion estimation has an effect on consumption and that education and training could reduce overconsumption of calories by selecting food portions. Discrimination training is an important educative component of better eating habits, making individuals more aware of the number of calories consumed. The study also found that the students were able to successfully generalize this behavior to novel foods, and a majority could still accurately estimate portion sizes during follow-up sessions.

Many behavioral interventions also include contingency management, typically in the form of monetary or tangible rewards. Washington, Banna, and Gibson (2014) enlisted 11 adults to wear Fitbit accelerometers for 3 weeks. Participants earned the opportunity to receive a prize (lottery-style) based on their physical activity. Percentile schedules were utilized to determine the prize-draw criteria, increasing the physical activity required to obtain participants' goal each day. The results showed participants increasing the number of minutes they were active per day as well as decreasing the latency between each bout of activity. Similarly, De Luca and Holborn (1992) implemented a variable-ratio reinforcement schedule with a changing criterion design with a group of preteen boys. The boys were given access to a stationary bike and told to exercise as long as they would like. During the treatment phase, each was rewarded with a point on a variable-ratio schedule for the number of rotations of the stationary bike wheel. Response rates were high for both the participants who were not obese and those who were. Though weight loss results were not specified, it was reported that one of the participants dropped four pant sizes over the course of the study.

Changing behavioral parameters, or directly altering target behavior topology (Foreyt & Goodrick, 1993), such as altering high-frequency behavior to incorporate physical activity, can be demonstrated through the concept of exergaming. Exergaming is the integration of physical activity into video games, capitalizing on the reinforcing effects of video games to promote physical activity. Multiple studies (Fogel, Miltenberger, Graves, & Koehler, 2010; Shayne, Fogel, Miltenberger, & Koehler, 2012; Van Camp & Hayes, 2012) have demonstrated that when the topography required to play a video game is altered (e.g., instead of pressing a button to move a character, the gamer must mime walking or alternate pressing sensors with their feet), there is a marked increase in physical activity compared to traditional video game play and compared to other forms of physical education interventions.

In short, the literature on behavioral interventions associated with obesity demonstrates an effective impact of the associated technologies on weight control at the behavioral level. However, the issues are global and require large-scale multifaceted solutions. It is not enough to design contingencies for an individual or even a single family. Lydon, Rohmeier, Yi, Mattaini, and Williams (2011) provide an elaborate overview of the health-related side effects associated with fast food consumption and offer potential solutions regarding altering the locations of fast food restaurants (i.e., rezoning) to combat obesity. The authors' discussion includes suggestions for systematic environmental engineering of neighborhoods such that the food items that are more readily available in neighborhoods are the ones likely to produce healthier, better balanced meals. The concept of rezoning is one way in which the leaders within a group or organization can promote change in the eating practices of consumers.

Cultural Behavior Analysis

Within behavior analysis several conceptual frameworks have been proposed from which one might draw in order to enact improvements in human well-being at large and obesity in particular. One of these is Glenn's (2004) conceptualization of culture and cultural practices more generally. The term *macrobehavior* is one that Glenn (2004) uses to refer to cultural practices. The macrobehavior of unhealthy eating involves the operant behavior of multiple individuals that together has a cumulative effect on the environment (i.e., an increased incidence and prevalence of obesity).

Glenn (2004) describes two kinds of contingencies: metacontingencies and macrocontingencies. The latter describe topographically similar behaviors in macrobehavior that operate independently of one another. For example, two neighbors who do not know each other eat unhealthy food on a routine basis. The cumulative effect of eating this food is to increase the cumulative amount of weight gain and likelihood of obesity prevalence across the community in the future.

Metacontingencies, however, describe selective contingencies that operate on interlocked patterns of behavior between one or more persons or groups of persons. When the behavior of one person (e.g., the salesperson in a fast food franchise) becomes interlocked with (i.e., dependent on) the behavior of another, a pattern of behavior emerges that Glenn (2004) describes as *interlocking behavioral contingencies* (IBCs). IBCs, when they occur, have a measureable effect on the aggregate outcome (e.g., hundreds of processed food items sold per day) and on the environment (an increased incidence and prevalence of obesity).

Glenn's perspective holds that cultural practices are composed of cumulative, non-interlocking behaviors that can vary in complexity from the cumulative fast food consumption of several individuals to the cumulative IBCs of workers in several fast food franchises producing fast food (Glenn, 2004, p. 140). Although the IBCs of organized entities (e.g., fast food franchises) may be maintained by a metacontingency, cumulative IBCs of a particular type (e.g., food manufacturers operating in relative isolation across a country) may prompt macrobehavior (e.g., unhealthy eating) and, hence, a cultural practice. When macrobehavior generates a cumulative product (e.g., cancer, diabetes, obesity), the relation between the two is called a *macrocontingency* (Glenn, 2004; Malott & Glenn, 2006).

Externalities and Cultural Behavior Analysis

Biglan introduced the economic concept of externality to the readers of the *Journal of Organizational Behavior Management* in 2009. Externality refers to "a cost imposed on society by the production or marketing of a good or service that the price charged for that good or service does not reflect" (Biglan, 2009, pp. 215–216). Organizational products that are potentially unhealthy yet are marketed as having good nutritional value can be considered externalities of the food industry (Brown & Houmanfar, 2015).

Among the factors preventing many organizational leaders from changing an organizational product (e.g., unhealthy to healthy food) are the size and complexity of the organization as well as the immediate adverse consequences, such as the cost associated with the investment in new products (Brown & Houmanfar, in press). The size and complexity (number of units and levels of hierarchy) of organizations affect their adaptability to environmental demands (Bar-Yam, 1997; Glenn & Malott, 2004). More specifically, as size and complexity increase, the level of adaptability decreases. Brown and Houmanfar (in press) also discussed the potential for the immediate consequence of higher cost associated with the adoption of new organizational practices (e.g., the design and production of a new product line) overshadowing the delayed positive consequences (e.g., healthy consumer choice, healthy eating practices of consumers, a decrease in obesity). Delay discounting is a ubiquitous characteristic of human behavior in choice situations, and stable patterns are seen in which people favor immediate rewards over those that are delayed but more valued. Decision making occurs as "the process by which future events are subjectively devalued by the decision maker" (Madden & Bickel, 2010, p. 3). The behaviors of consumers choosing immediate reinforcers over delayed but more significant ones are similar to those of organizational leaders acting to acquire immediate short-term profits over larger more delayed ones. Research (Kahneman & Tversky, 1979; Weatherly, Plumm, & Derenne, 2011) suggests that discounting is affected by how choices are labeled or framed and points to the language people use to present how choices can be crafted to nudge decisions toward various options. The popular book *Nudge* (Thaler & Sunstein, 2009) provides numerous examples of how relatively simple adjustments in antecedents can lead people to choices that better support their well-being.

A PROSOCIAL APPROACH TO CULTURAL CHANGE: FUNCTIONS OF ORGANIZATIONAL LEADERS

By drawing on our earlier definition of prosocial behavior as (a) operating in the context of positive reinforcement contingencies for others, (b) minimizing aversive or coercive conditions and contingencies of others while not explicitly operating as *part* of those conditions or contingencies, and (c) aiding others in identifying or achieving optimal levels or choice, let us turn our discussion to the role of organizational leaders in changing cultural practices outside and inside of organizations.

Houmanfar, Rodrigues, and Smith (2009) describe how the role of organizational leaders as a source for rule governance applies to the utility of the metacontingency as a guiding unit for cultural interventions. Rules are critical to the governance that affects consumption and sustains community resources (McGinnis & Ostrom, 2008; Ostrom, 1990) and are accounted for in the most recent conceptualization of the metacontingency. Residents of many communities do not have easy access to healthy food. Their neighborhoods are labeled *food deserts* with only processed and packaged food sold in local convenience stores. Their choices are restricted by the policies of community leaders and corporate directors that determine which food products are stocked on the shelves. The latest variation of the metacontingency consists of five terms: *cultural-organizational milieu, Socio-Interlocked Behaviors [socio-IBs], aggregate product, consumer practices,* and *group rule generation* (Houmanfar et al., 2010). The cultural-organizational milieu (factors such as resources, cultural practices, and societal infrastructure) includes all antecedent factors in the context in which an organization operates. Both factors external to the organization (such as resources, cultural practices, advocacy, and societal infrastructure) as well as internal factors of the organization itself (such as its resources and practices and infrastructure) define the context for the cultural-organizational milieu.

An aggregate product is a good (e.g., processed food) or service delivered by an organization (e.g., weight loss programs), created by the socio-IBs (coordinated behaviors of many employees) of the organizations, and not reducible to the behavioral level. Multiple, unique, and reoccurring behaviors are responsible for the good or service, and the good or service cannot be reduced to the behavior of an individual. In short, the interlocking socio-IBs (coordinated behavior of food manufacturing workers) in an organization contribute to the aggregate products (e.g., processed food) that are acquired by a receiving system (grocery shoppers). The receiving system is the consumer receiving the goods (e.g., processed food) or services (weight loss programs) that are produced by the socio-IBs.

The aggregate product (e.g., fast food) is consumed by individuals interacting with the product but not necessarily interacting with one another. The consumer side of an organization has been largely ignored within behavior analysis. Fortunately, a few ideas about this area lay substantial groundwork for an advanced analysis of consumer behavior (e.g., Foxall, 1999, 2001, 2010, 2015/this issue; Hantula, DiClemente, & Rajala, 2001). Most consumer research disregards the effect of the consumer setting on behavior and is often not grounded in empirically demonstrated principles. Behavior scientists working in economics would benefit from empirical explorations of consumer behavior, particularly in the areas of choice and alternative selections.

In their role as guides, leaders create new verbal relations between the current and future states of the organization, between the future organization and its niche in the future environment, and between current employees and the future organization (Houmanfar et al., 2009). Alavosius et al. (in press) note that many organizational leaders either ignore or, worse, mask the negative side effects of their production and supply chains from consumers and in so doing maintain historical practices. Examples in the food industry, the fashion/garment industry, and computer manufacturing have made headline news and reveal the efforts by some leaders to camouflage externalities associated with their organizations so that profits are valued above community health. For more positive examples, organizational and community leaders effective in shaping the health and safety of the community take into consideration the ever-evolving external environment and verbally evaluate the potential adaptations the organization can make to those possible futures. A fast food conglomerate might alter menus to include more healthy foods than burgers and fries and shape consumption of fruit and vegetables. These relations are based on a verbally constructed future that, for the leader at least, bears some connection with the current situation (Houmanfar et al., 2009). The verbal networks that would motivate healthy choice by organizational leaders are similar to those described for individual consumers, plus other factors specific to the organization, such as fiscal health, state and federal government policies, competitors' success, and peer opinions. The context for this population-level shift toward consumption of healthy food is vastly complex. The concepts of meta- and macrocontingencies are useful in describing the contingency networks that support prosocial changes in consumption and the language that facilitates such shifts.

Houmanfar et al. (2010) note that the consumer side of an organization has been largely ignored within behavior analysis. The behavior perspective model proposed by Foxall (1999, 2010) addresses this challenge adequately by examining the various influences on a consumer, including the social setting and history of consumption. The behavior perspective model examines the strength of social influence on a consumer's purchasing decisions along with the function of the behavior of purchasing a product. From this perspective, the consumer behavior setting consists of two kinds of consequences: utilitarian and informational. Utilitarian reinforcement comes from the practical outcomes of the purchase and consumption of a good or service. It consists not only of the usefulness of the product but also the feelings associated with owning and consuming it. Informational reinforcement, in contrast, relies on not just the response of the consumer but also the response of others to the consumer's purchasing decision. The social status, acceptance, or prestige that a product affords its buyer is informational reinforcement, which can vary dramatically from one culture to another.

In addition to the reinforcers that influence the behavior of consumers, there are the resources at their disposal. These resources may be viewed as establishing operations that increase the reinforcing effectiveness of certain products. Furthermore, social and cultural factors may influence the preferences of consumers, thus establishing the differential reinforcing effectiveness of different products for various individuals. The landscape of consumers and their preferences is the environment into which products and services are introduced. Similar products vie with one another for the attention of and purchase by consumers. Although there is certainly great complexity to the patterns and preferences of the buying public, they still bear consideration because of its importance in the survival or demise of products.

In short, a better understanding of the consumer response to the aggregate product and the various contingencies that affect that consumer response is critical to the generation of more effective organizational group rules (Houmanfar et al., 2010). Surveys and focus groups conducted by organizations are an aid to crafting useful group rules. The role of language here cannot be overstated. The recognition of the cultural milieu that consumers and the organization find themselves in; the assessment of organizational practices in terms of their efficiency and productivity; the rating of the aggregate product in terms of its quality and fit with consumer needs; the consumer response of choosing or rejecting a product based on marketing or price; and the designing of the mission, vision, and future direction of the organization and its socio-IBs are primarily verbal in nature. Language serves as an intermediary between these multiple processes and the delays between them.

Brown and Houmanfar (in press) provide a discussion of some variables that may promote organizational leaders' prosocial decision making pertaining to the production of healthy food products. According to the authors, incentives such as tax breaks and social awards may promote the adoption of pro-health-related practices. Negative consequences, such as higher taxes or acquiring the cost associated with the effect on the environment (e.g., BP covering the cost of the recent oil disaster), can provide an alternative solution (Biglan, 2009).

An important component of determining what products or practices contribute to externalities lies in the information that is available to organizational leaders (Brown & Houmanfar, in press). Research institutes and advocacy organizations can serve as sources of accurate, unbiased, and peer-reviewed data for organizations (Biglan, 2009). Biglan and Glenn (2013) also argue that the first step in change initiatives (specifically those that attempt to target behavior change to support healthier, prosocial environments) is to provide evidence about the prevalence and cost (to both the individual and society) of the problem. Given the critical role of organizational leaders in shaping the well-being of their consumers as well as employees, a discussion of leaders' behaviors in organizations is warranted. The following sections provide an overview of leadership behaviors in the organizational context.

Leadership Behavior and Management Behavior: A Distinction

In the analysis of leadership behavior, we consider various definitions and descriptions of leadership in the field of organizational behavior management. For instance, Daniels and Daniels (2005) state that the role of a leader is to promote conditions that motivate employees to execute the mission, vision, and values of the organization. In doing so, the leader must clearly specify which behaviors and results are critical to the survival of the organization. Similarly, Mawhinney and Ford (1977) write, "We consider the role of the leader to be that of organizing, specifying, and maintaining complex response chains of subordinates by communicating to them the contingencies of reinforcement . . . in the workplace" (p. 406). In addition, Abernathy (1996, 2000) note that a successful leader makes certain that employees understand what behaviors and outcomes are expected of them in order to promote organizational survival and provides the resources and means for them to accomplish these ends. In short, leadership behaviors include effectively communicating the mission and vision of an organization, cultivating a motivated workforce, and ensuring adequate resources for production. Leaders of the fast food industry, like the tobacco industry, measure success as the profit from sales. The health effects on consumers are secondary and deemed external to the organization's mission. Biglan (2009) argues for the critical role of advocacy organizations to represent the perspectives of the broader community and to curtail leaders' profit-driven focus that undervalues the externalities of the organization. An organization's management, in contrast, involves the implementation and maintenance of contingencies (Abernathy, 1996; Komaki, 1998) that sustain work functions under the leader's vision, whether it be prosocial or not. Thus, we consider prosocial leadership behaviors to be those that result in the organization's adaptation to the changing selective pressures of the broader culture in which the organization is localized. Management, in contrast, relates to those behaviors that arrange contingencies such that performance maintains during the interim of times of adaptation.

Leadership Values in Organizations

According to Skinner (1971/1990, p. 112), the term *values* is used when someone behaves with respect to contingencies arranged by others, so that individual's behavior reinforces the behavior of the person or persons who manages those contingencies. For example, the leadership of a church might arrange contingencies that reinforce church attendance and pious behavior and that punish the behaviors of drunkenness and adultery. One is then said to have values when he or she attends church, engages in prayer, and avoids situations in which sexual behavior and alcohol consumption are likely. Applying this to organizational leadership, we argue that organizational leadership demonstrates values when it creates an environment in which employees are encouraged to manage their own environment in accordance with a set of organizational goals and are reinforced for doing so (Herbst & Houmanfar, 2009). In other words, an organization is said to have values when its employees are granted the opportunity to change the organizational environment in ways that improve it and are reinforced for doing so. We recommend Abernathy's positive leadership model (Abernathy, 1996, 2000, 2009) by which this might be achieved.

The organizational behavior management literature has focused primarily on the financial value of organizational practices from a behavioral systemic perspective (Brethower, 2000; Gilbert, 2007). According to Brethower (2000) and Gilbert (2007), the performance of an organization is a function of interactions between the organization and the economic and social environment. Brethower asserts that the primary objective of any effective behavioral system is to add financial value to two marketplaces: the financial marketplace (i.e., owners, suppliers, investors, and employees) and the client service marketplace. Gilbert's behavioral systems engineering model promotes the systematic measurement of what is called "worthy performance." This process demonstrates the value-adding function (i.e., worthy performance) of an individual's performance as measured by the associated return on investment for the organization.

As an extension to Brethower's (2000) and Gilbert's (2007) perspectives, the main challenge of organizations in the 21st century is to interact with increasing environmental demands that are not only financial but also social in nature. The earth's population and its massive consumption of resources are served by hugely powerful corporations producing an endless stream of goods and services. The depletion of nonrenewable resources appears to be an unstoppable race to exhaust what is left. Future generations will suffer the consequences of this greed. As mentioned earlier, social responsibility emerges as a key feature of leadership decision making and citizenship behavior as the world's resources are depleted, as health and education crises increase, and as communities, societies, and cultures adapt to a new context.

The critical challenge for researchers and practitioners in applied behavior analysis is to determine the prosocial value in light of the financial value of their interventions. Enhancing human experience (inside and outside of organizational settings) entails thinking about the needs of not only current populations but future generations as well. Surveillance systems that track obesity rates, global warming, crime, drug use, gun deaths, and a host of other widespread social ills illuminate the social problems associated with cultural practices promoted by organizations and how many of these are escalating. These measures offer a metric to include when evaluating the social responsibility of organizations and their leaders for present and future generations.

ELIMINATING AVERSIVE ENVIRONMENTS

The most obvious suggestion for improving human well-being emerging across decades of writings by leading behavior analysts is to eliminate or decrease the prevalence of aversive conditions. This suggestion is echoed by Biglan and Glenn (2013). Fortunately, Biglan and Glenn report that empirical evidence for this kind of stressful environment (e.g., in schools and workplaces) has identified effective interventions. Similarly, there is evidence to suggest that changes in the current Millennial generation may positively affect levels of aversive conditions in companies while also pre-senting particular challenges for companies maintaining more traditional practices (Agnew, 2013; Schawbel, 2013). With the expanding role of social networks in the global landscape (e.g., Facebook, Twitter), opportunities for intra- and interindividual transmission of prosocial behavior inside and outside of organizations are limitless. One sees examples of this across the globe as communication technologies orchestrate social action in response to governments' restrictions of freedoms and other affronts to social groups.

With regard to the associated behavioral technology, evidence from organizational behavior management demonstrates the utility of primarily using positive reinforcement in the workplace (Abernathy, 1996, 2000, 2009; Daniels & Daniels, 2005), including in harsh work conditions such as fracking sites (Moran, 2013).

There is ample evidence to suggest that managing an environment that promotes flexible, creative behavior benefits employees beyond the imme-diate reinforcers that must be built into a system in order for it to thrive. In the industrial/organizational literature, numerous researchers have found that employees who experience a high degree of control over their work environment report more satisfaction (Greenberger, Strasser, Cummings, & Dunham, 1989), fewer health problems (Carayon & Zjilstra, 1999; Salanova, Peiro, & Schaufeli, 2002), and less stress (Van Yperen & Hagedoorn, 2003). Though most of the research in this area relates to self-reported experience of control, a system that is specifically designed to encourage control should result in similar benefits. Furthermore, arranging environments in this way should directly benefit the organization, as employees who report greater control tend to show less absenteeism (Smulders & Nijhuis, 1999).

Beyond the benefits that may directly accrue to organizations that adopt such practices, there should be benefits to the consumer practices that ultimately act as the selective mechanism for those entities (Houmanfar et al., 2010). In addition to the previously cited literature on obesity, numerous studies have found a predictive relationship between experienced work stress and substance abuse (e.g., Chopko, Palmieri, & Adams, 2013; Dawson, Grant, & Ruan, 2005; Grunberg, Moore, Anderson-Connolly, & Greenberg, 1999), though it should be noted that these relationships are not always found (e.g., Hodgins, Williams, & Munro, 2009; Mezuk, Bohnert, Ratliff, & Zivin, 2011). Furthermore, researchers have also pinpointed relationships between career and work stress and domestic violence (e.g., Cano & Vivian, 2003; Stith, Smith, Penn, Ward, & Tritt, 2004). With regard to obesity, costs associated with a loss in work productivity are estimated to be as high as $580 billion (Finkelstein et al., 2010). Though it is beyond the scope of this article to exhaustively review the literature pertaining to workplace stress, obesity, and societal problems, even a brief review points to the idea that creating an environment in which employees experience less stress would have significant effects on the well-being of society more generally.

When considering organizational values, however, one might look beyond how the organizational leadership behaves toward the people managed within the organization and toward the implications their leadership and management practices have for the culture more generally. As discussed earlier, as behavior is selected by its environment, cultural entities such as business organizations are selected based on the consequences supplied by the culture (Glenn, 1988; Glenn & Malott, 2004; Houmanfar et al., 2010; Malott & Glenn, 2006). Therefore, one can argue that an organization demonstrates values not only through the practices it has toward its employees but through the outcomes its practices have in relation to the culture more broadly. Thus, we consider value in terms of not only the reinforcers inherent in the product or service delivered but the delayed consequences that an organization's practices may have for the health of its members, their families, and the broader environment in which the organization operates. This broader perspective on the boundaries of assessments in organizational behavior management calls for enhancements to measures such as the Potential for Improving Performance (PIP) to include functional assessment of the societal impact of leaders' actions. Innovation in technologies such as social media and population-level surveillance systems offers mechanisms for reliably estimating human well-being and ties these within contingency networks affecting leaders' behavior. Resistance to this social intrusion on corporate practices will certainly occur, but some leaders might elevate the commonwealth above corporate profit. Consider the example set by Bill and

Melinda Gates and Warren Buffet via their foundation that invests billions of dollars globally to develop education, health care, and other essential supports to human well-being (http://www.gatesfoundation.org). Leaders like these demonstrate that social values can trump public displays of affluence when they invest accumulated wealth into worthy improvements to cultures to better lives now and in the future.

In short, the role of organizational leaders in our analysis of organizational practices is critical, as these leaders serve as the primary source for decision making and rule governance in organizations as they relate to the management of natural resources involved in producing the goods and services all people consume. As mentioned earlier, the role of advocacy organizations (Alavosius et al., in press; Biglan, 2009) is also critical, as they provide a counterweight to the profit-driven actions of organizational leaders and bring the perspective of communities harmed by the externalities of corporate practices as a factor in resource use decisions. The impact of many advocacy organizations needs to be strengthened to more effectively advance the public's interest, as the lobbyists who advocate alternative views are often well organized and richly funded and demonstrate a better way forward. This is an area that can be of focus for behavior analysts with an interest in organizational behavior management and cultural behavior analysis.

CONCLUSION

This article calls for future work in behavior analysis, emphasizing the importance of establishing organizational practices that support prosocial behavior and that eliminate aversive conditions within cultural systems. These are undoubtedly massively important steps. However, the issues we face globally require large-scale multifaceted solutions. It is not enough to eliminate aversive conditions for an individual or even a single family. Rather, it is necessary to arrange community and organizational interventions that can create environments that support the establishment and *maintenance* of prosocial behavior. Some organizational leaders, under mounting pressure from social forces, may seek to direct their organizations' resources toward broader social values. As briefly discussed in this article, behavior analysis informs pragmatic solutions that can alleviate some of the challenges humanity faces and offers prosocial corporate leaders a promising strategy for cultural change.

In keeping with Skinner's earlier enthusiasm, we believe that behavior analysis has the capability of having a significant impact on certain issues in which behavior change plays a vital function. Consumptive behaviors are fundamental to the obesity epidemic, global warming, and other huge threats to human well-being. The science of behavior has reached a point where we can contribute to understanding and shaping cultural change (Alavosius & Mattaini, 2011; Alavosius et al., in press; Biglan, 2009; Biglan & Glenn, 2013; Glenn, 1988; Glenn & Malott, 2004; Houmanfar et al., 2010; Malott & Glenn, 2006; Mattaini, 2013). In short, prosocial actions by individuals in positions of power are needed to create conditions for actions that apply behavior science at a scale envisioned by the founder of the discipline, B. F. Skinner. After all, as Skinner put it, "The way positive reinforcement is carried out is more important than the amount" (BrainyQuote, n.d.).

ACKNOWLEDGMENTS

Portions of this article were presented at the Special Seminar on Leadership and Cultural Change, May 23, 2014, in Chicago, Illinois.

REFERENCES

Abernathy, W. B. (1996). *Sin of wages*. Memphis, TN: PerfSys Press.

Abernathy, W. B. (2000). *Managing without supervising: Creating an organization-wide performance system*. Memphis, TN: PerfSys Press.

Abernathy, W. B. (2009). Walden two revisited: Optimizing behavioral systems. *Journal of Organizational Behavior Management, 29*, 175–192.

Agnew, J. (2013). *Managing Millennials: Can science help?* Retrieved from: http://aubreydaniels.com/pmezine/managing-millennials-can-science-help

Alavosius, M. P., & Mattaini, M. A. (2011). Editorial: Behavior analysis, sustainability, resilience and adaptation. *Behavior and Social Issues, 20*, 1–5.

Alavosius, M. P., Newsome, W. D., Houmanfar, R., & Biglan, A. (in press). A functional contextualist analysis of the behavior and organizational practices relevant to climate change. In R. D. Zettle, S.C. Hayes, D. Barnes-Holmes, & A. Biglan (Eds.), *Handbook of contextual behavior science*. New York, NY: Wiley.

Baer, D. M., Wolf, M. M., & Risley, T. R. (1968). Some current dimensions of applied behavior analysis. *Journal of Applied Behavior Analysis, 1*, 91–97. doi:10.1901/jaba.1968.1-91

Bar-Yam, Y. (1997). *Dynamics of complex systems*. Reading, MA: Addison-Wesley.

Biglan, A. (2009). The role of advocacy organizations in reducing negative externalities. *Journal of Organizational Behavior Management, 29*, 215–230.

Biglan, A., & Glenn, S. S. (2013). Toward prosocial behavior and environments: Behavioral and cultural contingencies in a public health framework. In G. J. Madden (Ed.), *APA handbook of behavior analysis* (pp. 255–275). Washington, DC: American Psychological Association.

Bond, F. W., & Bunce, D. (2000). Mediators of change in emotion-focused and problem-focused worksite management interventions. *Journal of Occupational Health Psychology, 5*, 156–163.

Bond, F. W., Flaxman, P. E., & Bunce, D. (2008). The influence of psychological flexibility on work redesign: Mediated moderation of a work reorganization intervention. *Journal of Applied Psychology, 93*, 645–654.

Bond, F. W., Hayes, S. C., & Barnes-Holmes, D. (2006). Psychological flexibility, ACT, and organizational behavior. *Journal of Organizational Behavior Management*, *26*(1–2), 25–54.

BrainyQuote. (n.d.). *B. F. Skinner quotes*. Retrieved from http://www.brainyquote. com/quotes/quotes/b/bfskinne385025.html

Brethower, D. M. (2000). A systematic view of enterprise: Adding value to performance. *Journal of Organizational Behavior Management*, *20*(3–4), 165–190.

Brinkborg, H., Michanek, J., Hesser, H., & Berglund, G. (2011). Acceptance and commitment therapy for the treatment of stress among social workers: A randomized controlled trial. *Behaviour Research and Therapy*, *49*, 389–398.

Brown, L., & Houmanfar, R. A. (in press). The cost of affluence: A closer look at the food industry. *Behavior and Social Issues*, *24*.

Cano, A., & Vivian, D. (2003). Are life stressors associated with marital violence? *Journal of Family Psychology*, *17*, 302–314.

Carayon, P., & Zjilstra, F. (1999). Relationship between job control, work pressure and strain: Studies in the USA and in The Netherlands. *Work and Stress*, *13*, 32–48.

Catania, A. C. (1975). Freedom and knowledge: An experimental analysis of preference in pigeons. *Journal of the Experimental Analysis of Behavior*, *24*, 89–106.

Chase, J., Houmanfar, R., Hayes, S., Ward, T., Plumb, J., & Follette, V. (2013). Values are not just goals: Online ACT-based values training adds to goal setting in improving undergraduate college student performance. *Journal of Contextual Behavioral Science*, *2*, 79–84.

Chopko, B. A., Palmieri, P. A., & Adams, R. E. (2013). Associations between police stress and alcohol use: Implications for practice. *Journal of Loss and Trauma*, *18*, 482–497. doi:10.1080/15325024.2012.719340

Daniels, A. C., & Daniels, J. E. (2005). *Measure of a leader*. Atlanta, GA: Performance Management.

Dawson, D. A., Grant, B. F., & Ruan, W. (2005). The association between stress and drinking: Modifying effects of gender and vulnerability. *Alcohol and Alcoholism*, *40*, 453–460. doi:10.1093/alcalc/agh176

De Luca, R., & Holborn, S. (1992). Effects of a variable-ratio reinforcement schedule with changing criteria on exercise in obese and nonobese boys. *Journal of Applied Behavior Analysis*, *25*, 671–679.

Ferster, C., Nurnberger, J., & Levitt, E. (1962). The control of eating. *Journal of Mathetics*, *1*, 87–109.

Finkelstein, E., DiBonaventura, M., Burgess, S., & Hale, B. (2010). The costs of obesity in the workplace. *Journal of Occupational and Environmental Medicine*, *52*, 971–976.

Finkelstein, E., Fiebelkorn, I., & Wang, G. (2009). National medical spending attributable to overweight and obesity: How much, and who's paying? *Health Affairs*, *28*, 822–831.

Fisher, W. W., & Mazur, J. E. (1997). Basic and applied research on choice responding. *Journal of Applied Behavior Analysis*, *30*, 387–410.

Fogel, V., Miltenberger, R., Graves, R., & Koehler, S. (2010). The effects of exergaming on physical activity among inactive children in a physical education classroom. *Journal of Applied Behavior Analysis*, *43*, 591–600.

Foreyt, J., & Goodrick, G. (1993). Evidence for success of behavior modification in weight loss and control. *Annals of Internal Medicine, 19*, 698–701.

Forman, E., Butryn, M., Hoffman, K., & Herbert, J. (2009). An open trial of acceptance-based behavioral intervention for weight loss. *Cognitive and Behavioral Practices, 16*, 223–235.

Foxall, G. R. (1999). The behavioural perspective model: Consensibility and consensuality. *European Journal of Marketing, 33*, 570–596.

Foxall, G. R. (2001). Foundations of consumer behaviour analysis. *Marketing Theory, 1*, 165–199.

Foxall, G. R. (2010). Invitation to consumer behavior analysis. *Journal of Organizational Behavior Management, 30*, 92–109.

Foxall, G. (2015/this issue). Consumer behavior analysis and the marketing firm: Bilateral contingency in the context of environmental concern. *Journal of Organizational Behavior Management, 35*.

Gallup. (2014). State of American well-being: 2013 state, community, and congressional district analysis. Retrieved from http://cdn2.hubspot.net/hub/162029/file-610480715-pdf/WBI2013/Gallup-Healthways_State_of_American_Well-Being_Full_Report_2013.pdf

Gilbert, T. (2007). *Human competence: Engineering worthy performance* (Tribute ed.). San Francisco, CA: Pfeiffer.

Glenn, S. S. (1988). Contingencies and metacontingencies: Toward a synthesis of behavior analysis and cultural materialism. *The Behavior Analyst, 11*, 161–179.

Glenn, S. S. (2004). Individual behavior, culture, and social change. *The Behavior Analyst, 27*, 133–151.

Glenn, S. S., & Malott, M. M. (2004). Complexity and selection: Implications for organizational change. *Behavior & Social Issues, 13*, 89–106.

Greenberger, D. B., Strasser, S., Cummings, L. L., & Dunham, R. S. (1989). The impact of personal control on performance and satisfaction. *Organizational Behavior & Human Decision Processes, 43*, 29–51.

Grunberg, L., Moore, S., Anderson-Connoly, R., & Greenberg, E. (1999). Work stress and self-reported alcohol abuse: The moderating role of escapist reasons for drinking. *Journal of Occupational Health Psychology, 4*, 29–36.

Hantula, D. A., DiClemente, D. F., & Rajala, A. K. (2001). Outside the box: The analysis of consumer behavior. In L. Hayes, J. Austin, R. Houmanfar, & M. Clayton (Eds.), *Organizational change* (pp. 203–223). Reno, NV: Context Press.

Hausman, N., Borrero, J., Fisher, A., & Kahng, S. (2014). Improving accuracy of portion-size estimations through a stimulus equivalence paradigm. *Journal of Applied Behavior Analysis, 47*, 485–499.

Hawkins, R. (1991). Is social validity what we are interested in? Argument for a functional approach. *Journal of Applied Behavior Analysis, 24*, 205–213.

Hayes, S. C., Bunting, K., Herbst, S., Bond, F. W., & Barnes-Holmes, D. (2006). Expanding the scope of organizational behavior management: Relational frame theory and the experimental analysis of complex human behavior. *Journal of Organizational Behavior Management, 26*(1–2), 1–23.

Hayes, S., Luoma, J., Bond, F., Masuda, A., & Lillis, J. (2006). Acceptance and Commitment Therapy: Model, processes and outcomes. *Behavior Research and Therapy, 44*, 1–25.

Hayes, S., Masuda, A., Bissett, R., & Guerrero, L. (2004). DBT, FAP, and ACT: How empirically oriented are the new behavior therapy technologies? *Behavior Therapy, 35,* 35–54.

Hayes, S. C., Strosahl, K. D., & Wilson, K. G. (1999). *Acceptance and commitment therapy: An experiential approach to behavior change.* New York, NY: Guilford Press.

Helliwell, J., Layard, R., & Sachs, J. (Eds.). (2013). *World happiness report.* New York, NY: Columbia University, The Earth Institute.

Herbst, S. A., & Houmanfar, R. (2009). Psychological approaches to values in organizations and organizational behavior management. *Journal of Organizational Behavior Management, 29,* 47–68.

Hodgins, D. C., Williams, R., & Munro, G. (2009). Workplace responsibility, stress, alcohol availability and norms as predictors of alcohol consumption-related problems among employed workers. *Substance Use & Misuse, 44,* 2062–2079. doi:10.3109/10826080902855173

Houmanfar, R. A., Rodrigues, N. J., & Smith, G. S. (2009). Role of communication networks in behavioral systems analysis. *Journal of Organizational Behavior Management, 29,* 257–275.

Houmanfar, R. A., Rodrigues, N. J., & Ward, T. A. (2010). Emergence and meta-contingency: Points of contact and departure. *Behavior and Social Issues, 19,* 78–103.

Kahneman, D., & Tversky, A. (1979). Prospect theory: An analysis of decision under risk. *Econometrica, 47,* 263–292.

Karsina, A., Thompson, R. H., & Rodriguez, N. M. (2011). Effects of a history of differential reinforcement on preference for choice. *Journal of the Experimental Analysis of Behavior, 95,* 189–202.

Komaki, J. L. (1998). *Leadership from an operant perspective.* New York, NY: Routledge.

Layng, T. V. J. (2006). Emotions and emotional behavior: A constructional approach to understanding some social benefits of aggression. *Brazilian Journal of Behavior Analysis, 2,* 155–170.

Lydon, C. A., Rohmeier, K. D., Yi, S. C., Mattaini, M. A., & Williams, W. L. (2011). How far do you have to go to get a cheeseburger around here? The realities of an environmental design approach to curbing the consumption of fast-food. *Behavior and Social Issues, 20,* 6–23. doi:10.5210/bsi.v20i0.3637

Madden, G. J., & Bickel, W. K. (2010). *Impulsivity: The behavioral and neurological science of discounting.* Washington, DC: American Psychological Association.

Malott, M. E., & Glenn, S. S. (2006). Targets of intervention in cultural and behavioral change. *Behavior and Social Issues, 15,* 31–56.

Mattaini, M. (2013). *Strategic nonviolent power: The science of Satyagraha.* Retrieved from: http://www.aupress.ca/books/120224/ebook/99Z_Mattaini_2013-Strategic_Nonviolent_Power.pdf

Mawhinney, T. C., & Ford, J. D. (1977). The path goal theory of leader effectiveness: An operant interpretation. *Academy of Management Review, 2,* 398–411.

McGinnis, M & Ostrom, E. (2008). Will lessons from small-scale social dilemmas scale up? In A. Biel, D. Eek, T. Gärling, & M. Gustaffson (Eds.), *New issues and paradigms in research on social dilemmas* (pp. 189–211). Berlin, Germany: Springer.

Mezuk, B., Bohnert, A. S. B., Ratliff, S., & Zivin, K. (2011). Job strain, depressive symptoms, and drinking behavior among older adults: Results from the Health and Retirement Study. *Journals of Gerontology: Series B: Psychological Sciences and Social Sciences, 66B*, 426–434. doi:10.1093/geronb/gbr021

Moran, D. J. (2013). *Building safety commitment*. Joliet, IL: Valued Living Books.

Ogdon, L. C., Caroll, M., Kit, K., B., & Flegal, M. (2014). Prevalence of childhood and adult obesity in the United States, 2011-2012. *Journal of the American Medical Association, 311*, 806–814.

Ono, K. (2000). Free-choice preference under uncertainty. *Behavioural Processes, 49*, 11–19.

Ono, K. (2004). Effects of experience on preference between forced and free choice. *Journal of the Experimental Analysis of Behavior, 81*, 27–37.

Organisation for Economic Co-operation and Development. (2013). *OECD guidelines on measuring subjective well-being*. Paris, France: Author. doi:10.1787/9789264191655-en

Ostrom, E. (1990). *Governing the commons*. New York, NY: Cambridge University Press.

Salanova, M., Peiro, J. M., & Schaufeli, W. B. (2002). Self-efficacy specificity and burnout among information technology workers: An extension of the job demand-control model. *European Journal of Work and Organizational Psychology, 11*, 1–25.

Schawbel, D. (2013). *10 ways Millennials are creating the future of work*. Retrieved from: http://www.forbes.com/sites/danschawbel/2013/12/16/10-ways-millennials-are-creating-the-future-of-work/

Schwartz, B. (2004). *The paradox of choice: Why more is less*. New York: Harper Perennial.

Shayne, R., Fogel, V., Miltenberger, R., & Koehler, S. (2012). The effects of exergaming on physical activity in a third-grade physical education class. *Journal of Applied Behavior Analysis, 45*, 211–215.

Sidman, M. (1989). *Coercion and its fallout*. Boston, MA: Authors Cooperative.

Skinner, B.F. (1938). *Behavior of organisms*. Acton, MA: Copley Publishing Group.

Skinner, B. F. (1948). *Walden two*. New York, NY: Macmillan.

Skinner, B. F. (1965). *Science and human behavior*. New York, NY: Macmillan. (Original work published 1953)

Skinner, B. F. (1987). Why we are not acting to save the world. In *Upon further reflection* (pp. 1–14). Englewood Cliffs, NJ: Prentice Hall.

Skinner, B. F. (1990). *Beyond freedom and dignity*. New York, NY: Bantam Books. (Original work published 1971)

Smulders, P. G. W., & Nijhuis, F. J. N. (1999). The job demands-job control model and absence behavior: Results of a 3-year longitudinal study. *Work & Stress, 13*, 115–131.

Stith, S. M., Smith, D. B., Penn, C. E., Ward, D. B., & Tritt, D. (2004). Intimate partner physical abuse perpetration and victimization risk factors: A meta-analytic review. *Aggression and Violent Behavior, 10*, 65–98. doi:10.1016/j.avb.2003.09.001

Stuart, R. (1971). A three-dimensional program for the treatment of obesity. *Behavior Research and Therapy, 9*, 177–186.

Stunkard, A. (1975). From explanation to action in psychosomatic medicine: The case of obesity [Presidential address, 1974]. *Psychosomatic Medicine, 37*, 195–236.

Suzuki, S. (1997). Effects of number of alternatives on choice in humans. *Behavioural Processes, 39*, 205–214.

Suzuki, S. (2000). Choice between single-response and multichoice tasks in humans. *The Psychological Record, 50*, 105–115.

Thaler, R. H., & Sunstein, C., R. (2009). *Nudge: Improving decisions about health, wealth, and happiness*. London, England: Penguin Books.

Van Camp, C., & Hayes, L. (2012). Assessing and increasing physical activity. *Journal of Applied Behavior Analysis, 45*, 871–875.

Van Yperen, N. W., & Hagedoorn, M. (2003). Do high demands increase intrinsic motivation or fatigue or both? The role of job control and social support. *Academy of Management Journal, 46*, 339–348.

Wang, Y., McPherson, K., Marsh, T., Gortmaker, L., & Brown, M. (2011). Health and economic burden of the projected obesity trends in the USA and the UK. *Lancet, 378*, 815–825.

Washington, W., Banna, K., & Gibson, A. (2014). Preliminary efficacy of prize-based contingency management to increase activity levels in health adults. *Journal of Applied Behavior Analysis, 47*, 231–245.

Weatherly, J. N., Plumm, K. M. & Derenne, A. (2011). Delay discounting and social policy issues. *The Psychological Record, 61*, 527–546.

Well-being. (n.d.). In Merriam-Webster's online dictionary. Retrieved May 12, 2014 from http://www.merriam-webster.com/dictionary/well-being

Withrow, D., & Alter, D. (2011). The economic burden of obesity worldwide: A systematic review of the direct costs of obesity. *Obesity Review, 12*, 131–141.

Wolf, M. M. (1978). Social validity: The case for subjective measurement or how applied behavior analysis is finding its heart. *Journal of Applied Behavior Analysis, 11*, 203–214. doi:10.1901/jaba.1978.11-203

Leadership and Culture

JON E. KRAPFL and BLINA KRUJA

*Leadership is defined as a broad menu of behaviors, some appro-
priate to one environment but not second. A number of the more
common leadership behaviors are discussed. The article goes on
to identify the process of learning some of the behaviors required to
lead. It is suggested that an individual build a leadership repertoire
based on personal background and experiences. Learning to lead
is then discussed as requiring experience, because leadership cannot be learned from a book. A review of several kinds of experience
models of instruction follows. Finally, the article addresses the issue
of culture and makes the point that organizational culture is based
on both the larger culture of which the organization is a part and
the behavior of the organization's leader. The article closes with
a recommendation that behaviorists not only learn about behavior
analysis but also learn something about the environments in which
the behavior analyst is likely to function.*

Businesses, nongovernmental organizations, nonprofit organizations, governments, academic institutions, and organizations of all kinds are in serious
need of effective leaders to guide them in today's increasingly unpredictable
world. According to a global risk report, financial crises, social and political
instability, and degrading environmental conditions represent but a few of
the threats to be faced over the next decade (Hjelmgaard, 2014).

Despite the need for individuals able to provide rapid, innovative solutions and willing to take measured risks to achieve positive results, society
is not very effective at producing young leaders. The current culture in
the United States produces young individuals who are less, rather than

TABLE 1 Needs of the Working World and Characteristics of Young Professionals

Students entering college	Needs of the working world
Passive consumers	Dynamic creators
Craving certainty	Seeing opportunity in uncertainty
Seeking the right answer	Asking the right questions
Doing as they are told	Seizing the day
Convergent thinking	Divergent thinking
Doing their best	Making it happen
Seeking technical solutions to manageable problems	Providing creative solutions to wicked problems

Note. From an unpublished report from the Mason School of Business at the College of William & Mary (Krapfl et al., 2012).

more, prepared to lead and take full responsibility for their lives. Moreover, generally speaking, higher education institutions do well with respect to specific disciplines, but fall short of the mark in preparing students to lead, manage, or otherwise deal with the emerging world of work, especially work carried out in organizational settings. As outlined in Table 1, an unpublished research paper at William & Mary's Mason School of Business identifies a number of dimensions to illustrate this claim (Krapfl et al., 2012).

Given the need to further understand the development of effective leadership, the current article aims to examine some of the factors involved in effective leadership. To this end, the article begins by providing a working definition of leadership, then identifies a number of behaviors deemed most likely to produce effective leadership in organizations. Finally, the article concludes by identifying some ideas that can be used in preparing students to become effective leaders.

LEADERSHIP DEFINED

Since the late 19th century, the scientific study of leadership has been a topic of interest among different disciplines (Galton, 1869). As a result, there exist several competing theories that attempt to define leadership and model leaders' skills or traits (for a review, see Northouse, 2012). Today, it is generally agreed that leadership refers to the process of influencing others (Vroom & Jago, 2007). The challenge in providing a more detailed universal definition of the concept stems from the findings that there exist multiple styles that are effective in different environments. A number of historical figures can help illustrate this point. Steve Jobs, the cofounder and former chairman and chief executive officer (CEO) of Apple Inc., is considered one the greatest leaders of the 21st century. According to biographies of his life, Jobs was notorious for easily losing his temper and verbally abusing and threatening employees and friends (Isaacson, 2011). Furthermore, he was uncomfortable and clumsy in social situations and had few personal friends. As a result, his leadership style clearly involved different forms of aversive control. Although Jobs did not exhibit many of the behaviors or characteristics usually associated with leadership, no one can deny that he was an effective leader. He demanded of his staff that they achieve what seemed impossible. Despite his temper, Jobs created an effective, collaborative, and enthusiastic work culture and was widely admired. Under his guidance Apple Inc. became the most highly valued company in the world. Similar to Jobs, there are a number of people, including General George Patton, Edward Hennesey, and Dame Margaret Thatcher, to name but a few, whose leadership styles were atypical.

Others have successfully led with very different repertoires. For example, Mahatma Gandhi secured India's freedom from colonial rule through civil disobedience. In a similar manner, Martin Luther King, Jr., led the effort to dismantle racism in the United States through nonviolent resistance, thus becoming a civil rights icon. Their leadership styles were founded on their ability to inspire large groups of people by communicating a vision of change.

These examples serve to demonstrate two key features of leadership. First, the concept of leadership is similar to the concept of personality. Both concepts serve as umbrella terms that entail a wide variety of behaviors. Thus, leadership is not an inherent attribute or trait within a person (Vroom & Jago, 2007). In fact, personality and social psychology studies attempting to identify and measure the "leader trait" have repeatedly failed (for a review, see Gibb, 1954; Stogdill, 1948). Skinner (1945) suggested that terms like *personality* or *leadership* should be dealt with in the form in which they are observed, namely, as verbal responses. Therefore, meanings, contents, and references are found among the determiners, not the properties of response (Skinner, 1945). Skinner clarifies this point by explaining that the question "What is length?" is answered by listing the circumstances in which the verbal response "length" is emitted. Similarly, the definition of leadership must consider the circumstances in which the term is used.

This brings up a second defining aspect of leadership: the context in which it is observed. As Skinner (1945) further points out, if a common verbal response is emitted under two quite different and separate sets of circumstances, then there are two responses having the form "leadership." That is to say that the verbal response class "leadership" cannot be defined by phonetic form alone but must also be defined by its functional relationships. Therefore, a holistic study of leadership should take into account the interaction between leaders and their reinforcement history (Stogdill, 1948). According to this school of thought, effective leaders are the product of the individuals' previous experiences and features of their environment. In addition, an individual's genetic background, for example a tendency to display an explosive temper, might provide him or her with a limited and unique behavioral repertoire, which may limit the range of leadership styles available to that person and may affect his or her ability to function as a leader in some contexts. In sum, leaders emerge when their behavioral repertoires coincide with the structure and features of the environment in which leadership is required (Fiedler, 1964).

Lastly, leadership requires the presence of followers (Jacobs & Jaques, 1991; Zaccaro, 2001). In contrast to other high-performing individuals, leaders are identified by the presence of followers. Thus, as demonstrated by the aforementioned examples, leaders' ability to influence others depends on both their skills and the environment to which those skills are to be applied. Differing circumstances and differing personal backgrounds can produce a successful leader in one situation yet be ineffective in another (Stogdill, 1948).

COMMON CHARACTERISTICS OF LEADERS

Having acknowledged that the successful leadership of any one individual in a particular environment depends on the individual's genetic makeup and his or her existing repertoire, previous studies have identified a number of behaviors often exhibited by effective leaders. To put it differently, it is possible to identify a "menu" of behaviors that often prove valuable in leading for a great variety of individuals and across a wide range of contexts. Furthermore, individual differences and histories facilitate or hinder one's ability to acquire certain behaviors on the proposed menu. So each individual may rely on well-developed behaviors in one menu area to compensate for lesser developed behaviors in another menu area. That said, the leadership menu offered here identifies a number of behavior classes deemed valuable for most leaders, and they are presented in order of our sense of their importance to the leadership process.

Leadership Behavior Menu

A VALUE PROPOSITION

It is the responsibility of the leader to evaluate the value proposition and, if necessary, articulate it or change it. A value proposition is something like a vision, but it is more than that. In a vision, a person specifies some future product or service to be offered by an organization or business. A value proposition does the same thing, but also identifies the likely reciprocal controlling relationships that would hold between the organizational culture and the larger culture of which it is a part. That is to say, it specifies how the product or service is likely to function as a reinforcer for the intended recipient and how, in turn, the members of the organization will be reinforced for providing the product or service. In addition, the value proposition positions the organization against its competitors, for example, it is the most reliable like Toyota, or the best designed like Apple, or the best value like Costco. Finally, the value proposition should generate for employees a sense of what the future performance should look like or produce, and what the likely personal payoff will be. The value proposition may be implicit in the organization and not explicitly stated.

Value propositions are generally not considered in either the behavioral or psychological study realms, so here are some examples. Neiman Marcus and Target are both successful retail merchants. Neiman Marcus has a value proposition that offers the highest quality merchandise and exceptional service at a cost that is high but appropriate for the level of quality and service offered. Target's value proposition is to provide merchandise that is considered to be of relatively high quality given the prices charged. Two retailing giants, Sears Roebuck and Montgomery Ward, were 20th-century companies that lost their value proposition because, as more alternatives became available, they could no longer be seen as the alternatives for the middle class.

An even better example is provided by the copying industry. In the early 1960s, the Xerox machine was invented. Until that time, the only alternative for producing copies of any page or document was to use carbon paper on a typewriter or to use a mimeograph machine. Most of you probably do not know what a mimeograph is. It was a machine on which a special kind of paper was used by typing on it and then placing the paper on a round drum that turned to produce copies. Errors in typing were costly to correct, and the entire process was time consuming and messy. If a professor, for example, wanted a secretary to make multiple copies of a test it could take 4 to 5 hr or more to get the copies made. The Xerox machine took only a few minutes to complete the entire process. The name of the company that produced the mimeograph was the A. B. Dick Company. Did you ever hear of it? No! The Xerox machine was far less costly, far less time consuming, and far less messy than the mimeograph. Try as they might, the A. B. Dick Company did not stand a chance. Its value proposition had been destroyed. Efforts were made to decrease prices, enhance sales, and improve efficiency, but with a poor value proposition, none of the efforts were successful. The same analysis could be provided for the typewriter.

There is a significant lesson to be learned here. In any attempt to lead an organization in a new direction, if the value proposition is not strong, the effort will ultimately fail. A business, a charity, a nongovernmental organization, or a government that does not have a strong value proposition is doomed to failure. Failing value propositions inevitably produce difficult working environments replete with aversive control.

Imagine that you, as a behavioral psychologist, were called into the A. B. Dick Company to improve sales or strengthen the culture. There was nothing that could be successfully done. The organization's value proposition was no longer valid. The reciprocal controlling relationship between the organization's culture and the larger external culture was shattered. If the value proposition is not strong, nothing else matters. Any effort to improve performance with the existing value proposition is doomed to failure.

The concept of the value proposition was one of the principal concepts that led to the formation of Corporate Behavior Analysts Inc., the company with which the primary author was associated for many years. Corporate Behavior Analysts Inc. functioned as change consultants but did so while also helping companies determine the strength of their value proposition and helping them reposition themselves, if necessary. Weak value propositions require strategic repositioning. Failed value propositions, like that of the A. B. Dick Company, require sea change strategies (i.e., the company must almost totally reinvent itself).

ETHICAL VALUES

There are two separate and equally important aspects of ethics. First, effective leaders behave with integrity and thus are trusted by their followers. With regard to leadership, trust extends beyond the employee observing concordance between what is said and what is done. It also includes the leader's demonstrated commitment to all of the organizational constituencies involved. Without trust, leadership, if possible at all, is typically weak. The second aspect of ethics relates to the long-term viability of the organization and its value proposition. A value proposition that either explicitly or implicitly indicates that the firm will remain valid over the longer term for the organization's consumers, for the organization itself, and for its employees can have an enhanced effect on the organization. Moreover, a value proposition that entails services or products regarded as both a good value and of high quality or noble by customers allows employees to be proud of their involvement and further strengthens their belief that the organization has enduring value. Therefore, ethical propositions create a positive culture, a good working environment, and a system that functions primarily on positive reinforcement.

EXECUTION SKILLS

In addition to having value propositions, visions, plans, and strategies, effective leaders must execute. Put very simply, they make things happen. A number of studies have found that leaders are more proactive compared to nonleaders (Crant & Bateman, 2000). In addition, execution skills are a factor in one's rise in the organization (Chan & Drasgow, 2001). Execution is typically not taught in school and is often found to be missing in the new college graduate. For many, especially among the more educated, there is an implicit assumption that once a concept or plan is understood and articulated, the implementation is a simple and straightforward process that requires no further attention. But ideas and plans cannot put themselves into effect. Lack of ability and experience in putting ideas and plans into working processes is one of the most often cited criticisms of new college graduates.

Innovation/Creativity

In an increasingly globalized world, much greater emphasis is placed on generating innovative products and processes. What is often referred to as "thinking outside the box" has become an essential skill in both academic and, especially, business environments (University of South Florida, n.d.). Entrepreneurs' ability to create new products and services has led to a profitable and dynamic economy in the United States. Over the past 25 years, innovative businesses have provided 80% of new jobs in the United States (Innovation Pessimism, 2013). However, over the past several years there has been a dramatic change in the U.S. position in the successful innovations index. From the 1960s through the 1990s, the United States ranked first in innovation and entrepreneurialism. In 2012, the United States slipped to 10th out of 34 Organisation for Economic Co-operation and Development countries (United Nations, 2012). Entrepreneurial and innovation skills may well become the most sought-after skills in the work environment over the next 20 years.

Communication skills

Communication skills are an undeniably important feature of the leadership process. Previous studies suggest that well-developed social and communication skills may be the key difference between effective leaders and other very intelligent or high-performing individuals (Yukl, 2006; Zaccaro, 2004). In addition to delivering the value proposition, creating and maintaining teams, and motivating followers, communication skills play a particularly important role in effective problem solving in the organizational setting (Mumford, Zaccaro, Harding, Jacobs, & Fleishman, 2000).

There are three important, yet often neglected, aspects of effective communication for a leader. First, effective leaders should provide employees with the big picture and include more information than is required for the immediate task. People work better when they see the big picture. For example, someone cutting rubber O-rings should understand where that O-ring fits in the assembly of a motor and therefore what kind of quality in the cutting is required to fulfill its purpose in keeping a motor running and reliable (i.e., the O-ring cutter is helping to build a motor). Second, communication must be clear. Effective messages are direct and concise yet communicate all of the critical information. Elaborate communications often obfuscate critical points. The most effective communications are usually short. It is not uncommon for CEOs to request a single-page report on a critical issue. The third point involves listening. Listening can inform the leader about how his or her message is understood and, furthermore, may result in some more advanced iteration of what the leader has proposed. Leaders who have a high rate of speaking and a low rate of listening are often people who have followers who are as little involved as possible.

ENABLING SKILLS

Enabling is a management and an instructional behavior. Management is often misunderstood as a control function because the manager is ultimately responsible for the organizational unit. However, effective leaders do not limit their influence to control. In fact, they spend more time on enabling. Enabling leaders use their position and authority to provide subordinates with opportunities to grow. Rather than taking responsibility directly, an enabling leader or manager delegates responsibility downward, offers support and guidance when requested or deemed necessary, provides feedback and advice, and tolerates error. The enabling leader also provides an opportunity for subordinates to perform in front of more senior executives. In this manner, the leader enables subordinates to develop professionally. It is worth noting that enabling leaders understand their responsibility to develop subordinates and recognize that both their personal position and the organization will benefit from that development.

TEAM-BUILDING SKILLS

A team differs from a group in that the team must collaborate on a shared objective. The composition of a team will significantly influence the leader's leading style. For example, Lowin and Craig (1968) showed that relative to leaders confronted with effective teams, leaders assigned ineffective teams behaved in a significantly less supportive and considerate manner in order to achieve results. Thus, the leader's primary task is not necessarily to lead the team himself or herself but rather to select team members based on expertise and past performance in working with others. For example, if the goal is to produce more creative ideas or products, a leader builds a highly diverse team whose members have widely varied backgrounds. Alternatively, teams required to execute are most effective when based on specific complementary skills and collaboration. An effective leader resembles an orchestra conductor who maintains the tempo and blends the various notes. Similarly, the leader directs his or her efforts to create the proper team for the task, establish trust, and keep members motivated and focused.

CONFRONTING ADVERSITY

Compared to other individuals, effective leaders are complex problem solvers (Mumford & Peterson, 1999). In addition to addressing adversity once it has risen, effective leaders constantly monitor the project's progress in order to prevent or prepare for possible problems. Moreover, relative to nonleaders, they tend to be more optimistic, more practical, and more capable of learning from past experience by building mental models that they in turn apply to new challenges (discussed by Mumford et al., 2000).

In addition to affecting performance, a leader's inability to correct or promptly address obstacles will result in a loss of trust. This is especially true when the leader fails to address the team's poor performance, despite its salience.

TENACITY

On a task of any length and complexity, the early stages, such as planning, are often points of exuberance, but as a project proceeds to implementation, ennui sets in, obstacles come to the fore, and tasks become more onerous. Effective leaders persist under these conditions and successfully influence others to do the same. Anyone who has implemented a strategy can tell you that, no matter the quality of the strategy, its implementation rarely goes as planned, and confronting unforeseen obstacles is something to be expected as a matter of course.

CULTURE-BUILDING SKILLS

Simply put, *culture* can be defined as "the way we do things around here." Under most circumstances a strong culture can be an advantage to effective leadership. A leader must complete several tasks in order to create a supportive and strong culture. First, the staffing of the organization is an important aspect of its cultural well-being. Employees who do not support the firm's culture must be addressed, even if this requires the removal or repositioning of an employee. New hires need to be vetted for fit as well as for competence. Second, trust, reliability, and contiguity of relationships all play a role in building a positive and well-maintained culture. The best cultures cannot be maintained without addressing the inevitable adversity that challenges virtually all cultures. Failure to perform or to fit, the shirking of responsibilities and duties—all of these things must be addressed directly and not allowed to fester. Leadership failure in these circumstances will produce a different kind of culture.

As a final note on the leadership menu, every leader must learn his or her personal leadership strengths and weaknesses. Knowing one's own capabilities makes it possible to secure the assistance of someone who possesses a complementary repertoire that fills a gap in the leader's repertoire.

LEARNING TO LEAD

Personal Assessment

Given the great differences in ways to lead and ways to approach the study of leadership, we believe that one must begin the task by assessing one's own repertoire. It is easier and more fruitful to build leadership skills on already existing strengths. Moreover, by identifying personal weaknesses, one can seek to overcome them or learn to recognize the complementary skills required to lead effectively. For example, making Steve Jobs sensitive and empathic would have been a near impossible task and may have been counterproductive in terms of achieving his vision. Steve, however, did need to complement his visionary skills, his forcefulness, and his passion for innovation with managers who could execute and who could develop cultures.

The question therefore arises of how to objectively assess oneself. Although behaviorists are able to change behavior, they are not particularly skilled at identifying which behaviors should be developed or altered. One possibility that might provide some guidance is the book *Strengths Finder 2.0* by Thomas Rath. Despite not being written from a behavioral point of view, it can assist one in identifying some broad classes of behavior in terms of the strengths and weaknesses in one's repertoire (Rath, 2007).

Alternatively, one might be able to ask friends or coworkers to speak candidly about what they have observed about one's behavior in the past. At the College of William & Mary, frequently solicited candid comments from faculty and fellow students provide students with honest feedback not only on intellectual performance but also on interpersonal and leadership performance in both a formal and an informal manner.

AN EXAMPLE OF PERSONAL ASSESSMENT

Another good way to learn about yourself is to ask yourself and others to describe or to characterize your position within a group or team. When admitted into William & Mary's master's of business administration (MBA) program, students are divided into teams of four or five. Over the course of the program, these teams are responsible for a significant number of tasks, and the students get to know one another quite well. As a result, they can easily identify the team leader, the best numbers person, the best communicator, the most helpful person, the person who makes the best judgments, and so forth. Several years ago, one of us mentored an MBA student who was a member of one of these teams. The student clearly aspired to the leadership role; however, after only a few weeks into the program, he recognized that his team members did not identify him as their leader. This led to a number of discussions about the differences between himself and the team's leader, who had seized that role and would not yield to anyone else. Given that the student did not want to jeopardize the team's performance and hinder future cooperation by aggressively competing for the leadership role, the situation was addressed by focusing on the differences between the chosen team leader and himself.

Upon looking at a number of relevant dimensions, the student recognized that he generated more ideas than the leader, and the team seemed to adopt the ideas proposed. The team respected his knowledge and skills.

Therefore, it was determined that the path to leadership for him was to become the advisor to the leader. In effect, he became the leader of the leader, working behind the scenes. The leader chosen by the team needed the public persona of a leader, but he was often uncertain about how to guide the team, and was happy for the council of the other student. In a business context, other students learned that they were more technically qualified, or more skilled at presenting or at writing, or more capable of consolidating disparate points of view into one agreed-upon position. Sometimes students led because they were extremely good at financial analysis. For them to lead with that strength, it was important for them to seek tasks that required that technical kind of leadership.

The presented example serves to illustrate three points. First, effective leaders attempt to lead through their strongest skills, and they delegate other tasks to people whose skills complement theirs. Second, different environments or challenges dictate different leadership styles. Third, one learns most about oneself by actually leading. And by recognizing skills, weaknesses, and interests, one can identify in what type of context one is most likely to succeed. For example, highly intelligent yet socially awkward individuals are not generally thought of as leaders. However, these individuals are more likely to lead in a highly technical environment or one associated with approaches that are orthogonal to those most readily displayed by most leaders.

Therefore, through self-assessment people should identify the strongest aspects of their behavior repertoire on which to build. Furthermore, they should learn to identify the kinds of environments or tasks in which they would most likely be successful as leaders. In addition to assisting him or her in further developing a leadership repertoire, this step also increases an individual's self-awareness and confidence in his or her abilities. These qualities are necessary for a leader, given that people are not likely to trust and follow someone who questions his or her place within a team.

Teaching Leadership in an Academic Institution

People cannot learn to be leaders by attending a class or reading a book any more than they can learn to play golf by reading a manual. Leadership is learned by leading. Ideally, this process should take place in a semiprotected environment in which students work with an experienced mentor who guides and provides them with advice when requested. In fact, this is precisely how academics train their students to fully comprehend their disciplines. Students are involved in conducting a professor's ongoing research, and in doing so gain a good deal more from lectures and other class experiences.

What ought to underlie all professional education programs is an analysis of what a student must know and do upon entering the work environment. This cannot be adequately taught without some practical experience. Some subjects, including behavior analysis and most sciences, have already adopted this model in their curricula, and students are encouraged to engage in a professor's research. However, experience is much more limited in areas outside of science. For example, a major criticism of law schools is that they offer almost no experiential instruction. In fact, law and business firms hiring new, young employees find that students are technically competent but unprepared for the practice of their profession. The practice of the experiential model is the norm only in medical schools, where 2 years of learning in a classroom setting are followed by 2 years of rotations, where learning takes place in on-the-job training.

LEADERSHIP AT THE MASON SCHOOL OF BUSINESS

In response to feedback from firms and employers, over the past 10 years, William & Mary's Mason School of Business has begun a number of initiatives to better prepare students to lead and manage. Upon entering the MBA program students begin working to select the kind of position and company in which they wish to be employed after graduation. During this time, they prepare a resume and ongoing analysis of where they stand in preparing for that position and identifying what additional work will be required. In their first year, when students are assigned to teams, they begin to focus on their various skills and weaknesses with regard to their leadership potential.

In addition, as part of their first-year program, students take a 1-credit course in which they identify, analyze, and propose a solution to a problem of their choosing. Moreover, they also identify something that they will build or create, such as a new company, a new division, a new product, or a new service. During the second year, students are expected to execute what they prepared in the previous semesters. As they start a new business or install a new process in an existing business, they are responsible for finding their own resources and collaborating with other students who possess critical skills that they lack.

When students want to work on Wall Street upon graduation, they spend a year working in the school's trading classroom, where they manage more than $500,000 worth of investments. Each student works with a mentor who is a corporate-level executive (chief executive officer, chief operating officer, chief information officer, chief financial officer, etc.) and is experienced and knowledgeable in the area of the student's creative endeavor. The students remain ultimately in charge of their decisions, which are not overridden by faculty or mentor.

In the first semester of their second year, students gain practical experience as they spend two sequential half-semester periods in career acceleration modules. In these modules, they study, work, and visit actual companies in their selected specialties. For example, finance students spend time on Wall Street or in national banks, marketing students are involved with big marketing companies like Procter & Gamble, whereas high-technology and entrepreneurial students spend time in the high-tech centers of Silicon Valley or northern Virginia. In addition, the executive partners and the Mason School of Business Entrepreneurship Center secure contracts for $20,000 from different businesses, and students work in teams of five or four and an executive partner to complete these contracts.

LEADERSHIP AT THE STANFORD INSTITUTE FOR DESIGN

Perhaps one of the best approaches that combines education and experience is provided by the Stanford Institute for Design. In the design model of instruction students of widely varying histories and experiences come together to brainstorm, design, and implement a solution to a problem provided by a professor. Generally students work on wicked social problems that cannot be addressed with simple solutions. (The term *wicked* is a term now rising in business that is intended to convey a sense that the problems are very serious, have proven intractable or insurmountable, and carry huge implications.) For example, one team was asked to address the high rate of infant death in India. The students discovered that this trend occurred mostly in the lower classes because, unlike upper class infants, these infants did not have access to incubators. Their first recommendation was to provide incubators for the lower class hospitals. However, on further investigating the issue, they found that rural, poor families did not have access to hospitals or, in many cases, electricity. This finding precluded the first suggestion of buying incubators. After brainstorming and considering a number of ideas they came up with a relatively inexpensive alternative that resembled a papoose carrier and proved to be very effective. Today, this same group manufactures these incubators at a reasonable price and sells them to governments, hospitals, and nonprofits interested in reducing the rate of infant death in less developed countries.

This group's result is not only an excellent example of sustainable social activity, but also an example of entrepreneurship, innovation, and leadership at its best. It further serves to illustrate the direction in which effective leadership can take our society.

Culture Building

This article is focused on leadership and culture, but culture building has yet to be addressed. The primary reason for this is that cultures are more influenced by the leader than any other single factor. Strong cultures tend to reflect or to react to the characteristics of the leader. Still, there remain some salient points to be made about building cultures.

There are conflicting megacomponents in an organization, of which culture is one. Culture is based on the past, whereas strategy tends to focus on the future. In the meantime, the organization continues to function in the present but is nearly always pulled in the other two conflicting directions. Culture is most often a byproduct of a variety of other factors. Rarely is culture a product of direct attempts to produce it as such. It would be difficult to build a valued culture without considering two broad factors that weigh heavily on it: the organization's senior leader and the culture in which it must function. An organization's culture exists within a larger culture of which it is a part. Therefore, it is important to consider external factors, of which only a few are addressed here. One of these is an external point of view. If an organization is not aligned with the external culture(s) of which it is a part, it cannot build an enduring organizational culture. Cultures are alive. They change. The organization must take these changes into account. If the organizational focus is inward, then different parts of the organization will be focused on different aspects of the culture, and the seeds of conflict will emerge. If the focus is external, primarily on customers but also on other beneficiaries of the organization's efforts, then there is a common focus and a basis is laid for both the development of a sound culture and an ability to adopt cultural changes as required. Take the value proposition, for example. If the value proposition is not sound, then it inevitably follows that aversive control will have a dramatic effect on the culture as inevitable conflicts emerge.

Strong cultures that provide a pleasant work environment can be seriously damaged if they do not respond to the external world. Take the example of IBM. From the 1950s to the 1980s IBM was recognized as having one of the finest cultures ever built. The company was inordinately successful. But IBM failed to recognize changes in the larger culture, a move away from mainframes to the personal computer, and IBM had to, in the end, adopt a sea change strategy and become a fundamentally different company. It was a painful process. IBM built such a strong culture that it began to look inward. It became a victim of its strong culture. Today IBM is back, but it is a fundamentally different company.

Never to be underestimated is the influence of the CEO on the culture. Often the CEO does not recognize this influence. In other instances the effects are intended. For example, a leader concerned only with organizational results regardless of how they are accomplished will inevitably hire people who will push the focus to internal variables, and thereby produce a lowered morale and conflict. Hiring practices must consider not only talent but also goodness of fit to avoid the seeds of cultural or organizational damage.

Closing

Leadership and culture are two of the most important topics for business and other organizations. Some organizations understand this; others do not.

In this ever more rapidly changing world, organizations are in an almost constant state of flux. Rather than being thought of as moving from one steady state to another, they should be thought of as moving along a vector. And even the direction of the vector may change. (The term *vector* implies both direction and speed. For example, Hewlett-Packard is currently growing revenues, but shedding or shrinking some hardware businesses while growing software businesses, and doing it all very rapidly.)

Behaviorists can and should have a strong role to play in business and in other kinds of organizations. To date, our impact has been very limited. To change this will require that behaviorists know not only about behavioral concepts and methods but also about business, about organization, and about a particular industry or field of endeavor. Only in this way will behaviorists begin to exert the level of influence they could have. When this understanding is absent, there is a good possibility that the behaviorist will move to solve the wrong problem. The "how" can be found in behaviorism. The "what," for the most part, is to be found outside the field as it currently exists. There is no limit to the growth of behavior analysis and to its impact on the world if behaviorists would combine their ability to bring about change with a deeper understanding of the kinds of organizations and cultures in which they plan to work.

REFERENCES

Chan, K. Y., & Drasgow, F. (2001). Toward a theory of individual differences and leadership: Understanding the motivation to lead. *Journal of Applied Psychology*, *86*, 481–498.

Crant, J. M., & Bateman, T. S. (2000). Charismatic leadership viewed from above: The impact of proactive personality. *Journal of Organizational Behavior*, *21*(1), 63–75.

Fiedler, F. (1964). A contingency model of leadership effectiveness. *Advances in Experimental Social Psychology*, *1*, 149–190.

Galton, F. (1869). *Hereditary genius*. New York, NY: Appleton.

Gibb, C. A. (1954). Leadership. In G. Lindsey (Ed.), *Handbook of social psychology* (pp. 877–917). Cambridge, MA: Addison-Wesley.

Hjelmgaard, K. (2014, January 16). *Ten greatest threats facing the world in 2014*. Retrieved from http://www.usatoday.com/story/news/world/2014/01/16/wef-biggest-risks-facing-world-2014/4505691/

Innovation Pessimism. (2013, January 12). *Has the idea machine broken down?* Retrieved from *The Economist* website: http://www.economist.com/news/briefing/21569381-idea-innovation-and-new-technology-have-stopped-driving-growth-getting-increasing

Isaacson, W. (2011). *Steve Jobs*. New York, NY: Simon & Schuster.

Jacobs, T. O., & Jaques, E. (1991). Executive leadership. In R. Gal & A. D. Mangelsdorff (Eds.), *Handbook of military psychology*. Chichester, England: Wiley.

Krapfl, J. E., Olver, J., Felton, E., Luchs, M., Adkins, C., & Harman, R. (2012). *The Center for Leadership & Management.* Unpublished document, College of William & Mary, Mason School of Business, Williamsburg, VA.

Lowin, A., & Craig, J. R. (1968). The influence of level of performance on managerial style: An experimental object-lesson in the ambiguity of correlational data. *Organizational Behavior and Human Performance, 3,* 440–458.

Mumford, M. D., & Peterson, N. G. (1999). The O*NET content model: Structural considerations in describing jobs. In N. G. Peterson, M. D. Mumford, W. C. Borman, P. R. Jeanneret, & E. A. Fleishman (Eds.), *An occupational information system for the 21st century: The development of O*NET* (pp. 21–30). Washington, DC: American Psychological Association.

Mumford, M. D., Zaccaro, S. J., Harding, F. D., Jacobs, T. O., & Fleishman, E. A. (2000). Leadership skills for a changing world: Solving complex social problems. *Leadership Quarterly, 11,* 11–35.

Northouse, P. G. (2012). *Leadership: Theory and practice.* Thousand Oaks, CA: Sage.

Rath, T. (2007). *Strengths Finder 2.0.* Gallup Press.

Skinner, B. F. (1945). The operational analysis of psychological terms. *Psychological Review, 52*(5), 270–277.

Stogdill, R. M. (1948). Personal factors associated with leadership: A survey of the literature. *Journal of Psychology, 25,* 35–71.

United Nations, World Intellectual Property Organization. (2012). *Global innovation index.*

University of South Florida, The Career Center. (n.d.). *The skills and abilities for the 21st century: A workforce readiness initiative.* Retrieved from http://www.coedu.usf.edu/zalaquett/workforce/sa.htm

Vroom, V. H., & Jago, A. G. (2007). The role of the situation in leadership. *American Psychologist, 62*(1), 17–24.

Yukl, G. A. (2006). *Leadership in organizations* (6th ed.). Upper Saddle River, NJ: Prentice Hall.

Zaccaro, S. J. (2001). *The nature of executive leadership: A conceptual and empirical analysis of success.* Washington, DC: American Psychological Association.

Zaccaro, S. J. (2004). Leadership. In C. Peterson & M. E. P. Seligman (Eds.), *Character strengths and virtues* (pp. 413–428). Oxford, England, and Washington, DC: Oxford University Press and American Psychological Association.

Collective Leadership and Circles: Not Invented Here

Mark Mattaini and Casey Holtschneider

ABSTRACT

Issues like police-community relations, violence—from neighborhood to global levels, economic inequality, and climate change have been only minimally addressed within behavior analysis, despite the oft repeated mantra that they are all at root behavioral. Disciplines determine the scope of their interests; behavior analysis and behavioral systems analysis have long claimed at least potential expertise in changing not only individual behavior, but also the collective and interlocking functioning of larger institutions and systems. In this paper we note that standard organizational behavior management (OBM) practices primarily emphasizing centralized leadership are unlikely to be adequate for such work. We therefore argue that collective leadership, a strategy that has not been emphasized in OBM, will be required to operationalize behavioral systems interventions in situations where centralized leadership is impossible or dangerous, and suggest circle processes as one behaviorally specifiable approach to constructing collective leadership, an approach that behavioral systems analysts are well-positioned to test and refine.

The need for systems/cultural level change addressing intractable and escalating social and environmental challenges is well established (Biglan, 2015; Mattaini & Aspholm, 2016). One of the attractions of behavior analysis for many has been the potential to have an impact on such challenges (certainly since Skinner, 1948, 1953). Issues like police-community relations, violence—from neighborhood to global levels, economic inequality, and climate change have been only minimally addressed within behavior analysis, despite the oft repeated mantra that they are all at root behavioral. Policy and advocacy work occurs constantly in and among governmental, corporate, and non-governmental organizations. However, little collective attention has yet been paid to that work within mainstream organizational behavior management (OBM), with the noticeable exception of efforts related to behavior analyst certification and licensure, and services for persons with disabilities served by behavior analysts. What attention has been paid over the past three decades (see, e.g., Biglan, 1995, 2015; Greene, Winett, Van Houten, Geller, & Iwata,

1987; Mattaini, 2013; Mattaini & Thyer, 1996) often calls for advocacy, policy change, and strategic planning based in a science of cultural and organizational practices, which remain seriously underdeveloped in areas of major social and environmental concern.

Decision making and leadership in the OBM literature are usually discussed in terms of management decisions in situations where data to guide decisions is available, and the primary work to be done involves ensuring that appropriate patterns of interlocking behavioral contingencies are in place to produce desired aggregate products meeting the requirements of receiving systems (Glenn et al., 2016). Relevant interlocking contingencies are often known, or can be estimated with a high probability of accuracy. There is a place for teamwork in such management, but the primary purpose of teams is typically held to "dramatically [increase] the opportunities for receiving positive reinforcement" (Daniels, 2000, p. 137). Daniels, for example, recommends a demand-pull model, in which "specific behaviors expected from team members, team leaders, and managers must be clearly spelled out" (p. 139) with a goal of increasing mutual reinforcement for desired behaviors, those largely identified by senior management. Komaki's Operant Model of Supervision similarly relies on increasing effective monitoring of desirable behaviors, arranging positive consequences, while minimizing antecedent only strategies (Komaki, 1998).

Models of this kind—demonstrably effective in conventional settings—often have limited applicability in settings in which centralized leadership is not realistic, and the interlocking contingencies required to produce desired outcomes and optimal rules to guide them remain largely unknown. Given this situation, some in behavior analysis have suggested that our limited disciplinary resources be directed to smaller projects (including modest laboratory analogues) in which our current knowledge is deeper, avoiding wicked problems like those mentioned in the first paragraph until much more basic science on which to build is in place. That is a defensible position, but not the one taken by the authors, who believe behavioral systems analysis in its current state is likely to have unique contributions to make in addressing contemporary social and global realities, the press of which requires immediate attention. At a minimum, we believe we know enough to propose system-level experiments, and to direct our well-established evaluation methods to those.

A key obstacle to a mainstream OBM emphasis, however, is that addressing community and larger societal issues usually requires some form of collective leadership. (A search indicates that the phrase "collective leadership" has not appeared in the *Journal of Organizational Behavior Management*.) Leadership is clearly necessary, but centralized leadership is not realistically possible in certain systems-level issues that involve multiple, often largely autonomous, cultural entities and powerful actors (Fawcett, Mathews, & Fletcher, 1980; Mattaini, 2013). Furthermore, because only limited knowledge is often available regarding realistic and sustainable solutions and the networks of interlocking contingencies required to achieve them, intervention is likely to require arrangements that encourage disciplined innovation and creativity. Histories of conflict and conflicting values among organizations, communities, and leaders are common, and powerful competing interests often at play in efforts to address our most difficult challenges (Biglan, 2015). The authors believe that some form of collective leadership is necessary under such circumstances (Ganz, 2009; Sharp, 2005). We will also suggest that circle processes, which originated in collective cultures, appear to be highly consistent with core behavior analytic and behavioral systems science principles, and may offer a realistic and testable technology supporting collective leadership. Finally, we will argue that behavioral systems science has unique potential to contribute to the evaluation and refinement of such processes.

Collective leadership

The concept of collective leadership is not unknown within behavior analysis. The fictional planner/manager model in *Walden Two* (Skinner, 1948) is probably the best known example, although Skinner offered limited detail regarding decision-making processes other than that they were firmly grounded in data and respect for individual preferences and differences. Stephen Fawcett's partnerships with communities around local issues emphasized collaborative and locally compatible partnerships for decision making (Fawcett, 1991; Fawcett, Mathews, & Fletcher, 1980). Increasing community participation has also been explored behavior analytically (Mattaini, 1993a), as has improving processes within a community board (Briscoe, Hoffman, & Bailey, 1975). The compendium *Behavior Analysis in the Community* (Greene et al., 1987) includes other valuable and related content. Nonetheless, most of the community and larger systems work that has been done within behavior analysis has focused on relatively discrete behaviors, with little emphasis on collective leadership or shaping complex systems of interlocking behavioral contingencies over time. There are, however, other literatures on which behavior analysts can draw that are largely consistent with a scientific perspective and offer some insight into operationalizing collective leadership.

Marshall Ganz, currently a lecturer in public policy at the Kennedy School of Government at Harvard University, previously director of organizing for the United Farm Workers (UFW), and an organizing and leadership advisor to the first Obama presidential campaign, published a book-length study of leadership and organization in the UFW (2009). In this study he contrasted the UFW with the less successful campaigns of the Teamsters and American Federation of Labor and Congress of Industrial Organizations (AFL-CIO), contextualized with other similar campaigns and related research. Ganz's focus was on "strategic capacity" within leadership teams; he identified two clusters of factors key to strategic capacity: biographical sources, and organizational sources. Biographical dimensions included diversity of life experiences, diversity of social networks, and diversity of tactical repertoires, all of which proved valuable in taking on new challenges where solutions were not yet known, and distinguished between the UFW and the AFL-CIO. (Although not discussed further, it appears that diverse and transdisciplinary experiences and repertoires will be essential in dealing with wicked problems like those identified above.) Particularly germane for our purposes, however, are Ganz's organizational sources, including processes of deliberation and decision making, resources, and accountability structures. The circle processes explored below provide operationalized approaches to deliberation and decision making, identifying and soliciting resources, as well as accountability in ways that are consistent with Ganz' findings as well as with behavior analytic principles—although clearly more research is needed, as discussed later, and behavior analysts are uniquely prepared to complete much of that research.

While early research indicated that traditional brainstorming, avoiding critical analysis, as developed by Alex Osborn, commonly produced solutions to problems inferior to those developed by individuals (Lehrer, 2012), there is considerable evidence within science that teams, collective problem solving, and collective leadership often yield improved solutions to complex or wicked problems (Lee, Brownstein, Mills, & Kohane, 2010; Nemeth & Ormiston, 2007; Wuchty, Jones, & Uzzi, 2007). Elements like the ability within the group to disagree and process that disagreement, physical proximity, and diversity within the group are among the characteristics that research has identified as important. Genuine innovators have in nearly all cases been "part of a movement, a school, a band of followers and disciples and mentors and rivals and friends who saw each other all the time and had long arguments over coffee" (Gladwell, 2002, p. 4).

Examples of structuring such arrangements include establishing architectural arrangements like Building 20 at MIT and Steve Jobs' structuring of Pixar headquarters to enforce interaction across disciplines and perspectives (Lehrer, 2012). In both cases these arrangements led to the clarification of positions, but also in many cases provided powerful motivative conditions for achieving common solutions (Lehrer). Geographic collocation is particularly valuable, due to the intensity of face-to-face contingencies present (Lee et al., 2010). For persons and cultural entities concerned with major social and global issues, structuring such intense, constructional (in Goldiamond's [1974/2002] terms), and creative arrangements can be a difficult challenge. Those concerned are commonly geographically dispersed, and often further divided by conflicting interests, complex political dynamics, and severe time limitations. Nonetheless, while those personally involved may not recognize this, in areas like climate change, economic inequality, and urban violence, long-term interests among many actors, organizations, and other cultural entities merge to a great extent. For example, police, neighborhoods, governmental actors, and inner city young people would all benefit from reduced urban violence, but behavioral and cultural histories and short-term contextual realities often obscure these common interests. Two ultimately compatible but immediately contesting approaches hold the most promise in these situations: collective nonviolent resistance (Aspholm & Mattaini, in press), and the construction of transcultural collective leadership. At least preliminary evidence suggests that variations of circle processes may be one valuable technology supporting nurturance of such leadership. In the material that follows, we first present basic concepts and references related to circle processes as described in the literature, including a brief summary of current evidence for their utility. We then examine possible convergences between circle processes as commonly described and core behavior analytic and behavioral systems concepts, leading to suggestions for further exploration and research supporting collective action on critical social and environmental issues.

Circle processes

Circle processes are traditional to many aboriginal and First Nations cultures around the world. While most commonly associated with restorative justice practices that foster healing as an alternative to punishment, the power of the circle method has been observed and documented in numerous other settings ranging from the court to the classroom to the boardroom.[1] Circles are a method of dialogue rooted in the values of interconnectedness, equality, and respect—principles that are often absent in contemporary decision making among persons of different cultures and power differentials. Circles bring together affected stakeholders through an organized behavioral process that can dramatically increase the probability that divergent perspectives can be understood, evaluated, and incorporated into collective planning and problem-solving. The circle process is at once highly structured and potentially creative; as discussed later, a core set of cultural practices and interlocking contingencies protects this potential.

Before discussing details of circle processes, it is important to clarify that indigenous circle processes (including for decision making, accountability, and healing) often were and are grounded in traditional spirituality and interlocking practices shaped and sustained within unique physical and interpersonal contextual realities. While there are times that such factors

---

[1] For accessible introductions, see Rupert Ross, *Returning to the Teachings: Exploring Aboriginal Justice* (2nd ed.) 2006); Carolyn Boyes-Watson, *Peacemaking Circles and Urban Youth: Bringing Justice Home* 2008); Jennifer Ball, Wayne Caldwell, and Kay Pranis, *Doing Democracy with Circles*.

are appropriately included in contemporary projects (e.g., coming of age programs for African-American youth), in most cases including practices like "smudging" in mainstream groups would be a little more than disrespectful cultural appropriation, and likely to be unnecessarily off-putting to many in mainstream society. The presentation suggests that our cultures have much to learn from others, but that this learning needs to be applied in ways that can be integrated into the values and contextual realities of contemporary societies and cultures.

The process of participating in a circle requires those present to shed often destructive conventional meeting norms by which some are able to monopolize the conversation (often risking silencing and alienating those most impacted by, and often with the most information about, the decisions being made). In the circle, opportunities for speaking rotate around the group and interruptions are excluded; thus responses must be held until a person's turn comes around. This potentiates and to a great extent enforces listening rather than speaking over, and considering responses rather than immediately reacting, thus allowing understanding and planning to evolve collectively and working toward achieving some level of consensus. Circles allow participants to practice (and reinforce) the skills required to create cultural entities that allow space for dialogue and understanding—communities built on the rule that "our fates are intertwined: what happens to one affects what happens to others" (Ball, Caldwell, & Pranis, 2010, p. 35). It is important to note that circles can be demanding and usually do not yield easy solutions; the issues involved typically are complex and often stressful. Recent work as discussed later, however, demonstrates that circle processes often provide opportunities and reinforcers for staying with issues until some level of resolution can be achieved, even if the final outcome is not precisely what any participant expected. As the data discussed below suggest, such resolutions, although they may take time, are more likely to be honored than those that are quickly leveraged by actors (persons or groups) with narrow (often self-) interests, as resistance by the excluded can be minimized—also a finding from long-standing Quaker practices.

Several types of circle processes can be specifically structured to foster collective leadership (see Ball et al., 2010, for details). Learning and understanding circles are conducted to share knowledge, develop more sophisticated and holistic understandings of an issue, and process information shared to move forward in the face of challenges. These processes can facilitate a more complete comprehension of a topic as sharing of information and values facilitates disclosure from multiple sources represented in the circle. Conflict resolution circles bring together individuals who initially see themselves as on opposing sides of an issue to clarify disagreements, explore options, and ultimately search for consensus on moving forward in a way that respects and is acceptable to all parties. The simple practices of sharing thoughts, feelings, and experiences with those you initially disagree with can facilitate understandings required for a positive resolution (Ball, Caldwell, & Pranis, 2010). Community-building circles create bonds and sustain relationships among persons and groups who share common lives or circumstances with the goal of constructing and sustaining a healthy common life.

Accountability circles have been applied in a range of settings including schools, workplaces, and communities, providing a structure for understanding, processing, and repairing harms that may have occurred among parties. Accountability circles also have particular value for ensuring that plans made among voluntary and activist groups working in areas of social responsibility are sustained by those involved (including in one form by Behaviorists for Social Responsibility). Such circles have also been widely used in juvenile and criminal justice settings, and in matrix and team projects within business and nonprofit settings in which they can offer opportunities to maximize targeted reinforcement practices.

Decision-making circles provide a useful strategy in a variety of settings in which groups are making decisions under conditions in which no single actor or representative has adequate knowledge to make optimal decisions. In these circles, established roles can be loosened so that, for example, legislators and constituents share knowledge and power, supervisors and employees have opportunities to hear each other and harness the information each brings to the work being done, or police and community members can establish plans that are acceptable to each. (For descriptions of other types of circles, refer to Ball et al., 2010.)

While circles have been utilized for diverse purposes, their basic structure is consistent across forms. Among essential practices for all participants in circles are (a) negotiating to establish common values; (b) listening attentively and quietly to other participants until one's own turn comes around (typically by circulation of a "talking piece," although variations fitting the setting are common); (c) sharing one's own perspective and responding to others' concisely, honestly, and respectfully; (d) verbally reflecting on one's own and the collective's performance; (e) providing reinforcement to others for their contributions; and (f) committing to continuing participation until the group reaches common understandings. Figure 1 depicts some key practices that structure effective circle processes; if the incidence of any of these is too low, the circle is unlikely to produce optimum outcomes.

Experiences over the past two decades suggest that certain structural arrangements support positive circle outcomes (Ball et al., 2010; Boyes-Watson, 2008; Pranis, Wedge, & Stuart, 2003; Riestenberg, 2012). In most circles, all participants are seated facing one another and only the individual holding the talking piece may speak, then when done, passes the talking piece to the person seated directly next to them. Although it is possible to

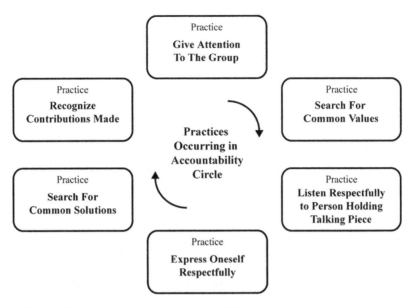

Figure 1. Key practices in effective use of accountability circles.

use only some elements of circle processes but not others, for example, passing a talking peace while using auditorium seating or at a conference table, doing so while facing each other without a barrier in between is generally reported to increase the intensity of participation. Typically circles have formal opening and closing rituals (moments of silence, statements of concern or commitment, even music) designed to focus attention on the present gathering, introductions, and searches for common values and guidelines to guide the circle. Circle processes are guided by one or two circle keepers who ensure that the values and practices of the circle are maintained. This is not a typical leader or facilitator role (although in some settings the labels "facilitator" or "guide" may be more appropriate than the "circle keeper"); there is a delicate balance, as in some settings words like "talking piece" or "keeper" may be uncomfortable, but the message that "what we are doing here is something really different" can also be empha- sized with new language. Nonetheless, language appropriate to the setting can and should be chosen. Regardless of title, circle keepers are equal participants in decisions and sharing, but with the added responsibility of holding the process intact. They are not usually outsiders with no invest- ment in the actions or decisions to be taken, rather they are members of the collective that has come together who have learned the skills of keeping the circle. This role, in fact, is often best rotated.

The core process of the circle centers on a series of questions posed to participants designed to bring perspectives, alternatives, and resolution to the issue at hand. Under most circumstances, circle participants (including circle keepers) speak in a clockwise order, responding to questions initially raised by the circle keeper, although other members may also raise questions (or anything else consistent with collectively developed guidelines) in their turns. Each member of the circle is invited to share how the topic being discussed directly impacts their situation as relevant, along with their perspective and experiences on the issue at hand. Effective circles are enacted to ensure that all voices can be heard, although participants can choose to pass if they do not feel they have something to contribute, or are not comfortable doing so. The goal is usually for solutions acceptable to all participants; some decisions made are therefore necessarily interim or experimental, with full recognition that more may need to be done at a different time or place.

In their primer on the use of circles in public planning, Ball et al. (2010) outline four stages of the circle process. The first is determination of the circle process as suitable for the task at hand. Are participants willing? Are well-prepared keepers and adequate space and time available? Are the intentions of those who have organized the circle prepared to listen to the perspectives, no matter how different, of all those participating? The more genuinely the intentions of participants are communicated, regardless of their differences, the more likely that circle will achieve meaningful outcomes. These questions should be considered in advance to minimize aversive conditions for participants that could interfere with achieving a successful outcome. The second stage Ball et al. (2010) refer to is that of preparation. This includes identifying, inviting, and preparing each participant, gathering as much information about the situation as possible, planning opening and closing rituals and solidifying the logistics for the circle such as time, place, and refreshments.

The third stage is the convening of the circle itself. Circle keepers welcome all participants and lead an opening ritual to help all present transition into a mindful space focused on the issue at hand. The first round of questions should typically include identifying the values (note the connections to Acceptance and Commitment Therapy [ACT] [Hayes, Strosahl, & Wilson, 2011]) that the group would like to hold throughout the circle, and clarifying guidelines that will help the group uphold these values. The circle then turns to rounds of introductions, and an invitation for each to share their experiences and perspectives on the topic being discussed. If participants stray from the guidelines during the circle, the keeper pauses the process and revisits the guidelines, engaging the group in examining whether there is a need for any changes. The work of the circle continues until closure on the issue is reached; a closing round or ritual that honors the process and celebrates connections and progress completes the meeting. Note that elements of circle processes can be incorporated into other meetings in which the whole process would be cumbersome or initially uncomfortable (Boyes-Watson, 2008), although the full process has considerable value. (In fact, such elements are likely to be facilitative in any collective leadership arrangement.) The steps taken during the circle are intended to minimize aversive conditions and reinforce participation by creating an environment where each participant experiences responses indicating that their voice is heard and respected, while being open to appropriate challenges by others. The final stage discussed by Ball et al. (2010) is ensuring that there is appropriate follow-up following the circle (or often sequence of circles). This may include providing a summary of what was discussed to all participants, keeping them updated as to how plans are moving forward, eliciting feedback on the process itself, and planning for follow-up circles where indicated.

Like any other complex repertoire, the skills of guiding and keeping circles require training and shaping as appropriate for various contexts and conditions. A good deal can be learned from literature and video materials, but there is considerable advantage to in situ training experiences, which are available in many large urban areas, most often from organizations significantly associated with juvenile justice, but often with a much broader mission of dissemination of circle processes.

Consistency with behavioral systems science

Although this may be evident to some readers, circle processes incorporate a number of practices and principles that are consistent with behavior analytic and behavioral systems analysis, and that are likely to account for the successes that have been reported.

Practices encouraging empathy

Recent work by Biglan and others on mindfulness and empathy indicates that high levels of empathy and the resulting forbearance lead to improved social and working relationships, reduced stress, and policies reducing conflict and coercion (Biglan, 2015). Well-implemented circle processes encourage empathic exchanges by structuring supporting motivative antecedents and reinforcers. Initial mutual introductions, sharing of values and experiences that bring people to the work of the circle often surface similarities and emotions supporting empathy, while the processes of only one speaking at a time and passing the opportunity around the circle increase the probability that commonalities will be heard. As discussions proceed, additional such opportunities commonly arise. Circle keepers also are positioned to model both sharing and reinforcing it when it occurs.

Practices encouraging acceptance and commitment

Acceptance and commitment therapy and training have become mainstream behavior analytic strategies for both clinical and developmental purposes (Biglan, 2015; Hayes et al., 2011). Carefully paced circle processes increase opportunities to hear and gradually accept the realities of the situations under discussion and of reactions to and positions on issues raised. The strong emphasis on core values both in the beginning and throughout circle work continually brings participants back to those values, thus offering multiple opportunities to commit oneself to collectively valued action, even when that may be uncomfortable. Enhanced empathy is also likely to increase the probability of collective commitment. Keepers have opportunities to shift discussions in these directions, and to bring them back when necessary, throughout the process.

Practices maximizing opportunities reinforcing cooperation and innovation

Overall rates of reinforcing and aversive exchanges have long been known to affect the quality of group functioning (Mattaini, 1993b; Rose, 1977). Discussion rounds within circles offer many opportunities to recognize or agree with contributions of others. Circle keepers, but in fact all members, also have many opportunities to provide motivative antecedents for and to reinforce acts of mutual encouragement, including by modeling and directing questions toward recognizing or increasing current rates of positive exchange. Questions initiated by keepers but also by group members can also be specifically directed toward new ideas, innovations, or how to move beyond current limitations arising in the discussion.

Practices minimizing aversives while encouraging differences

Circles have particular strengths in guiding group processes away from aversive exchanges while concurrently evoking and reinforcing discussions of differences in values, approaches, and desired outcomes. Initial collectively developed guidelines begin to shape these repertoires; the keeper is also empowered to shift discussion back to those guidelines at any point—not so much to "enforce" them, as to structure a discussion among all members (always one at a time around the circle) as to whether the group is satisfied that the guidelines are being followed at the present moment, and whether changes in guidelines should be explored prior to returning to the process. Compliance can and should also periodically be reinforced by keepers. Collectively developed guidelines almost always include listening with respect for others' positions, managing disagreements in honest ways, opportunities for each to speak "their truth," and willingness to hear new ideas. Combined with practices on the part of facilitating evocation of and reinforcement for innovation, a structure consistent with the research reported earlier on effective work groups is likely to emerge. The process of passing a talking piece (literally or figuratively) typically evokes full participation while encouraging deep exploration of multiple understandings and patterns of systemic transactional patterns that can guide decision making.

Common and interlocking practices structuring collective leadership

All of the above practices support the emergence of patterns of collective leadership by bringing the right people together, shaping mutual engagement, providing voice to all participants, evoking deep exploration of the patterns of interlocking system transactions involved in current issues and challenges, and developing and following up on plans to respond to those realities (patterns that behavior analysts have long recognized as challenges for some groups (e.g., Briscoe et al., 1975). Those who have had successful circle experiences often find that elements of those processes can be integrated into other group efforts (e.g., by eliciting comments from those who are silent—including those one expects to disagree with the directions a discussion is currently taking). Familiarity with circles within a collective shapes practices that with encouragement can be sustained outside the circle proper, and those practices can be integrated into daily and long-term interlocking practices within the specific collective, but potentially in its interlocking transactions with other behavioral systems as well.

It is important to note that circle processes are not always rapid; particularly in situations of conflict, even developing common guidelines may take significant time (Boyes-Watson, 2008; Pranis et al., 2003). If there is a real need for collective leadership as discussed above, however, the investment may often be worth the time required. There is a long-standing recognition going back at least to early Quaker processes, (Philadelphia Yearly Meeting, 2002) that decisions made in cases where there is substantial disagreement among important actors often face real challenges in implementation. The greater the agreement on the decision, the less likely such resistance will appear. These assertions, while they have substantial support in some settings, remain anecdotal as general principles. As discussed toward the end of the next section, behavioral systems analysts are particularly well-positioned to contribute to the knowledge base regarding the power and generalizability of circle processes across settings, and more broadly the dynamics of effective collective leadership.

Support for the utility of circle processes in organizations and communities

Data supporting the utility of circle processes in some areas are well developed, while support in others is currently largely anecdotal. Adequate evaluation relying on standard social science methods is in many cases difficult; this is an area in which behavior analytic science could be particularly helpful, given our expertise in interrupted time series and related methods. The strongest support for the use of circle processes is currently found in the restorative justice literature utilized within the criminal justice system. In their meta-analysis of restorative justice practices, most utilizing some form of circle processes, Latimer, Dowden, and Muise (2005) synthesized existing literature meeting criteria for rigor in a meta-analysis from 1980 to 2005. Twenty-two studies of 35 unique restorative justice programs were analyzed; the researchers found evidence that restorative programs were significantly more effective than standard justice processes across the four outcomes of victim and offender satisfaction, restitution compliance, and recidivism. With the exception of mixed findings of the impact of restorative justice approaches on reoffending (Weatherburn & Macadam, 2013), studies completed since the meta-analysis of Latimer and colleagues continue to report promising results for the use of circles as part of an alternative approach to traditional criminal prosecution and sentencing (Bergseth & Bouffard, 2012; De Beus & Rodriguez, 2007; Lambson, 2015; Leonard & Kenny, 2011; Sherman & Strang, 2007). Many of the studies included are limited, however, by a self-selection bias in that participants must agree to participate in the restorative process (Latimer et al., 2005); at the same time, the alternative is typically criminal prosecution, so agreement rates tend to be very high.

There is preliminary descriptive support for the use of circles in other multiple settings for equally varied purposes through numerous case studies. Circles have been used to improve integrated healthcare and thereby overall health outcomes by bringing together patients, their multiple providers, and support systems to work through stressful decisions and circumstances; encourage transparency and understand options for care; process the frustration and fatigue those with chronic illness face; share insights and information with the patient; and heal social relationships that go beyond the physical conditions with which they are struggling (Jordan, 2014; Mehl-Madrona & Mainguy, 2014). Circles have also successfully been used in bringing together community organizations, law enforcement, and youth involved in gangs in the prevention of violence (Boyes-Watson, 2008); increasing academic achievement and safety and reducing delinquency in schools (Hopkins, 2002; Porter, 2007); and intervening in domestic violence with both victims and offenders (Zakheim, 2011). In all of these cases, evaluation relying on pooling many cases and even randomized experiments is possible, often with increasingly rigorous designs as results accumulate.

Perhaps of most interest, circle processes have demonstrated utility for planning for property development in townships of farmers, residents, developers, and landowners with competing interests and concerns (Ball et al., 2010), and making operational decisions in board of directors meetings for corporations and nonprofit organizations (Baldwin, Linnea, & Wheatley, 2010).

In most cases, organizational contexts and change efforts in one setting are substantially different than in other settings, even within organizations with somewhat similar mandates and challenges. At best, a small number of similar cases may be available for study. Rigorous evaluation has therefore proven difficult up to now. Such situations are, however, ideal settings and occasions for the use of time-series designs within organizations and across small numbers of cases. The rigorous testing of circle processes in most organizational settings therefore awaits exactly the methods in which behavior analysts are highly skilled (Biglan, Ary, & Wagenaar, 2000).

Behavioral systems science has much to learn, and likely some things to teach, in the development of effective processes supporting productive collective leadership. Disciplines determine the scope of their interests; behavior analysis and behavioral systems analysis have long claimed at least potential expertise in changing not only individual behavior, but also the collective and interlocking functioning of larger institutions and systems. Given the historic challenges currently faced by human collectives and societies, it is time to test the hypothesis that we have something substantial to offer in these areas. Collective leadership will be required to operationalize behavioral systems interventions in situations where centralized leadership is impossible or dangerous. Circle processes are one behaviorally specifiable approach to constructing collective leadership that behavioral systems analysts are well-positioned to test.

References

Aspholm, R. R., & Mattaini, M. A. (in press). Youth activism as violence prevention. In P. Sturmey (Ed.), *Wiley handbook of violence and aggression*. Hoboken, NJ: John Wiley and Sons.

Baldwin, C., Linnea, A., & Wheatley, M. (2010). *The circle way: A leader in every chair*. San Francisco, CA: Berrett-Koehler Publishers, Inc.

Ball, J., Caldwell, W., & Pranis, K. (2010). *Doing democracy with circles: Engaging communities in public planning*. Saint Paul, MN: Living Justice Press.

Bergseth, K. J., & Bouffard, J. A. (2012). Examining the effectiveness of a restorative justice program for various types of juvenile offenders. *International Journal of Offender Therapy and Comparative Criminology, 57*, 1054–1075. doi:10.1177/0306624X12453551

Biglan, A. (1995). *Changing cultural practices*. Reno, NV: Context Press.

Biglan, A. (2015). *The nurture effect: How the science of human behavior can improve our lives and our world*. Oakland, CA: New Harbinger.

Biglan, A., Ary, D., & Wagenaar, A. C. (2000). The value of interrupted time series experiments for community intervention research. *Prevention Science, 1*, 31–49. doi:10.1023/A:1010024016308

Boyes-Watson, C. (2008). *Peacemaking circles and urban youth: Bringing justice home*. St Paul, MN: Living Justice Press.

Briscoe, R. V., Hoffman, D. B., & Bailey, J. S. (1975). Behavioral community psychology: Training a community board to problem solve. *Journal of Applied Behavior Analysis, 8*, 157–168. doi:10.1901/jaba.1975.8-157

Daniels, A. C. (2000). *Bringing out the best in people* (2nd ed.). New York, NY: McGraw-Hill.

De Beus, K., & Rodriguez, N. (2007). Restorative justice practice: An examination of problem completion and recidivism. *Journal of Criminal Justice, 35*, 337–347. doi:10.1016/j.jcrimjus.2007.03.009

Fawcett, S. B. (1991). Some values guiding community research and action. *Journal of Applied Behavior Analysis, 24*, 621–636. doi:10.1901/jaba.1991.24-621

Fawcett, S. B., Mathews, R. M., & Fletcher, R. K. (1980). Some promising dimensions for behavioral community technology. *Journal of Applied Behavior Analysis, 13*, 505–518. doi:10.1901/jaba.1980.13-505

Ganz, M. (2009). *Why David sometimes wins*. Oxford, England: Oxford University Press.

Gladwell, M. (2002, November 25). Group think. *The New Yorker*, p. 4.

Glenn, S., Malott, M., Andery, M., Benvenuti, M., Houmanfar, R., Sandaker, I., ... Vasconcelos, L. (2016). Toward consistent terminology in a behaviorist approach to cultural analysis. *Behavior and Social Issues, 25*, 11–27. doi:10.5210/bsi.v25i0.6634

Goldiamond, I. (1974/2002). Toward a constructional approach to social problems: Ethical and constitutional issues raised by applied behavior analysis. *Behavior and Social Issues, 11*, 108–197. (Originally published in *Behaviorism, 2*, 1–84.) doi:10.5210/bsi.v11i2.92

Greene, B. F., Winett, R. A., Van Houten, R., Geller, E. S., & Iwata, B. A. (1987). *Behavior analysis in the community, 1968-1986, from the journal of applied behavior analysis*. Lawrence, KS: Society for the Experimental Analysis of Behavior.

Hayes, S. C., Strosahl, K. D., & Wilson, K. G. (2011). *Acceptance and commitment therapy: The process and practice of mindful change* (2nd ed.). New York, NY: Guilford.

Hopkins, B. (2002). Restorative justice in schools. *Support for Learning, 17*, 144–149. doi:10.1111/1467-9604.00254

Jordan, M. (2014). Healing circles: An ethnographic study of the interactions among health and healing practitioners from multiple disciplines. *Global Advances in ... Health and Medicine, 3*(4), 9–13. doi:10.7453/gahmj.2014.035

Komaki, J. L. (1998). *Leadership from an operant perspective*. Abingdon-on-Thames, England: Routledge.

Lambson, S. H. (2015). *Peacemaking circles: Evaluating a native American restorative justice practice in a state criminal court setting in Brooklyn*. New York, NY: Center for Court Innovation.

Latimer, J., Dowden, C., & Muise, D. (2005). The effectiveness of restorative justice practices: A meta-analysis. *The Prison Journal, 85*, 127–144. doi:10.1177/0032885505276969

Lee, K., Brownstein, J. S., Mills, R. G., & Kohane, I. S. (2010). Does collocation inform the impact of collaboration? *Plos ONE, 5*(12), e14279. doi:10.1371/journal.pone.0014279

Lehrer, J. (2012, January 30). Groupthink: The brainstorming myth. *The New Yorker*. Retrieved from www.newyorker.com/magazine/2002/12/02/group-think

Leonard, L., & Kenny, P. (2011). Measuring the effectiveness of restorative justice practices in the republic of Ireland through a meta-analysis of functionalist exchange. *The Prison Journal, 91*, 57–80. doi:10.1177/0032885510389561

Mattaini, M. A. (1993a). Behavior analysis and community practice: A review. *Research on Social Work Practice, 3*, 420–447. doi:10.1177/104973159300300405

Mattaini, M. A. (1993b). *More than a thousand words: Graphics for clinical practice*. Washington, DC: NASW Press.

Mattaini, M. A. (2013). *Strategic nonviolent power: The science of Satyagraha*. Edmonton, AB: Athabasca University Press.

Mattaini, M. A., & Aspholm, R. R. (2016). Contributions of behavioral systems science to leadership for a new progressive movement. *The Behavior Analyst, 39*, 109–121. doi:10.1007/s40614-015-0043-4

Mattaini, M. A., & Thyer, B. A. (Eds.). (1996). *Finding solutions to social problems: Behavioral strategies for change*. Washington, DC: American Psychological Association Press.

Mehl-Madrona, L., & Mainguy, B. (2014). Introducing healing circles and talking circles into primary care. *The Permanente Journal, 18*(2), 1–9.

Nemeth, C. J., & Ormiston, M. (2007). Creative idea generation: Harmony versus stimulation. *European Journal of Experimental Social Psychology, 37*, 524–535. doi:10.1002/ejsp.373

Philadelphia Yearly Meeting. (2002). *Faith and practice*. Philadelphia, PA: Philadelphia Meeting of the Religious Society of Friends.

Porter, A. (2007, June 6). Restorative practices in schools: Research reveals power of restorative approach. *Restorative Practices E-Forum*. Retrieved from https://www.iirp.edu/iirpWebsites/web/uploads/article_pdfs/schoolresearch2.pdf

Pranis, K., Wedge, M., & Stuart, B. (2003). *Peacemaking circles: From conflict to community*. St. Paul, MN: Living Justice Press.

Riestenberg, N. (2012). *Circle in the square: Building community and repairing harm in school*. St. Paul, MN: Living Justice Press.

Rose, S. D. (1977). *Group therapy: A behavioral approach*. Upper Saddle River, NJ: Prentice-Hall.

Ross, R. (2006). *Returning to the teachings: Exploring aboriginal justice* (2nd ed.). Toronto, ON: Penguin Canada.

Sharp, G. (2005). *Waging nonviolent struggle: Twentieth century practice and twenty-first century potential*. Boston, MA: Extending Horizons Books.

Sherman, L., & Strang, H. (2007). *Restorative justice: The evidence*. London, UK: The Smith Institute. Retrieved from: http://www.iirp.edu/pdf/RJ_full_report.pdf

Skinner, B. F. (1948). *Walden two*. New York, NY: Macmillan.

Skinner, B. F. (1953). *Science and human behavior*. New York, NY: Free Press.

Weatherburn, D., & Macadam, M. (2013). A review of restorative justice responses to offending. *Evidence Base, 1*, 1–20.

Wuchty, S., Jones, B. F., & Uzzi, B. (2007). The increasing dominance of teams in production of knowledge. *Science, 316*(5827), 1036–1039. doi:10.1126/science.1136099

Zakheim, S. F. (2011). Healing circles as an alternative to batterer intervention programs for addressing domestic violence among orthodox jews. *Partner Abuse, 2*, 484–496. doi:10.1891/1946-6560.2.4.484

Integrating Organizational-Cultural Values With Performance Management

Carl Binder

ABSTRACT

Early analyses of organizational culture used and an approach derived from cultural anthropology to provide guidance for leaders, managers, and employees, but lacked units of analysis congruent with behavior science. More recent approaches identify values and practices, the latter being behavior which can be analyzed. However, the abstract language of this approach limits our ability to set specific performance expectations and relies on post-hoc recognition and reinforcement. This article outlines an approach that anchors performance analysis in the valuable work outputs (accomplishments) produced by behavior, and uses value statements to adjust expectations for work outputs and behavior. With this approach we can define how specific values apply to specific work outputs and behavior, and set clear performance expectations. The author proposes that performance analysis anchored in work outputs may improve our ability to set expectations and arrange conditions for optimizing values-driven performance in organizational or societal contexts.

Introduction

The recent special issue of *Journal of Organizational Behavior Management* on leadership and culture change (Houmanfar & Mattaini, 2015) covered topics and perspectives related to how we define, strengthen, lead, change, and contribute to culture—whether in societies at large or within specific organizations. Many contributors to the field of organizational behavior management (OBM) have become involved personally or professionally in efforts to contribute to society; to change things for the better; and to address pressing societal issues, such as environmental sustainability, poverty, and so on.

At the same time, those interested in leadership and culture change have sought to define the repertoires of leaders needed to drive change in organizations and communities. Thus, the discussion of culture applies to specific companies and nonbusiness organizations in which cultural values such as *focus on the customer, environmental sustainability, innovation*, or *diversity* are often stated and sometimes lived. It also applies to communities and societies as a whole, in which shifts in cultural values can contribute to or obstruct progress toward societal or environmental goals or visions. This article describes a recently emerging approach for integrating cultural values (whether societal or organizational) into descriptions of specific performance to set expectations for leaders, managers, and those being managed or led.

Previous approaches to organizational culture

In their classic treatment of organizational culture, Deal and Kennedy (1982) approached organizations as social anthropologists. Identifying values, legends, rituals, heroes, and other elements of traditional culture analysis, the authors encouraged readers to be aware of these cultural factors as key contributors to organizational effectiveness and results. They offered descriptions and examples following this anthropological analysis with recommendations for those entering, seeking to understand, and hoping to survive and thrive in organizations. They proposed that leaders examine their organizations with these factors in mind and take advantage of them while adjusting them in ways to optimize performance.

Although this approach was interesting and novel at the time, it was not as actionable as an organizational performance improvement professional might like. Nonetheless, such anthropological analyses, language, and metaphors continued in the business literature for some time and are still sometimes part of the vocabulary of those concerned about understanding and managing variables that drive organizational performance.

The emerging attention to culture alerted leaders and consultants to the fact that there is more to overall organizational success than straightforward operational efficiency and productivity or financial management. Culture, which has often been described as "how we do things around here," was recognized as a critical success factor, in some cases more important than the relatively cut and dried operational influences per se. Case studies highlighting different cultural values and their impact on organizational performance and employee satisfaction described how leaders and employees behave in different types of organizations and profiled cultures as reflecting degrees of risk taking, individualism, pace of activity, and so on (Deal & Kennedy, 1982).

Much like competency models used by human resources professionals in the current era (Teodorescu & Binder, 2004), these general descriptors were useful up to a point for analysis and description. But they ultimately fell short of the specificity or precision needed for systematic performance management. These high-level, abstract descriptions of cultural characteristics were difficult to apply precisely in day-to-day operations.

There have been various treatments of organizational culture in the general business literature since 1982, and discussion among behavior analysts about culture aligned with contingencies and metacontingencies of reinforcement for decades (e.g., Glenn, 2004; Houmanfar, Alavosius, Morford, Herbst, & Reimer, 2105; Skinner, 1956). An immediate precursor for the current article, however, was a model advanced by Tosti and Jackson (1994, 1997a), two thought leaders in the International Society for Performance Improvement. Both Tosti and Jackson had been active in early applications of behavior science to instructional design and development and over time had become involved at more strategic levels in organizations, working with executives and their teams to improve performance from the top down. Their analysis, similar to that in the present article, was less technically behavior analytic and more pragmatic, using terminology often found among business stakeholders rather than at the level of analysis applied by OBM scholars and practitioners.

Their organizational alignment model (Tosti & Jackson, 1994) depicted how operational performance should be aligned with organizational culture. They claimed that organizational culture could sometimes account for more than half of the variance in performance among companies. They engaged stakeholders at the highest levels and across entire organizations in the analysis, clarification, and modification of organizational culture.

Tosti and Jackson (1994) identified *values* and *practices* as key elements for analyzing and improving organizational culture. They did not define values in the ways in which previously cited behavior analysts have done, focused on a functional analysis of consequences to determine value. Rather, they identified *values*, or *value statements*, as words or phrases that describe generally how people are expected to work; what they should prioritize; and how they should behave in relation to one another, customers, and society at large. In other words, they attempted to put the words and phrases so commonly posted on the walls of large organizations, listed in company literature and on websites, and referenced in training and management gatherings into practice through the day-to-day behavior of employees. They defined *practices* as the habitual or routine forms of behavior that put values into action, the types of behavior that characterize "how we do things around here." This is similar to, but not precisely the same as, Glenn's (2004) description of organizational practices as macrobehavior.

Tosti (Tosti & Jackson, 1997a) often cited an engagement with British Airways in which he and his colleagues worked from the top down in the organization to install the value of *openness* with a key practice for application in daily activities. The airline was suffering in comparison to its competitors from a lack of agility in the marketplace and too little innovation or adaptation in the competitive landscape. Analysis determined that the company lacked *openness* in its culture and that employees were often restrained and less than forthcoming in their communications with one another. Such behavior was consistent with, and perhaps an extreme form of, the British national culture at the time. This obstruction to free communication was thought to slow down operational processes and change. Thus, the value of *openness* was selected as a focus for strategic reasons.

The consultants worked in a series of workshops to gain agreement from the top to the bottom of the organization for the practice *openness* in 1:1 or group. Using an elegantly printed "openness card" supplied to everyone for immediate access in their pockets, the leadership encouraged employees to "pull the openness card" in meetings by reciting text on the card that read, "In the spirit of openness I'd appreciate your hearing me out and giving me your full considered opinion" (Tosti & Jackson, 1997b). With agreement established to comply with the protocol and thank those who followed the practice, the behavior of freely exchanging information became a widespread practice in the organization, with a culture scan some months later indicating a change in this general category of behavior. Eventually people misplaced their cards and simply used approximations of the language. But over time this new practice took hold and was sustained. It was judged by the executive leadership and through employee surveys to have led to acceleration of innovation and problem solving across the company.

When my colleagues and I first learned about this approach from Tosti and Jackson in the early 1990s, we were impressed by how they had been able to identify an antidote to a behavioral problem (constrained communication) and establish a widespread form of behavior in conversations and meetings designed to change "how we do things around here" on a daily basis. This was a significant change in culture, accomplished in relatively short order. Combined with Tosti's observation that much of organizational performance depends on culture, this approach was compelling and actionable, framed as a type of organizational development intervention.

We began to seek opportunities for this kind of project, even discussing with Tosti possible partnering with him and his team. Over time, however, we realized that opportunities for this type of work are rare. Such projects are typically restricted to consultants working at the top of large organizations, senior executives themselves, or those able to work with smaller organizations in which the entire management team is accessible for and interested in the effort. In other words, we learned that despite the seeming power of the approach, it might not be as easy to implement as we had originally thought. We began to recognize other, more technical challenges as well.

Working with culture: Challenges and opportunities

As we sought opportunities to address cultural issues or define and strengthen culture in organizations, the problem of finding the right level of generality became a challenge. That is, the problem with words and phrases that describe organization-wide (or societal) values is that they must by definition refer to very wide arrays of specific situations in order to be useful. In that respect such value statements resemble poorly defined concepts, with large sloppy sets of examples and nonexamples used to define and teach recognition and application. Although British Airways was fortunate to find a pervasive issue to address with a specific but broadly applicable practice (i.e., following the openness protocol in virtually every meeting with others), it is not always easy to identify behavior that will have so much leverage across a wide range of operational performance situations.

Often value statements such as *focus on the customer* or *quality first* read well on posters and presentation slides but are not so easy to pin down for all of the people and situations in the organization where they might apply. They likely require different specific behavior in different job roles or in the execution of different processes. A symptom of this problem of using abstract words and phrases (generalizations) to pinpoint different forms of behavior is that it can resemble the infamous film censors who said about pornography, "I can't tell you what it is. But I know it when I see it."

To identify and recognize exemplary practice of values across entire organizations, leaders and human resources professionals often design interventions that include the following:

- Communicating value statements and engaging leaders and managers as models and evangelists
- Illustrating values and teaching practices with examples and nonexamples, testimonials, readings, and so on
- Identifying exemplary instances of practicing the values post hoc, using awards, video testimonials, and descriptions about how people behaved in particular situations to serve as models and encouragement for others

The challenge is to provide a sufficient range of models, or expectations, for performance. Although we can identify exemplary cases in retrospect, doing so is a slow process likely to illustrate only some possible types of values-based practice. Such efforts are likely to lose momentum over time unless continuously reinforced and refined. Many cultural initiatives either fade away with the impression that they have helped or continue in forms that resemble employee-of-the-month award programs, offering little or no reinforcement for most people's practice of the values. This is not a formula for rapid behavior change.

Additional challenges beyond the problem of abstraction or generality include the likely necessity of implementing across whole organizations at once. Even if there is an attempt at multiple-baseline implementation and evaluation across business units or departments, cultural interventions of the

Tosti and Jackson variety are likely to require the attention of senior leadership and will tend to bleed from one part of the company to others, not always effectively or with great fidelity. This means that an organization must devote significant high-level executive and management attention and allocate significant resources for consulting or internal staff work. In most cases, we would expect challenges related to the level of generality in the language of value statements and the inability to crisply characterize what the value looks like as it is practiced across different job roles, teams, processes, and so on.

Even in the example of openness cited by Tosti and Jackson, implementation was preceded by months of high-level alignment meetings, departmental discussions, and related activities to be sure that everyone was on board. For most value statements, there will be greater variety in the types of behavior needed to practice the values than in the case of openness in meetings. Does *focus on the customer* look the same in customer service as it does in product development? Of course it does not. Use of abstract terms to describe behavior leaves application open to wide interpretation for any individual, team, department, or process.

A technical solution to the level of generality problem

A key to addressing these challenges lies in anchoring analyses and descriptions of human performance on the products of behavior rather than starting with descriptions of behavior itself. There are many reasons to appreciate the contributions of Thomas F. Gilbert (1978) and his colleagues. One of Gilbert's most important contributions was his critique of the "cult of behavior" (Gilbert, 1978, p. 7) and his efforts to shift our focus in the analysis of performance from behavior to what he called *accomplishments*. Accomplishments, in Gilbert's terms, are the *valuable products of behavior*. To be clear, his reference to accomplishments (what I call *work outputs*) did not necessarily mean that for the individuals or groups producing them the accomplishments were reinforcers, technically defined. Rather, he meant that accomplishments were valuable to the organization to the extent that they contributed to organizational or business results.

Thus, he distinguished between accomplishments and incentives, which might or might not be the same, and listed incentives as one of the variables in his behavior engineering model that influence behavior (Gilbert, 1978), not assuming that accomplishments themselves would be functional consequences for those who produce them. Reinforcement of behavior might come from other sources, including social consequences or incentives arranged by the organization. Gilbert pointed out that in organizations, the value we create or pass on resides in the products of behavior, not in the behavior itself. He criticized the cult of behavior as the mistaken belief that behavior should be the focus of performance improvement, in contrast to his view that behavior is valuable only to the extent that it produces valuable accomplishments.

Organizationally, financially, and even metabolically speaking, behavior is *costly*, whereas accomplishments are *valuable*. Gilbert described the worth of a performance intervention as being equal to the value of the incremental accomplishments it produces divided by the cost of establishing and supporting the behavior that produces the accomplishments, these days often described as return on investment. This assertion can be tested against any number of scenarios, for example, the value of an important decision versus the cost of the behavior to produce it, or the value of a new product prototype versus the cost for behavior to produce it. We see this in our personal lives as well, in which we invest significant amounts of our behavior into relationships that we seek to establish and maintain. Viewed through the lens of performance analysis, those relationships are accomplishments (work outputs) that either do or do not meet implicit criteria for "good." Examples abound in the business world, where the work outputs that people deliver to the organization are what enable it to succeed (see Figure 1).

Based on this insight from Gilbert, we (Binder, 2005) developed a model called the *Performance Chain*, which delineates the elements of performance and their sequential dependencies as simply as possible. As part of developing the model, we labeled it with plain English words and phrases that virtually anyone can understand and apply. *Behavior influences* are the variables that enable or obstruct behavior. *Behavior* includes the tasks and tactics—the activities, whether overt or covert—that produce work outputs. *Work outputs* are the products of behavior, what Gilbert called *accomplishments*. And *business results* are the organization-level outcomes that define the success of the organization or business in relation to its mission and goals. In operation, each element of the chain affects the element to its right, while we analyze and plan from right to left.

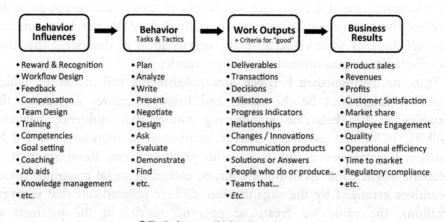

© The Performance Thinking Network

Figure 1. The Performance Chain.

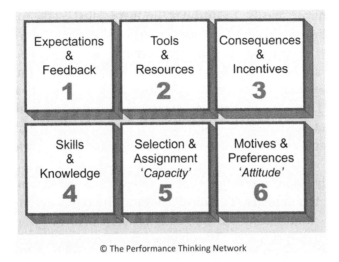

© The Performance Thinking Network

Figure 2. The Six Boxes® Model.

The Performance Chain model defines the performance to which we apply the variables identified in the Six Boxes® Model of behavior influence (Binder, 1998). The Six Boxes Model is a descendent of Gilbert's behavior engineering model, improving on his model with user-tested plain English labels to accelerate learning, communication, and application. This model, developed in the mid-1980s in response to stakeholder confusion about Gilbert's behavior engineering model terminology, enables analysis and communication among stakeholders at all levels in organizations about the factors that influence behavior (see Figure 2).

Although we do not teach our clients the intricacies or terminology of functional behavior analysis, the Six Boxes Model provides a framework in which skilled behavior analysts can apply what they know about the contingencies of reinforcement in the context of other variables such as existing employee repertoires (skills and knowledge), tools and resources, employee selection factors, and the identification of individual and group preferences. We can also use the Six Boxes Model as a framework for *teaching* more precise application of the findings and concepts of behavior science. Our claim, which has proven so far to be true, is that any variable one can identify that influences behavior can fit into one of the cells of this model, or relationships among the cells (e.g., expectations aligned with consequences). Although a detailed description of that formulation is beyond the scope of this article, the reader can refer to white papers and publications at the website sixboxes.com for more information.

Our focus in developing both of these models in the mid 1980s was on simplicity and plain language for the sake of easy learning and communication. We discovered that the language of Gilbert's (1978) models did not communicate easily to ordinary nonspecialist stakeholders, so we began changing terms and phrases until we arrived at what we have now. We user-tested the language in iterations as we refined the models for several years between about 1984 and 1988. A client, Tom Hogan, who brought street-smart sales and marketing savvy to his job as sales vice-president at Dun and Bradstreet, suggested that we call it the Six Boxes Model, a label that stuck. We ultimately trademarked the name to protect its integrity and ensure consistent use of language in any reference to the model.

Accordingly, there are differences in language between our two models and Gilbert's terminology. The most relevant difference here is that we use the phrase *work output* rather than *accomplishment* to describe the valuable products of human behavior. We changed this language for several reasons. First, dictionary definitions of *accomplishment* generally include at least one reference to behavior (e.g., "an activity that a person can do well, typically as a result of study or practice") (Soanes, Hawker, & Elliott, 2009). Second, and perhaps related to the dictionary definition, we found that people often confuse *accomplishments* with *behavior*. This is a common and understandable confusion, and the phrase *work output* does not seem to occasion descriptions of behavior quite so often, at least among our audiences of ordinary organizational employees, educators, and others.

We insist that work outputs are *things*, tangible or less tangible things that can be described as countable nouns (e.g., documents, widgets, decisions, new ideas, relationships that meet specific criteria). We emphasize nouns rather than verbs, including passive verbs. We find even in sophisticated performance improvement and OBM groups descriptions of accomplishments such as *procedure completed*—a passive verb rather than a countable noun that is the product of behavior. Following Gilbert's lead, we prefer to anchor our analyses of performance on the valuable products of behavior, what is left after the behavior is finished, not mere completion of the behavior itself. In early attempts to teach people the distinction, we found that the phrase *work output* resulted in fewer category errors than the word *accomplishment*.

Once we define a work output, stakeholders work to agree on criteria for a "good" instance of the work output—characteristics of the work output itself that make it valuable. Those might include details of magnitude, quality, timeliness, or other factors that specify what "good" means—often defined by downstream users or recipients of the work outputs. As mentioned previously, we insist that work outputs be *countable*, a guideline not shared by some of our colleagues in the fields of OBM and performance improvement. We have seen many examples of accomplishments described as *information*, *advice*, or *support* or in other ways that are not *countable* nouns. We believe that until a work output is countable—specifying what could be called a *unit of analysis*—it is difficult to determine whether it is "good" or "not good." We must know for each work output—whether a deliverable, a decision, a new idea, a widget, a relationship, or something else—what a good one looks like. Once we define work outputs and criteria, we can more easily pinpoint the behavior needed to produce work outputs to criterion and measure (count) the work outputs that do and do not meet criteria. This approach is similar to common practice in manufacturing process improvement.

It is important to note that work outputs might include *people who can do or produce something specific* (the work output of a trainer) or things produced by a manager designed to be behavior influences for others (e.g., goals, feedbacks, consequences). We find that it is possible to adequately describe any role/job title or individual's work with a list of major work outputs far more easily than with endless (or truncated) descriptions of behavior. We can likewise pinpoint the intermediate and final work outputs produced by the steps in any process.

We use the Performance Chain and the Six Boxes Model in our proprietary programs to teach performance improvement to leaders, managers, coaches, consultants, and staff performance professionals in many specialties (e.g., human resources, training and development, process improvement, quality, organizational development, performance consulting). They begin by capturing the language used by leaders and investors/owners to define the organization-level business results (e.g., profit, revenue, employee engagement, regulatory compliance, quality) at the right end of the Performance Chain. Once they know what is at stake for the whole organization, they identify the work outputs involved in the performance their clients or teams seek to establish, improve, manage, or support. They define criteria for a *good* instance of each work output ("what good looks like") and describe the behavior needed to produce work outputs at whatever level of detail is needed.

These steps start with the end in mind, using elements of the Performance Chain to define existing and/or desired performance. Business results define success for the organization, work outputs that contribute to those business results identify value delivered by people and processes, and behavior is what people must do in order to produce the valuable work outputs. Once we identify critical behavior, we can analyze and arrange behavior influences to optimize performance, framed by the cells of the Six Boxes Model. This is the Performance Improvement Logic that we teach, based on simple models of the elements of performance and the variables that influence it.

Given this synopsis of our technical approach to performance analysis, let us proceed to a discussion of how we apply it in work with organizational culture and potentially with societal culture as well.

How cultural values can influence performance expectations

As mentioned previously, our work with culture and culture change has been driven more by the definitions of values and practices advanced by Tosti and Jackson (1994) than by the extensive analyses of behavior, macrobehavior, and metacontingencies conducted by Skinner (1956), Glenn (2004), Houmanfar et al. (2015), and others. Although we acknowledge the excellent analyses conducted by these and other scholars, our vocabulary derives more from plain English discussions of values and practices that we encounter among stakeholders and leaders in organizations than from the scholarly literature.

As noted previously, most descriptions of cultural practices are open to wide interpretation by those attempting to apply them to *their* jobs or processes. Such lack of specificity undermines the ability of leaders and managers to set clear expectations for individuals and groups of employees. It muddies the waters for measurement of how people apply cultural values, and it makes detailed implementation planning and management of cultural change or cultural strengthening more difficult at the individual, departmental, or process levels of the organization, where practices associated with value statements might differ significantly.

Using the Performance Chain as a guide to identify the valuable work outputs that any job or process must deliver, and the behavior needed to deliver it, we can create a framework for setting specific performance expectations, providing feedback, enabling performance with tools and resources, accelerating behavior with positive consequences, and so on. Over the past several years, in our work to develop leaders and managers in several Korean conglomerates, in which cultural differences and culture change are high priorities, we realized that there are only two points on the Performance Chain at which a cultural value can influence desired performance. Practice of the value may change *criteria* considered to be "good" for any given work output, and it will certainly change or refine descriptions of the *behavior* needed to produce the work output. In addition, a given cultural value might or might not be relevant to a particular work output. For example, the new Korean corporate value of *challenging fixed ideas* probably does not apply to many work outputs in accounting departments but certainly applies to work in research and development.

Consider the following three examples of how organizational values might affect the definition of desired performance specified by work outputs and behavior.

Example 1: Impact of openness on decisions

In the Tosti and Jackson (1997a) example from British Airways, the value of *openness* was practiced in meetings between people. A typical work output from such meetings might be a *decision*, or perhaps a *recommendation*. Note

Table 1. Impact of the Value *Openness* on Decisions.

Cultural value	Work output	Criteria for "good"	Behavior
Openness	Decision in a 1:1 meeting	Based on full mutual disclosure	Say and gain agreement: "In the spirit of openness, I'd appreciate your hearing me out and giving me your full considered opinion."
Career advancement	Decision in a 1:1 meeting	What I want	Only disclose what is necessary to sway opinion and do not disclose any contrary information.

that although the process of deciding might entail many different types of behavior, when that behavior is successful, it produces a work output called a *decision*. In a culture that practices *openness*, criteria for what would be considered a "good" decision might be (in addition to its producing the desired organizational impact) that it reflects or takes into account the fully considered opinions of those involved in the meeting. This might be in contrast to a decision made in a culture in which participants do not practice openness and consequently only reveal information beneficial to their own particular careers or desired outcomes. In arriving at decisions in those two cultures, people will behave quite differently, and their work outputs will differ accordingly. Table 1 summarizes this analysis.

This example may remind some readers of meetings in which they have participated, with the behavior in those meetings driven more by the individual goals of people in the meetings and not so much by collective organizational or cultural values. Definitions of a "good" decision, and the behavior for producing it, vary depending on values.

Example 2: Impact of fairness to customers on pricing agreements

For one of our clients, a supply chain and transportation logistics company that seeks to distinguish itself from the competition, executive leaders stress the value *fairness to customers* as part of the corporate culture. They articulate this value to ensure that their employees' actions will put customers first in providing services considered to be fair and beneficial as a long-term strategy for customer retention. Table 2 analyzes how they apply this value to a particular work output—the *pricing agreements* that account managers periodically renegotiate with major clients.

This case is striking because the company, through its articulation and practice of *fairness to customers*, did the opposite of what many organizations would do: It intentionally lowered its own short-term profits to maximize long-term client retention and revenue. Leaders in the company cited this as differentiator from their competitors, whom they characterized as "cigar-chomping backroom dealmakers" likely to raise prices just short of losing the customer. In this context, the value reflects a strategic decision.

Table 2. Impact of the Value *Fairness to Customers* on Pricing Agreements.

Cultural value	Work output	Criteria for "good"	Behavior
Fairness to customers	Pricing agreement with customers	Priced as low as possible for the customer as long as we can ensure a minimum overall profit	Optimize spreadsheet values for different types of shipments to calculate the lowest possible overall pricing plus a specified minimum profit margin.
Profitability	Pricing agreement with customers	As profitable as possible without losing the client to price competition	Raise pricing as high as you can, checking to be sure it does not produce sticker shock and loss of the customer.

Example 3: Impact of differing values on the final feature set in a software release

Although the following is not a documented example from our work with clients, readers will recognize how it reflects the historical values and products of two well-known high-tech companies. In one company, driven by a cultural value of *cool technology* (sometimes described by its founder and former chairman as "neat features"), decisions about the final feature set to be included in each release of a software product were weighted toward including as many features as possible. In the other company, driven by the value of *user experience*, feature set decisions were weighted toward elegance and the elimination or redesign of features that undermined simplicity of user experience. The late founder and chairman emphasized saying "No!" to as many features and add-ins as possible, quite a different way of arriving at a final feature set than packing in as many bells and whistles as could be made tolerably navigable. Table 3 summarizes this analysis.

Although these examples only hint at what is possible, they illustrate a straightforward approach to defining and communicating performance expectations in relation to cultural values for specific types of performance. With this level of analysis it is possible for any job or any process to identify whether and how a given cultural value might influence what are considered "good" work outputs and what behavior will be expected to produce the work outputs. Added to or highlighted in descriptions of desired operational behavior, this lays a foundation for culture-driven performance management.

Table 3. Impact of Values on Decisions About Software Feature Set for Release.

Cultural value	Work output	Criteria for "good"	Behavior
Cool technology	Decision about software feature set for a given release	Includes as many features as possible and tolerably navigable	Incorporate as many neat features as we can possibly include, with tolerable means of navigating them.
User experience	Decision about software feature set for a given release	Elegant, beautiful, and as simple to use as possible while delivering maximum value to the user	Get rid of as many features and add-ins as possible. Revise to ensure a positively pleasant user experience.

That is, it will be possible to set expectations and deliver feedback and consequences based on conformance to defined criteria for "good" work outputs and specific forms of behavior.

How organizations can apply this approach

For any given job, a cultural value might be relevant to some work outputs and irrelevant to others. The same applies to a given process, in which a value might influence criteria and behavior for some work outputs or milestones and not others. This approach enables leaders, managers, supervisors, and performance professionals to focus on the areas of performance in which values can be practiced and to determine specific performance expectations, work output by work output.

Organizations need not always conduct the type of top-down effort illustrated by Tosti and Jackson's work at British Airways. They can apply this approach from the bottoms up in an organization, albeit with new expectations, tools, incentives, and skills/knowledge that may be provided from a central organization. If the organization decides from the top down that a given value statement should drive performance, then leaders and managers of each department or team can define expected work outputs and behavior for job roles or processes, examine whether and how the value statement(s) might alter criteria for "good" instances of the work outputs and desired behavior, and then manage performance to those modified expectations.

Although specification of the value statements themselves would be from to top down, the identification of exactly how the values apply to particular types of performance could be managed from the bottom up, starting with department heads or even team leaders. The initiative can begin in certain departments, in important processes, at specific levels of management, and so on. Management and leadership development programs might teach this approach. And if leaders and managers count (measure) key work outputs that meet culture-driven criteria and those that do not, they will be able to apply a multiple-baseline evaluation approach across work outputs, teams, departments, or other units and to refine how they engage various levels and groups of individuals in the effort. This approach will enable them to be as specific as they need to be as they communicate expectations, measure performance and provide feedback, provide tools and resources, arrange consequences, and develop the skills and knowledge needed for people to perform well.

The prerequisite for those who would apply this approach is that they must become fluent in the analysis of performance into its elements: specific work outputs that contribute to business results and the behavior needed to produce them. We teach this form of analysis both to staff human resources and performance professionals in various specialties and to leaders and managers, to the point that it becomes second nature. Thus, any manager, leader, or staff professional can work with individuals and groups in any part of an organization to define performance with organizational values in mind and to use that performance definition to set expectations for their people.

Although we have only begun to develop this approach, we believe that the practical implications may be significant. For example, in so many organizations these days, values such as *Customer First* or *Quality Across the Enterprise* are proudly proclaimed on posters, in presentations, and in various types of employee and customer documents. These phrases alone give only the most general hints for how employees should proceed. But in a relatively simple exercise that can be facilitated in the beginning by consultants or staff performance professionals, managers and leaders, department heads, process owners, and self-managed teams can deconstruct their jobs and processes into major work outputs and arrive at agreements about how cultural value statements should affect criteria for each work output and/or the behavior needed to produce it.

A research and development team, for example, might determine that the organizational value of *Customer First* will determine certain elements of their product designs and the activities they complete in order to be sure that their new products are customizable, are easy to use, or incorporate features that allow customers to obtain rapid product support. Applying that same organizational value, a customer service department might determine that any solution offered to customers needs to align with stated customer preferences and surpass customer expectations in specific ways. Naturally, how people behave in producing and configuring these work outputs would have to incorporate tasks and tactics designed to meet criteria.

Strategies for implementing this approach

One of our colleagues, a Six Boxes® Practitioner at Insperity, Inc., working as a consultant to the owner of a small information systems asset management company, was able to begin with a single department. She helped the manager redefine performance expectations based on two stated organizational values. The effort focused on work outputs that were part of the client lifecycle and used the organizational value statements *delivering value* and *stewardship* to specify criteria for the work outputs and specific forms of behavior for producing work outputs to criteria.

Although the experiment is not complete, the initial experience suggested that it is feasible and relatively straightforward for managers to identify how stated values apply to performance within their scope of control (individuals, teams, processes) and to manage the performance of their people accordingly. The performance consultant recognized the importance of starting small, developing a prototype implementation for a segment of the organization, and then expanding to other departments and cross-functional processes.

Such an effort can be accompanied by some degree of central staff oversight if there is a concern about consistency and alignment across the organization. But unlike the anthropological approach of the 1980s or the company-wide values and practices methodology described by Tosti and Jackson (1994, 1997a), this can be applied one job or process at a time, and even one work output at a time. We will see how the application unfolds as we encounter more organizations interested in approaching organizational culture in a proactive way.

By zeroing in on specific work outputs and behavior, this approach enables what might otherwise seem to be an overwhelming and resource-demanding focus on culture development to become a pilot, a small step, or an initial lab from which insights and improvements can be extended to work with other groups. It is an example of how simplicity and specificity in the analysis of performance can make behavior science and performance technology available to ordinary team leaders, managers, and department heads, not merely to consultants or staff specialists conducting large projects.

Conclusion

This article is a preliminary examination of a potentially powerful and straightforward technique for defining and strengthening organizational culture. It seems clear that identifying work outputs with criteria for "good" ones and the behavior needed to produce them offers a path for better defining cultural expectations and supporting behavior at a societal level as well. It is a good example of how Gilbert's (1978) shift of the focus in performance analysis from behavior to its valuable products (*accomplishments* or *work outputs*) provides leverage and clarity in performance management and the application of behavior science and performance technology to important organizational and societal outcomes.

Acknowledgments

Additional information about this approach can be found at www.SixBoxes.com.

Performance Thinking and Six Boxes are registered trademarks of The Performance Thinking Network and should not be used to label products or services provided by other organizations or individuals. I request that those who cite these models or this approach acknowledge copyright and trademarks, as applicable, and refer to www.SixBoxes.com in their citation.

References

Binder, C. (1998). The Six Boxes*: A descendent of Gilbert's behavior engineering model. *Performance Improvement, 37*(6), 48–52. doi:10.1002/pfi.4140370612

Binder, C. (2005). *What's so new about the Six Boxes* model?* [White paper]. Retrieved from The Performance Thinking Network website: http://www.sixboxes.com/_customelements/uploadedResources/160039_SixBoxesWhatsSoNew.pdf

Deal, T. E., & Kennedy, A. A. (1982). *Corporate cultures: The rites and rituals of corporate life.* Reading, MA: Addison-Wesley.

Gilbert, T. F. (1978). *Human competence: Engineering worthy performance.* New York, NY: McGraw-Hill Book Company.

Glenn, S. S. (2004). Individual behavior, culture, and social change. *The Behavior Analyst, 27,* 133–151.

Houmanfar, R. A., Alavosius, M. P., Morford, Z. H., Herbst, S. A., & Reimer, D. (2015). Functions of organizational leaders in cultural change: Financial and social well-being. *Journal of Organizational Behavior Management, 35*(1–2), 4–27. doi:10.1080/01608061.2015.1035827

Houmanfar, R. A., & Mattaini, M. A. (Eds.). (2015). Leadership and cultural change [Special issue]. *Journal of Organizational Behavior Management, 35*(1–2). doi:10.1080/01608061.2015.1036645

Skinner, B. F. (1956, November 30). Some issues concerning the control of human behavior: A symposium. *Science, 124,* 1057–1066. (Reprinted in *Cumulative Record*, pp. 25–38. New York, NY: Appleton-Century-Crofts).

Soanes, C., Hawker, S., & Elliott, J. (2009). Oxford dictionary of current English. Retrieved from http://www.encyclopedia.com/The+Oxford+Pocket+Dictionary+of+Current+English/publications.aspx?pageNumber=1

Teodorescu, T. M., & Binder, C. (2004). Competence is what matters. *Performance Improvement, 43*(8), 8–12. doi:10.1002/pfi.4140430805

Tosti, D. T., & Jackson, S. F. (1994, April). Organizational alignment: How it works and why it matters. *Training Magazine, 5,* 8–64.

Tosti, D. T., & Jackson, S. F. (1997a). *Changing organizational culture.* Sausalito, CA: Vanguard Consulting.

Tosti, D. T. & Jackson, S. F. (1997b). Changing Organizational Culture. Presented at the annual conference of the International Society for Performance Improvement, April 14-18, 1997, Anaheim, California.

Selection of Business Practices in the Midst of Evolving Complexity

Maria E. Malott

ABSTRACT

I admire leaders who, with little experience and training, create organizations that make major contributions in their industries, especially given that a great number of businesses fail. Some fail spectacularly, in headline-grabbing fashion, but most failed businesses implode quietly. In the United States alone, half of small businesses do not survive beyond 5 years; each year more than 1 million file for bankruptcy, and another 1.5 million-plus await bankruptcy resolution. For an organization to survive, the recurring and nonrecurring interlocking behavior of the organization members must ultimately adapt to the complex and dynamic demands of the organization's external environments. Based on an understanding of behavioral dynamics, this article offers a perspective on how leaders can identify realistic improvements inside their organizations and orchestrate their implementation to better adapt to the requirements of the external environment.

Business leaders and managers have both my admiration and my sympathy. I especially admire those who, with little or no tools to assist them, create successful organizations. Hendrik Meijer is an example: He arrived as a young man in Holland, Michigan, from The Netherlands in 1907. For the next 22 years he made a living at odd jobs and as a barber. By then he had saved enough money to buy a small building to generate rental income (Meijer, 1984). He subdivided it into several rental units, but no one would rent the one located at the back of the building. So he opened a small grocery store—that store eventually grew into Meijer, Inc., one of the largest privately held retail business in the United States, operating 204 stores in the Midwest (Murthy, 2015).

Not far from Meijer's headquarters, in Grand Rapids, Michigan, Melville and Anna Bissell invented a carpet sweeper to keep their small crockery shop free of sawdust. They patented their design and opened a manufacturing business in 1876 that revolutionized the cleaning industry. The Bissells' company would become the world's largest seller of vacuum and floor

Color versions of one or more of the figures in the article can be found online at www.tandfonline.com/WORG.

cleaners. Bissell's slogan, "Clean, meet easy," is also an elegant assessment of their success (Bissell, 2015).

Nearby in Kalamazoo, Michigan, orthopedic surgeon Homer Stryker had ideas for devices that improved medical care. In 1941, while still in practice, he started a small company to manufacture products, including the Stryker frame, a mobile hospital bed that rotated 360 degrees to change the position of injured patients while keeping them motionless. Today Stryker Corporation produces more than 60,000 medical products and services, sells them in more than 100 countries, generates nearly $10 billion in revenue, and employs more than 26,000 people (Stryker, 2014).

There are many other inspiring stories: Steve Jobs (1955–2011) and Steve Wozniak (1950–) started Apple Inc. in the garage of Jobs' parents' house; Bill Gates (1955–), a college dropout, founded Microsoft Corporation. I marvel at the many leaders whose accomplishments far surpass what any organization change expert could expect or claim.

But of course, many businesses fail. The 1988 Hollywood movie *Tucker: The Man and His Dream* recounts the story of Preston Tucker (1903–1956), an innovator in the automotive industry. After producing 51 prototypes of the 1948 Tucker Sedan, he was forced to close his company (Fuchs, Roos, & Coppola, 1998). Tucker's story lives on in museums and through his cars, now valued antiques (e.g., Tucker Model 1043 sold for $2.91 million in 2012). But most businesses that fail are not well known. In the United States, half of small businesses do not survive beyond 5 years (Small Business Administration, Office of Advocacy, 2012). Furthermore, in 2013 alone, more than 1 million filed for bankruptcy, and another 1.5 million-plus were awaiting bankruptcy resolution (United States Federal Courts, 2013). More than 10.5 million middle managers find themselves battered by constantly changing directions and an inability to help their businesses succeed (Nisen, 2013). My sympathies go out to these leaders and managers pressured to thrive in the midst of highly complex and dynamic business environments with little or no training. This article is written to recognize and cast light on the dynamic complexities that surround and embed their organizations.

Environmental complexity and selection

About 30 years ago, a friend and I were stranded at the Santiago International Airport in Chile. During our previous 6 weeks of travel, a new visa requirement had been introduced to enter Peru—our next destination. To allow us time to secure visas, our airline changed our flight and covered four nights and incidentals at the most expensive hotel in the city—and provided limousine transportation between the airport and hotel!

Travel experiences today are dramatically different. My recently cancelled flight to Caracas left hundreds of passengers stranded in Miami. Instead of a complimentary hotel stay, I got a good luck wish; instead of limousine service, I was directed to a taxi. I reached my destination 48 hr later than scheduled—without luggage.

Complexity

As a passenger, I am disappointed with how airline service has changed in three decades. But I am awestruck when I realize that commercial passenger aviation has only been in existence for a little more than 100 years. Between the first commercial flight in 1914 and 2014, flights went from connecting just two cities (St. Petersburg, Florida, to Tampa, Florida) to connecting 40,000, travel distance went from 30 kilometers to 80.4 million kilometers, and the number of passengers increased from 1 to 8.5 million (International Air Transport Association, 2014). As of January 2012, there were 531 airlines around the world offering more than 59,000 routes between more than 3,200 airports (United States Department of Transportation, Bureau of Transportation Statistics, 2005; Northwestern University, 2012; Patokallio, 2016).

Many factors affect the airline industry. For instance, the economic recession of 2008 and 2009 caused a significant decrease in the number of passengers. Consequently, revenues declined by $82 billion in 2008 and by $482 billion in 2009 (International Air Transport Association, 2015). Industry regulations also have a significant impact. In 1938, the Civil Aeronautics Board began to regulate airfare based on average cost and routes. Airlines competed through the services they provided, given that fares were relatively constant; this explains, perhaps, why I got such great treatment in Chile 30 years ago. In 1978, the U.S. Airline Deregulation Act lifted federal control over fares and routes, opening the door to market competition. Air safety and traffic control regulations imposed by the Federal Aviation Administration have also dramatically changed airlines' processes over the years (Allianz Global Corporate & Specialty SE, 2014).

As a result of extensive competition, airlines have diversified services and reduced costs, benefiting passengers. However, cost reductions have also negatively affected the provision of other services that travelers could previously expect (Grandeau, 1995).

Terrorism has affected air travel. For instance, al-Qaeda's assault on the United States on September 11, 2001, resulted in a $19.6 billion decrease in ticket sales from 2001 to 2002. The price of oil also affects the industry, as oil constitutes approximately 29% of airlines' expenses (Blokhin, 2015; Burger, 2013; International Air Transport Association, 2011). Internal factors in oil-producing countries—wars and political struggles—can disrupt access to fuel.

Weather, natural disasters, and contagious illnesses can also cause interruptions in service (Delta Investor Relations, 2016).

The economy, industry and federal regulations, competition, fuel prices, terrorism, weather, and the spread of disease are just examples of the many environmental variables that affect the airline industry. But influence is not one sided; it is reciprocal. Changes to the industry also affect external entities (Biglan, 2009). For instance, the decline in demand for air travel after the September 11 terrorist attacks affected the U.S. government's expenditure by necessitating unplanned economic aid to the airline industry ($5 billion in aid and $10 billion in future loan guarantees). Most human systems, industries, and organizations have permeable boundaries; that is, there is reciprocal influence between their dynamics and those of their external environments.

Selection

In the midst of ongoing changes, some airlines have adjusted and grown and others have not. In the past 20 years, approximately 200 airline companies filed for bankruptcy protection. Some recovered, including American (2012), Delta (2005), Northwest (2005), United (2002), and US Airways (2004). Others went under, such as Continental, Pan American, and World Airways (Veselinovic, 2016). Why do some succeed and others fail?

In essence, airlines are selected through their customers' purchases—without sales to sustain them, they will not endure. Organizations are complex adaptive systems that must meet the demands of their external environments if they are to survive. Customers are *selectors*, and, along with the income they generate, they constitute the *selecting environment*. Because many variables in the external environment affect customers, the airlines themselves, and other essential aspects of the industry, airlines have to adjust their internal processes to meet ongoing demands (De Neufville, Odoni, Belobaba, & Reynolds, 2013).

Airlines like Pan American, a major airline in the 1950s, could not adjust to environmental demands and collapsed under growing competition. Surviving airlines were able to cope with environmental complexities; this includes Delta, which is now the largest U.S. carrier, generating more than $34.7 billion in sales in 2015 (Delta, 2016).

Delta offers 15,000 daily flights to 328 destinations in 57 countries. These flights are Delta's main *aggregate products* and result from the combined behavior and products of 80,000 employees operating over 800 aircrafts. The type and number of behaviors involved are countless, and each employee's behavior is maintained by its consequences. For instance, a flight attendant's boarding announcement results in passengers approaching the departure gate, because this is what has happened in the past. This recurrence of the behavior/consequence relationship over time for each individual constitutes an *operant lineage*, which is the locus of change in behavior analysis (Glenn, 1991, 2003, 2004; Glenn & Madden, 1995).

Focusing on how the behavior of each individual affects the overall performance of Delta, day in and day out, is fruitless; for the most part, the behavior of a single individual is too far removed from the airline's total aggregate product. There are exceptions, of course. An individual's act of terrorism can have rippling effects in the airline industry. The faulty performance of an aircraft safety procedure might result in a crash.

It is more practical and expedient to focus on the aggregate product of interest and then study the *interlocking behavioral contingencies* (IBCs) that generate it. IBCs consist of lineages of interrelations among multiple individuals' behavior that generate an aggregate product. The relations are interlocking because one element of the behavioral contingency of one individual (i.e., antecedent, behavior, or consequence) or his product also constitutes an element of the behavioral contingency or product of another individual. So the processes of arranging flight operations, maintenance, airframe engineering, forecasting, reservations, airport operations, scheduling, and so on, take place repeatedly, as many times as needed to offer 15,000 daily flights. Roughly the same group of individuals participate in specific processes over time, although with some variations. For instance, employees might be absent and others cover for them, or specific actions are altered because of unexpected weather.

The relationship between the aggregate products and their generating IBCs constitutes a *culturant* (term first mentioned by Hunter, 2012; also described in Glenn et al., 2016; M. E. Malott, 2015). The relation between a culturant and its selected environment constitutes a *metacontingency* (Glenn, 1988). Figure 1 shows a metacontingency depicting selection of the Delta airlines culturant by

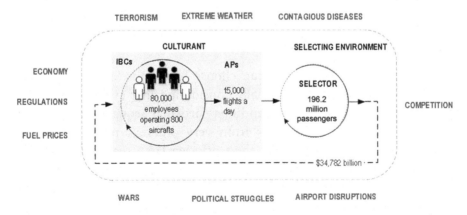

Figure 1. Metacontingency depicting selection of the Delta Airlines culturant by its customers. IBCs = interlocking behavioral contingencies; APs = aggregate products.

its customers. The figure identifies the culturant (i.e., IBCs/aggregate products relations), the selecting environment, and the external factors that might affect selection. The arrows in the circles symbolize repetitions over time.

More often than not, business leaders are aware of environmental complexities that affect their organizations. They are less cognizant of what needs to change inside their organizations to adapt to the demands of their external environment. Furthermore, when they identify the required internal changes, they struggle on how to actually implement them through the web of their inner IBCs expediently and efficiently.

Some organizations, such as Delta, succeed in reacting internally to external demands. In 1924, Delta was the world's first aerial crop dusting company. Since then, it has diversified its services; acquired routes, networks, and aircrafts; created partnerships; and purchased other airlines. Delta continues to exist despite filing for bankruptcy protection, pleading for subsidies, merging with Northwest, and avoiding a hostile takeover by US Airways. Its survival has necessitated restructuring, process reengineering, layoffs, and other drastic internal changes. How can an organization this complicated adjust to drastic external changes?

Part of the answer involves synchronizing external selection with internal selection practices. This alignment requires navigating through the organization's internal complexities and establishing IBCs that support adaptive practices, which is the focus of the next section.

In conclusion, organizations are selected by the demands of their external environment and are vulnerable to its evolving complexities. Leaders should watch closely for environmental factors that might affect their organizations to focus on areas of improvement. Then they should implement internal changes that facilitate their business survival and growth, which necessitates an appreciation of internal complexity and selection.

Internal complexity and selection

It is astounding that consumers can choose from more than 100 different kinds of cereal at the store, especially considering that every brand is carefully located on a particular shelf and in a particular sequence; that the same store carries about 200,000 items from very different product lines; that merchandise arrives from all over the world via land, sea, and air; that the parent business has more than 200 stores located in different regions with consumer patterns that are markedly diverse; and that nearly 76,000 associates make it possible for the stores to remain open 24 hr a day, 7 days a week (Murthy, 2015). How does such a business adapt its complex internal processes to external demands?

Complexity

As businesses grow, they become more complex, they develop more components and more part–whole relationships, and they become increasingly vulnerable to their external environments. What begins as a relatively simple exercise of ordering merchandise to place on a shelf develops into a conglomerate of countless interrelated behavioral contingencies of many individuals.

Many entrepreneurs start by creating one-person-does-it-all operations. They wear different hats: chief executive officer, sales representative, administrator, and so on. As sales increase, the workload increases. The founder hires an assistant to manage financial transactions. When operations become too much, she hires a salesperson, who brings new customers. When selling becomes laborious, the salesperson asks for regional sales representatives ... and so on. The business grows with the addition of staff and differentiation of functions needed to cover costs and generate the profits that then fund development.

Functions tend to be organized as departments delineated by aggregate products. With the growth in demand for goods, Merchandising allocates buyers to different product lines. Buying toys is different from buying food. And within food, buying perishable goods is different from buying canned foods. As products diversify within a line, buyers may require a more specialized function that collects and analyzes trend data on customer preferences, market share, and sales to help guide their purchasing decisions, giving birth to yet another functional unit within Merchandising called *Category Analysis*. Other functional units emerge, and these smaller units also divide into subcomponents. Both a department and any internal subcomponent can be conceived as metacontingencies with different levels of complexities.

The web of interrelations develops to serve the essential function of a brick-and-mortar retail system—to purchase goods from vendors and sell them to customers. Basic functions are performed by four departments: Merchandising purchases the goods, Warehouse & Logistics delivers the goods to the stores, Operations sells to customers, and Merchandise Planning & Control replenishes goods sold. These are essential functions and *core departments* because without them the business would not generate income and could not exist (M. E. Malott, 2003).

Other functions organize into departments that support the core. Information Technology provides technology infrastructure and applications that transform data into information; Human Resources hires and trains team members; and Finances sets the corporate budget, facilitates budget control, and audits the financial system. These departments ought to interact with all others, as all functions require useful information, necessitate human resources, and carry financial implications. Other support functions evolve to help some departments, not all. Properties, for instance, might design and build innovative stores.

When examined, this maze of interconnected metacontingencies can sometimes be found to impede rather than enable core departments' functions. For instance, instead of Merchandising getting what it needs from supporting departments, Information Technology may ask buyers to prepare technology specifications for applications, because developers do not understand merchandising. But writing technology specifications is not buyers' expertise. (And also, this is a job in itself!) So overwhelmed buyers find themselves incapable of doing either job well, resulting in the development of technologies that complicate rather than facilitate purchasing. They are asked to support Information Technology and are blamed if things go poorly. Similarly, Human Resources expects buyers to write job descriptions, identify candidates, and interview because buyers know what they need. In truth, they continue using Microsoft Excel rather than the expensive applications developed by Information Technology, and they recruit candidates who share their own outdated expertise. Support departments begin to behave as though they are the core. Essential business processes become increasingly difficult not only because of their inherent complexities but because of complications brought by other departments. Added to these dysfunctionalities can be difficulties of strong personalities and turf wars, forming internal kingdoms.

When Merchandising does not get what it needs from supposed support departments, it provides for itself by creating redundant jobs. For instance, assistants may be hired to transfer the information that buyers enter in Excel into the hugely expensive technology application and to assist with hiring; programmers are hired to find ways around the new technology absurdities. This is how businesses give birth to functional redundancies and walls between departments. This phenomenon was well illustrated by Rummler and Brache (1995).

It is hard to improve processes when the organization has many internal walls and redundancies. For instance, the process that determines the location of specific cereals on stores' shelves requires the coordinated work of several departments. In Merchandising, buyers approve the concept of the display for a trial set with the input of category analysts who create planograms. They physically implement the trial set in one store in conjunction with one of the cereal vendors; in Operations, team leaders approve the trial set so that it can be implemented in other stores. Subsequently, order writers maintain the integrity of the set by ordering products as they sell, and stockers place products on the shelves in the exact location determined in the trial set. Other departments are involved as well. In a dysfunctional system, Merchandising might develop planograms that cannot be implemented in the stores, and vendors might be making the order writer's job more challenging.

What might be obvious from a distance can be tough to accomplish because functional units, separated by territorial walls, do not normally work in concert to streamline processes. Departments become oblivious to how their actions affect other departments. Those participating continue doing what they are accustomed to doing regardless of whether their actions contribute to the well-being of the business. Consequently, employees tend to lose sight of the business's mission and can engage in practices detrimental to its overall performance.

Selection

Many tombstones lay in the graveyard of the retail industry. The F. W. Woolworth Company (1879–1997), a five-and-dime retailer with discount department stores, went out of business after 100 years. Other innovators and successful retailers have had similar misfortune, including Montgomery Ward (1872–2001), Musicland (1955–2006), Builders Square (1984–1999) and Hollywood Video (1988–2010, Fidlin, 2011). One that particularly saddens me is the demise of Borders, my favorite weekend destination. After 40 years in business (1971–2011), it liquidated its remaining 400 stores to pay off creditors. Borders President Mike Edwards confessed to his employees, "Borders has been facing headwinds for quite some time, including a rapidly changing book industry, eReader revolution, and turbulent economy." He concluded, "We put in a valiant fight, but regrettably, in the end we weren't able to overcome these external forces" (National Retail Federation, 2011; Week Magazine, 2011). This business lost enough customers and market share that sales could no longer maintain operations. And the "valiant fight" was not timely or effective. Why couldn't they survive?

It is challenging for a business to meet external demands when internal and external selection are incongruent. Internal culturant selection can be far removed from external selection. For instance, it is possible that while a retailer is losing market share, its Merchandising department meets internal demands from other departments: Warehouse & Logistics demands specification of volume, means of transportation, and routes to deliver goods to stores; Operations demands days of arrival, prices, dimensions, and planograms to sell; Merchandise Planning & Control demands projected sales by day and week to replenish goods sold. Other departments become Merchandising's selectors, while Merchandising also serves as a selector for other departments' culturants. Merchandising demands shipping costs from Warehouse & Logistics to determine sale prices, for instance. Therefore, a department's culturants both are selected and serve as selectors. Figure 2 shows a high-level depiction of the internal

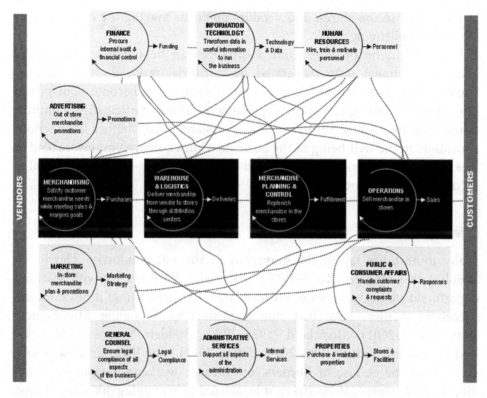

Figure 2. Functional depiction of the internal metacontingencies of a retail business.

metacontingencies of a retail business. It illustrates the internal web of interrelated metacontingencies in which functions organized into departments both are selected by other departments and serve as selectors. If one were to do a deeper analysis, one would find that webs of interactions multiply exponentially.

To meet the never-ending twists and turns of the external environment, businesses are forced to react quickly and implement adaptive changes through their web of internal complexities. Navigating internal complexity is like peeling an onion—one can analyze large components, then their subcomponents, then components of the subcomponents, and so on. It is necessary to cross through the web of internal metacontingencies. To avoid getting lost in that web, one should focus on the trends of main aggregate products, for instance, cereal sales in the entire business. When trends are not as expected, one can measure aggregate products of relevant subcomponents, like on-time delivery and accurate planogram implementation. Once a person identifies culturants that are at the root of the problem, he or she needs to examine the corresponding IBCs and redesign them. Today's top four larger retailers, Wal-Mart, Kroger, Target, and Walgreens (National Retail Federation, 2011), are able to adjust internal complexities to external demands with enough efficiency and speed to prosper. Such fortune, however, might change.

Sometimes businesses need major surgery to internal processes to survive. After a 10-year absence, Steve Jobs saved Apple by reducing 350 projects to 10 and focusing on the release of the iMac, the iPod, iTunes, and the iPhone. In 2005, Richard Clark (1950–) found Merck in turmoil when its arthritis drug Vioxx was removed from the market for its association with heart attacks and death. He closed five manufacturing plants, cut 7,000 jobs, and focused on the approval of eight new drugs. Merck remains one of the largest drug manufacturing companies in the world. Ideally organizations adjust internal complexities on an ongoing schedule before being forced to make a dramatic change and running the risk of bankruptcy.

Businesses do not die sudden deaths; more often, they die slowly. The poet Stanley Kunitz (1995) wrote about the process of death in "King of the River": "The great clock of your life is slowing down, and the small clocks run wild" (p. 55). As in "King of the River," when inefficiencies are sustained over time, internal metacontingencies run without orchestration. Organizations can tolerate some degree of ineffectiveness in their internal web of metacontingencies, but if these are extreme and prolonged they can threaten survival. They are like a crack in the middle of an iceberg that goes undetected until it creates an avalanche.

In conclusion, the growth of internal complexity is often accompanied by the emergence of territorial wars, bureaucracy, and inefficiencies. Organizations can tolerate some dysfunctionality, but in the face of excess dysfunctionality adaptation becomes impossible. Some businesses succeed in implementing dramatic and sudden change, but this is risky. Instead, organizations are better off managing internal complexities on an ongoing basis. They should measure trends in critical aggregate products and adjust the internal IBCs to better match external demands, before it is too late.

Unique nonreplicable phenomena

> I will build a car for the great multitude. It will be large enough for the family, but small enough for the individual to run and care for. It will be constructed of the best materials, by the best men to be hired, after the simplest designs that modern engineering can devise. But it will be so low in price that no man making a good salary will be unable to own one.... (Ford & Crowther, 1922, p. 73)

This was Henry Ford's (1863–1947) vision. With Ford Motors, he revolutionized the automobile industry in 1908 with the creation of the Ford Model T. What used to be a privilege of the wealthy became attainable by the middle class. By conceiving the manufacturing of completely interchangeable auto parts and the assembly line, Ford Motors mass produced cars at an affordable price. The Model T accounted for 40% of all of the cars sold in the United

States during its manufacture (History, n.d.) and became one of the 10 most sold cars of all times—16.5 million Model T cars were sold between 1908 and 1927 (Holweg, 2008; Siu, 2012).

Cusps

The creation of the Model T resulted from the interlocking behavior of several individuals. Charles Sorensen (1881–1968), who wrote *My Forty Years With Ford* (Sorensen, 1956), innovated foundry practice for mass production and developed the assembly line with a plant foreman. Joseph Galamb (1881–1955) designed many components of the Model T, including its clutch, transmission, drive shaft, and differential (Encyclopedia of World Biography, 2005). Harold Wills (1878–1940), Ford's principal shop assistant, appreciated the strength and lightness of nickel-chrome vanadium steel in car manufacturing. Goldstone (2016, p. 222) said, "It is impossible to disentangle Ford's work from that of Wills." Others, like J. Kent Smith, chief metallurgist of the American Vanadium Company, shared with Ford his expertise in creating vanadium alloy steel (History, n.d.). Although history tends to aggrandize individual accomplishments, there are always others who help make them possible (Gladwell, 2008).

The interlocking behavior of these individuals had no lineage, and it was not replicable. Nevertheless, their aggregate product left a tremendous legacy for car manufacturing and changed the way of life of most middle-class Americans. This phenomenon constitutes a *cultural cusp*—an aggregate product with significant and far-reaching cultural impact generated by interlocking behaviors of multiple individuals that have no lineage (Glenn et al., 2016; M. E. Malott, 2015). (For behavioral cusps, see Bosch & Fuqua, 2001; Rosales-Ruiz & Baer, 1997.) There are many examples of cultural cusps in the business history of the United States.

Cultural cusps can result from undesirable circumstances. For example, no one predicted that Enron Corporation, one of the world's major electricity, natural gas, and communications companies, would build its fame by falsely reporting profits, hiding losses, and engaging in other improper maneuvers. In addition to the indictment of Enron's chief financial officer Andrew Fastow (1961–) and prosecution of chief executive officer and former chairman Kenneth Lay (1942–2006), who died before he was sentenced, the discovery of Enron's well-disguised fraud led to the finding of other notable cases of fraud, such as WorldCom's, and to the approval of the Sarbanes–Oxley Act in 2002. That act changed accepted accounting principles for public companies in the United States in such a way that boards, management, and accounting firms bear more responsibility in financial reporting (Wikipedia, n.d.).

Incidents

Many events that take place in organizations involving the unique and nonreplicable interlocking behavior of multiple individuals do not have a long-lasting impact as do cultural cusps. For lack of a better term, I call these interactions *cultural incidents*—aggregate products generated by the interlocking behaviors of multiple individuals that have no lineage. People do not hear about these because they rarely make history. However, they are part of the fabric of all human systems and need to be taken into account when dealing with organizational change. Political maneuvers to be promoted and the incorporation of new policies in organizations are just two examples.

In conclusion, not all of the interlocking contingencies existing in organizations involve lineages; they are cultural cusps or incidents. Yet they emerged from complex cultural phenomena and should be studied.

Conclusions

A quick search for "leadership" on Amazon.com returns about 30,000 titles offering formulas for success. A popular theme is to describe what successful and failed organizations have done and conclude with lists of must-do and must-avoid tips (Collins, 2001; Collins & Porras, 1997; De Geus, 2007; Peters & Waterman, 1982). Case studies can be informative and inspirational, but what works for one business does not necessarily work for others. Furthermore, what has worked in the past will not necessarily work in the present. Cookbook recipes for organizational change are ineffective and have been widely critiqued (Chapman, 2007; Rosenzweig, 2007).

Organizations are inherently unique; they have different members, different internal processes, and different vulnerabilities. They are complex and dynamic behavioral systems, and it is not possible to predict with certainty the impact of interventions on overall performance. One cannot find control systems or conduct rigorous behavioral experimentation. Instead, change initiatives rely on taking calculated risks and trial and error because of the always-changing complexities of organizations' external and internal environments. To me, it is this inherent dynamic and uncertain nature of systems that makes leading and managing change so interesting.

Having served traditional roles as manager, vice-president, president, and chief executive officer and as lead consultant to large-scale organizational change initiatives, I have felt fortunate to have been trained in behavior systems analysis. I became convinced that environmental selection is at the core of behavioral change. Rather than relying on the internal motivation of individuals, which is hard to observe, focus should center on configuring environments that are more likely to target behavioral change. This perspective was brought by the work of B. F. Skinner (1904–1990) with his study on the behavior of organism (Skinner, 1938, 1953, 1971, 1974, 1981). Many studies show the effect of environmental manipulations on behavior in a great array of populations and settings. Examples of behavioral change in single individuals are abundant in behavioral journals such as *Journal of Applied Behavior Analysis, Behavior Analysis in Practice, Journal of Experimental Analysis of Behavior,* and *Journal of Organizational Behavior Management.* Many classical textbooks summarize the principles of behavior derived from Skinner's work and the supporting behavioral research (examples include Cooper, Heron, & Heward, 2007; R. W. Malott, 2008; Martin & Pear, 1999; Miltenberger, 2001).

Although the scientific behavioral community is my home, I have found it limiting to focus on individual behavioral change when trying to improve organizations. I find comfort and utility in Sigrid Glenn's concept of metacontingency (Glenn, 1988, 1991, 2003, 2004) because it helped me focus on what the interrelations of multiple individuals produce. Focusing on the behavior of single individuals as the starting point, which I have tried many times, has never been fruitful. There is a lot of irrelevant behavior in organizations that does not add up to much. And also, it is easy to get lost in behavioral minutiae and never see the impact of single behaviors on the bottom line. If the intent is to help businesses survive and thrive, it is more practical to focus on external environmental demands as the starting point and adjust the organization's culturants to meet those demands. This would necessitate changing lineages of IBCs between departments and management levels.

The field is indebted to the pioneering work of Brethower (2000), Gilbert (1978/1996), and Rummler and Brache (1995) on complex behavioral systems. They argued that organizational systems are selected by their environments. The concept of metacontingency brings additional insight into units of selection from a behavioral perspective—IBCs and their correspondent aggregate products. I am encouraged by the analyses, studies, and applications of the concept of metacontingency as well as the efforts to address cultural analysis from a behavioral perspective (Baker et al., 2015; Glenn & Malott, 2004; Houmanfar, Alavosius, Morford, Herbst, & Reimer, 2015; Houmanfar, Rodrigues, & Smith, 2009; Houmanfar, Rodrigues, & Ward, 2010; M. E. Malott, 2003; M. E. Malott & Glenn, 2006; Marques & Tourinho, 2015; Mattaini, 2004a, 2004b; Ortu, Becker, Woelz, & Glenn, 2012; Pennypacker, 2004; Sandaker, 2009, 2010; Smith, Houmanfar, & Louis, 2011; Tadaiesky & Tourinho, 2012; Todorov, 2013; Todorov & Vasconcelos, 2015; Tourinho, 2013; Ulman, 2004; Velasco, Benvenuti, & Tomanari, 2012; Vichi, Andery, & Glenn, 2009). Other types of cultural selection not addressed in this article are important to consider (Glenn et al., 2016). I see this line of work as an opportunity for major development of behavior analysis as a discipline.

As people see day after day, businesses that do not adapt to environmental complexities fail. Business practices are maintained by existing contingencies, and those that maintain behaviors involved in setting direction and those involved in implementing direction are different and affect different individuals. Leaders at the highest levels of an organization experience more closely pressures from the market, from the environment, and from their stakeholders. They are in a better position to appreciate the external threats than those working at lower levels. Often leaders respond to such pressures by launching initiatives, which brings promise of change for the better, without really appreciating the implications of those decisions. Talking is easier than doing, and when too many change efforts are initiated at the same time, more often than not, they cannot be implemented. These efforts encounter employees already swamped in their daily jobs, whose behaviors are maintained by existing contingencies. Not only do business practices continue as usual and the initiatives remain where they started, but unsuccessful efforts often leave a trail of turmoil, discontent, and lack of trust in leadership.

Rather than feeling victimized by seemingly impossible circumstances, or blaming others for the failure of implementation, leadership should take a systems approach. Focus on the mismatches between external and internal selection and deconstruct the complexities of internal IBCs to identify how to correct the disparity. One fruitful area of investigation is determining whether core functions are driving internal processes or whether other, less critical functions are. Solutions must be dynamic and adapt to ongoing changes. Static solutions do not work. Companies invest tremendous resources in technologies and training programs that become obsolete in the midst of their implementation.

All businesses have some degree of inefficiencies, but if these affect the ability to adapt and the inefficiencies are sustained for extensive periods of time, they may cause total failure. Organizations do not die overnight; most failed businesses implode quietly. It is like a cancer that is diagnosed too late, as has happened to businesses like Borders. The good news is that if major impediments are detected in time they can be corrected, as done by Delta, Apple, and Merck.

But metacontingencies do not explain everything. Indeed, much of what happens in a business does not involve lineages of IBCs, and yet these must be an object of study of behavioral systems. For instance, bringing new trends to the market often involves the unique and nonreplicable interrelated behavior of several individuals. Walt Disney (1901–1966) imagined a one-of-a-kind amusement park where adults and children could share experiences previously nonexistent, attracting families from all over the world. The *Oprah Winfrey Show* brought a distinctive television format for sharing intimate personal accounts for the goal of self-improvement, which resonated so thoroughly that it made Oprah Gail Winfrey (1954–) one of the most famous talk show hosts of all time. Business history is filled with examples of organizations that emerged by exploiting opportunities that were available to all but only a few took on (Brands, 2003).

Businesses like Disney and the *Oprah Winfrey Show* created aggregate products with unique processes that have a tremendous impact on the culture—they constitute cultural cusps. However, many of these unique interrelations do not have such an impact; they are cultural incidents that do not count as much at the end yet are part of the fabric of each organization that should be examined. Indeed, most of what are identified now as cultural cusps in retrospect might have started as incidents. Regardless of the end result, those who want to make a difference in the business world should realize early on that they need others to succeed and should bring complementary talents and partnerships to help them pursue their vision.

In conclusion, there is no simple trick to and no magic in leading organizations. It is essential to focus on critical aspects by engaging in careful and systematic analyses, identifying realistic improvements based on the interrelations of what people do, and orchestrating their implementation. Such efforts must be ongoing, as systems are always evolving. There is not an end to progress.

Acknowledgments

I thank Ramona Houmanfar for her invitation and encouragement to participate in this special issue. As well, I am indebted to Thomas Breznau and Majda Seuss for their careful comments on a draft of this article.

References

Allianz Global Corporate & Specialty SE. (2014). *Global aviation safety study*. Retrieved from http://www.agcs.allianz.com/assets/PDFs/Reports/AGCS-Global-Aviation-Safety-Study-2014.pdf

Baker, T., Schwenk, T., Piasecki, M., Smith, G. S., Reimer, D., Jacobs, N., ... Houmanfar, R. A. (2015). Cultural change in a medical school: A data-driven management of entropy. *Journal of Organizational Behavior Management*, 35, 95–122. doi:10.1080/01608061.2015.1035826

Biglan, A. (2009). The role of advocacy organizations in reducing negative externalities. *Journal of Organizational Behavior Management*, 29(3–4), 215–230. doi:10.1080/01608060903092086

Bissell. (2015). *Our history*. Retrieved from http://www.bissell.com/about-us/our-history

Blokhin, A. (2015). *To what extent will changing fuel costs affect the profitability of the airline industry?* Retrieved from http://www.investopedia.com/ask/answers/052515/what-extent-will-changing-fuel-costs-affect-profitability-airline-industry.asp#ixzz42nc9933P

Bosch, S., & Fuqua, R. W. (2001). Behavioral cusps: A model for selecting target behaviors. *Journal of Applied Behavior Analysis*, 34, 123–125. doi:10.1901/jaba.2001.34-123

Brands, H. W. (2003). *The masters of enterprise: American business history and the people who made it.* Prince Frederick, MD: Recorded Books.

Brethower, D. M. (2000). A systemic view of enterprise: Adding value to performance. *Journal of Organizational Behavior Management, 20*(3/4), 165–190. doi:10.1300/J075v20n03_06

Burger, A. (2013, September 10). *4 huge ways 9/11 impacted the American economy.* Retrieved from http://www.gobankingrates.com/personal-finance/ten-years-after-economic-impacts-9-11/

Chapman, J. (2007). *In search of stupidity: Over twenty years of high tech marketing disasters* (2nd ed.). New York, NY: Apress.

Collins, J. C. (2001). *Good to great: Why some companies make the leap—and others don't.* New York, NY: HarperBusiness.

Collins, J. C., & Porras, J. I. (1997). *Built to last: Successful habits of visionary companies.* New York, NY: HarperBusiness.

Cooper, J., Heron, T. E., & Heward, W. L. (2007). *Applied behavior analysis* (2nd ed.). New York, NY: Pearson Education.

De Geus, A. (2007). *Living company: Habits of survival in a turbulent business environment.* Boston, MA: Harvard Business School Press.

De Neufville, R., Odoni, A. R., Belobaba, P. P., & Reynolds, T. G. (2013). *Airport systems: Planning, design, and management* (2nd ed.). New York, NY: McGraw-Hill. Retrieved from http://accessengineeringlibrary.com/browse/airport-systems-planning-design-and-management-second-edition

Delta. (2016, January 19). *Delta Air Lines announces December quarter and full year 2015 profit news.* Retrieved from http://ir.delta.com/news-and-events/news/news-release-details/2016/Delta-Air-Lines-Announces-December-Quarter-and-Full-Year-2015-Profit/default.aspx

Delta Investor Relations. (2016, February 5). *Annual report for fiscal year ended December 31, 2015.* Retrieved from http://d1lge852tjjqow.cloudfront.net/CIK-0000027904/082dbd71-0d08-4ce4-b155-3f7bb2018395.pdf

Encyclopedia of World Biography. (2005). *Joseph Galamb.* Retrieved from the Encyclopedia.com website: http://www.encyclopedia.com/doc/1G2-3435000079.html

Fidlin, D. (2011, December 17). *10 notable retail stores that went out of business.* Retrieved from http://listosaur.com/miscellaneous/10-notable-retail-stores-that-went-out-of-business/

Ford, H., & Crowther, S. (1922). *My life and work.* Garden City, NY: Garden City.

Fuchs, F., & Roos, F. (Producers), & Coppola, F. F. (Director). (1988). *Tucker: The man and his dream* [Motion picture]. United States: Lucasfilm.

Gilbert, T. F. (1996). *Human competence: Engineering worthy performance.* Amherst, MA: HRD Press. (Original work published 1978)

Gladwell, M. (2008). *Outliers: The story of success.* New York, NY: Little, Brown.

Glenn, S. S. (1988). Contingencies and metacontingencies: Toward a synthesis of behavior analysis and cultural materialism. *The Behavior Analyst, 11,* 161–179.

Glenn, S. S. (1991). Contingencies and metacontingencies: Relations among behavioral, cultural, and biological evolution. In P. A. Lamal (Ed.), *Behavioral analysis of societies and cultural practices* (pp. 39–73). New York, NY: Hemisphere Press.

Glenn, S. S. (2003). Operant contingencies and the origin of cultures. In K. A. Lattal & P. N. Chase (Eds.), *Behavior theory and philosophy* (pp. 223–242). New York, NY: Kluwer Academic/Plenum.

Glenn, S. S. (2004). Individual behavior, culture, and social change. *The Behavior Analyst, 27,* 133–151.

Glenn, S. S., & Madden, G. J. (1995). Units of interaction, evolution, and replication: Organic and behavioral parallels. *The Behavior Analyst, 18*(2), 237–251.

Glenn, S. S., & Malott, M. E. (2004). Complexity and selection: Implications for organizational change. *Behavior and Social Issues, 13,* 89–106. doi:10.5210/bsi.v13i2.378

Glenn, S. S., Malott, M. E., Andery, M. A. P. A., Benvenuti, M., Houmanfar, R., Sandaker, I., ... Vasconcelos, L. (2016). Toward consistent terminology in a behaviorist approach to cultural analysis. *Behavior and Social Issues, 25,* 11–17. doi:10.5210/bsi.v.25i0.6634

Goldstone, L. (2016). Drive!: Henry Ford, George Selden, and the race to invent the auto age. New York, NY: Ballantine Books.

Grandeau, S. C. (1995). *The processes of airline operational control* (Master's thesis, Massachusetts Institute of Technology). Retrieved from http://dspace.mit.edu/bitstream/handle/1721.1/68117/FTL_R_1995_02.pdf

History. (n.d.). *Model T.* Retrieved from http://www.history.com/topics/model-t

Holweg, M. (2008). The evolution of competition in the automotive industry. In G. Parry & A. Graves (Eds.), *Build to order* (pp. 13–34). New York, NY: Springer. doi:10.1007/978-1-84800-225-8

Houmanfar, R. A., Alavosius, M. P., Morford, Z. H., Herbst, S. A., & Reimer, R. (2015). Functions of organizational leaders in cultural change: Financial and social well-being. *Journal of Organizational Behavior Management, 35,* 4–27. doi:10.1080/01608061.2015.1035827

Houmanfar, R., Rodrigues, N. J., & Smith, G. S. (2009). Role of communication networks in behavioral systems analysis. *Journal of Organizational Behavior Management, 29*(3), 257–275. doi:10.1080/01608060903092102

Houmanfar, R. A., Rodrigues, N. J., & Ward, T. A. (2010). Emergence and metacontingency: Points of contact and departure. *Behavior and Social Issues, 19,* 78–103. doi:10.5210/bsi.v19i0.3065

Hunter, C. S. (2012). Analyzing behavioral and cultural selection contingencies. *Revista Lationomericana De Psicología, 44,* 43–54.

International Air Transport Association. (2011). *The impact of September 11 2001 on aviation.* Retrieved from http://www.iata.org/pressroom/Documents/impact-9-11-aviation.pdf

International Air Transport Association. (2014). *100 years of commercial flight.* Retrieved from http://www.flying100years.com/#1997

International Air Transport Association. (2015, June 5). *Economic performance of the airline industry.* Retrieved from https://www.iata.org/whatwedo/Documents/economics/IATA-Economic-Performance-of-the-Industry-mid-year-2015-report.pdf

Kunitz, S. (1995). *Passing through.* New York, NY: Norton.

Malott, M. E. (2003). *Paradox of organizational change: Engineering organizations with behavioral systems analysis.* Reno, NV: Context Press.

Malott, M. E. (2015). What studying leadership can teach us about the science of behavior. *The Behavior Analyst, 39*(1), 1–28. doi:10.1007/s40614-015-0049-y

Malott, M. E., & Glenn, S. S. (2006). Targets of intervention in cultural and behavioral change. *Behavior and Social Issues, 15*(1), 31–56. doi:10.5210/bsi.v15i1.344

Malott, R. W. (2008). *Principles of behavior* (6th ed.). Upper Saddle River, NJ: Prentice Hall.

Marques, N. S., & Tourinho, E. Z. (2015). The selection of cultural units by non-contingent cultural events. *Behavior and Social Issues, 24,* 126–140. doi:10.5210/bsi.v24i0.4283

Martin, G., & Pear, J. (1999). *Behavior modification: What it is and how to do it* (6th ed.). New York, NY: Prentice Hall.

Mattaini, M. A. (2004a). Systems, metacontingencies, and cultural analysis: Are we there yet? *Behavior and Social Issues, 13*(2), 124–130. doi:10.5210/bsi.v13i2.20

Mattaini, M. A. (2004b). Toward a natural science of cultural analysis. *Behavior and Social Issues, 13,* 85–88.

Meijer, H. (1984). *Thrifty years: The life of Hendrik Meijer*. Grand Rapids, MI: Eardmans.

Miltenberger, R. G. (2001). *Behavior modification: Principles and procedures*. Stanford, CT: Wadsworth, Thomson Learning.

Murthy, A. (2015, October 28). *Top 20 largest private companies of 2015*. Retrieved from the *Forbes* website: http://www.forbes.com/companies/meijer/

National Retail Federation. (2011). *Top 100 retailers*. Retrieved from https://nrf.com/resources/top-retailers-list/top-100-retailers-2011

Nisen, M. (2013, August 7). *Life is hard for America's 10.5 million middle managers*. Retrieved from the *Business Insider* website: http://www.businessinsider.com/problems-with-middle-management-2013-8

Northwestern University. (2012, June 1). *Researchers develop method that shows diverse complex networks have similar skeletons*. Retrieved from http://phys.org/news/2012-06-method-diverse-complex-networks-similar.html#jC

Ortu, D., Becker, A., Woelz, T. A. R., & Glenn, S. S. (2012). An iterated four-player prisoner's dilemma game with an external selecting agent: A metacontingency experiment. *Revista Latinoamericano De Psicologia, 44*(1), 111–120.

Patokallio, J. (2016, February 12). *Airport, airline and route data*. Retrieved from http://openflights.org/data.html#airline

Pennypacker, H. S. (2004). Complexity and selection: A template for nation-building? *Behavior and Social Issues, 13*, 134–135. doi:10.5210/bsi.v13i2.22

Peters, T. J., & Waterman, R. H. (1982). *In search of excellence: Lessons from America's best-run companies*. New York, NY: Harper & Row.

Rosales-Ruiz, J., & Baer, D. M. (1997). Behavioral cusps: A developmental and pragmatic concept for behavior analysis. *Journal of Applied Behavior Analysis, 30*, 533–544. doi:10.1901/jaba.1997.30-533

Rosenzweig, P. M. (2007). *The halo effect—and the eight other business delusions that deceive managers*. New York, NY: Free Press.

Rummler, G. A., & Brache, A. P. (1995). *Improving performance: How to manage the white space on the organizational chart*. San Francisco, CA: Jossey-Bass.

Sandaker, I. (2009). A selectionist perspective on systemic and behavioral change in organizations. *Journal of Organizational Behavior Management, 29*(3–4), 276–293. doi:10.1080/01608060903092128

Sandaker, I. (2010). Some comments on "emergence and metacontingency." *Behavior and Social Issues, 19*, 90–93. doi:10.5210/bsi.v19i0.3222

Siu, J. (2012, February 9). *Top 10 best selling cars of all time*. Retrieved from http://www.autoguide.com/auto-news/2012/02/top-10-best-selling-cars-of-all-time.html

Skinner, B. F. (1938). *The behavior of organisms*. New York, NY: Appleton-Century-Crofts.

Skinner, B. F. (1953). *Science and human behavior*. New York, NY: Free Press.

Skinner, B. F. (1971). *Beyond freedom and dignity*. Cambridge, MA: Hackett.

Skinner, B. F. (1974). *About behaviorism*. New York, NY: Random House.

Skinner, B. F. (1981, July 31). Selection by consequences. *Science, 213*, 501–504. doi:10.1126/science.7244649

Small Business Administration, Office of Advocacy. (2012, June). *Small business facts*. Retrieved from www.sba.gov/advocacy

Smith, G. S., Houmanfar, R. A., & Louis, S. J. (2011). The participatory role of verbal behavior in an elaborated account of metacontingency: From conceptualization to investigation. *Behavior and Social Issues, 20*, 122–146.

Sorensen, C. E. (1956). *My forty years with Ford*. Detroit, MI: Wayne State University Press.

Stryker. (2014). *2014 annual review*. Retrieved from http://www.stryker.com/2014/assets/pdf/Stryker_2014_Annual_Review.pdf

Tadaiesky, L. T., & Tourinho, E. Z. (2012). Effects of support consequences and cultural consequences on the selection of interlocking behavioral contingencies. *Revista Latinoamericana De Psicología, 44*, 133–147.

Todorov, J. C. (2013). Conservation and transformation of cultural practices through contingencies and metacontingencies. *Behavior and Social Issues, 22*, 64–73. doi:10.5210/bsi.v22i0.4812

Todorov, J. C., & Vasconcelos, I. (2015). Experimental analysis of the behavior of persons in groups: Selection of an aggregate product in a metacontingency. *Behavior and Social Issues, 24*, 111–125. doi:10.5210/bsi.v24i0.5424

Tourinho, E. Z. (2013). Cultural consequences and interlocking behavioral contingencies: Selection at the cultural level. *Behavior and Philosophy, 41*, 60–69.

Ulman, J. D. (2004). Institutions and macrocontingencies: Comments on Glenn and Malott's "Complexity and Selection." *Behavior and Social Issues, 13*, 147–151. doi:10.5210/bsi.v13i2.28

United States Department of Transportation, Bureau of Transportation Statistics. (2015, March 26). *Summary 2014 U.S.-based airline traffic data* (Press Release No. BTS 15-15). Retrieved from http://www.rita.dot.gov/bts/press_releases/bts015_15

United States Federal Courts. (2013, September 30). *Table 7.1—U.S. bankruptcy courts judicial facts and figures (September 30, 2013).* Retrieved from http://www.uscourts.gov/statistics/table/71/judicial-facts-and-figures/2013/09/30

Velasco, S. M., Benvenuti, M. F. L., & Tomanari, G. Y. (2012). Metacontingencies, experimentation and nonhumans: Searching for conceptual and methodological advances. *Revista Latinoamericana De Psicología, 44*, 25–34.

Veselinovic, J. (2016, October 16). *11 most profitable airlines in the world: Will it last?* Retrieved from http://www.insidermonkey.com/blog/11-most-profitable-airlines-in-the-world-will-it-last-376243/

Vichi, C., Andery, M. A. P., & Glenn, S. S. (2009). A metacontingency experiment: The effect of contingent consequences on patterns of interlocking contingencies of reinforcement. *Behavior and Social Issues, 18*, 41–57. doi:10.5210/bsi.v18i1.2292

Week Magazine. (2011, July 20). *Why Borders failed and Barnes & Noble hasn't: 4 theories.* Retrieved from http://theweek.com/articles/483158/why-borders-failed-barnes–noble-hasnt-4-theories

Wikipedia. (n.d.). *Sarbanes–Oxley Act.* Retrieved from https://en.wikipedia.org/wiki/Sarbanes%E2%80%93Oxley_Act

Consumer Behavior Analysis and the Marketing Firm: Bilateral Contingency in the Context of Environmental Concern

GORDON R. FOXALL

Consumer behavior analysis provides an operant understanding of consumption as the result of the scope of the consumer behavior setting and the pattern of reinforcement that maintains it. The theory of the marketing firm shows how organizations respond to consumer behavior by managing the consumer behavior setting scope and pattern of reinforcement. Environment-impacting consumption and corporate attempts to reverse its impact can therefore be understood in operant terms. The question remains how we can understand the relationship between a complex contextual system like a firm, the behavior of which is predictable and controllable by considering its emergent operant consequences, and the collective behaviors of consumers, each of whom is a contextual system responding uniquely to the peculiar pattern of contingencies that shapes and maintains its behavior. This article seeks the solution in terms of bilateral contingencies and seeks to relate these to issues arising from the theory of metacontingency and macrobehavior.

If behavior analysis is to contribute to the amelioration of those aspects of environmental despoliation that are the result of consumption, it is necessary to show systematically that the consumer behaviors in question are contingent on their consequences and that environmental management strategies can be systematically addressed to their modification. But we cannot do

---

Color versions of one or more of the figures in the article can be found online at www.tandfonline.com/worg.

research that addresses complex human behavior and complex human problems with the same conceptual apparatus and investigative methods that are so well suited to experimental research into animal behavior. Methodological progression is inevitable as the principle of selection by consequences is progressively applied to the investigation of natural selection, operant conditioning, and cultural evolution (Skinner, 1981). This does not mean that we have to abandon the basic tenets of behavior analysis, but it does require that we acknowledge the differences of degree and of kind between behavior that can be examined in the closed setting of the operant laboratory and that encountered in the world at large. There is a clear progression from the experimental space, the realm of individual behavior, through the organization, to society in general. Increasing methodological complexity is inevitable as we move from contingencies to metacontingencies to cultural contingencies.

It is this third area, defined in terms of cultural contingency, with which we are concerned when we seek to effect broad societal change. But seeking to act directly on cultural contingencies may not be the surest way to succeed. To use an idea that is commonplace among chemical engineers, we need to scale up from the situations that are more directly under our control to those that we wish to influence, even though they are not. Scaling up requires intermediate models that elaborate without replacing the three-term contingency, but which render it more appropriate for the analysis of behavior beyond the confines of the operant chamber. Such models must be empirically testable if they are to provide a basis for interpretation. Hence, the fact that we are involved in the process of behavioral interpretation does not give us license to arbitrarily label events we observe as discriminative stimuli, responses, and reinforcing stimuli. Our interpretations rely for their validity and reliability on a model of environment–behavior relationships that can be empirically demonstrated, preferably with the full rigor of an experimental analysis. Two such models are used in this article: the behavioral perspective model (BPM) of consumer choice and that of the marketing firm.

CONSUMER BEHAVIOR ANALYSIS AND THE MARKETING FIRM

First, this article explores consumer choice as the outcome of operant contingencies (Foxall, 1990/2004), which has been supported by a wide range of empirical research, experimental and nonexperimental, in behavioral economics and marketing science. Second, it addresses the behavior of the organizations that respond to consumer choice: marketing firms. The concept of the marketing firm (Foxall, 1999a) proposes that the raison d'être of the business organization is marketing (i.e., creating and keeping a buyer by responding appropriately to buyer behavior). A key tenet is that the behavior of the marketing firm can be predicted from and explained by its supra-personal consequences, predominantly the effectiveness of the marketing mixes—product, price, promotion, and place utilities—it supplies to the market.[1] In other words, the firm is a contextual system or operant system, one predictable from its learning history and the behavioral outcomes made possible by its current situation (Foxall, 1999b). This feature of organizational behavior analysis finds resonance in work on metacontingencies (e.g., Glenn, 1991, 2004).

The essence of metacontingency theory is that the behavior of an organization is greater than or different from that of the combined repertoires of its members. The behavioral components of the system are enmeshed in *interlocking behavioral contingencies*. The supra-individual behavior of the system is inferred from the outputs it produces. Hence, each element of the marketing mix—the product, the price, the promotional communications, and the distribution system—can be used to infer behaviors or behavior programs that denote the salient actions of the organizational system. Biglan and Glenn (2013, p. 257) state that "the term *metacontingencies* can describe the contingent relations between [interlocking behavioral contingency] lineages with their products, on the one hand, and the consequent actions of their external environment on the other." Metacontingency theory and the concept of the marketing firm have much in common if two emphases of the latter, with which this article is centrally concerned, are appreciated. First, what metacontingency theory refers to as the product of the supra-personal behavior of organizations is actually in the context of the marketing firm the product, price, promotion, and place that make up the marketing mix. Second, the concept of the marketing firm places a strong emphasis on the exchange relationships that bind the marketing firm and its consumerate together, which it analyzes in terms of bilateral contingencies (Foxall, 2014a, b).

The starting point is that both individuals and organizations such as the marketing firm can be considered contextual systems (Foxall, 1999b); that is, their behavior can be predicted from their learning history[2] and current

---

[1] While the marketing department or function is responsible for the technical devising and implementation of marketing mixes, these can be optimally directed toward the profitable fulfillment of customer requirements only in the context of a customer-oriented perspective that the marketing firm supplies. Therefore, this article refers to the provision of marketing mixes as a corporate-level responsibility of the marketing firm as a whole.

[2] The question of how an organization can be said to have a learning history requires an answer that goes beyond the limits of this article. An organization's learning history might simply be that of its leader or leaders; it might be that of a dominant coalition within the firm or consist of the tacit and explicit knowledge base within the enterprise, the procedures to which its members' behavior patterns conform, or the set of verbal behaviors and rules that govern its activities. For considerations that arise within behavior analysis, see Houmanfar, Rodrigues, and Smith (2009). The conceptualization at which this passage hints, however, is broader than these, consisting of an abstraction of learning processes that influence the entire conduct of the firm within its market place.

behavior setting. The marketing firm is an evolved environment that comprises a system of interlocking internal behavioral contingencies. It is also, by definition, an organization that is linked by a nexus of contingencies with an external public. The interdependence of the marketing firm and its customer base that is the subject of this article has been analyzed through the concept of bilateral contingencies (Foxall, 1999a; Vella & Foxall, 2011, 2013). This article explores the nature of bilateral contingencies that link a complex organization that is a contextual system in its own right with a public that consists of a myriad of individual contextual systems. Rather than doing so in abstract terms, however, it concentrates on attempts to engender prosocial consumption to mitigate environmental damage. The aim of the discussion is not to provide novel solutions to this problem, though the analysis may clarify some of the issues involved; it is to elucidate the nature of the contingencies that account for the behavior of each of these types of contextual system not in isolation but as they form the exchange transactions that characterize market economies.

In turn, the marketing firm model benefits from the distinction Biglan and Glenn (2013) make between the behavioral outputs of organizations that are metacontingencies and those of collectivities of persons who form the firm's consumerate. (For discussion of the notion of consumers as collectivities, see Houmanfar et al., 2009.) The firm's being a metacontingency means, then, that its behavioral output *emerges* from the behaviors of its members and is different from and greater than its members' combined behaviors. This behavior evolves in its own right as its consequences are selected or deselected by the environment, in this case by the firm's customers and potential customers. The behavior of those consumers is of a different order, however. The behavioral output of the mass of consumers is simply the aggregated behavioral output of them all. We may perform statistical operations on measures of this behavior—aggregate it, average it, relate it to other measures—but however we treat it, it does not amount to anything but individual operant behavior. It is simply "the operant behavior of many people that has a cumulative and measurable effect on the environment" (Biglan & Glenn, 2013, p. 256). Crucially, it does not evolve as an entity in itself. It does not produce behavioral outputs over and above those of consumers *en masse* that can be differentially acted on by a selective environment. Such behavior, albeit the behavioral output of a large collectivity, is simply macrobehavior (Glenn, 2004).

ENVIRONMENT-IMPACTING CONSUMPTION

Environment-impacting consumption is notorious for its broader physical and social consequences, such as fossil fuel depletion; air pollution and health disbenefits that result from excessive reliance on transportation systems; esthetic, health, and economic demerits of indiscriminate waste disposal; depletion of fossil fuels and contribution to global warming in the case of overconsumption of domestic energy; and depletion of natural resources in the case of excessive water consumption (van Vliet, Chappells, & Shove, 2005). These broader societal outcomes define the cultural contingencies that Skinner (1981) and others have drawn attention to. They involve a "tragedy of the commons," in Hardin's (1968) words, exemplified by the fact that farmers who share rights to common land feel no added burden if one of their number increases their flock by a single sheep but that all suffer severe disadvantages when every farmer does so (Foxall, 1979). It is in these circumstances that some management theorists and behavior analysts have advocated social marketing to address these concerns (Foxall, Oliveira-Castro, James, Yani-de-Soriano, & Sigurdsson, 2006). However, it is legitimate to question whether the direct assault on cultural contingencies is the most effective strategy for change, to advocate a more intermediate level of analysis, and to examine the practical and theoretical implications of this approach.

PLAN OF THE ARTICLE

The section "Consumer Behavior Analysis" shows how consumer behavior is contingent on patterns of reinforcement that derive from the functional and symbolic benefits of products and services. A behavior analytical model of consumer choice, the BPM, predicts economic dimensions of consumption such as product and brand choice, the sensitivity of demand to price, and the kinds of utility that consumers maximize; it also predicts consumers' emotional reactions to retail and consumption situations. This model is used in "Environment-Impacting Consumption" to interpret environment-impacting consumption in the spheres of private versus public transportation, waste disposal, the overexploitation of domestic energy, and the domestic consumption of water, all themes that have been well researched by applied behavior analysts. "The Marketing Firm" illustrates the ways in which marketing firms respond to consumer demands by showing how a parallel behavior analytic model, this time the concept of the marketing firm, describes how marketing-oriented management can be interpreted in behavior analytical terms. "Responses to Environment-Impacting Consumption" outlines how marketing firms have responded to problems of environmental despoliation. This makes possible an exploration of the bilateral contingencies joining marketing firms and their customer bases, which in turn permits an extension of metacontingency theory into the realm of cultural contingencies in "Symmetry and Asymmetry Between Contextual Systems."

CONSUMER BEHAVIOR ANALYSIS

Consumer behavior analysis is the application of behavioral psychology and behavioral economics to understanding the market place of human purchase and consumption behaviors (Foxall, 2001, 2002b).

The BPM

The BPM (see Figure 1) is an elaboration of the three-term contingency to sensitize it to the analysis of human consumption in the market place (Foxall, 1990/2004). The setting in which consumer choice takes place consists not of a single stimulus but of an array of discriminative stimuli and motivating operations that set the scene for consumption. The topography of consumer behavior settings is diverse, from stores and restaurants through automated teller machines and online banking to cultural events and lectures. Consumer behavior settings vary too in the extent to which they encourage or inhibit specific responses. A bar or a bookstore offers multiple choices from among which to make our selection, and we are not even constrained to remain in the setting. Consumer behavior settings like these that offer multiple responses are relatively open settings. Banks and cinemas, by contrast, allow rather more restricted behavior or patterns of behavior, gyms and emergency rooms even more so. Settings like these that offer one or at most a few behavioral options are relatively closed.

We have, therefore, a continuum of consumer behavior settings from the most open to the most closed that we can analyze in terms of discriminative stimuli and motivating operations as well as their *scope:* their openness/closedness and its implications for consumer choice. The scope of the setting is influenced by the way in which the consumer's learning history impinges on the stimulus setting to influence the probability of

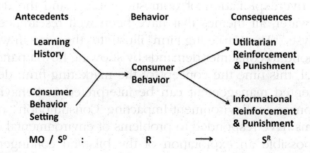

FIGURE 1 Summative behavioral perspective model. MO = motivating operation; S^D = discriminative stimulus; R = response; S^R = reinforcing stimulus. *Source:* Foxall (1990/2004). Adapted with permission.

Informational Reinforcement

		Low	High
Utilitarian Reinforcement	High	Hedonism	Accomplishment
	Low	Maintenance	Accumulation

FIGURE 2 Patterns of reinforcement and operant classes of consumer behavior. *Source:* Foxall (1990/2004). Adapted with permission.

certain behaviors taking place and others remaining dormant. The learning history brings meaning to the behavior setting. The intersection of the consumer's learning history (or experience) with the behavior setting that defines the *consumer situation* is the immediate precursor of consumer behavior.

Human social and economic behavior is shaped and maintained by two sources of reinforcement. Almost any watch will provide us with the time. That is the utility we expect from a timepiece. However, for many people, a Rolex watch offers so much more: social status, self-esteem, honor, prestige. *Utilitarian* reinforcement, which we share with other organisms, is the receipt of functional benefits that confer material satisfactions, the utility of orthodox microeconomic theory, contributors to biological fitness in evolutionary theory. *Informational* reinforcement is performance feedback, an indication of how well the consumer is doing. As well as being positively reinforced by the consumer's acceptance of utilitarian and informational reinforcers or the avoidance of or escape from aversive consequences, consumer behavior is also punished by *aversive* consequences. For example, a luxury cruise is positively reinforced by the utility it supplies (the results of sunshine, rest, good food, etc.) and informationally (by the status it confers). Using a stain remover is negatively reinforced by the erasure of the mark on the carpet to which it is applied. Both consumer behaviors meet with aversive consequences, however: the surrender of hard-earned money in the first case and the energy that has to be expended in the second. We can define consumer behavior in operant terms by reference to the relatively high or relatively low levels of utilitarian and informational reinforcement that maintain it (see Figure 2). In summary, consumer behavior is shaped and maintained by (a) the scope of the consumer behavior setting and (b) the pattern of reinforcement provided by available products and services.

ENVIRONMENT-IMPACTING CONSUMPTION

Environment-impacting consumption can be analyzed in terms of the BPM. That is, we can understand environment-impacting consumption in terms of the scope of the consumer behavior setting and the pattern of reinforcement that maintains the behavior. We have a unique set of research findings that provide an independent analysis of these contingencies as they relate to (a) private transportation, (b) waste disposal (specifically, littering), (c) domestic energy consumption, and (d) domestic water consumption. The applied behavior analysts who conducted this research, particularly in the 1970s and 1980s, used different terminology from that of the BPM, but the sources of reinforcement are similar: *Incentives* correspond to what we would call utilitarian reinforcement, *feedback* to informational reinforcement, and *prompts* perhaps to discriminative stimuli and rules. Moreover, the applied behavior analysis (ABA) research has had the goal of changing the behaviors it has investigated by the manipulation of the contingencies: As a result, we have a dynamic demonstration of the contextual factors that actually modify these behaviors.[3]

Discouragement of Private Transportation

The goal here has been to modify consumers' private transportation behavior in order to reduce fuel consumption, urban congestion, and pollution by discouraging unilateral use of private cars and promoting public or shared transportation. The evidence is that only high levels of incentives *and* feedback have had an appreciable effect on the number of miles travelled in private cars or the amount spent on fossil fuels.

Although the discouragement of car travel can reduce mileage travelled by as much as half, the provision of feedback plays a strong role in reducing driving if it is combined with appropriate incentives. Each of these rewards relies on the provision of the other in order to be effective, and it is the interaction of financial savings and feedback on changed performance that, as a combined source of reinforcement, influences driving behavior. Hence, feedback alone (on the number of miles travelled, operating costs, depreciation, social costs, etc.) exerts little if any effect on mileage travelled; performance feedback influences behavior by encouraging the driver to monitor behavior in order to achieve the incentives contingent on behavior modification.

In summary, both utilitarian reinforcement and informational reinforcement at high levels are required to change behavior, and the appropriate

---

[3]   Relevant reviews to the ABA literature on environmental conservation include Foxall (1994, 2002a, 2002c, 2013) and Foxall et al. (2006). There are also excellent comprehensive reviews by Cone and Hayes (1980) and Geller, Winett, and Everett (1984). The present exposition summarizes the results of these reviews.

operant class of consumer behavior is therefore *accomplishment*. This is borne out by consideration of the benefits of private transportation. *Private transportation* supplies high levels of both utilitarian and informational reinforcement: utilitarian reinforcement in the form of control, comfort, flexibility, reliability, privacy, speed, fun, safety, and protection; informational reinforcement in the form of travel time reduction, cargo capacity, predictability, and above all autonomy and social status, including self-esteem. It has important aversive consequences too: putting up with traffic congestion, stress, costs of purchase and maintenance, and adverse comment. Moreover, a measure of the strength of this pattern of reinforcement on consumer behavior is apparent from the level of aversive consequences that the individual is willing to incur in order to continue with this product choice. In the case of private transportation, these are high.

Waste Disposal

The goal here has been to reduce littering in public places by encouraging the use of waste bins, to stimulate the recycling of irreplaceable materials, and to enlist consumers in a process of waste recovery. Attempts at reducing littering have relied heavily on the use of prompts. The results have been generally disappointing except where the target behaviors were facilitated by the provision of bins and rewarded by incentives (Nootebloom, 2009; Posner, 1995). In field experiments conducted by applied behavior analysts, even the provision of a dime or a ticket for a movie had a considerable effect on recycling behavior. Exhortations, lectures, and relevant general education have proved largely ineffective.

In summary, the relevant operant class is *hedonism:* Utilitarian reinforcement is high, whereas informational reinforcement is relatively low. This is borne out by considering the utilitarian reinforcement of littering, predominantly ease of disposal, and the informational reinforcement, which consists perhaps of conspicuous consumption, social prestige, and social status. The aversive consequences are also apparent: social disapproval (if noticed by others). The consumer behavior in question (littering, indiscriminate waste disposal) is maintained by immediately-acting contingencies that are countered by the availability of alternative methods of disposal, such as rubbish bins. The adverse consequences apparently have little effect on a consumer who is adding litter or other waste to an already-infested site. The tragedy of the commons is only too apparent.

Domestic Energy Consumption

The objective in this case has been to reduce overconsumption of domestic energy derived from fossil fuels, notably electricity for heating and lighting, through the provision of prompts pointing out the long-term consequences, feedback on individuals' and households' recent consumption levels, and financial and other incentives for reduced usage.

Attempted modification of consumers' domestic energy consumption has incorporated antecedent prompting, feedback, and incentives, separately and in combination. Prompting alone (e.g., information about environmental effects of pollution caused by overconsumption of electricity at peak periods) had little if any effect on peak usage. The greatest behavior change was effected by consumer self-monitoring of current energy use. Energy usage proved especially sensitive to feedback, especially if this was frequent: Daily feedback on energy usage, especially when combined with group feedback and mild social commendation for prosocial behavior, is particularly effective, the combination of prompts and feedback with incentives even more so. This is an area of consumption in which a high level of utilitarian reinforcement in the form of instant power, heating, and lighting is taken for granted; there is no opportunity for tradeoffs here between lower prices and less efficient provision.

In summary, the operant class is *accumulation:* Utilitarian reinforcement is essential, but behavior change is particularly sensitive to informational reinforcement. Utilitarian reinforcement takes the form of warmth, use of electrical and electronic appliances, comfort, and convenience; informational reinforcement, of status and self-esteem (these derive from the direct availability of energy and, indirectly, from the ability to acquire and operate gadgets or appliances). The principal aversive consequence is the financial outlay necessary.

Domestic Water Consumption

The objective has been to reduce domestic consumption of water, especially in washing, cleaning, and gardening. There is less directly generated ABA experimental evidence for the behavioral economics of water consumption and conservation than for the other commodities and products considered, but the limited evidence confirms the pattern of results found for other commodities. In Perth, Australia, water consumption decreased by more than 30% in both an experimental group provided with daily feedback on water use and a rebate proportionate to demand reduction and a control group provided only with feedback, though change in climatic conditions may also have affected the results. The low elasticity of demand for water makes financial rebates less appropriate than for other classes of consumer behavior.

In summary, the operant class is *maintenance:* There are relatively low levels of utilitarian reinforcement and informational reinforcement. Utilitarian reinforcement stems from water use, cleanliness, hygiene, and prevention of disease, whereas informational reinforcement is apparent in status and social approval. The aversive consequences are also considerable and include local taxes, charges, rationing, pricing, and metering.

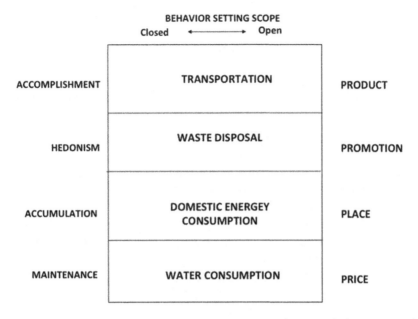

FIGURE 3 Environment-impacting consumption: Operant classes and dominant marketing mix elements. *Source:* Foxall (2010). Adapted with permission.

SUMMING UP

The main conclusions of this discussion are summarized in Figure 3. The question that arises now is how society responds to consumer behavior, and in particular what form of response to environment-impacting consumption has been forthcoming. The marketing firm is the means of organizational response to consumer behavior, and the response to environment-impacting consumption has been uncannily sympathetic to the findings of ABA.

THE MARKETING FIRM

The Marketing Firm in Context

The organization that responds to consumer choice is the marketing firm. The idea of the marketing firm, which reflects aspects of the thought of Coase (1937), Drucker (2007), and Simon (1976, 1987), posits that the primary rationale for firms, given the structural nature of modern markets, is to undertake customer-oriented management—that is, to respond to the general economic and social conditions that make production orientation unprofitable and that compel a customer-oriented strategy on not only the part of the marketing department or function, but of the entire enterprise. The marketing firm is not therefore simply a firm that undertakes marketing activities, nor does the term refer to the marketing department or function of the enterprise. It is the entire firm as it responds to the opportunities to satisfy consumer wants and the competitive threats enjoined on it by the structural economic and social conditions that compel marketing-oriented management. (For elaboration, see Foxall, 1999b; Hodgson & Knudsen, 2010; Vella & Foxall, 2011.) The conditions that compel customer orientation are (a) supply or potential supply exceeding aggregate demand, (b) high levels of discretionary income, (c) intense interindustrial competition among suppliers, and (d) consumer sophistication (Foxall, 1981/2015). These circumstances necessitate marketing planning and research; product development; market segmentation strategies (rather than the attempt to satisfy the entire market); and assiduity in planning and producing, implementing and managing, integrated marketing mixes that meet corporate goals (e.g., Kotler, Keller, Brady, Goodman, & Hansen, 2012). All of these are matters are so closely intertwined with the raison d'être of the firm—why it exists, what it does—that the relationship of marketing and corporate strategies is more than alignment: It is coincidence. Both strategic perspectives involve answers to the questions famously raised by Drucker (2007): What business are we in? Who is our customer? Who will be the customer? The shelter of the corporate environment is required to ensure that these tasks are undertaken without their being observed by competitors. Whatever the historical basis for the existence of firms (e.g., Coase, 1937; Nooteboom, 2009; Sautet, 2000), this philosophy of management provides their contemporary rationale.

Only Marketing?

It is natural to ask why the marketing firm has been given a single function when surely firms produce, consult, and practice as well as market. The marketing firm concept is an extension of Coase's (1937) realization that firms exist because they minimize transaction costs, an insight that has become central to the definition of economic institutions and the delineation of their unique nature. Transactions will be incorporated within the firm when the costs of coordination they entail become thereby smaller than if they were undertaken through individual contracting among independent producers. Coase's recognition of the implications of costs of transacting in the market place transforms understanding of the nature of business behavior and of the business enterprise itself. It is possible, however, to extend his analysis to incorporate characteristics of the modern corporation that do not figure, at least not prominently, in his work. In particular, in Coase's purview, the firm is essentially a unit of production, and although he uses the term *marketing costs* (rather than *transaction costs*), his analysis says little of the firm as a marketing entity. This was conveyed by both the title and the tenor of his 1991 Nobel Lecture (Coase, 1993): Even allowing for the inclusion of marketing activity within the term *production,* this usage fails to discriminate the various kinds and functions of marketing costs understood as those of coordinating marketing intelligence and the profitable provision of consumer benefits. If we extend Coase's insight to include the marketing operations of firms, however, this leads to the bolder claims that, because the pursuit of marketing-oriented management is the prime motive for their current rationale, all firms are necessarily marketing firms; in short, marketing provides the raison d'être of the contemporary corporation. Another way of putting this is that Coasean analysis concentrates on the inputs to the firm's productive processes; the concept of the marketing firm extends the analysis by, first, incorporating the subset of these inputs that are ultimately involved in output decisions, and, second, considering the outputs themselves as entities that need to be coordinated as much as the inputs.

Bilateral Contingency

In general terms, firms attempt to manage their relationships with their customers. The *marketing firm* can be defined as an organization that responds to consumer behavior by producing marketing mixes that influence consumer choice by managing the pattern of reinforcement of the consumer and the scope of the consumer behavior setting. This entails the formation and management of *marketing relationships,* which are characterized by *literal exchange,* exchange of legal title to a product or service on the one hand and whatever it is exchanged *for* (usually money) on the other (Foxall, 1999a). This general observation translates well into an account of the activities of the marketing firm viewed in behavior analytic terms. We have seen that consumer behavior is a function of the scope of the consumer behavior setting and the pattern of reinforcement that shapes and maintains choice. The behavior of the marketing firm may be represented as a response to consumer demand that involves managing the scope of the consumer behavior setting so that the brand marketed by the firm becomes a more salient member of the consumer's consideration set and managing the pattern of reinforcement by providing appropriate responses to the operant classes of accomplishment, hedonism, accumulation, and maintenance shown by consumers (Vella & Foxall, 2011, 2013).

The way in which marketing firms respond to consumer behavior is by attempting to effectively manage the bilateral contingencies that link them with their customer bases (see Figure 4). Firms undertake this by researching consumer behavior and wants and designing and implementing marketing mixes that use product, price, promotion, and place as effectively as possible in order to achieve corporate objectives by profitably meeting consumer requirements. Consumers respond by buying or rejecting the offerings of firms and thereby fulfilling or thwarting the financial objectives of the enterprise. The behavior of marketers thus provides as its outputs the

MARKETER

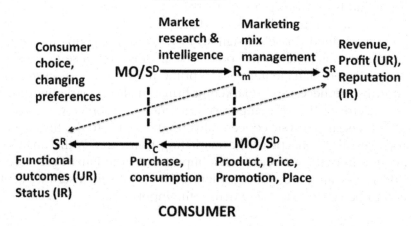

FIGURE 4 Bilateral contingency. MO = motivating operation; S^D = discriminative stimulus; Rm = response of the marketer; Rc = response of the consumer; S^R = reinforcing stimulus; UR = utilitarian reinforcement; IR = informational reinforcement. *Source:* Foxall (1999a). Adapted with permission.

discriminative stimuli and motivating operations that embody the behavior setting of the consumer and the satisfactions (we would say, *reinforcers*) that shape and maintain consumer choice; in turn, the behaviors of consumers provide as their outputs the revenues and profits that influence corporate planning and operations.

The essence of *bilateral* contingency is that the parties are sufficiently closely connected to read clearly the behaviors of each other and for these, and their outcomes, to act as discriminative stimuli and reinforcers/punishers for further behavior (Foxall, 1999a, 2014b). Although these relationships depend heavily on rule-governed behavior as well as that which is directly contingency shaped, the bilateral contingencies involved allow the behavior of one party to be responsive with some immediacy to that of the other, to be in touch with the other party by virtue of proximal rather than distal, concrete rather than highly symbolic, reinforcements (Foxall, 2013).

RESPONSES TO ENVIRONMENT-IMPACTING CONSUMPTION

Actual attempts to redress problems of environment-impacting consumption have followed the prescriptions of both ABA and the suggestions of the marketing firm. (European examples have been chosen because they facilitate the comparison of nations and cultures for which similarly based measures apply. But these are supplemented by studies for the United States and Australia.)

Private Transportation

It is predicted on the basis of the preceding analyses in terms of ABA research and the marketing firm that the crucial marketing mix element will be the product; the pattern of reinforcement that must be maintained or enhanced is high utilitarian reinforcement and high informational reinforcement: accomplishment. The actual marketing response: provision of benefits previously in the province of private transportation—comfort, speed, and reliability combined with enhancement of status. It is likely, however, that charges for the new services, whether recovered by pricing or taxation, have risen.

Changes in mode and frequency of transportation can be implemented by fiat (e.g., by banning cars with particular index numbers from the streets on certain days). The approach known as voluntary travel-behavior change (VTBC), as used in Australia, Germany, Japan, The Netherlands, Sweden, the United Kingdom, and the United States, is claimed effective even though it does not rely on compulsion (Friman, Pedersen, & Garling, 2012). Drawing on recent research by Friman, Larhult, and Gärling (2013), Friman et al. (2012), Redman et al. (2013), and Richter, Friman, and Gärling (2010, 2012), I would like to summarize the results of these so-called "soft" transport policies (in contrast to "hard" policies (which entail the use of punitive pricing, legislation, and investment in infrastructure) in order to show how they approach the consumer. I want also to distinguish *market-based measures* from *coercion* and to draw attention to the fact that general cultural contingencies will favor one or the other depending on the society involved. Market-based measures include road and congestion charging, kilometer/mileage charges, fuel duty and parking charges, and public transport discounts and travel vouchers. Coercion includes taxation, road closure, punitive pricing, and so on. Most societies—perhaps *all* societies—combine market-based and coercive measures (Cairns et al., 2008).

Another approach is voluntary travel behavior change (VTBC), which encourages drivers to make a voluntary switch toward a more sustainable travel mode. There may be no such thing as voluntary behavior, but we can easily understand these measures as offering drivers alternative behavior patterns that are positively reinforced, thereby expanding the scope of their consumer behavior settings. VTBC can be combined with either market-based or coercive policies, or all three can be incorporated in a comprehensive policy. There is indeed evidence of synergy between the hard and soft measures such a policy requires. Studies in the United States and The Netherlands showed that VTBC alone resulted in reductions of 5% to 15% in car travel, whereas reductions in car use by 20% to 25% were apparent when VTBC was used in combination with hard measures such as parking management and bus subsidy.

All of these types of measures involve either a corporate metacontingency or a government metacontingency or a combination of the two transacting with individual consumers. The behavior of road users reflects patterns of reinforcement imposed by others. It remains that of individual drivers. If we aggregate it, it remains macrobehavior that does not evolve in its right. The actions of the metacontingencies in this case, however, are instrumental in extending rather than restricting the scope of the consumer behavior setting.

Waste Disposal

ABA and the marketing firm lead to the prediction that the crucial predicted marketing mix element is place; the pattern of reinforcement that must be maintained or enhanced is high utilitarian reinforcement and low informational reinforcement: hedonism. The actual marketing response has been more concentrated provision of bins that seeks to change behavior by enhanced utilitarian reinforcement. In addition, the agencies responsible have emphasized that greener areas promote pride.

It is unlikely that the effects of littering or more destructive forms of indiscriminate waste disposal can be assuaged by the market alone. Most anti-litter interventions are the result of action by local government or facility owners/managers, but in either case they are enforced ultimately by systems of fining malfeasants that require central government involvement. The emphasis on punishment (fines) may well encourage visitors to dispose of litter more carefully though still illegally. A study by Keep America Beautiful revealed that only two variables are significantly related to littering: the availability of receptacles and amount of litter present (Keep America Beautiful, 2009, p. 22). It has also proved possible to segment litterers (Lyndhurst, 2012). And so, the behavior of individual consumers/disconsumers is aggregated into macrobehavior albeit at the level of the segment. Such behavior does not evolve.

Domestic Energy

The predictions of ABA and the marketing firm are that the crucial marketing mix element is promotion, where the pattern of reinforcement that must be maintained or enhanced is low utilitarian reinforcement and high informational reinforcement: accumulation. The actual marketing response has been smart metering giving (near-) instant feedback on consumption, allowing costs paid to be controlled by the consumer without reducing the overall utilitarian benefits obtained. The crucial factor is informational reinforcement. In addition, utilitarian reinforcement has been maintained by lagging, double glazing, insulation, and building regulations.

In energy there is a concerted consumer-oriented program that has incorporated sound research and the encouragement of metering of domestic energy supplies. A summary of 21 studies on feedback between 1975 and 2000 indicated, in complete agreement with the earlier ABA research, that *direct* feedback constitutes the most effective means of generating savings in domestic electricity consumption. The greatest savings (approximately 20%) were attained through providing consuming households with a tabletop interactive cost- and power-display unit, a smartcard reader for prepayment of electricity, and an indicator showing the cumulative cost of operating an electric cooker. Indirect feedback in the form of enhanced billing also influenced savings. The 21 studies between 1975 and 2000 showed that these direct interventions were responsible for up to 20% savings. *Indirect* feedback includes such factors as more frequent bills based on meter readings and historical feedback on consumption and costs of electricity (European Environment Agency, 2013). These interventions are generally less effective than direct measures.

All of these measures involve the identification and management of contingencies that influence the behavior of individual customers or households. The behavior of these individuals/units is then influenced by skillful management of these contingencies to produce an overall level of macrobehavior that fulfills corporate projections. Such macrobehavior does not evolve; it adjusts to changing contingencies imposed from without. We would say in terms of the BPM that the consumer behavior setting is relatively closed, therefore. The consumer has little or no option but to conform to the contingencies imposed, and although he or she may do so willingly (i.e., he or she is responding to positive rather than negative reinforcement), the scope of the consumer behavior setting remains highly restricted. Central agencies such as the European Environment Agency can monitor and encourage the progress of whole nations in adopting an appropriate strategy. But the pattern of engagement is always between a corporate metacontingency and the behavior and macrobehavior of numerous individuals or households. The aim of the managerial intervention is to manipulate the pattern of reinforcement the consumer faces and to effect closure of the scope of the consumer behavior setting.

Domestic Water Consumption

The ABA-derived predictions in terms of the marketing firm are that the crucial marketing mix element is price (or perhaps value for money) whereas the pattern of reinforcement that must be maintained or enhanced is low utilitarian reinforcement and low informational reinforcement: maintenance.

The actual marketing response has been the installation of metering to provide instant or almost instant feedback on consumption and costs, and its judicious use provides close links between consumption and the benefits obtained. This enables the cost incurred by obtaining utilitarian benefits to be minimized and encourages use of less water. Water conservation measures also rely heavily on metering, so many of these considerations apply there too. The criteria for achieving sustainability in this area have been set out for the United Kingdom by Hetherington (2007), who, in a report to the World Wide Fund for Nature (WWF), encapsulates them in several rules, of which the most indicative of the approach taken are that as a generalization the entire cost incurred by a water utility should be charged to consumers; water should be metered so that household tariffs avoid fixed annual charges (which are inefficient and encourage waste); and, ideally, the benchmark price of metered water prices should be the marginal cost of providing it (i.e., the extra cost of one more unit).

All of these rules respond to water consumers or households as individuals. Again, the macrobehavior of these units is the input to the corporate planning and operations of the utility companies, which are metacontingencies. The import of treating households as if they were units of consumption is that they are not expected to produce outputs other than the collective behavior of the individuals who compose them. The marketing mix is aimed at the management of the contingencies responsible for the pattern of individual behavior; this management is achieved by the provision to consumers of a pattern of reinforcement that will have the desired behavioral effects; the consumer's/household's behavior setting scope is reduced by the provision of a single pattern of behavior that will be overwhelmingly preferred. I am not making any judgment about the benignity of these measures, or the conduct of the utility companies, or the economic system in which they operate. My interest is solely academic: the relevance of metacontingencies and bilateral contingencies to our understanding consumer and marketer behaviors.

Principles of Contingency Management

It is apparent from this that several principles of corporate response are consonant with the prescriptions of metacontingency theory. First, it is necessary to maintain a similar pattern of contingencies to that currently maintaining less prosocial behavior, though consideration should be given to the levels of utilitarian reinforcement and informational reinforcement being enhanced. *This is in line with Biglan and Glenn's (2013) principle that prosocial behavior should be richly reinforced.* Second, the consumer behavior setting scope needs to be modified. One may see this as a closure of the setting in that at present the consumer has the choice between a problem behavior and the prosocial pattern we wish to engender, whereas we are seeking to restrict his or her choice to the latter. *This view would be in line with Biglan and Glenn's principle of setting limits for problem behavior.* Or it could be seen as enhancing the degree of choice available to the consumer by offering a new behavior pattern and thereby increasing the number of options available to the consumer. *This is in line with Biglan and Glenn's principle that prosocial behavior is encouraged by reducing or removing toxic conditions.* Insofar as the remoter, more long-run consequences of environment-impacting consumption are toxic, we are ultimately providing a more open setting for consumer behavior.

SYMMETRY AND ASYMMETRY BETWEEN CONTEXTUAL SYSTEMS

The examination of how marketing firms have actually approached environmental problems permits further investigation of the relevance of metacontingency and bilateral contingency to the analysis of firm–consumerate interactions. These relationships can be understood in terms of their being symmetrical or asymmetrical.

Symmetry

By *symmetry* I mean the interaction of two organizations each marked by metacontingency such that their behavior can be analyzed in terms of an overarching metacontingent system. The advantage of symmetry is that there is a degree of equality between the parties to a transaction. If both parties to the transaction are metacontingencies, each has an output/product that enables the other to tailor its marketing mixes appropriately. For example, in the case of a marketing firm interacting with a corporate customer, each can read the other's behavior in terms of a unified marketing mix or purchasing policy from which it can infer the strategy of the other and respond to it strategically. This leads to more appropriate marketing mixes and acquisition strategies, greater efficiency, and long-term relationships that enhance product development. Each organization has control of its behavior setting to a considerable (though of course not absolute) degree. Each organization matters to the other sufficiently for its strategic ends to be taken into consideration in large degree by the other. Each party has the opportunity to assert its strategic aims, and if it chooses not to transact with the other, this will have tangible effects on the other's fortunes. The result is a long-term relationship between the transacting organizations, so-called relationship marketing.

Asymmetry

Asymmetry, however, is marked by an inequality of interaction in the following sense. If only one party to the transaction is a metacontingency (i.e., the marketing firm), it might be said that each member of the consumerate is pitched against the marketing output of an organization that has the resources to plan a marketing mix that is to some degree imposed on the consumerate. In all of the cases we have considered, the relationships are asymmetrical—there is considerable inequality of status between the marketing firm and individual consumer or household. The consumerate is not in a position to develop a strategic stance let alone to act as a metacontingency that has strategic outputs. (A household might be considered a small metacontingency, but it is not able to exert market power vis-à-vis the marketing firm.) There is no need in principle for the marketing firm to seek long-term relationships with its individual consumers in this case. As long as the marketing firm achieves its revenue, profit, or other goals, it is immaterial whether it seeks to meet the requirements of each available market segment let alone each consumer. *However,* the exercise of environmental conservation by marketing firms has in practice been effective, and many of the provisions (such as metering) have been welcomed by customers.

The explanation suggested here derives from the existence of bilateral contingencies that in a market economy ensure that consumers' setting scope is sufficiently open to allow them to transfer their business to another supplier. The nature of the bilateral contingencies that bind firms and their consumers also offers an explanation of the different kinds of relationships we have identified (see Figure 5). Bilateral contingencies differ in the extent to which they are firm or fragile, that is, the extent to which they promote orderly exchange between customers and suppliers. Figure 5 places the four areas of consumption ordinally on a continuum from firm to fragile bilateral contingencies. *Energy* consumption is marked by a moderately firm bilateral contingency. Consumption occurs in a situation in which consumers have a choice of supplier because there is competition among providers. But they also have the option of overconsuming if they prefer as long as they can pay for the energy they use. Metering does control consumption very effectively, however. *Water* consumption is marked by an even more firm bilateral contingency: There may not be competition for particular consumers among suppliers, even though providers may be regulated by national bodies to provide an acceptable level of service. Despite some similarities in consumption and marketing between energy and water, water belongs closer to the *firm* pole of the continuum because of the low elasticity of demand that characterizes this commodity and the lack of competition among suppliers. Neither of these is true of energy consumption and provision. *Transportation* occurs in an even more open setting because of the high levels of competition among providers and the alternative of private motoring if the high levels of utilitarian and informational reinforcement that consumers demand are not otherwise met. Finally, most open of all is the setting in which *littering* is a possibility. There is no long-term relationship between marketers

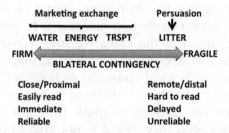

FIGURE 5 Bilateral contingency in the context of environmental concern. TRSPT = transportation.

and their consumerate; indeed, we are dealing with a fleeting relationship that does not entail marketing in any generally understood sense. There is no possibility of policing green areas such that littering will be eliminated. The contingencies are distant; one has to get caught; the fines seem remote and unlikely; and although everyone says they prefer a clean environment, the fact that littering increases where there is already litter undermines this. There is no immediacy of mutual reinforcement.

How do the bilateral contingencies vary among these marketing and consumption patterns? Those at the *firm* end of the continuum are close or proximal (dovetailing the behaviors of marketers and consumers). They involve easily read stimulus profiles (the elements of supplier behavior that act as motivating operations or discriminative stimuli for customer behavior are very apparent and vice versa), they are immediately acting (especially in the case of metered commodities), and they are reliable. At the *fragile* end, however, contingencies are remote or distal, not easily read, delayed, and unreliable (chances are I will not be caught for littering). Moreover, the relationships between water and energy utilities and transport organizations entail genuine marketing relationships: The exchanges are literal and embrace the whole of the marketing mix. Those involved in the reduction of littering rely principally on persuasion, and there is no literal exchange, though metaphorical analogs may be suggested. These fragile bilateral contingencies signal a sphere of behavior change that does not invoke marketing at the intermediate levels considered in this article so much as real social marketing and cultural contingencies.

CONCLUSIONS

Environmental concern often stems from problems of consumption. If behavior analysis is to contribute to the solution of these problems, we need to understand what environment-impacting consumption is contingent on, how response to environment-impacting consumption works, and how environment-impacting consumption and that response are related. Consumer behavior is contingent on patterns of reinforcement and the consumer behavior setting scope; environment-impacting consumption is similarly contingent. Response to environment-impacting consumption is undertaken by the marketing firm, which seeks to influence consumer choice via the modification of patterns of reinforcement and setting scope. Firms also manage bilateral contingencies that link them via networks of close contingency with their consumerates. Whereas marketing firms are metacontingencies, consumerates are composed of a mass of individual consumers whose combined activity is better characterized as macrobehavior. The relationships between marketing firms and consumerates are asymmetrical, but the skillful management of bilateral contingencies can ensure that consumers remain involved in the process of alleviating environmental concern.

Metacontingency and Bilateral Contingency

Each of the marketing programs we have examined involves an organization (a single contextual system) interacting with its customer base (a large number of contextual systems). The marketing firm generates a marketing mix, not for each of the consumers it seeks to respond to or influence, but for each segment of the market that is measurable, accessible, justifiable, differentiable, and actionable (Kotler et al., 2012). This does not mean that it envisions each segment of its customer base as a metacontingency; rather, a segment is characterized precisely by what Biglan and Glenn (2013) call macrobehavior: To the firm it is an aggregate of consumers who will act similarly in the face of the marketing mix the firm designs and implements for it. Each member of a segment responds to the marketing mix in a predicted way, and as the contingencies contained in the mix vary, the individual consumer's behavior will vary. But there is no overall output of the consumer base's behavior that is other than an aggregate of the behavior of each of its members. It is the marketing mix that produces sales, not any one element of it but the emergent bundle. It is unlikely that marketing firms know what their consumers are buying, and although this may not matter if the market for widgets is large enough in the short to medium term, it will affect the marketing firm's fortunes in the long term if technological advance overtakes its product offering. This amorphous nature of the marketing mix, the inability of the marketing firm to pin down precisely what generates its sales, is especially important for business-to-business marketing.

How would this be different if the marketing firm were transacting with a corporate customer? The customer in this case would itself be a metacontingency, a complex of interlocking *internal* behavioral contingencies out of which would emerge a purchasing strategy that specified the kinds of products/services it required and its conception of value (i.e., what it would be willing to pay); this strategy would be revealed in negotiations with the marketing firm and would be an output of the behavior not of any individual or group but of the overall organization. This strategy would be a behavior pattern of the organization that would have consequences of its own in the market place in terms of the effectiveness with which it contributed to the overall strategic goals of the customer organization in which it originated. The relationships between the marketing firm and its customer would then be an interaction of metacontingencies. The amorphousness of the marketing firm's marketing mix is compounded by the amorphousness of the customer firm's purchasing strategy.

The marketing mix that is the supra-personal behavioral output of the marketing firm is met, in the market place, by the purchasing strategy of the firm that is its customer. In this case, although the marketing firm may produce a mix for each segment it serves, it is likely to tailor the mix for each customer firm, each of which has it own requirements that are profitable for the marketing firm to meet separately. At the theoretical level, however, the interesting outcome is that the marketing firm is dealing with an emergent output from its customer that may be difficult to describe definitively.

Practical Implications

There will only be greater symmetry in the relationships between marketing firms and their ultimate consumerates if consumers join forces by forming an association that develops as an output a policy or strategy to guide its members' behaviors with respect to the marketer that is over and above the aggregate behaviors of individual consumers. If this occurred, the consumerate would become a metacontingency and its relationship with marketing firms would be more equal. The strategic output of the consumer association would evolve to meet consumers' changing requirements.

The attempt to use social marketing—defined as an attempt to alter cultural or macrocontingencies directly—brings new organizations into play, the interests of which may not be those of the consumerate. This does not necessarily meet the need of the consumerate to develop countervailing power vis-à-vis marketing firms. There is no obvious bilateral contingency between the social marketer in this sense and the consumerate. There is clearly a need for behavior analytical research to address this practical issue. Fortunately, the concepts of metacontingency and bilateral contingency have proved consonant with each other, giving hope that further research will develop further their theoretical and practical implications.

ACKNOWLEDGMENTS

This article was presented as "Consumer Behavior Analysis and Cultural Change in the Context of Environmental Conservation" at the Association for Behavior Analysis International Seminar on Leadership and Cultural Change, May 23–25, 2014, in Chicago, Illinois.

I am grateful to Kevin Vella for helpful comments on an earlier draft.

REFERENCES

Biglan, A., & Glenn, S. S. (2013). Toward prosocial behavior and environments: Behavioral and cultural contingencies in a public health framework. In G. J. Madden, W. V. Dube, T. D. Hackenberg, G. P. Hanley, & K. A. Lattal (Eds.), *APA handbook of behavior analysis* (Vol. 2, pp. 255–275). Washington, DC: American Psychological Association.

Cairns, S., Sloman, L., Newson, C., Anable, J., Kirkbride, A., & Goodwin, P. (2008). Smarter choices: Assessing the potential to achieve traffic reduction using "soft measures." *Transport Reviews, 28,* 593–618.

Coase, R. H. (1937). The nature of the firm. *Economica*, *4*, 386–405.

Coase, R. H. (1988). *The firm, the market and the law*. Chicago, IL: University of Chicago Press.

Coase, R. H. (1993). Nobel Lecture 1991: The institutional structure of production. In O. E. Williamson & S. G. Winter (Eds.), *The nature of the firm: Origins, evolution, and development* (pp. 227–235). New York, NY: Oxford University Press.

Cone, J. D., & Hayes, S. C. (1980). *Environmental problems/behavioral solutions*. Belmont, CA: Wadsworth.

Drucker, P. F. (2007). *The practice of management*. London, England: Routledge.

European Environment Agency. (2013). *Achieving energy efficiency through behaviour change: What does it take?* (EEA Technical Report No. 5/2013). Copenhagen, Denmark: Author.

Foxall, G. R. (1979). On the management of "commons." *Journal of Agricultural Economics*, *30*, 55–58.

Foxall, G. R. (1988). Marketing new technology: Markets, hierarchies, and user-initiated innovation. *Managerial and Decision Economics*, *9*, 237–250.

Foxall, G. R. (1994). Environment-impacting consumer behaviour: A framework for social marketing and demarketing. In M. J. Baker (Ed.), *Perspectives on marketing management* (Vol. 4, pp. 27–53). Chichester, England: Wiley.

Foxall, G. R. (1999a). The contextual stance. *Philosophical Psychology*, *12*, 25–46.

Foxall, G. R. (1999b). The marketing firm. *Journal of Economic Psychology*, *20*, 207–234.

Foxall, G. R. (2001). Foundations of consumer behaviour analysis. *Marketing Theory*, *1*, 165–199.

Foxall, G. R. (2002a). Consumer behavior analysis and social marketing. In G. Bartels & W. Nelissen (Eds.), *Marketing for sustainability: Towards transactional policy-making* (pp. 304–320). Amsterdam, The Netherlands: IOS Press.

Foxall, G. R. (Ed.). (2002b). *Consumer behaviour analysis: Critical perspectives in business and management*. London, England: Routledge.

Foxall, G. R. (2002c). Social marketing for environmental conservation. In G. R. Foxall (Ed.), *Consumer behaviour analysis: Critical perspectives in business and management* (Vol. 3, pp. 460–486). London, England: Routledge.

Foxall, G. R. (2004). *Consumer psychology in behavioral perspective*. Frederick, MD: Beard Books. (Original work published 1990).

Foxall, G. R. (2010). *Interpreting consumer choice: The Behavioral Perspective Model*. New York: Routledge.

Foxall, G. R. (2013). *Interpreting consumer choice: The behavioral perspective model* (2nd ed.). New York, NY: Routledge.

Foxall, G. R. (2014a). Cognitive requirements of neuro-behavioral decision systems: Some implications of temporal horizon for managerial behavior in organizations. *Frontiers in Human Neuroscience*, *8*, 184. doi:10.3389/fnhum.2014.00184

Foxall, G. R. (2014b). The marketing firm and consumer choice: Implications of bilateral contingency for levels of analysis in organizational neuroscience. *Frontiers in Human Neuroscience*, *8*, Article 472, 1–14. doi:10.3389/fnhum.2014.00472

Foxall, G. R. (2015). *Strategic marketing management*. London and New York: Routledge. (Original work published 1981).

Foxall, G. R., Oliveira-Castro, J. M., James, V. K., Yani-de-Soriano, M. M., & Sigurdsson, V. (2006). Consumer behavior analysis and social marketing: The case of environmental conservation. *Behavior and Social Issues*, *15*, 101–124.

Friman, M., Larhult, L., & Gärling, T. (2013). An analysis of soft transport policy measures implemented in Sweden to reduce private car use. *Transportation*, *40*, 109–129.

Friman, M., Pedersen, T., & Garling, T. (2012). *Feasibility of voluntary reduction of private car use* (Karlstad University Studies 2012:30). Karlstad, Sweden: Karlstad University, Faculty of Economic Sciences, Communication and IT.

Geller, E. S., Winett, R. A., & Everett, P. B. (1984). *Preserving the environment: New strategies for behavior change.* New York, NY: Pergamon.

Glenn, S. S. (1991). Contingencies and metacontingencies: Relations among behavioral, cultural, and biological evolution. In P. A. Lamal (Ed.), *Behavioral analysis of societies and cultural practices* (pp. 39–73). New York, NY: Hemisphere.

Glenn, S. S. (2004). Individual behavior, culture, and social change. *The Behavior Analyst*, *27*, 133–151.

Glenn, S. S., & Malott, M. E. (2004). Complexity and selection: Implications for organizational change. *Behavior and Social Issues*, *13*, 89–106.

Hardin, G. (1968). The tragedy of the commons. *Science*, (13 December), *162*, 3859, 1243–1248.

Hetherington, P. (2007). *Waste not, want not: Sustainable water tariffs.* Bristol, England: Centre for Sustainable Energy.

Hodgson, G. M., & Knutsen, T. (2010). *Darwin's conjecture: The search for general principles of social and economic evolution.* Chicago, IL: Chicago University Press.

Houmanfar, R., Rodrigues, N. J., & Smith, G. S. (2009). Role of communication networks in behavioral systems analysis. *Journal of Organizational Behavior Management*, *29*, 257–275.

Keep America Beautiful (2009). *Littering Behavior in America: Results of a national study.* San Marcos, CA: Action Research.

Kotler, P., Keller, K. L., Brady, M., Goodman, M., & Hansen, T. (2012). *Marketing management.* Harlow, England: Pearson.

Lyndhurst, B. (2012). *Rapid evidence review of littering behaviour and anti-litter policies.* Stirling, Scotland: Zero Waste Scotland.

Nooteboom, B. (2009). *A cognitive theory of the firm.* Northampton, MA: Edward Elgar.

Posner, R. A. (1995). *Overcoming law.* Cambridge, MA: Harvard University Press.

Redman, L., Friman, M., Gärling, T. and Hartig, T. (2013). Quality attributes of public transport that attract car users. *Transport Policy*, *25*, 119–127.

Richter, J., Friman, M. and Gärling, T. (2010). Review of evaluations of soft transport policy measures. *Transportation: Theory and Application*, *2*, 5–18.

Richter, J., Friman, M. and Gärling, T. (2011). Soft transport policy measures: Gaps of knowledge and research needs. *International Journal of Sustainable Transportation*, *5*, 199–215.

Sautet, F. E. (2000). *An entrepreneurial theory of the firm.* London, England: Routledge.

Simon, H. A. (1976). *Administrative behavior* (3rd ed.). New York, NY: Macmillan.

Simon, H. A. (1987). Rational decision making in business organizations. In L. Green & J. H. Kagel (Eds.), *Advances in behavioral economics* (Vol. 1, pp. 18–47). Norwood, NJ: Ablex.

Skinner, B. F. (1981). Selection by consequences, *Science, 213*, (3 July), 501–504.

van Vliet, B., Chappells, H., & Shove, E. (2005). *Infrastructures of consumption: Environmental innovation in the utility industries*. Oxford, England: Routledge.

Vella, K. J., & Foxall, G. R. (2011). *The marketing firm: Economic psychology of corporate behavior*. Northampton, MA: Edward Elgar.

Vella, K. J., & Foxall, G. R. (2013). The marketing firm: Operant interpretation of corporate behavior. *The Psychological Record, 62*, 375–402.

Job Satisfaction: The Management Tool and Leadership Responsibility

DONALD A. HANTULA

Job satisfaction's tenuous relationship to a variety of work behaviors is reviewed from the perspective of a management tool and as a leadership responsibility. It may be viewed a management tool for accomplishing certain organizational objectives related to reducing absenteeism and tardiness. However, job satisfaction's importance is neither limited to nor justified by its somewhat weak relationship to certain organizational outcomes. Rather, job satisfaction is analyzed as a leadership responsibility with effects that extend far beyond the bounds of any given organization. Some fundamental assumptions surrounding job satisfaction are reviewed, and an argument for job satisfaction as an ethical imperative that results from organizational and management practices that emphasize positive reinforcement, not aversive control, is advanced.

Job satisfaction is the most widely researched variable in industrial-organizational psychology (Spector, 1997). This literature is bursting with studies of assorted antecedents, mediators, and moderators of job satisfaction. It is also filled with copious correlates of job satisfaction, such as various organizationally important attitudes and behaviors, primarily as an argument for its importance (Judge, Piccolo, Podsakoff, Shaw, & Rich, 2010; Judge, Thoresen, Bono, & Patton, 2001). The present article is less concerned with these issues, which view job satisfaction as a management tool, but rather approaches job satisfaction as a leadership responsibility, organizational leadership obligation, and ethical imperative (Hocutt, 2013; Mawhinney, 1984, 1989, 2011) and as a necessary outcome of successful organizational behavior management (OBM) interventions. Rather than sliding into scholasticism regarding the mensurational and definitional issues surrounding job satisfaction, the working definition adopted herein is quite simple: following Spector (1997, p. 2), "the extent to which people like (satisfaction) or dislike (dissatisfaction) their jobs," or job satisfaction = affective response to work, workplace conditions, and the work environment.

BEGINNING WITH A QUIZ

As is common in many academic endeavors, we will begin with a quiz.

Where do adults in industrial and postindustrial societies spend the majority of their conscious, waking hours?

What is perhaps the largest influence on adults' daily emotional well-being?

What is a substantial determinant of adults' health, quality of family life, and community involvement?

The answer to all of the above is "the workplace." According to the Gallup Work and Education Poll (Saad, 2014), in 2013–2014 salaried employees in the United States worked an average of 49 hr/week and 50% worked more than 50 hr/week. Hourly employees worked an average of 44 hr/week, with 26% working more than 50 hr/week. Similarly, the American Time Use Survey (Bureau of Labor Statistics, 2014) showed that adults in the United States spend more time working than engaging in any other conscious activity; sleep occupies only slightly more time.

Work, the workplace, working conditions, and the daily experience of work are fundamentally important, or possibly the most critically important factors in adult psychological functioning. By extension, a parent's work experience may also well be one of the most significant foundations of children's emotional, intellectual, and social development, because parents' daily encounters at work directly affect their interactions with their children when they come home. The economic benefits that work brings dictate the quality of neighborhoods, schools, and opportunities, and adults' modeling of work-related behavior and reactions to work might serve as powerful instructions and examples to their children. Indeed, it can be argued that the workplace is the single greatest influence on human psychology in postindustrial daily life. The growing literature on work–life balance makes these points abundantly clear (Bulger & Fisher, 2012; Kossek, Valcour, & Lirio, 2014).

A MANAGEMENT TOOL, BUT PERHAPS NOT A MANAGEMENT RESPONSIBILITY

To many, the "happy productive worker" is the holy grail of organizational behavior research (Staw, 1986; Wright & Staw, 1999). Historically speaking, interest in job satisfaction stemmed from pecuniary purposes, an implicit or sometimes explicit assumption that morale and productivity were causally connected; or as the old adage goes, the contented cow gives the best milk. However, research shows that correlations of behavioral outcomes such absenteeism and turnover with job satisfaction are low (Schleicher, Hansen, & Fox, 2011). Expecting any correlation between job satisfaction and job performance is held to be dubious at best because job satisfaction is a fairly narrow construct whereas job performance is a very diffuse construct (Fisher, 1980). Indeed, the relationship between job satisfaction and job performance has been found to be nonexistent (Bowling, 2007; Brayfield & Crockett, 1955; Riketta, 2008) to low (Iaffaldano & Muchinsky, 1985) to weak (Christen, Iyer, & Soberman, 2006) to moderate (Judge et al., 2001), with no causal conclusions regarding the relationship between the two. Nevertheless, the search for mediators and moderators of job satisfaction and various organizationally important attitudes and behaviors continues unabated, with well over 10,000 studies published to date.

A presumed job satisfaction–job performance link is ideologically convenient, especially if job satisfaction is assumed to be dispositional in nature (Staw, Bell, & Clausen, 1986; Staw & Ross, 1985). If job satisfaction can be argued to cause job performance (despite evidence to the contrary), and if it is further presumed that job satisfaction is an intrinsic internal property of the individual (as a dispositional approach holds, to at least some extent), job performance (or the lack thereof) may then be assumed to be primarily the individual's fault. According to this perspective, on occasion, a manager may be able to arrange matters so that job satisfaction (and hence productivity) improves, but if such efforts fall short, the onus is on the individual employee, not the manager, because whether or not any such change in the workplace actually alters job satisfaction is primarily a function of presumably more powerful internal factors. Of course such a dispositional approach suggests strongly that individuals who score high on job satisfaction measures should be preferred and may be selected on that basis.

Research on the potential hereditability of job satisfaction lends credence to such a dispositional approach. Job satisfaction is moderately correlated in monozygotic twins reared apart (Arvey, Bouchard, Segal, & Abraham, 1989) but more highly correlated than in dizygotic twins (Arvey, McCall, Bouchard, Taubman, & Cavanaugh, 1994), which is taken as evidence for a genetic basis for job satisfaction. Such genetic determinism is often assumed to be immutable by those unfamiliar with behavioral genetics and thus is invoked as an argument against managerial responsibility for job satisfaction—simply, some people are just born that way. However, as Arvey et al. (1994) caution, the heritability correlations found in their studies are modest, and such correlations do not suggest that job satisfaction is in any way unchangeable. In addition, there is no evidence showing that any dispositional characteristics constrain the effects of environmental or organizational efforts to improve job satisfaction at all (Gerhart, 2005).

However, despite contradictory evidence, or at least evidence arguing for a more tenuous and nuanced interpretation, a dispositional approach to job satisfaction remains popular. In this case, job satisfaction may then be seen as a potential managerial tool whose efficacy is constrained not by management ineptitude but by much more potent, largely innate, employee characteristics. Furthermore, such an approach to job satisfaction removes much, if not all, of the responsibility for individual employee job satisfaction from management. That is, in a dispositional approach, job satisfaction may have some utility as a management tool, but it most likely is not a management responsibility.

QUESTIONING ASSUMPTIONS

The assumed job satisfaction–job performance causal link is questionable at best. The correlations between job satisfaction and other employment-related behaviors are modest, and causality is again muddled. Four other assumptions surrounding job satisfaction—(a) a difference definition, (b) a presumption that work must be unpleasant, (c) an equating of rewards with reinforcers, and (d) the normalcy of aversive control—may also wilt under further scrutiny.

Difference Definition

Implicit in many job satisfaction measures is an assumption of a deficit in affective reaction to work; that is, job satisfaction equals the gap between what one wants or expects from work and what one actually receives. Indeed, in one of the original investigations of job satisfaction, Thorndike (1917) explored the decline in "satisfyingness" over time: Workers were most satisfied at the beginning of work, and their satisfaction declined linearly over time until the end of the work period. This difference definition of job satisfaction may also be found in more current treatments of the topic, such as the well-cited volume by Cranny, Smith, and Stone (1992), who define *job satisfaction* as "an emotional state resulting from an employee's comparison of actual and desired job outcomes" (p. 148). This definition begs a question: Why must work be assumed to be less satisfying than individuals may expect or desire?

Work Is Unpleasant

Perhaps one reason for this deficit definition of job satisfaction may be an assumption that work is, or must necessarily be, intrinsically unpleasant. An early investigation of job satisfaction (Thorndike, 1917) clearly proceeds from such an assumption, which may have been the case a century ago. Similarly, the Marxist critique of the capitalist system holds that work in the industrial world will be inherently unpleasant because of the alienation of the worker from the product of labor, the act of producing, and the worker as a producer; or in behavioral terms, a lack of immediate consequences such as positive reinforcement for work. Skinner (1986) called this "estrangement" from work, a condition in which a worker is separated from the positive reinforcement that may accrue from work activities. Implicit in Marx's critique and made explicit in Skinner's is a recognition that work in the absence of positive reinforcement will be unpleasant and furthermore such a lack of positive reinforcement will necessarily lead to a system of aversive control. This analysis raises a question: In a postindustrial world, must such estrangement (in Skinner's terms) and its attendant aversive control systems continue?

Rewards Are Reinforcers

Many researchers and most of the lay public believe that job satisfaction causes job performance (Bowling, 2007). The entire "satisfaction causes productivity" argument leads to the inevitable conclusion that in order to increase productivity, one must increase satisfaction, and if satisfaction is largely equivalent to happiness or morale, the path to productivity involves making people happy. In this view, a surefire way to make people happy is to reward them. Unfortunately, even if this were to be the case, managers are not particularly accurate when it comes to identifying or predicting what employees may find rewarding (Wilder, Harris, Casella, Wine, & Postma, 2011; Wilder, Rost, & McMahon, 2007; Wine, Reis, & Hantula, 2014), possibly because employee preferences for rewards vary over time (Wine, Gilroy, & Hantula, 2012; Wine & Axelrod, 2014; Wine, Kelley, & Wilder, 2014). Hence, a well-intentioned effort to increase morale may backfire if the rewards offered are not in fact rewarding to the recipient; or more to the point, if such "rewards" do not in fact reinforce behavior. This confusion of rewards and reinforcers may also underlie the pernicious "rewards undermine intrinsic motivation" myth (Mawhinney, Dickinson, & Taylor, 1989), but there may be a grain of truth here. Rewards that are in fact reinforcing do not undermine motivation, but rewards that are not reinforcing may be the culprit (Eisenberger & Cameron, 1996). Finally, a reinforcer, by definition, strengthens behavior; specifically, it strengthens the behavior that precedes it. If people are rewarded, what behavior (if any at all) is reinforced is questionable; however, if work-related behavior is reinforced, that behavior will be strengthened, and people may be happier. Reinforcement is rewarding, but reward is not necessarily reinforcing. Must this confusion continue?

Normalcy of Aversive Control

Skinner (1986) pointed out that work for wages that do not directly reinforce behaviors will inevitably lead to a system of aversive control (see also

Abernathy, 2014). Seemingly ubiquitous aversive control in organizations may lead people to believe that such a system is preordained or normal. An organization exists as a formal means of behavior control; a Hobbesian perspective on organizations would argue that employees consent to such control in exchange for a paycheck because without it an organization would devolve into disorder and chaos. That is, it may not be possible to be productive without aversive control, which is akin to a Marxist critique of an industrial system. However, as Skinner (1955, 1975) observes, it is possible for people to be productive, happy, and free, but this requires an erosion of aversive control in favor of positive reinforcement. A major contribution of the positive behavior support movement (Tincani, 2011) is that teachers can control or even eliminate challenging behavior in classrooms through establishing a culture of positive reinforcement, rather than aversive contingencies, the point being that aversive control is aberrant, not customary. Why cannot this model be extended to formal organizations?

JOB SATISFACTION AS A MANAGERIAL RESPONSIBILITY, ORGANIZATIONAL LEADERSHIP OBLIGATION, AND ETHICAL IMPERATIVE

Organizational leaders and managers are responsible for the work environment. This is self-evident. It is also codified legally. Managers can be held civilly liable for harm to employees from a host of work environment malfunctions from negligent hiring ("Hidden Liability," 2013) to sexual harassment (Zachary, 2014). Sometimes organizational leaders and managers can be held criminally liable for workplace accidents (Pryor, 2014). These legal examples underscore two fundamental facts: Demonstrated control of the work environment confers responsibility for the work environment, and employees do not surrender their basic human rights when they enter the workplace. Employees have the right to not be harmed physically by the work environment. Their physical well-being must be protected. Employees have the right to not be harassed sexually or ethnically in the work environment. Their psychological well-being in this respect must be protected.

Responsibility Revisited

A meta-analysis of 485 studies showed clearly that job satisfaction is related to a myriad of health outcomes, including cardiovascular disease (Faragher, 2005). Higher job satisfaction is negatively correlated with occupational injury rates (Barling, Kelloway, & Iverson, 2003), perhaps bringing job satisfaction into the realm physical harm prevention. A large-scale panel study showed that employees high in job satisfaction have both higher subjective and objective health indicators (Fischer & Sousa-Poza, 2009). Tying both the organizational and social benefits, research shows that job satisfaction is highly negatively correlated with sickness absence (Böckerman & Ilmakunnas, 2008; Munch-Hansen, Wieclaw, Agerbo, Westergaard-Nielsen, & Bonde, 2008; Roelen, Koopmans, Notenbomer, & Groothoff, 2008, 2011). Sickness absence is a combination of both employee self-report of illness (or perhaps willingness to go to work) as well as the presence of physical illness. When faced with an excusable inconvenience such as a snowstorm, employees low in job satisfaction are more likely to be absent (Mawhinney, 1989); it is likely that the same result may occur if employees low in job satisfaction awaken with equivocal evidence of an illness. But furthermore, not only is job satisfaction associated with the behavioral manifestation of illness in terms of absence, but low job satisfaction is also associated with increased common infection (Mohren, Swaen, Kant, van Schayck, & Galama, 2005) as well as natural killer cell immunity (Nakata, Takahashi, Irie, & Swanson, 2010). That is, low job satisfaction may make employees more likely to fall ill and then more likely to be absent when symptoms of sickness are experienced.

Job satisfaction as a social good (or lack thereof) extends beyond the workplace into the family and community. Low levels of job satisfaction are related to depression and burnout (Faragher, 2005; Ybema, Smulders, & Bongers, 2010), which may diminish the degree to which individuals engage constructively with their communities and families. Indeed, job satisfaction is a major factor in work–family interface and life satisfaction (Simone et al., 2014). Job satisfaction level is correlated with marital satisfaction and also with affect at home, and the more highly integrated individuals' work and family roles, the more pronounced the positive and negative effects become (Ilies, Wilson, & Wagner, 2009). The negative spillover is real and destructive, for example making spouses too burned out and exhausted to talk to each other in the evening (Hewlett & Luce, 2006). It does not require a large inductive leap to see how such exhausted employees are much less likely to interact with their children, help with homework, participate in community activities, or do much of anything beyond watch television and self-medicate.

Organizational Leadership Obligation

Ensuring safety and preventing harassment are managerial duties. These are the bare minimum. The degree to which job satisfaction may contribute to certain organizationally important outcomes may then become the degree to which job satisfaction is seen as a management tool. This is barely over the minimum. In both cases, people are treated essentially as commodities to be used and risks to be mitigated, not as human beings. The managerial charge may well begin and end within the boundaries of the organization, but the leadership responsibility extends beyond the confines of the organization into the society and culture at large. Management's responsibilities to the organization are well delineated; however, there are equally important implied duties to employees. The argument herein is not that managers and organizational leaders are obligated to transform the workplace into an adult amusement park, nor is it another call for corporate social responsibility. Rather, the argument is that demonstrated control of the work environment implies a management responsibility and leadership imperative to use this control not only for the good of the organization but also for the greater social good. Improving organizational productivity and efficiency is a social good. Promoting occupational heath and safety is a social good. Accomplishing these in a positive manner is also a social good. Emotionally healthy employees are a social good. Management is about working in the present; leadership is about striving for the future.

Working Toward a Solution

The zero to modest correlations found between measures of job satisfaction and various typical measures of work-related behavior may lead to a conclusion that these variables are largely orthogonal, and the wisdom of expecting much of a relationship is dubious at best. Or, small relationships may exist but are obscured by an individual-level analysis; rather, they are emergent when organizational-level dependent variables are used (Ostroff, 1992). Alternatively, as Mawhinney (2011) argues, any such relationships may be constrained by Hobson's choice on the part of individual employees and restriction of range in the data. There is a further point here to pursue: The vast majority of job satisfaction/work-related behavior studies are correlational. Independent variables are not manipulated in correlational studies. Thus, the full range of the independent variable and its effects on the dependent variable are not known. What is known is that a miasma of aversive control is associated with both low affective reaction to the environment in which aversive control occurs (job satisfaction) and a tendency behave in a manner that meets the bare minimum required to avoid the aversive control (work-related behavior). It may be that both job satisfaction and work-related behaviors (and also organizational performance) can be increased not by actions targeting each directly but by taking action to change a third variable. The dual goal of high-performing organizations and high job satisfaction may be achieved by eroding the paradigm of aversive control. There is some evidence to support this idea.

Taken a step further, the principles and practices of OBM may be the most positive and humanizing ways to achieve this solution (Crowell, 2004), OBM interventions can work synergistically with more traditional organizational interventions (Crowell, Hantula, & McArthur, 2011). Ethical leadership increases job satisfaction (Kim & Brymer, 2011; Pettijohn, Pettijohn, & Taylor,

2008), as does supportive leadership (Schyns, van Veldhoven, & Wood, 2009). Stock in trade OBM interventions such as feedback not only can increase job performance but can also increase job satisfaction (Anseel & Lievens, 2007; Palmer & Johnson, 2013; Sommer & Kulkarni, 2012), as can a goal-setting and feedback package intervention (Wilk & Redmon, 1998). Indeed, more systemic interventions such as the balanced scorecard (Abernathy, 1997) have been shown to increase job satisfaction (Molina, Gonzalez, Florencio, & Gonzalez, 2014). Unfortunately, most OBM interventions do not include measures of job satisfaction, or if such measures are included they are neither standardized nor validated (Mawhinney, 2011). Development and inclusion of theoretically (i.e., behavior analytic) based measures is an important future direction for OBM research.

Properly administered positive reinforcement–based interventions can make for more productive, humanized, and satisfying organizations. Perhaps the most compelling evidence for the sheer power of a highly reinforcing work environment is the audacious question of whether a job can be made so reinforcing that drug addicts will refrain from using in order to gain access to the workplace—that is, the work environment is more reinforcing than cocaine or heroin. The therapeutic workplace, which serves substance abusers and requires employees to provide a daily clean urine sample to gain access to a highly reinforcing work environment. Evidence shows that in fact a workplace can be made to be more reinforcing than drugs over a period of years (Aklin et al., 2014; Holtyn et al., 2014; Koffarnus et al., 2011; Silverman et al., 2002, 2005). And furthermore, such an arrangement can be extended to low-income adults, in that it has been found that positive reinforcement in the form of performance-based pay increases both job performance and job satisfaction (Koffarnus, DeFulio, Sigurdsson, & Silverman, 2013).

Indeed, highly reinforcing management and leadership practices can accomplish the following: make workplaces more productive and safe, make employees more emotionally healthy, reduce psychopathology, prevent cancer and heart disease, reduce (maybe cure) substance abuse, make families happier, reduce domestic violence, and make communities better. Consequences are the key. Behavior analysis provides the theoretical basis for such a solution, and OBM supplies the technology for accomplishing it. It is within our grasp.

Conclusion

Demonstrated control of the work environment implies responsibility for the same. Organizational psychologists as a whole, and OBM practitioners in particular, have the knowledge, skills, and abilities to construct reinforcing workplace interventions. Organizational scientists and practitioners hold much influence over the manner in which organizations treat their employees. People deserve to be treated well. Doing no harm is not good enough;

this goes far beyond social validity and is a call to lead by action, to show that it can in fact be done, repeatedly. Those who have the power to do good have the obligation to act; improving affective reaction to work is within our realm and becomes our duty. Work need no longer be a four-letter word. Depending on where one's sentiments may lie, the ethical imperative may be summed up either by Spiderman's dictum "With great power comes great responsibility" or by St. Luke's aphorism "To whom much is given, much is expected." It is now time to lead.

REFERENCES

Abernathy, W. (1997). Balanced scorecards make teamwork a reality. *Journal for Quality & Participation, 20*(5), 58–59.

Abernathy, W. B. (2014). Beyond the Skinner box: The design and management of organization-wide performance systems. *Journal Of Organizational Behavior Management, 34*(4), 235–254.

Aklin, W. M., Wong, C. J., Hampton, J., Svikis, D. S., Stitzer, M. L., Bigelow, G. E., & Silverman, K. (2014). A therapeutic workplace for the long-term treatment of drug addiction and unemployment: Eight-year outcomes of a social business intervention. *Journal of Substance Abuse Treatment, 47*, 329–338.

Anseel, F., & Lievens, F. (2007). The long-term impact of the feedback environment on job satisfaction: A field study in a Belgian context. *Applied Psychology, 56*(2), 254–266.

Arvey, R. D., Bouchard, T. J., Segal, N. L., & Abraham, L. M. (1989). Job satisfaction: Environmental and genetic components. *Journal of Applied Psychology, 74*(2), 187–192.

Arvey, R. D., McCall, B. P., Bouchard, T. J., Taubman, P., & Cavanaugh, M. A. (1994). Genetic influences on job satisfaction and work value. *Personality and Individual Differences, 17*(1), 21–33.

Barling, J., Kelloway, E. K., & Iverson, R. D. (2003). High-quality work, job satisfaction, and occupational injuries. *Journal of Applied Psychology, 88*(2), 276–283.

Böckerman, P., & Ilmakunnas, P. (2008). Interaction of working conditions, job satisfaction, and sickness absences: Evidence from a representative sample of employees. *Social Science & Medicine, 67*, 520–528.

Bowling, N. A. (2007). Is the job satisfaction-job performance relationship spurious? A meta-analytic examination. *Journal of Vocational Behavior, 71*(2), 167–185.

Brayfield, A. H., & Crockett, W. H. (1955). Employee attitudes and employee performance. *Psychological Bulletin, 52*, 396–424.

Bureau of Labor Statistics. (2014). *ATUS 2013 ACTIVITY SUMMARY FILE* [Computer file].

Bulger, C. A., & Fisher, G. G. (2012). Ethical imperatives of work/life balance. In N. P. Reilly, M. J. Sirgy, & C. A. Gorman (Eds.), *Work and quality of life: Ethical practices in organizations* (pp. 181–201). New York, NY: Springer Science + Business Media.

Christen, M., Iyer, G., & Soberman, D. (2006). Job satisfaction, job performance, and effort: A reexamination using agency theory. *Journal of Marketing*, *70*(1), 137–150.

Cranny, C. J., Smith, P. C., & Stone, E. F. (1992). *Job satisfaction: How people feel about their jobs and how it affects their performance*. New York, NY: Lexington.

Crowell, C. R. (2004). Beyond positive reinforcement: OBM as a humanizing approach to management practices. *Journal of Organizational Behavior Management*, *24*(1–2), 195–202.

Crowell, C. R., Hantula, D. A., & McArthur, K. L. (2011). From job analysis to performance management: A synergistic rapprochement to organizational effectiveness. *Journal of Organizational Behavior Management*, *31*, 316–332.

Eisenberger, R., & Cameron, J. (1996). Detrimental effects of reward: Reality or myth? *American Psychologist*, *51*, 1153–1166.

Faragher, E. (2005). The relationship between job satisfaction and health: A meta-analysis. *Occupational and Environmental Medicine*, *62*, 105–112.

Fischer, J. A. V., & Sousa-Poza, A. (2009). Does job satisfaction improve the health of workers? New evidence using panel data and objective measures of health. *Health Economics*, *18*(1), 71–89.

Fisher, C. D. (1980). On the dubious wisdom of expecting job satisfaction to correlate with performance. *Academy of Management Review*, *5*, 607–612.

Gerhart, B. (2005). The (affective) dispositional approach to job satisfaction: Sorting out the policy implications. *Journal of Organizational Behavior*, *26*(1), 79–97.

Hewlett, S. A., & Luce, C. B. (2006). Extreme jobs: The dangerous allure of the 70-hour workweek. *Harvard Business Review*, *84*(12), 49–59.

Hidden liability: Understand the risks of negligent hiring. (2013). *HR Specialist: New York Employment Law*, *8*(8), 4.

Hocutt, M. (2013). A behavioral analysis of morality and value. *The Behavior Analyst*, *36*(2), 239–249.

Holtyn, A., Koffarnus, M. N., DeFulio, A., Sigurdsson, S. O., Strain, E. C., Schwartz, R. P., . . . Silverman, K. (2014). The therapeutic workplace: A bridge to methadone treatment and drug abstinence for injection heroin users [Abstract]. *Drug & Alcohol Dependence*, *140*, e90–e91.

Iaffaldano, M. T., & Muchinsky, P. M. (1985). Job satisfaction and job performance: A meta-analysis. *Psychological Bulletin*, *97*, 251–273.

Ilies, R., Wilson, K. S., & Wagner, D. T. (2009). The spillover of daily job satisfaction onto employees' family lives: The facilitating role of work-family integration. *Academy of Management Journal*, *52*(1), 87–102.

Judge, T. A., Piccolo, R. F., Podsakoff, N. P., Shaw, J. C., & Rich, B. L. (2010). The relationship between pay and job satisfaction: A meta-analysis of the literature. *Journal of Vocational Behavior*, *77*(2), 157–167.

Judge, T. A., Thoresen, C. J., Bono, J. E., & Patton, G. K. (2001). The job satisfaction-job performance relationship: A quantitative and qualitative review. *Psychological Bulletin*, *127*, 376–407.

Kim, W. G., & Brymer, R. A. (2011). The effects of ethical leadership on manager job satisfaction, commitment, behavioral outcomes, and firm performance. *International Journal of Hospitality Management*, *30*, 1020–1026.

Koffarnus, M. N., DeFulio, A., Sigurdsson, S. O., & Silverman, K. (2013). Performance pay improves engagement, progress, and satisfaction in computer-based job skills training of low-income adults. *Journal of Applied Behavior Analysis*, *46*, 395–406.

Koffarnus, M. N., Wong, C. J., Diemer, K., Needham, M., Hampton, J., Fingerhood, M., . . . Silverman, K. (2011). A randomized clinical trial of a therapeutic workplace for chronically unemployed, homeless, alcohol-dependent adults. *Alcohol and Alcoholism*, *46*, 561–569.

Kossek, E. E., Valcour, M., & Lirio, P. (2014). The sustainable workforce: Organizational strategies for promoting work-life balance and wellbeing. In P. Y. Chen & C. L. Cooper (Eds.), *Work and wellbeing* (Vol. 3, pp. 295–318). Hoboken, NJ: Wiley-Blackwell.

Mawhinney, T. C. (1984). Philosophical and ethical aspects of organizational behavior management: Some evaluative feedback. *Journal of Organizational Behavior Management*, *6*(1), 5–31.

Mawhinney, T. C. (1989). Job satisfaction as a management tool and responsibility. *Journal of Organizational Behavior Management*, *10*(1), 187–192.

Mawhinney, T. C. (2011). Job satisfaction: I/O psychology and organizational behavior management perspectives. *Journal of Organizational Behavior Management*, *31*, 288–315.

Mawhinney, T. C., Dickinson, A. M., & Taylor, L. A. (1989). The use of concurrent schedules to evaluate the effects of extrinsic rewards on "intrinsic motivation." *Journal of Organizational Behavior Management*, *10*(1), 109–129.

Mohren, D. C. L., Swaen, G. M. H., Kant, I. J., van Schayck, C. P., & Galama, J. M. D. (2005). Fatigue and job stress as predictors for sickness absence during common infections. *International Journal of Behavioral Medicine*, *12*, 11–20.

Molina, M. Å. C., Gonzalez, J. M. H., Florencio, B. P., & Gonzalez, J. L. G. (2014). Does the balanced scorecard adoption enhance the levels of organizational climate, employees' commitment, job satisfaction and job dedication? *Management Decision*, *52*, 983–1010.

Munch-Hansen, T., Wieclaw, J., Agerbo, E., Westergaard-Nielsen, N., & Bonde, J. (2008). Global measure of satisfaction with psychosocial work conditions versus measures of specific aspects of psychosocial work conditions in explaining sickness absence. *BMC Public Health*, *8*, 270. doi:10.1186/1471-2458-8-270

Nakata, A., Takahashi, M., Irie, M., & Swanson, N. G. (2010). Job satisfaction is associated with elevated natural killer cell immunity among healthy white-collar employees. *Brain, Behavior, and Immunity*, *24*, 1268–1275.

Ostroff, C. (1992). The relationship between satisfaction, attitudes, and performance: An organizational level analysis. *Journal of Applied Psychology*, *77*, 963–974.

Palmer, M. G., & Johnson, C. M. (2013). The effects of task clarification and group graphic feedback on early punch-in times. *Journal of Organizational Behavior Management*, *33*, 265–275.

Pettijohn, C., Pettijohn, L., & Taylor, A. J. (2008). Salesperson perceptions of ethical behaviors: Their influence on job satisfaction and turnover intentions. *Journal of Business Ethics*, *78*, 547–557.

Pryor, D. (2014). Operators may face criminal charges after accidents. *Rock Products*, *117*(1), 54–55.

Riketta, M. (2008). The causal relation between job attitudes and performance: A meta-analysis of panel studies. *Journal of Applied Psychology, 93*, 472–481.

Roelen, C. A. M., Koopmans, P. C., Notenbomer, A., & Groothoff, J. W. (2008). Job satisfaction and sickness absence: A questionnaire survey. *Occupational Medicine, 58*, 567–571.

Roelen, C. A. M., Koopmans, P. C., Notenbomer, A., & Groothoff, J. W. (2011). Job satisfaction and short sickness absence due to the common cold. *Work: Journal of Prevention, Assessment & Rehabilitation, 39*(3), 305–313.

Saad, L. (2014). *The "40-hour" workweek is actually longer—by seven hours.* Retrieved from http://www.gallup.com/poll/175286/hour-workweek-actually-longer-seven-hours.aspx

Schleicher, D. J., Hansen, S. D., & Fox, K. E. (2011). Job attitudes and work values. In S. Zedeck (Ed.), *APA handbook of industrial and organizational psychology: Vol. 3. Maintaining, expanding, and contracting the organization* (pp. 137–189). Washington, DC: American Psychological Association.

Schyns, B., van Veldhoven, M., & Wood, S. (2009). Organizational climate, relative psychological climate and job satisfaction: The example of supportive leadership climate. *Leadership & Organization Development Journal, 30*, 649–663.

Silverman, K., Svikis, D., Wong, C. J., Hampton, J., Stitzer, M. L., & Bigelow, G. E. (2002). A reinforcement-based therapeutic workplace for the treatment of drug abuse: Three-year abstinence outcomes. *Experimental and Clinical Psychopharmacology, 10*(3), 228–240.

Silverman, K., Wong, C. J., Grabinski, M. J., Hampton, J., Sylvest, C. E., Dillon, E. M., & Wentland, R. D. (2005). A Web-based therapeutic workplace for the treatment of drug addiction and chronic unemployment. *Behavior Modification, 29*, 417–463.

Simone, S., Lampis, J., Lasio, D., Serri, F., Cicotto, G., & Putzu, D. (2014). Influences of work-family interface on job and life satisfaction. *Applied Research in Quality of Life, 9*, 831–861.

Skinner, B. F. (1955). Freedom and the control of men. *American Scholar, 25*, 47–65.

Skinner, B. F. (1975). The steep and thorny way to a science of behavior. *American Psychologist, 30*(1), 42–49.

Skinner, B. F. (1986). What is wrong with daily life in the Western world? *American Psychologist, 41*, 568–574.

Sommer, K. L., & Kulkarni, M. (2012). Does constructive performance feedback improve citizenship intentions and job satisfaction? The roles of perceived opportunities for advancement, respect, and mood. *Human Resource Development Quarterly, 23*(2), 177–201.

Spector, P. E. (1997). *Job satisfaction: Application, assessment, causes, and consequences.* Thousand Oaks, CA: Sage.

Staw, B. M. (1986). Organizational psychology and the pursuit of the happy/productive worker. *California Management Review, 28*(4), 40–53.

Staw, B. M., Bell, N. E., & Clausen, J. A. (1986). The dispositional approach to job attitudes: A lifetime longitudinal test. *Administrative Science Quarterly, 31*(1), 56–77.

Staw, B. M., & Ross, J. (1985). Stability in the midst of change: A dispositional approach to job attitudes. *Journal of Applied Psychology, 70*, 469–480.

Thorndike, E. L. (1917). The curve of work and the curve of satisfyingness. *Journal of Applied Psychology, 1*(3), 265–267.

Tincani, M. (2011). *Preventing challenging behavior in your classroom: Positive behavior support and effective classroom management.* Waco, TX: Prufrock Press.

Wilder, D. A., Harris, C., Casella, S., Wine, B., & Postma, N. (2011). Further evaluation of the accuracy of managerial prediction of employee preference. *Journal of Organizational Behavior Management, 31,* 130–139.

Wilder, D. A., Rost, K., & McMahon, M. (2007). The accuracy of managerial prediction of employee preference: A brief report. *Journal of Organizational Behavior Management, 27*(2), 1–14.

Wilk, L. A., & Redmon, W. K. (1998). The effects of feedback and goal setting on the productivity and satisfaction of university admissions staff. *Journal of Organizational Behavior Management, 18*(1), 45–68.

Wine, B., & Axelrod, S. (2014). The effects of progressively thinning high-preference item delivery on responding in employees. *Journal Of Organizational Behavior Management, 34*(4), 291–299.

Wine, B., Gilroy, S., & Hantula, D. A. (2012). Temporal (in)stability of employee preferences for rewards. *Journal of Organizational Behavior Management, 32,* 58–64.

Wine, B., Kelley, D. P., III, & Wilder, D. A. (2014). An initial assessment of effective preference assessment intervals among employees. *Journal of Organizational Behavior Management, 34,* 188–195.

Wine, B., Reis, M., & Hantula, D. A. (2014). An evaluation of stimulus preference assessment methodology in organizational behavior management. *Journal of Organizational Behavior Management, 34,* 7–15.

Wright, T. A., & Staw, B. M. (1999). Affect and favorable work outcomes: Two longitudinal tests of the happy-productive worker thesis. *Journal of Organizational Behavior, 20*(1), 1–23.

Ybema, J. F., Smulders, P. G. W., & Bongers, P. M. (2010). Antecedents and consequences of employee absenteeism: A longitudinal perspective on the role of job satisfaction and burnout. *European Journal of Work and Organizational Psychology, 19*(1), 102–124.

Zachary, M.-K. (2014). Sexual harassment policies—No guarantee of protection. *Supervision, 75*(10), 20–24.

Seven Life Lessons From Humanistic Behaviorism: How to Bring the Best Out of Yourself and Others

E. SCOTT GELLER

Seven evidence-based guidelines for improving the quality and increasing the frequency of desirable behavior are described and illustrated as relevant for benefiting human welfare and well-being. If practiced extensively, these life lessons would most assuredly improve overall quality of life by reducing interpersonal conflict and bullying; preventing the occurrence of unintentional injuries and fatalities; and enhancing work productivity, environmental sustainability, and life satisfaction. The first three guidelines reflect the applied behavioral science principles of positive reinforcement, observational learning, and behavior-based feedback. The subsequent four life lessons are essentially derived from humanism. Techniques for operationalizing these humanistic guidelines are presented, demonstrating social validity in integrating select principles from humanism with behaviorism. The result: humanistic behaviorism—the application of some humanistic fundamentals to make behaviorism more acceptable, effective, and sustainable on a large scale.

Suppose you were asked to define and explain the top seven lessons you have learned from studying the literature on behavioral and psychological science. Not just the most memorable, most important, or most researched lessons, but those evidence-based lessons you believe should be taught and disseminated worldwide to benefit human welfare and quality of life. Which would you choose? Before reading further, it would be beneficial to ponder this question and derive your own list of seven life lessons. Then compare your list with those discussed here, noting similarities and discrepancies.

Obviously there is no right answer to the question, "What are seven crucial life lessons from psychological science?" Answers certainly will be biased by personal experience, including idiosyncratic reading of a diverse literature and varied research experiences at an educational and/or research institution and beyond. The seven life lessons presented here are derived from my selective perception, which evolved from intensive and extensive study of human dynamics—5 years in graduate school and 45 years as a teacher and researcher of psychology at Virginia Tech.

The first three lessons connect directly to applied behavioral science (ABS) and will likely be included in the lists of most readers. The remaining four life lessons reflect humanism and are likely not among the life lesson lists created by readers of the *Journal of Organizational Behavior Management*. However, an aim of this article is to convince you that these life lessons should be accepted, even deemed important, by students and teachers of ABS and organizational behavior management (OBM). Perhaps some readers will consider the life lessons derived from humanism to be an overly radical departure from behaviorism.

Recall that the adjective *radical* in *radical behaviorism* was used to denote deviance from the narrow methodological behaviorism advocated by Watsonian psychologists to infer the absence of unobservables. As explained by Ogden Lindsey (1991), this is "nothing-else-behaviorism" for "those who say there is only observable behavior, nothing else" (p. 452). In contrast, "Skinner's new radical behaviorism not only accepted thoughts and feelings, but also put their causes in the environment along with outer behavior's causes" (p. 453). So how radical is humanistic behaviorism?

HUMANISTIC BEHAVIORISM

To be sure, this article is not the first to entertain the concept of humanistic behaviorism. More than 40 years ago, F. William Dinwiddie (1975) proposed humanistic behaviorism as "a working model for modern, dynamic, and successful treatment centers for children (because) . . . behaviorism modulated by traditional humanistic approaches helps in the molding of an efficient helping environment for children" (p. 259). Similarly, Carl E. Thoresen (1972) claimed, "Humanistic psychology offers directions for the kind of behavior that individuals should be able to engage in; contemporary behaviorism offers principles and procedures to help individuals increase their humanistic actions" (p. 4).

In fact, a number of behavioral scientists in the 1970s considered themselves humanists (e.g., Day, 1971; Hosford & Zimmer, 1972; Kanfer & Phillips, 1970; Lazarus, 1971; MacCorquadale, 1971; Staats, 1971; Thoresen & Mahoney, 1974; Ullmann & Krasner, 1969) because they (a) focused on individual behavior under *present* circumstances; (b) emphasized the role of learning in explaining and resolving human problems; (c) examined how environments can be changed to prevent or alleviate human problems; and (d) used the scientific method to develop and improve intervention techniques (Thoresen, 1972). Given these criteria, B. F. Skinner would be considered a humanist, and indeed he was honored with Humanist of the Year in 1972 by the American Humanist Association, founded in 1941 to be a clear and democratic voice for humanism in the United States and to develop and advance humanistic thought and action (American Humanist Association, 2008).

Yes, integrating humanistic and behavioristic concepts was proposed by several scholars in the 1970s, but since then there has been very little discussion of this notion, especially for behavior change beyond the clinic. Few if any students in introductory psychology courses read about or hear the term *humanistic behaviorism*. Instead, most introductory psychology textbooks focus on explicating distinct differences between the humanistic and behavioristic approaches to clinical therapy.

It is not difficult to find critics of integrating humanism and behaviorism. Newman (1992) censured an alliance between humanism and behaviorism, claiming, "The unfortunate truth is that many problems in living will not be alleviated by empathy, a supportive environment or even unconditional positive regard" (p. 47). Plus, after reviewing Newman's book *The Reluctant Alliance: Behaviorism and Humanism,* Houts (1993) concluded, "Based on the evidence we have thus far, there is little reason to believe that integrating humanistic psychotherapy and education with behavior analysis will do anything but attenuate the efforts of behavior analysis" (p. 70).

Please note that this critique of a humanistic behaviorism alliance occurred more than two decades ago within the context of clinical therapy. Plus, the integration of humanism and behaviorism proposed in this article selects certain (not all) concepts from humanism to augment the impact of behavior-focused intervention. These humanistic concepts are included as life lessons based on empirical evidence (e.g., perceptions that increase self-motivation and a sense of empowerment); others are not included for lack of research support (e.g., unconditional positive regard).

Bottom line: The notion of humanistic behaviorism is certainly not new, and integrating these seemingly disparate domains to develop sustainable behavior-change interventions for the large-scale benefit of individual and group health and well-being is not particularly innovative. Thus, the seven life lessons derived from humanistic behaviorism are not that radical from radical behaviorism.

1. EMPLOY THE POWER OF POSITIVE CONSEQUENCES

Skinner's concern for people's feelings and attitudes was reflected in his antipathy toward the use of punitive consequences to motivate behavior. "The problem is to free men, not from control, but from certain kinds of control" (Skinner, 1971, p. 5). Skinner proceeded to explain that control by negative consequences must be reduced to increase perceptions of personal freedom.

The same situation can usually be viewed as (a) control by penalizing unwanted behavior or (b) control by rewarding desired behavior. Some students in my university class, for example, are motivated to avoid failure (e.g., a poor grade), whereas other students are motivated to achieve success (e.g., a good grade or increased knowledge). Which students feel more empowered and in control of their class grade? Which have a better attitude toward the class? Of course, you know the answer. Reflect on your own feelings or attitude in similar situations in which you perceived your behavior was influenced by either positive or negative consequences.

Figure 1 depicts four distinct achievement typologies defined by Covington (1992) and derived from the seminal research of Atkinson (1957, 1964). These four classifications have been researched to explain differences in how people approach success and/or avoid failure (Covington & Roberts, 1994). It is most desirable to be a *success seeker*. These are the optimists who respond to setbacks (e.g., to corrective feedback) in a positive and adaptive manner. They are self-confident and willing to take risks, as opposed to avoiding challenges to avoid failure. They wake up each day to an *opportunity* clock rather than an *alarm* clock. It is a mindset or attitude toward life you can influence in yourself and others with situational manipulations.

Failure avoiders have a low expectancy for success and a high fear of failure. They do whatever it takes to protect themselves from appearing incompetent. They often use self-handicapping and defensive pessimism to shield themselves from experiencing failure (Berglas & Jones, 1978). These individuals are motivated but are not happy campers. They are the students

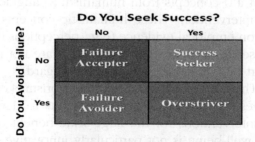

FIGURE 1 The four motivational typologies defined by achieving success versus avoiding failure.

who say, "I've *got* to go to class; it's a *requirement*," rather than, "I *get* to go to class; it's an *opportunity*."

Bottom line: Applying soon, certain and positive consequences is the most efficient way to improve behavior and attitude at the same time. Of course, every reader of this article knows this and also knows the term *positive reinforcer* should only be used if the positive consequence increases the frequency of the target behavior. But even when positive consequences do not result in an observable change in behavior, they are still useful. They might, in fact, affect an unobserved behavior, and they likely benefit an attitude or person-state, possibly enhancing a success-seeking mindset. These consequences are called *rewards,* as you know.

Using this life lesson on a daily basis is both critical and challenging. Why? Because we seem to live in a click-it-or-ticket culture that relies on negative reinforcement and punishment to manage behavior, from the classroom and workplace to our homes, and during our travel in between. The government approach to behavior management is to pass a law and enforce it. It is not enough to understand and believe this life lesson; we need to act accordingly. Thus, our next life lesson.

2. EXERCISE OBSERVATIONAL LEARNING

If you want to be better at what you do, watch someone who performs that behavior better than you. Of course, we all realize the power of observational learning. Indeed, a large body of psychological research indicates that this type of learning is involved to some degree in almost everything we do (Bandura, 1969). Our actions influence others to a greater extent than we realize. Children learn by watching us at home, and our colleagues are influenced by our actions at work. We are often unaware of such influence. Consider what children learn by watching the driving behavior of their parents, including their parents' verbal behavior.

It is likely that observational learning is key to the dramatic success of behavior-based safety (BBS) in preventing injuries. Consider the basic BBS process: (a) Coworkers develop a checklist of critical safe and at-risk behaviors on their job, termed a *critical behavior checklist* (CBC); (b) they observe each other while working and systematically check the safe and at-risk behaviors they observe; and (c) the observer shows the completed CBC to the worker observed, and they discuss the results.

The role of observational learning is obvious. The observers note safe work practices and might learn new ways to work safely in the process. They also observe at-risk behaviors to avoid, perhaps behaviors they themselves perform all too often. This representation of observational learning suggests BBS observers will subsequently work more safely on similar work tasks. Yes, this logical supposition from observational learning has been demonstrated empirically (e.g., Alvero & Austin, 2004; Alvero, Rost, & Austin, 2008). Of course, a most important component of the BBS peer-to-peer observation process is behavioral feedback—our third life lesson.

3. GIVE AND RECEIVE BEHAVIORAL FEEDBACK

"Practice makes perfect" is not true; practice makes permanence. Only with behavior-based feedback can practice improve behavior. Sometimes behavioral feedback is a natural consequence, as when the golfer or tennis player see where their ball lands after swinging a golf club or tennis racket. But even when we observe the outcome of our behavior, behavioral feedback from an observer (e.g., a coach) is necessary for proper behavioral adjustment and improvement.

Most readers of this article would include this life lesson among their top seven. Indeed, most effective OBM interventions include some form of behavioral feedback, as does BBS. The letters of COACH say it all: *C* for Care, *O* for Observe, *A* for Analyze, *C* for Communicate, and *H* for Help (Geller, 2001).

It all starts with *caring*. "Know I *care* and you'll care what I know. I care so much, I'm willing to *observe* you and record occurrences of desirable and undesirable behavior." The observer records occasions of designated behaviors and notes environmental factors that may be influencing the observed behavior, from antecedent conditions to behavioral consequences. This is the *analysis* phase of coaching.

Next we have interpersonal *communication*—the delivery of information gained from the prior *observation* and *analysis* steps. Most people want to improve, but many people resist giving and receiving the kind of communication that is critical to beneficial behavior change. Some people perceive feedback that implies personal change as an indictment of their current work style, job skills, or diligence. This reaction is most likely to happen when someone is being asked to change dramatically and when current procedures have been followed for years. To overcome this resistance, effective behavior improvement coaches steer clear of disruptive and dramatic communication and emphasize incremental fine tuning or successive approximations. They also facilitate beneficial change to both behavior and attitude by accentuating the positives—occurrences of desirable behavior.

Like client-centered or humanistic therapy (Rogers, 1942), the focus is on the perceptions and feelings of the individual being coached. Behavioral and environmental conditions are observed from this person's perspective, and feedback communication is supportive and nondirective. Feedback is typically not delivered to direct behavior change but to empower personal acceptance and self-accountability for designated behavioral improvement.

If the interpersonal communication goes well, the last letter of COACH—*help*—is accomplished. The behavioral feedback was accepted and will be used to improve the pinpointed behaviors. Note how the four letters of HELP—Humor, Esteem, Listen, Praise—reflect strategies to increase the probability a coach's advice, directions, or feedback will be appreciated.

4. REPLACE THE GOLDEN RULE WITH THE PLATINUM RULE

We have all been exposed to the Golden Rule: "Treat others the way you want to be treated." Let us consider the Platinum Rule (Allesandra & O'Connor, 1996): "Treat others the way *they* want to be treated." This viewpoint reflects the idiographic philosophy of both humanism and behaviorism. The uniqueness of each person is considered, and generalization across people and their experiences is avoided. It is psychology as the study of the individual—not the group. Indeed, Skinner's experimental study of single rats and pigeons in a within-subjects ABA reversal design implies an idiographic approach to behavioral science (Skinner, 1938, 1953).

Using the Platinum Rule positions us to better serve and meet the specific needs of others. This is essential to establishing a brother/sister keepers' culture of people looking out for the welfare of one another. It enables the development of authentic interpersonal relationships and the community spirit needed for behavioral feedback to be given and received frequently, constructively, and in a nonadversarial manner. When these relationships develop in the workplace, the ability to inspire and influence the achievement of all business objectives is optimized.

5. EMBRACE AND PRACTICE EMPATHY

The rationale for using more positive than negative consequences to motivate behavior is the differential feeling states provoked by positive versus negative reinforcement and punishment. Similarly, the way in which an intervention process is implemented can increase or decrease feelings of empowerment, build or destroy trust, and cultivate or inhibit a sense of teamwork or belonging (Geller, 2005). It is important to assess person-states or perceptions occurring concomitantly with an intervention process. This can be accomplished informally through one-on-one interviews and group discussions or formally with a perception survey (O'Brien, 2000; Peterson, 2001).

Decisions regarding which ABS intervention to implement, and how to refine existing intervention procedures, should be based on both objective observations of behaviors and subjective evaluations of feeling states. Often, it is possible to use *empathy* to evaluate the indirect internal impact of an intervention. Imagine yourself going through a particular set of intervention procedures. Then ask yourself, "How would I feel?"

A Personal Example

Two decades ago when my daughter wanted to drive my car to her high school I installed a large sign on the back with the bold message, "How's my driving? Call my Dad: 540-626-7712." I bolted the sign to my vehicle after she had received a percent safe score of 100% on three consecutive coaching sessions with our CBC, as described under Life Lesson 2. We had this if/then contingency: "Achieve a perfect score on three consecutive trips with the CBC, and you may drive my car to school."

I was sure she would accept the addition of the sign on my vehicle. Note how this activator is more than an awareness prompt; it implies a consequence. We had talked frequently about the value of positive or supportive consequences, so I thought Krista would view this sign as a fun and positive approach to promoting safe driving. "Let's be optimistic about this," I said to her, "and see how many positive phone calls I get about your safe and courteous driving behavior."

"Are you kidding me, Dad? There's no way I'd park that car and sign at my high school," Krista retorted. "I'd be the laughingstock of the whole school. I'll talk to Mom about this."[1] My lesson: Do not assume you know how a well-intentioned intervention will be received by the participant(s); ask first.

Empathic listening, diagnosing, and action planning take patience. Conversations at this level are often not efficient, but they are always most effective. Through questioning and listening, the objective is to first learn what it is like to be in the other person's situation. Then the objective shifts to developing a corrective intervention that fits the circumstances as mutually understood by everyone involved in the conversation. If commitment to follow through with a specific action plan is stated, you were an empathic behavioral coach.

A Critical Caveat

Before proceeding to the next life lesson, consider a crucial exception to an intervention approach implied by these latter humanism-derived life lessons—practicing empathy to follow the Platinum Rule. Can you think of circumstances in which treating others the way *they* want to be treated could do more harm than good? Are there times when adherence to the Platinum Rule is detrimental to human welfare?

---

[1] Subsequently Krista earned a PhD in Human Development and teaches each of these life lessons as the Global People-Based Safety and Human Performance-Improvement Manager for Bechtel Corporation.

Parents, teachers, and readers who have used ABS to improve the behavior of children can list numerous situations in which the behavioral target of an intervention had to be defined by the parent, teacher, coach, or behavior analyst, not by the child. Simply put, children do not always know what is good for them, and when they do (e.g., complete house chores or a homework assignment), they might not choose that behavior to be the focus of a behavior-change intervention.

How about BBS? Treating workers the way they want to be treated implies they should be allowed to take risky shortcuts and avoid wearing uncomfortable personal protection equipment. And, if we listened with empathy to the public, vehicles would not even have safety belts, let alone laws requiring their use; and drivers could travel at any speed they deem safe while engaging in all sorts of distracting behaviors. Plus, cigarette smokers could practice their unhealthy behavior wherever they wanted.

Obviously, the Platinum Rule can be stretched to absurdity. There are numerous occasions when people of all ages should not be treated the way *they* want to be treated. Behaviors defined for the public good often conflict with egoistic wishes, and in these cases the Platinum Rule cannot work. But the traditional Golden Rule is also irrelevant if the person doing the "treating" is also egotistically disregarding a policy or rule (e.g., a safety or health regulation) or performing a self-serving but publicly destructive behavior (e.g., smoking a cigarette in a public setting or driving a vehicle while intoxicated).

To influence people to sacrifice personal pleasures detrimental to public welfare, interventions must be implemented to increase the frequency of behaviors that benefit large-scale well-being. But these behaviors might not be intrinsically reinforcing to the individual. Here is where the first three life lessons—positive consequences, modeling, and behavioral feedback—are paramount. In this regard, please note a critical incongruity between behaviorism and humanism.

The first life lesson uses positive consequences conditional on the occurrence of a desirable behavior, whereas the humanistic therapy of Carl Rogers (1942) features *unconditional* positive regard. Although a love-them-anyway approach can work at times, readers of this article realize the behavior change advantages of *conditional* positive regard. Thus, the life lessons explicated here implicate some but certainly not all tenets of humanism.

6. DISTINGUISH BETWEEN MANAGING BEHAVIOR AND LEADING PEOPLE

Management is not the same as leadership. Yes, both are critically important to bringing the best out of people. Simply put, managers hold us accountable for performing desirable behavior and avoiding undesirable behavior. Leaders inspire us to hold ourselves accountable to do the right thing. Managers control behavior with an external (or extrinsic) accountability intervention or system. Leaders facilitate self-motivation by influencing person-states (e.g., perceptions, attitudes, and/or emotions) that facilitate self-motivation. Self-motivation (or self-directed behavior) often leads to discretionary behavior (Daniels & Daniels, 2005)—behavior beyond that which is required.

Self-Motivation

The *C* words of *Choice, Competence,* and *Community* were used by Geller and Veazie (2010) in their narrative to illustrate the three evidence-based perceptions or person-states that determine self-motivation. Dispositional, interpersonal, and environmental conditions that enhance these states, presumed to be innate needs by some psychologists (Deci, 1975; Deci & Flaste, 1995; Deci & Ryan, 1995), increase personal perceptions of self-motivation. Guidelines for enhancing perceptions of choice, competence, and community are given elsewhere (Geller, 2014a, 2014b), and many of these are consistent with the life lessons discussed here. Consider, for example, how proper application of Lessons 1, 2, 3, and 5 can increase one's perception of competence and hence fuel self-motivation. Consider also how our language can affect each of these perceptions.

WATCH YOUR LANGUAGE

Your language should suggest minimal external pressure. The common phrases "Safety is a condition of employment," "All accidents are preventable," and "Bullying is a rite of passage" reduce one's sense of autonomy. In contrast, the slogan "Actively caring is a core value of our organization" implies personal authenticity, interpersonal relatedness, and human interaction.

The common phrase "random acts of kindness" (Editors of Conari Press, 1993) has a disadvantage when describing or promoting prosocial behavior. Random implies the behavior happens by chance, suggesting it is beyond individual choice or control. The kind act may appear random to the recipient, but it was likely performed intentionally and was self-motivated. An alternative is "intentional acts of kindness." The language we use to prescribe or describe behavior influences our perceptions of its meaningfulness and its relevance to our lives. Language impacts culture and vice versa.

OPPORTUNITIES FOR CHOICE

Participative management means employees have personal choice during the planning, execution, and evaluation of their jobs. People have a need for autonomy regardless of dispositional and situational factors. In the workplace, managers often tell people what to do rather than involving them in the decision-making process. Referring to language again, should managers give "mandates" or set "expectations"? Should they request "compliance" or ask for "commitment"?

In schools, students are often viewed as passive learners because teachers plan, execute, and evaluate most aspects of the teaching/learning process. Students' perceptions of choice are limited. Yet cooperative teaching/learning—in which students contribute to the selection and presentation of lesson material—is most beneficial over the long term (Chance, 2008).

INVOLVING THE FOLLOWERS

Autonomy is supported with rules that are established by soliciting input from those affected by the regulation (Deci & Flaste, 1995). Employees are more likely to comply with safety regulations they helped to define. Shouldn't they have substantial influence in the development of policy they will be asked to follow? Those on the front line know best what actions should be avoided versus performed in order to optimize the safety and quality of their production system.

Similarly, before a rule or regulation is implemented in an educational system, those affected (i.e., faculty and/or students) should certainly be given opportunities to offer suggestions. In a family, as the children mature, certain rules should be open to discussion before being imposed. This takes more time, but the marked increase in effectiveness justifies the loss in efficiency.

Empowerment

In the management literature, *empowerment* typically refers to delegating authority or responsibility or to sharing decision making (Conger & Kanungo, 1988). In other words, when a manager says, "I empower you," he or she usually means, "Get 'er done." In contrast, the empathic leader first assesses whether the empowered individual *feels* empowered. "Can you handle the additional assignment?" Proper assessment of feeling empowered involves asking three questions, as derived from social learning theory (Bandura, 1997).

As depicted in Figure 2, the first question, "Can I do it?" asks whether the empowered individual or group has the resources, time, knowledge, and ability to handle the assignment. The knowledge and ability components refer to training, and the term *self-efficacy* places the focus on personal belief. An observer might think an individual has the competence to complete a task, but the empowered person might feel differently. Thus, a "yes" answer

FIGURE 2 The three beliefs that determine empowerment (adapted from Bandura, 1997).

implies a belief of relevant personal effectiveness by those who received the assignment or who set a performance-improvement process goal.

The second question, the response-efficacy question, asks whether those empowered believe pursuing and accomplishing the assignment or attaining the process goal (i.e., performing the required behaviors) will contribute to a valued mission of the organization, work team, or individual. Regarding workplace safety, this translates to believing a particular injury prevention process (e.g., a BBS observation-and-feedback process) will contribute to achieving the vision of an injury-free workplace.

A sports team would answer "yes" to this question if the members believe their new workout routine or competition strategy would increase the probability of winning a game. And a student studying for an exam would give a "yes" answer to response-efficacy if he or she believes the study strategy would contribute to earning a higher exam grade. Of course, the behavioral outcome for these two examples could be more distal and substantive, like having a winning season or obtaining a college degree, respectively.

Whereas a "yes" answer to the self-efficacy question might require more training, education might be needed to obtain a "yes" answer to the response-efficacy question. In other words, people might believe they can accomplish a particular process or task but not believe such accomplishment will make a difference in an ultimate outcome. In this case, education is needed, including an explanation of an evidence-based principle or theory and perhaps the presentation of convincing data.

The third empowerment-assessment question targets motivation. Is the expected outcome worth the effort? The performance of relevant behavior is motivated by anticipating a positive consequence to achieve or a negative consequence to avoid. Referring back to the first life lesson, recall that people feel more choice and are more likely to be self-motivated when they are working to achieve a positive consequence than when they are responding to avoid a negative consequence.

EMPOWERING GOALS

Readers of this journal are well aware of the beneficial role of behavior-focused goal setting as an activator of process activities aimed at achieving a particular outcome. They are also likely aware of a popular acronym used to define the characteristics of an effective goal: SMART. There are actually a few variations of the words reflected by these acronym letters, with *M* representing Measurable or Motivational and *T* referring to Timely or Trackable, for example.

I proposed the following acronym words—*S* for Specific, *M* for Motivational, *A* for Attainable, *R* for Relevant, and *T* for Trackable (Geller, 2005, 2008a)—later adding *S* (i.e., SMARTS) for Shared, because special support can increase commitment to work toward reaching a goal (Geller, 2014c). A rationale and procedural details for each component of effective goal setting are provided elsewhere (Geller, 2005, 2014c). Here it is instructive to note the connection between SMARTS goals and the empowerment model introduced earlier.

Specifically, SMARTS goals are empowering because they are attainable ("I can do it"), motivational ("It's worth it"), and relevant ("It will work"). This connection makes it clear that both empowerment and goal setting are similar behavioral antecedents, setting the stage for (or activating) certain behavior(s). Each of these establishing operations refers to motivation as the anticipation of a desirable consequence or outcome.

EMPOWERMENT VS. SELF-MOTIVATION

It is important to consider a critical distinction between these two person-states. Empowerment is a behavioral antecedent or establishing operation (Michael, 1982), whereas self-motivation reflects the impact of consequences. In other words, feeling empowered means the individual is ready (or activated) to work toward achieving a given goal. In contrast, a self-motivated person is anticipating or has received a consequence that supports self-directed rather than other-directed behavior (Watson & Tharp, 1997).

Although the initial proponents of self-motivation (Deci, 1975; Deci & Ryan, 1995) did not connect self-motivation with behavioral consequences, a behavioral scientist naturally associates consequences with motivation, as implied by Skinner's legacy "selection by consequences" (Skinner, 1981). With this perspective, consequences that reflect personal choice, competence, and/or a sense of social support or community should enhance self-motivation and thereby increase the durability of a behavior-change intervention that uses positive reinforcement. Thus, an intervention that applies positive consequences to increase the occurrence of a target behavior should have a longer-term impact if the intervention inspires self-motivation by linking the behavioral consequence(s) with a perception of choice, competence, and/or community. Perhaps some readers will view this as a hypothesis worthy of ABS research.

7. PROGRESS FROM SELF-ACTUALIZATION TO SELF-TRANSCENDENCE

This final life lesson connects most obviously to humanism, but without ABS it is just a theory with limited practical value. Indeed, a transition to self-transcendence could be key to saving the world from itself (Skinner, 1971).

A Hierarchy of Needs

Probably the most popular theory of human motivation is the hierarchy of needs proposed by humanist Abraham Maslow (1943). Categories of needs are arranged hierarchically. It is presumed people do not attempt to satisfy needs at one stage or level until the needs at the lower stages are satisfied.

First, we are motivated to fulfill physiological needs. This includes food, water, shelter, and sleep for basic survival. After these needs are met, we are motivated by the desire to feel secure and safe from future dangers. When we prepare for future physiological needs, we are working proactively to satisfy our need for safety and security.

Next, we have our social acceptance needs—the need to have friends and feel like we belong. When these needs are gratified, our concern shifts to self-esteem, the desire to develop self-respect, gain the approval of others, and achieve personal success. Now we have self-actualization, right? Is this the highest level of Maslow's hierarchy of needs? No, it is not.

Maslow's hierarchy of needs is illustrated in Figure 3. Note that self-actualization is not at the top. Maslow revised his renowned hierarchy shortly before his death in 1970, placing self-transcendence above self-actualization (Maslow, 1971). Transcending the self means going beyond self-interest to actively care for others.

It seems intuitive that various self-needs require satisfaction before self-transcendent or actively-caring-for-people (AC4P) behavior is likely to occur. But scant research supports the ranking of human needs in a hierarchy. It is possible to think of many examples in which individuals performed various AC4P behaviors before satisfying all of their personal needs. Mahatma Gandhi put the concerns of others before his own. He suffered imprisonment, extensive fasts, and eventually assassination in his 50-year struggle to help his poor and downtrodden compatriots.

Note the connection between the need hierarchy and various potentially-reinforcing consequences, as well as our discussion of self-motivation and sustaining the impact of a behavior change intervention.

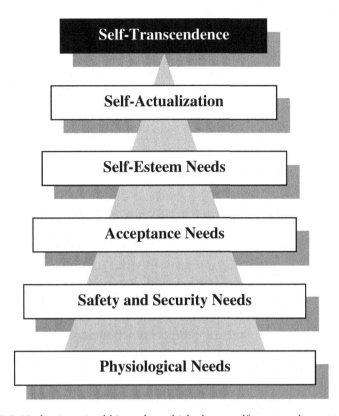

FIGURE 3 Maslow's revised hierarchy, which shows self-transcendence at the top.

An individual's position in the hierarchy certainly determines what types of consequences are likely to be most reinforcing at a particular time. Without food, shelter, or sleep, for example, most people will focus their efforts on satisfying these needs. But if this need level is satisfied (i.e., an establishing operation of satiation), the motivation of human behavior requires consequences related to higher-level needs.

As we climb Maslow's hierarchy, need states are reached that implicate consequences linked to self-motivation. For example, consequences that boost one's sense of connection with others (i.e., community) satisfy the need for acceptance or social support, and consequences that certify a person's belief in his or her personal competence to perform worthwhile work are associated with the self-esteem and self-actualization needs. Plus, it is intuitive that reaching beyond self-needs to help others through AC4P behavior can contribute to satisfying a person's need for social acceptance and self-esteem, and even self-actualization.

Question: When does one's need for social acceptance, self-esteem, and self-actualization get satisfied? In other words, at what point does a person become satiated on consequences linked to these need states? Yes, these are rhetorical questions, posed to reiterate the value of delivering rewarding consequences that reflect the three *C* words of self-motivation (i.e., Competence, Choice, and Community) and enhance need states in Maslow's hierarchy that are difficult to satiate. In other words, behavioral consequences that foster perceptions of personal competence, self-worth, interpersonal belongingness, and/or autonomy also facilitate self-motivation and self-directed behavior and are thus likely to have a longer-term impact than consequences unrelated to these person-states.

The AC4P Movement

I coined the term *actively caring* in 1990 when working with a team of safety leaders at the Exxon chemical facility in Baytown, Texas (Geller, 1991). The vision was to cultivate a brother/sister keepers' culture in which everyone looks out for one another's safety—people routinely going above and beyond the call of duty to benefit the health, safety, and/or welfare of others.

"Actively caring for people" was an ideal description for this site-wide paradigm shift. Most people care about the well-being of others, but relatively few act on their feelings of caring. The challenge was to get everyone to *actively care*—to take effective action based on their caring. The vision: a company with more interpersonal empathy, compassion, and AC4P behavior.

Following the Virginia Tech campus shooting rampage on April 16, 2007 that took the lives of 33 students and faculty and injured 17 others (Geller, 2008b), the mission of AC4P took on a new focus and prominence for me and my students. In a time of great uncertainty and reflection, those most affected by the tragedy were not thinking of themselves. They acted to help classmates, friends, and even strangers. This collective effort was manifested in an AC4P Movement for worldwide culture change.

For more than 20 years, I promoted the use of a green wristband embossed with the words *Actively Caring for People* to recognize individuals for their AC4P behavior. During those years, I had distributed about 50,000 of these wristbands following my keynote addresses at conferences and organizations. Recently, my students have used this recognition approach to reduce bullying by promoting and rewarding AC4P behavior in various educational settings (McCarty & Geller, 2011; McCarty, Teie, McCutchen, & Geller, in press).

For these latter applications, the AC4P wristbands were redesigned to include a different identification number per wristband, and a website (http://www.ac4p.org) was developed for people to (a) share their AC4P stories (with the number of the wristband they gave or received), (b) track worldwide where a particular AC4P wristband has been, and (c) order more AC4P wristbands to reward others for their AC4P behavior.

It is recommended that the delivery of an AC4P wristband be accompanied with words that serve higher level needs. For example, never suggest the wristband is a "payoff" for AC4P behavior; rather, the wristband is only a token of appreciation for the "special servant leadership exemplified by the observed act of kindness." Plus, the wristband recipient is told he or she is now one of many who have joined the AC4P Movement—a flourishing worldwide effort to cultivate cultures of interpersonal compassion and interdependent AC4P behavior.

To date, more than 4,000 AC4P stories have been shared on this website, and more than 100,000 AC4P wristbands have been purchased, with proceeds going to the Actively Caring for People Foundation, Inc. It is hoped this particular accountability system for activating and rewarding AC4P behavior will help to spread the AC4P paradigm worldwide and inspire the development of AC4P cultures in various settings.

IN SUMMARY

This article introduced seven life lessons derived from behaviorism and humanism, and presumed to benefit human well-being and quality of life wherever they are practiced. The first three lessons are used in almost every successful intervention developed and evaluated by OBM researchers and practitioners. The next four connect directly to the principles of humanism, and it is likely most readers of this journal will consider these to be beyond the empirical, behavior-based domain of OBM.

However, operational definitions were included with each of these humanistic lessons, making it possible to bring them to life with a behavior-focused intervention. For example, the concept of self-transcendence was discussed in terms of interpersonal AC4P behavior, and a practical application of Life Lesson 1 (i.e., the AC4P wristband) was illustrated to increase the frequency of AC4P behavior en route to achieving an AC4P culture.

Although a number of effective AC4P applications of the life lessons reviewed here have successfully improved human welfare (cf. Geller, 2014a, 2014b), we have merely scratched the surface of societal problems that could be solved in part by large-scale applications of these life lessons. We have so much more to learn from the synergistic integration of ABS and humanistic psychology—*humanistic behaviorism.*

ACKNOWLEDGMENTS

This article was adapted from my keynote presentation at the Association for Behavior Analysis International Seminar on Leadership and Cultural Change, May 25, 2014. I am grateful for informational and inspirational feedback from the following individuals who read a prior draft of this article: Katya

Davydova, Cory Furrow, Rob Holdsambeck, Georgiana Lee, Shane McCarty, Micah Roediger, and two anonymous reviewers.

REFERENCES

Allesandra, T., & O'Connor, M. S. (1996). *The platinum rule: Discover the four basic business personalities and how they can lead you to success.* New York, NY: Warren Books.

Alvero, A. M., & Austin, J. (2004). The observer effect: The effects of conducting behavioral observations on the behavior of the observer. *Journal of Applied Behavior Analysis, 37,* 457–468.

Alvero, A. M., Rost, K., & Austin, J. (2008). The safety observe effect. *Journal of Safety Research, 39*(4), 365–373.

American Humanist Association. (2008). American Humanist Association. Retrieved June 16, 2014 from http://www.americanhumanist.org/

Atkinson, J. W. (1957). Motivational determinants of risk-taking behavior. *Psychological Review, 64,* 359–372.

Atkinson, J. W. (1964). *An introduction to motivation.* Princeton, NJ: Van Nostrand.

Bandura, A. (1969). *Principles of behavior modification.* New York, NY: Holt, Rinehart & Winston.

Bandura, A. (1997). *Self-efficacy: The exercise of control.* New York, NY: Freeman.

Berglas, S., & Jones, E. E. (1978). Drug choice as a self-handicapping strategy in response to noncontingent success. *Journal of Personality and Social Psychology, 36,* 405–417.

Chance, P. (2008). *The teacher's craft: The 10 essential skills of effective teaching.* Long Grove, IL: Waveland Press.

Conger, J. A., & Kanungo, R. N. (1988). The empowerment process: Integrating theory and practice. *Academy of Management Review, 13,* 471–482.

Covington, M. V. (1992). *Making the grade: A self-worth perspective on motivation and school reform.* New York, NY: Cambridge University Press.

Covington, M. V., & Roberts, B. W. (1994). Self-worth and college achievement: Motivational and personality correlates. In P. R. Pintrich, D. R. Brown, & C. E. Weinstein (Eds.), *Student motivation, cognition, and learning: Essays in honor of Wilbert J. McKeachie* (pp. 157–187). Hillsdale, NJ: Erlbaum.

Daniels, A. C., & Daniels, J. E. (2005). *Measure of a leader.* Atlanta, GA: Performance Management.

Day, W. F. (1971). Humanistic psychology and contemporary humanism. *The Humanist, 31,* 13–16.

Deci, E. L. (1975). *Intrinsic motivation.* New York, NY: Plenum.

Deci, E. L., & Flaste, R. (1995). *Why we do what we do: Understanding self-motivation.* London, England: Penguin Books.

Deci, E. L., & Ryan, R. M. (1995). *Intrinsic motivation and self-determinism in human behavior.* New York, NY: Plenum.

Dinwiddie, F. W. (1975). Humanistic behaviorism: A model for rapprochement in residential treatment milieus. *Child Psychiatry and Human Development, 5*(4), 254–259.

Editors of Conari Press. (1993). *Random acts of kindness*. Emeryville, CA: Conari Press.

Geller, E. S. (1991). If only more would actively care. *Journal of Applied Behavior Analysis, 24,* 763–764.

Geller, E. S. (2001). *The psychology of safety handbook*. Boca Raton, FL: CRC Press.

Geller, E. S. (2005). *People-based safety: The source*. Virginia Beach, VA: Coastal Training Technologies.

Geller, E. S. (2008a). *Leading people-based safety: Enriching your culture*. Virginia Beach, VA: Coastal Training Technologies.

Geller, E. S. (2008b). The tragic shooting at Virginia Tech: Personal perspectives, prospects, and preventive potentials. *Traumatology, 14*(1), 8–20.

Geller, E. S. (Ed.). (2014a). *Actively caring at your school: How to* make *it happen*. Newport, VA: Make-A-Difference.

Geller, E. S. (Ed.). (2014b). *Actively caring for people: Cultivating a culture of compassion*. Newport, VA: Make-A-Difference.

Geller, E. S. (2014c). The psychology of self-motivation. In E. S. Geller (Ed.), *Actively caring for people: Cultivating a culture of compassion* (pp. 73–75). Newport, VA: Make-A-Difference.

Geller, E. S., & Veazie, R. A. (2010). *When no one's watching: Living and leading self-motivation*. Virginia Beach, VA: Coastal Training and Technologies.

Hosford, R. E., & Zimmer, J. (1972). Humanism through behaviorism. *Counseling and Values, 16,* 1–7.

Houts, A. C. (1993). Review of "The reluctant alliance: Behaviorism and humanism." *Child & Family Behavior Therapy, 15*(4), 69–85.

Kanfer, F. H., & Phillips, J. S. (1970). *Learning foundations of behavior therapy*. New York, NY: Wiley.

Lazarus, A. (1971). *Behavior therapy and beyond*. New York, NY: McGraw-Hill.

Lindsey, O. R. (1991). From technical jargon to plain English for application. *Journal of Applied Behavior Analysis, 24,* 449–458.

MacCorquodale, K. (1971). Behaviorism is a humanism. *The Humanist, 31,* 12–13.

Maslow, A. H. (1943). A theory of human motivation. *Psychological Review, 50,* 370–396.

Maslow, A. H. (1971). *The farther reaches of human nature*. New York, NY: Viking.

McCarty, S. M., & Geller, E. S. (2011). Want to get rid of bullying? Then reward behavior that is incompatible with it. *Behavior Analysis Digest International.* 23(2), pp. 5, 7.

McCarty, S., Teie, S., McCutchen, J., & Geller, E. S. (in press). Actively caring to prevent bullying in an elementary school: Prompting and rewarding prosocial behavior. *Journal of Prevention and Intervention in the Community.*

Michael, J. (1982). Distinguishing between discrimination and motivational functions of stimuli. *Journal of Experimental Analysis of Behavior, 37,* 149–155.

Newman, B. (1992). *The reluctant alliance: Behaviorism and humanism*. Buffalo, NY: Prometheus Books.

O'Brien, D. P. (2000). *Business measurements for safety performance*. New York, NY: Lewis.

Peterson, D. (2001). *Authentic involvement*. Itasca, IL: National Safety Council.

Rogers, C. (1942). *Counseling and psychotherapy*. New York, NY: Houghton Mifflin.

Skinner, B. F. (1938). *The behavior of organisms: An experimental analysis*. Acton, MA: Copley.

Skinner, B. F. (1953). *Science and human behavior*. New York, NY: Macmillan.

Skinner, B. F. (1971). *Beyond freedom and dignity*. New York, NY: Knopf.

Skinner, B. F. (1981, July 31). Selection by consequences. *Science, 213*, 501–504.

Staats, A. W. (1971). *Child learning, intelligence and personality*. New York, NY: Harper & Row.

Thoresen, C. E. (1972, April). *Behavioral humanism* (Research and Development Memorandum No. 88). Stanford, CA: Stanford University, School of Education.

Thoresen, C. E., & Mahoney, M. J. (1974). *Behavioral self-control*. New York, NY: Holt, Rinehart & Winston.

Ullmann, L. P., & Krasner, L. (1969). *A psychological approach to abnormal behavior*. Englewood Cliffs, NJ: Prentice Hall.

Watson, D. C., & Tharp, R. G. (1997). *Self-directed behavior: Self-motivation for personal adjustment* (7th ed.). Pacific Grove, CA: Brooks/Cole.

An Industry's Call to Understand the Contingencies Involved in Process Safety: Normalization of Deviance

KEVIN BOGARD

TIMOTHY D. LUDWIG

CHRIS STAATS

DANIELLE KRETSCHMER

Marathon Petroleum Company (MPC), Illinois Refining Division (IRD) adopted a behavior science approach to its safety operations becoming one of the first sites accredited for its behavioral safety program by the Cambridge Center for Behavioral Studies (CCBS). Beyond success in managing personal safety, there is increased and intense attention toward Process Safety in the oil and gas industry where equipment, processes, and behavior are managed to reduce the potential for catastrophic loss, damage, and impact on human life and livelihood. The oil and gas industry is increasingly looking to the behavior science community to understand the contingencies related to "normalization of deviance", where behaviors begin to drift from process standards and become the norm among work teams over time. Further, the oil and gas industry seeks to understand how interlocking contingencies may both shape and maintain normalization of deviance, as well as how systemic interventions can address the issue.

Portions of this manuscript were presented at the Symposium for Leadership and Cultural Change, May 23, 2014, Chicago, Illinois.

Marathon Petroleum Company (MPC) is a Fortune 30 company and is Responsible Care Certified (American Chemistry Council, 2014) for its environmental stewardship, safety programs, process safety management systems, security initiatives, and product quality. The Illinois Refining Division (IRD) has maintained the Occupational Safety and Health Administration's (OSHA) Voluntary Protection Program (VPP) STAR Site since 1999 (OSHA, 2014a).

This safety performance was not always the standard at MPC's IRD. OSHA requires that injuries needing care beyond first aid be recorded and submitted as a ratio, in which total cases are multiplied by 200,000 and then divided by exposure hours (Bureau of Labor Statistics, 2013). In 1995, the OSHA recordable rate at IRD was 3.63 for refinery employees, which was roughly consistent with the industry norm. Investigation into the factors maintaining this rate indicated that trust and communication between management and the hourly workforce was generally viewed as low, and was seen as a barrier to reducing injuries.

An employee-driven team was formed in 1996 and implemented a behavioral safety program in 1997 named Areas Communicating Trust in Safety (ACTS). The ACTS process combined research and practice from behavioral science that built behavioral safety (Geller et al., 1990; Hermann, Ibarra, & Hopkins, 2010; Ludwig & Geller, 2000; McSween, 1995; Myers, McSween, Medina, Rost, & Alvero, 2010; Sulzer-Azaroff & Austin, 2000) with practices from Total Quality Management (Deming, 1982) and other team-based performance improvement movements that seek to empower employees. The ACTS process is not run from the top down; it is owned and managed by hourly personnel. Managers, supervisors, and foreman are not in charge of the ACTS process, they are simply a part of it.

Data on safety and at-risk behaviors are collected by trained observers performing peer-to-peer job observations. These observers provide feedback on their peer's performance and identify barriers—antecedents and consequences—associated with these actions. Data are then analyzed to determine the highest frequency of at-risk behaviors among the workforce or work group. These behaviors and their barriers are reviewed in detail during employee safety meetings and with management. Problem solving around the at-risk behaviors at these meetings leads to targeted interventions in the refinery, including focused safety meetings, training initiatives, and the purchasing of new safety equipment. As an example, based on its data, the ACTS team discovered a trend indicating that workers were engaging in more at-risk behaviors and sustaining injuries an hour before and after lunch, as well as an hour before they left for the day. To combat this problem, the ACTS team held brief safety meetings to discuss pertinent safety topics based on the data on at-risk behaviors occurring around lunch and the end of the shift. This was associated with a decrease in recordable incidents from six per year to zero during this period. Trend analyses such as this are also given to shift supervisors to present the information to their respective work groups. This cycle of collecting and distributing information creates a proactive approach to improving safety.

It is standard practice in the oil and gas industry, along with most industries, not to include contractor workforce injuries in published safety statistics. However, MPC's IRD chose to report contractor injuries in addition to its own and commit to helping its contractors with implementing and refining their own behavioral safety processes. Contractors attended a 4-hr class on the ACTS behavior-based safety process and were encouraged by the refinery general manager to stop jobs if they felt the task put themselves or their coworkers at risk. After including contractor injury statistics, training their personnel, and using their dedicated observers to collect and distribute data, they experienced an initial 30% to 40% decrease in first aids and incidents.

To formalize contractor participation in behavioral safety, MPC's IRD began to sponsor another committee in 2005 run by contractor employees to manage their own behavioral safety processes. The Contractor Advisory Panel is made up of 11 contract companies that participate in similar behavioral safety processes. A substantial increase in behavioral observations was realized subsequent to the formal onset of contractor behavioral safety processes. Since then, MPC's IRD and its contractors have recorded tens of thousands of observations annually (28,883 in 2013) as the number of safety incidents has declined (see Figure 1).

Since 2005, MPC's IRD and its contractors have succeeded in keeping their injury rate below 0.50 in five separate years. In 2013, IRD's OSHA recordable rate was 0.40 (0.00 for MPC employees and 0.84 for the contractor workforce). Because of the substantial reduction in injuries associated with their application of behavioral science to safety programming, the Cambridge Center for Behavioral Studies (CCBS) has accredited MPC's IRD as a best-in-practice behavioral safety program since 2005 (CCBS, 2014). In addition, nine of the contractors participating in the Contractor Advisory Panel have also been accredited by CCBS or have received a certificate in pursuit of accreditation.

PROCESS SAFETY

Maintaining this level of excellence is challenging, as each year brings new obstacles. However, one constant in the oil and gas industry, as in other

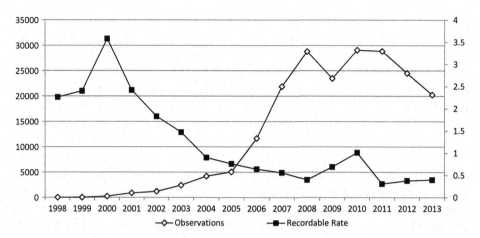

FIGURE 1 Marathon Petroleum Company, Illinois Refining Division, number of behavioral safety observations (left axis) overlaid with Occupational Safety and Health Administration recordable rates (right axis), from 1998 through 2013, for both Illinois Refining Division employees and contractor workforces combined.

industries, is the threat of catastrophic incidents. The focused management of these potential incidents is an area referred to as process safety management (OSHA, 2014b). Whereas personal safety pertains to an injury that impacts an individual, process safety incidents occur when many individuals are injured because of a problem resulting from equipment. Regarding process safety incidents, people on a worksite and in the surrounding community may become seriously injured and fatalities may occur because of breakdowns in process safety. Environmental disasters are also associated with incidents. Although equipment failure is often a cause of process safety incidents, human behavior is often associated with the event. The interaction of equipment failure and behavioral errors can result in an incident, sometimes undetectable, that can then cascade into larger and sometimes fatal consequences. Process safety impacts workers, the community, and the industry.

Process safety has changed the business landscape for many industries, especially oil and gas. Society has a negative view of oil and gas industry companies due to a negative public image resulting from process safety issues. This includes injuries, fatalities, and environmental disasters. Impacts of these events are widespread, and people have become less tolerant of these issues—as they should. Fifteen people were killed in an explosion at the BP Texas City refinery in 2005 (Mufson, 2007). Three were seriously injured in the Valero refinery propane fire in 2007 (U.S. Chemical Safety and Hazard Investigation Board, 2008), two others were seriously injured in the Veolia flammable vapor explosion in 2009 (U.S. Chemical Safety and Hazard Investigation Board, 2010), and one person was critically injured in a CITGO refinery hydrofluoric acid release in 2009 (U.S. Chemical Safety and Hazard Investigation Board, 2009). Eleven were killed in a vapor cloud explosion at an Indian Oil Corporation terminal in Jaipur in 2009 (Center for Chemical Process Safety, 2012). Seven died in an explosion and fire at a Tesoro refinery in 2010 (U.S. Chemical Safety and Hazard Investigation Board, 2014). The explosion on the Deepwater Horizon in the Gulf of Mexico cost 11 lives in 2010, catastrophic environmental damage, and billions of dollars to BP Oil (Deepwater Horizon Study Group, 2011). Recently, West Fertilizer experienced an explosion and fire that resulted in 14 fatalities (U.S. Chemical Safety and Hazard Investigation Board, 2013).

The very public investigations of these disasters have indicated that a normalization of deviance often occurs. Often several safeguards break down and are never discovered because of lack of vigilance. The root causes can be traced to actions taken in the past by previous workers. Management systems break down, and the leadership is often unaware of the hazard and growing problem. The prevention and mitigation actions that leaders think are being done are not because systems are cumbersome to workers and shortcuts have replaced the engineered process. Thus, deviant behaviors, through either intentional shortcuts or unintentional omissions, contribute to process safety incidents.

Normalization of deviance was initially described by Diane Vaughan (1996), a sociologist who studied the Challenger Space Shuttle explosion, as a long-term process in which individuals or teams accept a lower standard of performance until that lower standard becomes acceptable. This reflects an acceptance of risk shaped over time by deviant behavior that is never corrected because it is ignored or never detected. (Note that ignoring deviant behavior is a deviant behavior in its own right.) When enough deviant behavior has been ignored, it becomes accepted or normalized, from a sociological standpoint. Ultimately, no reaction is accepted as the appropriate reaction to deviant behavior, and the deviant behaviors themselves may come to be regarded as normal.

Normalization of deviance can be described in the context of the BP Texas City refinery explosion that caused 15 fatalities, 180 injuries, and 43,000 community citizens to be sheltered after evacuation. The refinery was starting up its isomerization unit when the raffinate splitter tower overfilled. Relief valves opened into an atmospheric blowdown stack. Flammable liquids then released from the stack, which led to an explosion and fire. The Baker Panel findings (Mufson, 2007, p. 15) cited BP as having no "common unifying process safety culture," a lack of operating discipline, and a toleration of serious deviation from safe operation practices leading to complacency around process safety risk. This normalization of deviance at BP was evident in the Baker Panel report: Operators accepted inoperable instrumentation, procedures were routinely not followed, operators were not adequately trained and the training staff was cut over time, nonessential workers were allowed to be near the process, and everyone accepted the faulty atmospheric blowdown stack arrangement.

Normalization of deviance happens frequently within any refining environment. Hazards are inherent in the processes of refining. People working in and around a refinery become so accustomed to being around these hazards that they become complacent in their inaction. For example, in any of the 139 refineries in the United States, one can observe the following scenario: An alarm sounds and people just turn it off. These alarms are connected to sophisticated pressure-monitoring systems that track chemicals as they travel through different parts of the refinery. Alarms are triggered whenever equipment experiences deviations beyond defined standards. The first time new workers experience a triggered alarm they tend to panic, but after a year, they hardly orient toward the console monitor before disabling the alarm. The management system failed to direct the mitigation behaviors it was designed to do. For example, forms used to inspect critical equipment can get pencil whipped (Ludwig, 2014), in which the inspector falsifies the form by filling it out without proper inspection. Safety equipment, such as eye wash and safety showers, can be left unmaintained. The list of management system failures can be extensive, resulting in most process safety risks unconsidered.

Consider the following example of process safety deterioration. At the IRD, there is a routine task of conducting surveys of pressure readings. While an operator was performing this task, he came across a bleeder line that was plugged. This bleeder line was designed to drain equipment and was not part of the pressure test. The operator decided to be proactive and unplug the bleeder, but he did not use the available bleeder tool because this tool had not been maintained and was no longer functional. He had witnessed most operators in the past use a simple screwdriver or wire to clear the bleeders and not experience a problem. In this case, the use of the wrong tool caused the plugged material of the bleeder to blow out and cause a vapor release. Fortunately, this vapor did not ignite; otherwise, the result would have been an explosion and fire. IRD's normalization of deviance was evident in that the proper tool was not maintained and the use of work-around tools was the norm.

Another incident occurred at the refinery coker. While an operator was making his normal rounds inspecting various equipment, he noticed a small vapor release from an insulated line near the thermowell. Operations decided to remove the insulation to get a better look at the leak, at which time inspectors were then contacted to investigate the issue. While they were inspecting the line, the leak worsened and a hydrocarbon vapor cloud filled a pump room. Fortunately, again, the vapor did not ignite, but this did cause an emergency unit shutdown.

Because these were significant near misses, causal analyses were conducted. The refinery personnel conducted what they considered a routine task but did not conduct a proper hazard recognition process. Improper tools were used for these tasks as well. Management systems also contributed to the near miss, in that leaders had not conducted an adequate risk-versus-reward analysis of the type of inspection mitigation the inspector performed. Because of this, small leaks were considered manageable, even though they actually represented a high risk. Indeed, smaller risk tasks require work permits, but this high-risk task did not. The normalization of deviance became clear: Pressure surveys became routine work, and the process of removing insulation became the norm. Management systems, such as hazard analyses and work permits, had not been updated because leaders had become complacent with the risk as well.

The oil and gas industry, along with its fellow industries in mining, food distribution, construction, and others, is actively seeking solutions to these behavioral challenges. With this in mind, it is clear that the behavior science community and its industry partners must build on what has been accomplished with personal safety and replicate and extend it to process safety. Industries need to replicate the use of behavior science, the identification of critical behaviors, the growth of a culture willing to report deviations, the development of a process-driven measurement system able to analyze deviance, and the ultimate reduction in the probability of incidents.

Managing to reduce normalization of deviance will take a greater understanding of the behavioral systems that lead to the actions associated with process safety risk. Adding behavior analyses to an understanding of normalization of deviance may help design new behavioral safety processes that can help reduce process safety incidents.

Many behaviors that deviate from the engineered work process are behaviors that simplify the work process (i.e., shortcuts). These shortcuts are directed through antecedents offered by the work context, the management systems, and sometimes the culture of the workforce (Mawhinney, 1992). For example, the work context and supervisory systems may create a perceived pressure to achieve a desired outcome based on past experiences or rumors. Management systems such as adequate training, proximal work instructions, and hazard analyses could be antecedents to direct proper behaviors. When these management systems are lacking sound behavioral processes, deviance occurs. Otherwise, poorly designed management systems, such as overly detailed and time-consuming work permit processes or lockout tagout procedures, may be antecedents for behaviors that result in less response cost. Finally, more simplistically, when appropriate tools are not available, the nearest tool becomes an antecedent itself. Over time, many of these antecedents become discriminative stimuli for shortcuts because of their association with reduction of response cost consequences.

There are often no immediate punishing consequences for engaging in the shortcut because the behavior rarely results in a process safety issue. In addition, because of their own normalization of deviance, supervisors do not discipline the operator for the shortcut. This makes the punishing consequence far less probable (Daniels & Bailey, 2014; Petrock, 1978), and the operator is rarely going to contact the punishing consequence. Instead, most shortcut behaviors (e.g., using the improper tool that is available, beginning work before completing a hazard form) will be reinforced because the response effort of the work is reduced, in that it is simpler, more convenient, or perhaps more physically comfortable, and the work gets done quicker, which may be further reinforced by supervisors or other employees.

In addition, behavioral systems analysis (Brethower, 1982; Diener, McGee, & Miguel, 2009; Harshbarger & Maley, 1974; Ludwig & Houmanfar, 2010; Malott, 2003) allows one to map how the action (e.g., improper tool use) or inaction (e.g., failing to conduct a hazard analysis) of the employee is occasioned by the interlocking contingencies (Glenn, 1988; Glenn & Malott, 2004; Malott & Glenn, 2006) surrounding the employee. Indeed, the behaviors of leaders fail to build systems that may set the context to direct and reinforce successful hazard mitigation behaviors of their employees. The behaviors of supervisors fail to provide more immediate direction and reinforcement. In fact, the behaviors of leaders may lead the supervisors to focus on other tasks (e.g., paperwork and meetings) at the expense of alternative behaviors directed at mitigating employee risk. In addition, the actions of people in other operational functions can impact the context of the operator (e.g., the warehouse function not procuring or maintaining the proper tools). Finally, one can assess how the behaviors of other operators who do the same task contribute to the behavioral drift that becomes the norm. It is clear that this drift can become a problematic, self-sustaining cycle.

The oil and gas industry is seeking the assistance of behavior science in studying, understanding, and mitigating these dramatic events associated with human behavior. The challenges for the behavior analysis community are to (a) research the behavioral root causes of normalization of deviance, (b) create behavioral interventions to reduce normalization of deviance, and (c) identify the system factors that would promote the behaviors necessary to avoid the development of normalization of deviance.

Basic behavior research can help understand this phenomenon, and applied research building practical behavioral methodologies can move these efforts forward. The oil and gas industry and MPC in particular have been successful in reducing personal injuries through hazard mitigation and risk reduction. The industry needs to move beyond an engineering approach to process safety and truly address its little understood behavioral components. The industry therefore calls on behavioral science researchers to study and understand the behaviors and reinforcement contexts that drive and maintain normalization of deviance, determine its root causes, and develop interventions to counteract the problem. MPC wants to use behavioral science to further its safety agenda, to ensure that workers go home uninjured, to keep host communities unaffected by negative externalities (Biglan, 2009), and to stop relying on luck. Personal and process safety hazards need to be studied and addressed. Researchers, practitioners, and industry employees must continue to collaborate in order to produce cutting-edge research that reduces human suffering.

REFERENCES

American Chemistry Council. (2014, July 8). *Responsible care*. Retrieved from http://responsiblecare.americanchemistry.com/?gclid=CjwKEAjwre6dBRC94d-Gma7g3wcSJACNatZesLbSepFHxbgPwDYYHDZZfloXF3CiUheZ5mON_urydxo CQqDw_wcB

Biglan, T. (2009). The role of advocacy organizations in reducing negative externalities. *Journal of Organizational Behavior Management*, *29*, 155–174.

Brethower, D. M. (1982). The total performance system. In R. M. O'Brien, A. M. Dickinson, & M. P. Rosow (Eds.), *Industrial behavior modification: A management handbook* (pp. 350–369). New York, NY: Pergamon Press.

Bureau of Labor Statistics. (2013, November 7). *How to compute a firm's incidence rate for safety management*. Retrieved from http://www.bls.gov/iif/osheval.htm

Cambridge Center for Behavioral Studies. (2014, July 8). *Companies achieving behavioral safety accreditation*. Retrieved from http://www.behavior.org/resource. php?id=327

Center for Chemical Process Safety. (2012, April 4). *Characteristics of the vapour cloud explosion incident at the IOC terminal in Jaipur, 29 October 2009*. Retrieved from http://www.aiche.org/ccps/resources/chemeondemand/ conference-presentations/characteristics-vapour-cloud-explosion-incident-ioc-terminal-jaipur-29th-october-2009

Daniels, A., & Bailey, J. (2014). *Performance management: Changing behavior that drives organizational effectiveness* (5th ed.). Atlanta, GA: Performance Management.

Deepwater Horizon Study Group. (2011, March 1). *Final report on the investigation of the Macondo well blowout*. Retrieved from http://ccrm.berkeley.edu/ pdfs_papers/bea_pdfs/dhsgfinalreport-march2011-tag.pdf

Deming, W. E. (1982). *Quality, productivity, and competitive position*. Cambridge: Massachusetts Institute of Technology, Center for Advanced Engineering Study.

Diener, L. H., McGee, H. M., & Miguel, C. (2009). An integrated approach to conducting a behavioral systems analysis. *Journal of Organizational Behavior Management*, *29*, 108–135.

Geller, E. S., Berry, T. D., Ludwig, T. D., Evans, R. E., Gilmore, M. R., & Clarke, S. W. (1990). A conceptual framework for developing and evaluating behavior change interventions for injury control. *Health Education Research: Theory and Practice*, *5*, 125–137.

Glenn, S. (1988). Contingencies and metacontingencies: Toward a synthesis of behavior analysis and cultural materialism. *The Behavior Analyst*, *11*, 161–179.

Glenn, S. S., & Malott, M. E. (2004). Complexity and selection: Implications for organizational change. *Behavior and Social Issues*, *13*, 89–106.

Harshbarger, D., & Maley, R. F. (1974). *Behavior analysis and systems analysis: An integrative approach to mental health programs*. Kalamazoo, MI: Behaviordelia.

Hermann, J. A., Ibarra, G. V., & Hopkins, B. L. (2010). A safety program that integrated behavior-based safety and traditional safety methods and its effects on injury rates of manufacturing workers. *Journal of Organizational Behavior Management, 30*, 6–25.

Ludwig, T. D. (2014). The anatomy of pencil whipping. *Professional Safety, 59*, 47–50.

Ludwig, T. D., & Geller, E. S. (2000). Intervening to improve the safety of delivery drivers: A systematic behavioral approach. *Journal of Organizational Behavior Management, 19*(4), 1–124.

Ludwig, T. D., & Houmanfar, R. (Eds.). (2010). *Understanding complexity in organizations: Behavioral systems.* Philadelphia, PA: Routledge.

Malott, M. E. (2003). *Paradox of organizational change.* Reno, NV: Context Press.

Malott, M. E., & Glenn, S. S. (2006). Targets of intervention in cultural and behavioral change. *Behavior and Social Issues, 15*, 31–56.

Mawhinney, T. C. (1992). Evolution of organizational cultures as selection by consequences: The Gaia hypothesis, metacontingencies, and organizational ecology. *Journal of Organizational Behavior Management, 12*(2), 1–25.

McSween, T. E. (1995). *The values-based safety process: Improving your safety culture with a behavioral approach.* New York, NY: Wiley.

Mufson, S. (2007, January, 17). *BP failed on safety, report says.* Retrieved from http://www.washingtonpost.com/wp-dyn/content/article/2007/01/16/AR2007011600208.html

Myers, W. V., McSween, T. E., Medina, R. E., Rost, K., & Alvero, A. M. (2010). The implementation and maintenance of a behavioral safety process in a petroleum refinery. *Journal of Organization Behavior Management, 30*, 285–307.

Occupational Safety and Health Administration. (2014a, April 30). *Industries in the VPP federal and state plans.* Retrieved from https://www.osha.gov/dcsp/vpp/sitebynaics.html

Occupational Safety and Health Administration. (2014b, July 8). *Process safety management.* Retrieved from https://www.osha.gov/SLTC/processsafetymanagement/

Petrock, F. (1978). Analyzing the balance of consequences for performance improvement. *Journal of Organizational Behavior Management, 1*(3), 197–205.

Sulzer-Azaroff, B., & Austin, J. (2000). Does BBS work? Behavior-based safety and injury reduction: A survey of the evidence. *Professional Safety, 45*, 19–24.

U.S. Chemical Safety and Hazard Investigation Board. (2008). *Investigation report: LPG fire at Valero-McKee refinery.* Retrieved from http://www.csb.gov/assets/1/19/CSBFinalReportValeroSunray.pdf

U.S. Chemical Safety and Hazard Investigation Board. (2009, July 19). *CITCO refinery hydrofluoric acid release and fire.* Retrieved from http://www.csb.gov/citgo-refinery-hydrofluoric-acid-release-and-fire/

U.S. Chemical Safety and Hazard Investigation Board. (2010). *Case study: Explosion and fire in West Carrollton, Ohio.* Retrieved from http://www.csb.gov/assets/1/19/Veolia_Case_Study.pdf

U.S. Chemical Safety and Hazard Investigation Board. (2013). *West Fertilizer explosion and fire.* Retrieved from http://www.csb.gov/west-fertilizer-explosion-and-fire-/

U.S. Chemical Safety and Hazard Investigation Board. (2014). *Investigation report: Catastrophic rupture of Heach exchanger*. Retrieved from http://www.csb.gov/ assets/1/7/Tesoro_Anacortes_2014-May-01.pdf

Vaughan, D. (1996). *The Challenger launch decision: Risky technology, culture, and deviance at NASA*. Chicago, IL: University of Chicago Press.

Leadership and Crew Resource Management in High-Reliability Organizations: A Competency Framework for Measuring Behaviors

Mark P. Alavosius, Ramona A. Houmanfar, Steven J. Anbro, Kenneth Burleigh and Christopher Hebein

ABSTRACT

High-reliability organizations (HROs) have emerged across a number of highly technical, and increasingly automated industries (e.g., aviation, medicine, nuclear power, and oil field services). HROs incorporate complex systems with a large number of employees working in dynamic, and potentially dangerous environments. Effectively managing contingencies in HROs, to simultaneously promote safe and efficient behaviors is a daunting task. Crew Resource Management (CRM) has emerged in HROs as a highly effective approach to training and sustaining essential skills within work teams operating across a large workforce. CRM provides a competency framework that enables adherence to standard work instructions while, at the same time, encourages adaptive variance in responding to effectively manage current environmental circumstances that depart from normal routines. This paper considers the development of CRM across several high-reliability industries, develops a behavior analytic account of CRM behaviors, and describes an approach to measuring behaviors within simulated and actual work environments.

The Deepwater Horizon oil rig disaster on April 20, 2010 is a bellwether event in the oil services industry signaling that dire consequences may result when workers in a highly technical, dynamic work setting lose control of complex operations. Eleven people lost their lives that day on the BP managed oil rig in the Gulf of Mexico, and the environmental catastrophe affected millions of people residing along the Gulf coast. The financial impact is estimated to be as high as 60 billion dollars to cover losses and mitigate damage. The Deepwater Horizon Study Group, from the Center for Catastrophic Risk Management (2011), reports that a history of at-risk safety behaviors by workers on the oil rig contributed to the disaster. This event received worldwide attention, which contributed to a renewed focus on human (behavioral) factors that affect operational integrity in increasingly technical, automated contexts where failure can be catastrophic. High-risk industries such as oil field services are becoming increasingly automated but the human elements that remain have the potential to either avert or assist the evolution of a disaster.

High-reliability organizations (HROs) grow from settings in which managerial and operational behaviors are interlocked across levels of the organization in a systematic effort to learn from incidents and accidents and institutionalize corrections to improve safety and performance (Dekker & Woods, 2009). These institutionalized corrections involve highly engineered work settings where processes include redundancies, failsafes, and back-up systems so that nearly error-free technical operations are sustained. In these environments, failures are more likely to result from a complex set of interwoven, organized factors rather than some single component fault. HROs are uniquely challenging work environments as crew members' behaviors interact with automated expert systems to sustain the integrity of processes. HROs include settings that emphasize maintaining operational integrity in the face of challenges inherent in continuous, 24 hour/day operations (e.g., aviation, nuclear power plants, medical settings, and oil rigs). Human factor challenges in these environments may include fatigue due to extended shifts, loss of situational awareness (SA) in the context of complex automated processes with multivariate data streams to guide decisions, and novel contexts that invite behavioral variation from standard workpractices.

HROs utilize humans to monitor data streams, comprehend patterns in complex data, respond to alarms and signals, and sometimes approve or override automated adjustments. Pilots of commercial aircraft monitor preset flight plans run by autopilots and somewhat infrequently control flight maneuvers manually. A similar role is developing for surgeons, train engineers, nuclear power plant operators, oil rig personnel, and other HRO managers where expert technologies conduct many operations. The behavioral challenges in HROs are perhaps unique as the context for work is highly organized and sources of behavioral variance are within the complexity of interlocked contingencies.

Oil service companies aspire to performance levels achieved by the best HROs so that disasters such as the BP event in the Gulf of Mexico are averted (Flin & O'Connor, 2001; IOGP, 2014a, 2014b). A number of high tech industries are leading the way with the development of replicable methodologies to prevent human error and system failure. Transfer of behavioral technologies across these industries offers opportunties to study and understand work behaviors within the context of highly organized processes. Commercial aviation is the exemplar HRO as airlines maintain excellent (in relation to other industries) safety records across millions of hours of operation. Much of this is the result of sophisticated automated flight controls; some is the highly developed competencies of flight crew trained in high-fidelity simulators who learn to step in when automation reaches the limit of its design in a particular situation. The extraordinary example of Captain Chesley Sullenberger, who landed his disabled airliner in the Hudson River with no loss of life, illustrates how humans can fluently interact with technology to solve seemingly insurmountable problems (Sullenberger & Zaslow, 2009).

A challenge to industries aspiring to be top tier HROs is to adopt behavior scientific methodologies into their industry's technologies that resemble those developed in aviation, but systematically adapt the methodologies to the indiocyncracies of their industry. Medicine, for example, is emulating aviation with the developiment of simulators of surgery and patient care (Simon et al., 2000; Zeltser & Nash, 2010). Behavior science provides a coherent framework for identifying sources of behavioral variaton in these settings and helps to develop effective interventions that establish and sustain operational integrity by medical teams. Oil rigs are representative of work in other dynamic contexts such as transportation industries (e.g., commercial aviation, railways), medicine (e.g., surgical teams), and nuclear power (e.g., nuclear power plants) as they integrate highly trained personnel with advanced technologies. Oil rigs are distributed across the planet both on land and at sea and their workforce is often multicultural. Crew members' behaviors required to operate these rigs must interlock as team-level efforts and also engage with off-site personnel (e.g., suppliers, engineers, etc.) who provide ancillary services.

The purpose of this paper is to examine how Crew Resource Management (CRM) has developed as a methodology for managing crew in HROs, and outline a behavior analytic conceptualization of leadership within the context of CRM. We also discuss leadership in the context of interlocking behavioral contingencies, competency in managing behavioral systems, and organizational governance models needed to optimize procedural integrity. CRM offers a useful perspective on leadership and management of HROs as it operates within defined environments (e.g., oil rigs, surgical suites, cockpits, etc.) where the operational boundaries are relatively clear, behaviors can be objectively defined, and the interlocking with other organizational settings (e.g., mission control rooms) can be articulated with a high degree of precision.

Leadership competency for CRM in HRO settings faces two fundamental challenges. First, leaders need to maintain procedural integrity and ensure that crew members adhere to intricate and precise procedures. Control of deviations from desired practice is paramount as teams conduct prescribed duties within defined parameters. On oil rigs, for example, workers follow a prescribed drilling plan that is engineered to reach oil reserves that can be thousands of meters below the Earth's surface. The drilling plan dictates parameters (e.g., depths, pressures) of operations conducted by shifts of workers who drill continuously for weeks or months until the reserve is tapped. Oil rig worker behavior is channeled by rigid parameters that greatly constrain deviation. Second, on occasion, leaders must manage unanticipated events (e.g., excessive pressures) that disrupt well-laid plans. These deviations may escalate to crisis-level events that threaten not just the task at hand, but the lives of the crew and the environment in which they operate. Such was the case on the Deepwater Horizon where the crew lost control of the well and a blowout occurred that could not be contained by engineered fail-safe systems. In these crisis situations, the leader and crew must detect and track the changing context and adapt their responses to address the emerging crisis. Failure to adjust in a timely way can be catastrophic. Thus, CRM entails rigid adherence to standardized work that must also flex to alternative responses when conditions change and standard work is no longer effective. Similar events occur in commercial aviation, nuclear power, and medicine where standard work generally achieves the desired result, but on occasion, conditions emerge that require nonstandard responses to achieve the goal of operations. The behavioral challenges in sustaining routine operations, but also adapting to rapidly changing conditions are considerable (Alavosius, Houmanfar, & Rodriquez, 2005) and call for a competency model that bridges these two fundamental features of CRM (rigid compliance with rules, and flexibility in tracking changing conditions and adapting to them—see Wulfert, Greenway, Farkas, Hayes, & Dougher, 1994 for discussion of rule governed rigidity).

Finally, we present an inventory (Table 1) to illustrate the resources that HROs are applying to enhance crew leader's ability to manage coordinated work. Rules are central to CRM as the crew working in dynamic, high-risk settings may encounter ambiguity due to unexpected events that can be catastrophic if behaviors do not adapt to the changing, complex relationship between stimuli, response choices, and consequences that likely follow each choice. The paper concludes by discussing opportunities for researchers to study these variables affecting leadership and CRM in HROs

Definition of CRM

According to the Industry of Oil and Gas Producers (IOGP, 2014a) "a step-change improvement in operational safety and efficiency of well operations teams (i.e., the full spectrum of drilling, completions, work-overs, and interventions) can be achieved through effective development and application of *nontechnical skills*, also known as Crew Resource Management (CRM)." Crew leaders must not only manage the engineered technical aspects of oil field operations (Flin & O'Connor, 2001) but also interlock the behaviors of team members in light of the competencies and skills of crew members that vary as a function of the work demands. CRM can be viewed as a cascading chain of behavioral events where the leader and crew members effectively utilize available resources to:

(1) plan a work process,
(2) brief everyone on roles/functions,
(3) monitor the process as it occurs,
(4) detect and report deviations from the plan,
(5) communicate corrections from the top down,
(6) adjust actions as needed,

Table 1. Features of CRM and SA in Leading Industries.

CRM/SA effort	Oil field services	Aviation	Medicine	Nuclear
CRM training	Emerging efforts in simulators and CRM training for well site personnel	Advanced: codified and scheduled	Mid-level: beginning to interlock medicine and nursing staff	Advanced: based on aviation and military systems
		Pilot licensing		Train individual and crew competence
		Annual checks		
Simulators	Mid-fidelity: rig floor, drill shack replicas in classrooms	High fidelity: simulated cockpit matches actual aircraft	Mid-high fidelity: surgery suites and treatment rooms	Mid-high fidelity: control room replicas in classrooms with link to external resources
			Mannequins simulate patient	
SA definitions	Cognitive/ contextual	Cognitive framework	Cognitive framework	Cognitive framework
	Developing metrics of competency in context	Foundation work in SA— advanced instrumentation	Individual and group definitions	Individual and group definitions
	BEM identifies sources of variation		Implicit biases being examined	
Behavior metrics in training sites	Emerging competency framework—pre/ post tests of knowledge and skills	Multiple measures and rating scales	Cognitive/behavioral measures	Cognitive/ behavioral measures
		Pass/fail score in practical tests		Pre/post tests of knowledge and skills
Behavior metrics in work sites	Unknown	Unknown	Unknown	Unknown
CRM in incident investigations	Unknown	Black box to collect data— open reporting and documentation	Emerging—culture of suppression of reporting	Data records, communications, and logs
Emerging efforts	WSL interlocks with Driller and crew members Automation, HCI	Automation, HCI	Implicit attitude and bias in CRM—assess and mitigate	HCI

Note. CRM = Crew Resource Management; SA = situational awareness; BEM = Behavior Engineering Methodology; HCI = human–computer interaction.

(7) debrief at important moments (at significant change or conclusion of work), and

(8) learn to refine the human-machine interface.

In complex and dynamic situations, CRM orchestrates cooperation among crew members that have different vantage points on the process. Combined, these perspectives optimize adaptive behaviors by all members of the team and may include the input of remote personnel who monitor the process from afar (e.g., from mission control settings). The behaviors involved in CRM can be observed in several key events involved in managing a complex and dynamic process. A chain of CRM behaviors often begins with a briefing meeting during which the team leader informs the crew members of the task ahead, reviews their individual and collective roles and responsibilities, and provides objectives to gage progress. Following the briefing, the crew members conduct the task and work together to assess progress and meet project objectives. Unexpected events may thwart progress and crew members communicate their observations, per-haps in the format of a debriefing meeting, to decide on an adjusted course of action. Upon completion of the task or other significant event (e.g., handoff to another crew at shift change) a debriefing is held to share updates on progress, review actions taken and summarize lessons learned for future operations. These three events (briefing, operations, debriefing) provide useful vantage points for assessors to examine competency by leaders and crew members in context.

CRM is described in the aviation literature as "the effective use of all resources, including hardware, software, and people, to achieve the highest possible level of safety" (Northwest Airlines, 2005). Essentially, CRM can be viewed as a systemic model of training and behavioral change that results in a reduction of human error through the use of all relevant and available resources (Kanki, Helmreich, & Anca, 2010). From its origin in aviation, CRM targets several key processes or skills: situation awareness, communication skills, teamwork, task allocation, and deci-sion making (U.S. FAA, 2004). Among different airlines, this list of key processes or skills differs in organization but all focus on defining optimal interpersonal interactions of crew members working cooperatively within a dynamic environ-ment. To facilitate analysis of critical variations in CRM behavior, these skills can be grouped together into six core skill sets that can be measured as the crew interact with their operational environments:

(1) communication,
(2) situational awareness,
(3) decision making,
(4) teamwork,
(5) management of limits of crew members' capacities, and
(6) leadership.

Each of these six competency domains can be deconstructed into more mole-cular definitions of behavior within some defined context and viewed within the briefing, operations, and debriefing milestones. Leadership serves an essential integrative function of all elements, without which, CRM would not sustain or lead to desirable outcomes in an organization. Before examining these domains in detail in pursuit of measurable dimensions of these competencies, we briefly review how several HRO industries approach CRM. From this overview, a behavioral account of CRM can be offered.

History and development of CRM

On December 29, 1972, a commercial airliner crashed into the Florida everglades, resulting in 101 fatalities. On March 27, 1977, two commercial airliners collided on a runway at the Tenerife Airport in the Canary Islands, resulting in over 500 fatalities. The Tenerife Airport Disaster holds the record for highest casualties in any single aviation accident. Investigations into these catastrophic events, along with others, revealed a common pattern: an estimated 60–80% of incidents were due to human error. These errors resulted from faulty leadership behaviors from captains (e.g., the breakdown of effective interpersonal communication, and poor decision making) (Wagener & Ison, 2014). Following these findings, CRM was introduced into the aviation industry as a means of addressing these issues and preventing similar incidents.Since its inception in aviation, CRM has been adapted by other high-risk industries. CRM research has generally focused on a particular component, SA, and much of this research is conducted from a cognitive perspective. A review of this research relating to components of CRM is presented below, with a focus on three high-risk industries: aviation, medicine, and nuclear power to illustrate the diffusion of CRM across HROs.

Aviation

The introduction of CRM into aviation facilitated a dynamic culture shift among the crew working in this industry. Historically, the hierarchies within aviation were the driving force behind the organizational culture. A captain was seen as the ultimate authority figure of a flight crew. A captain's word was law, and should never be questioned or challenged. In such hierarchical structures, human error can still occur, as the captain is not exempt from making poor decisions. Therefore, it is crucial that effective, clear, two-way communication exists between the captain and any subordinates to take advantage of all available resources (their knowledge, observations of current conditions, interpretations of data, etc.) that crew members have to offer. CRM's approach to communication has historically been simplified by major airlines using four key words: "*authority* with *participation*, and *assertiveness* with *respect*" (Northwest Airlines, 2005). Throughout airline CRM training, crew members are taught to speak up *before* an incident occurs, rather than to place blame *after* an incident occurs. For instance, if a copilot notices some deviance from standard operating procedures (SOPs), it is their obligation to speak up and it becomes the captain's obligation to take the co-pilot's observation into account.

As previously described, SA is an essential component of CRM. One common feature of training SA in aviation is the utilization of high-fidelity simulators. In some airlines, pilots are required to participate in simulator training as often as every nine months, for a period of two days at a time. At-home computer modules are released on a quarterly basis to complement this hands-on simulator training. During the simulator training, pilots are exposed to a variety of scenarios in which instrument malfunctions, adverse weather conditions exist, or other adverse events are present. Pilots must then respond in ways that incorporate all available information in order to maneuver their simulated aircraft to safety. Their ability to successfully engage in these behaviors are measured and subjectively scored by expert instructors (e.g., using a 1–5 grading scale).

The use of cockpit simulators in the context of SA research is strengthened by the high fidelity of these simulators. Research demonstrates that when using simulator training, the configuration of data needs to be designed in simple ways that make it easily accessible for pilots (Jenkins & Gallimore, 2008), the use of objective measures such as physiological readouts and explicit questions during simulation freezes lead to greater SA (Vidulich, Stratton, Crabtree, & Wilson, 1994), and there may also be some utility in the design and implementation of subjective questionnaires with regard to measuring SA (Waag, 1994).

Systemic application of CRM has made commercial aviation the leading industry in transportation safety, with an average of 0.07 passenger fatalities per billion passenger miles (Savage, 2013). SA training within organizations in high-reliability industries such as aviation allows for the development of a safety culture, whereby the behaviors, practices, policies, and structural components seen within a given organization combine to emphasize increased levels of safety (Meshkati, 1997).

Medicine

CRM was first adopted within the medical field by anesthesiologists and labeled Anesthesia Crisis Resource Management (ACRM; Howard, Gaba, & Fish, 1992). The goal of ACRM was to bring CRM into the medical field and train anesthesiologists to handle crisis scenarios while working on interdisciplinary teams (Howard et al., 1992). ACRM also utilizes high-fidelity simulators for the purpose of training. Simulated operating rooms are large enough to accommodate entire teams (e.g., other physicians, nurses, and technicians) rather than only one person (like a pilot in aviation) and an instructor (Gaba, Howard, Fish, Smith, & Yasser, 2001). While ACRM has a substantial history of use in the medical field, we found no published study to date that empirically demonstrates the impact ACRM has on patient care (Zeltser & Nash, 2010).

MedTeams, an emergency department training program that incorporates CRM procedures into the medical field, is designed to reduce medical errors via the training of different professionals working together in an emergency department (Morey et al., 2002). Similar to CRM, MedTeams identifies system-level variables as a common source of error to be addressed through team-oriented behaviors and communication. In this application of CRM to medicine, resources used to establish competency include classroom instruction, video scenarios, and a 4-hour supervised practicum (Simon et al., 2000). The MedTeams' curriculum shows a strong effect on reducing clinical errors; one study across seven emergency departments showed an average decrease of clinical errors from 30.9% to 4.4% as a result of this training program (Morey et al., 2002).

A more recent application of CRM principles and strategies in the medical field is TeamSTEPPS (Team Strategies and Tools to Enhance Performance and Patient Safety). This protocol was developed by the Agency for Healthcare Research and Quality in collaboration with the Department of Defense. TeamSTEPPS focuses on training four core skill sets to improve overall patient care and safety in the hands of inter-professional teams working in dynamic settings (Epps & Levin, 2015; King et al., 2008):

(1) leadership,
(2) situation monitoring [SA],
(3) mutual support, and
(4) communication.

Research using the TeamSTEPPS methodology demonstrates reductions in medical errors (Cima et al., 2009; Haig & Sutton, 2006; Mann, Marcus, & Sachs, 2006) as well as improved communication and teamwork skills (Turner, 2012; Ward, Zhu, Lampman, & Stewart, 2015). Within the medical field, the majority of the applied SA research tends to focus on the implementation of TeamSTEPPS, as described above. Specific procedures within the TeamSTEPPS training include call outs, check backs, the two-challenge rule, and "CUS" words (Haynes & Strickler, 2014). Call outs involve publicly broadcasting a patient's vital signs, such that all members of a team receive the information at once. Check backs utilize closed-loop communication, whereby the receiver of information repeats key points back to the speaker. The two-challenge rule is where a team member voices a particular concern twice, and if ignored they move up the chain of command with their concern; this promotes the breakdown of hierarchies to the extent that everyone can be heard. "CUS" words, derived from the acronym, "I'm Concerned; I'm Uncomfortable; I don't feel like this is Safe!" (Haynes & Strickler, 2014) are a way any member of the team can halt an ongoing situation, via communicating concern, so that it can be reassessed. As with CRM, a major focus is on building team communication and breaking down hierarchical barriers.

Maraccini (2016) designed a behavior analytic intervention—to train values and perspective-taking skills—that was combined with TeamSTEPPS-related technology, to create an interprofessional education (IPE) training package for medical and nursing students. They used descriptive analysis methods—from the behavior analytic literature—to compare communication performance prior to and following the completion of the training package during a simulated hand-off task, versus that of a control task. Results demonstrated significant improvements in interprofessional communication accuracy and frequency during patient handoffs, independent of package type.

While much of this research is in its conceptual stage, there are several applied demonstrations of SA training in the medical field. One study that focused on shared, rather than individual, SA involved 500+ hours of observation in surgical settings over a 6-month period with data suggesting that one of the most crucial components to building up SA is the inclusion of explicit, distributed, and timely communication among team members (Gillespie, Gwinner, Fairweather, & Chaboyer, 2013). Behaviors such as self-talk, closed-loop communication, and overhearing conversations were identified as specific ways teams build shared SA.

Nuclear power

As work in nuclear power becomes more automated, increasingly complex technologies guide operators, often in conjunction with parallel monitoring of several data streams. However, even with advanced control systems, safety protocols, and accident mitigation software, human operators are still ultimately responsible for assessment. CRM integration in the nuclear industry has the primary goal of interfacing human, process, and technology elements by optimizing skilled behavior (individual repertoires) within these systems. Hamilton, Kazem, He, and Dumolo (2013) describe a systematic approach to safety and human factors that includes the integration of both engineering and human error data. Within the nuclear industry, human-computer interaction (HCI) and human reliability assessments (HRA) are applied through each component of a project's life cycle. Assessment methods include task analysis to identify critical behaviors, reviews of an operator's experience (behavior repertoires and ability), and functional allocation of resources.

Measuring SA in HROs often includes the use of published measurement tools including direct probe measures like the Situational Awareness Global Assessment Technique (SAGAT) and the Situation Present Assessment Method (SPAM), and qualitative measures like the Situational Awareness Rating Scale (SART) and others (Endsley, 1988, 1995b). These assessments are typically customized to specific scenarios common to the industry and conducted in simulators where raters score crew members' detection of variation in critical features of the work environments. Measurements include latency of responding to changing signals, accuracy of reporting deviations, and comprehension of the consequences of detected variations. Naderpour, Lu, and Zhang (2016) designed and tested the Situational Awareness Support System (SASS) to establish a semiautonomous technology to increase human reliability. The four major elements of this design model include data collection, assessment, recovery of safety failures, and HCI.

Using technology to reduce workload can reduce error and prevent operators from being overwhelmed with data; however, HCI that reduces variability or error in one domain can set the occasion for new types of human error in others (Yang, Yang, Cheng, Jou, & Chiou, 2012). SA and response planning are contextual human factors that reduce error by discriminating critical environmental cues (Naderpour, Lu, & Zhang, 2016). Chase and Bjarnadottir (1992, p. 191) classify two kinds of situations that can produce behavioral variability. First is an environmental change, where behavioral change as a response to that environmental change will produce reinforcement; or second, situations where stimuli changes occur only as a result of behavioral change. With effective discrimination, more precise identification of context and behavior can increase response flexibility. Flexibility training can successfully adapt the human response in ways that control room safety technologies cannot.

Kim and Byun (2011) studied two licensed crew members of nuclear power operators in simulators. Operators were required to mitigate problems by coordinating team members with personnel outside the control room and expert raters scored their individual and team performance using a selection of measurement tools. Their nontechnical competencies were evaluated as attitudes (questionnaires), individual performance (video recording), and collective performance (video recording and simulator records). Results showed that CRM training increased "coordination, communication, and team-spirit" most notable at the level of collective (team) performance. However, the impact was not significant when examined at the level of each individual. This suggests that all (or most) crew members need to be engaged in CRM training, not just the team leader, for positive results to be achieved.

CRM as a behavioral event

Behavior science provides a coherent perspective on the management of human behaviors needed to prevent catastrophe in HROs (e.g., well control on oil rigs). As equipment, automation, and engineering controls become increasingly sophisticated in HROs, the behavior of humans who operate the equipment looms as the most critical factor accounting for catastrophic failure. Behavioral engineering (Gilbert, 1978, 2007) offers a systematic method to identify categories of behavioral variation and institute controls that reduce risk for deviations causing catastrophic losses. The competency of crew leaders and crew members are critical as their behaviors interlock to maintain the integrity of operations, even as conditions change that might undermine the quality and safety of work. The leadership of the crew is a behavioral event that can be examined through the lens of behavior science so that variations are constrained below levels that result in catastrophic failure. Training to fluency aims (Binder, 1996), established by measuring the CRM behaviors of exemplary crew members, offers a structured approach to continuously improving the performance of HROs as managers better understand the behavioral challenges involved in achieving and sustaining effective operations.

Measurement of CRM competencies

Our review of the psychological literature on CRM indicates competency is defined in somewhat different ways across industrial/organizational psychology and behavior analysis. Industrial/organizational psychology might be labeled "the cognitive perspective" and considers competency as a set of enduring traits or characteristics of a person that are emitted across environments. A competent person, from this perspective, is regarded as one who emits adaptive behavior because their cognitive apparatus is sufficiently developed to permit expert behavior regardless of setting. A somewhat different perspective is taken in behavior science ("the operant perspective") where a person is competent if he/she has learned via training and experience to engage in adaptive behavior *within a given context*. Here, competency is assessed within the parameters of a given situation and generalization of skills across settings is not assumed to be automatic. Direct observation of behavior in context defines competency and no effort is made to posit features of the workers' mental facilities.

Both approaches hold merit and convey the notion that competency is a complex set of measures of expert behavior. The cognitive perspective lends itself to selecting workers who fit the task; the operant perspective focuses on assessing supports (job aids, feedback, instructions, training) to enable average workers to become experts. For maximum utility of a competency framework, it needs to consider sources of behavioral deviation if it is to be optimally predictive of adaptive behavior. For example, consider pedestrians walking in New York's Times Square or London's Trafalgar Square. The New Yorker is highly competent to navigate NYC traffic and avoid collision with vehicles; in London, this person might be seriously disoriented by 'foreign" traffic patterns and step in front a lorry. Likewise, the Londoner walks safely through UK traffic but is tentative and uneasy in NYC as swarms of yellow cabs drive on the "opposite" side of the road. The same considerations arise when assessing competency of personnel (e.g., Well Site Leaders [WSLs] on oil rigs). Some basic competencies likely extend across all well sites (e.g., comprehension of drilling parameters) but other critical competencies (e.g., instructing and supervising crew) might be unique to cultural features of geographic locations (a WSL might encounter different forms of crew communications in North Dakota than they would in Chad).

The "soft or nontechnical" behavioral components of CRM are areas of focus across each of the industries reviewed above. Each industry confronts challenges by objectively measuring the technical skills of personnel (e.g., the engineering prowess of field engineers, the "stick and rudder" skills of pilots) and the "human factors" of behavioral interactions of crew members within technical and dynamic environments. Simulators are helpful in measuring the technical and nontechnical competence of individuals and crew members as they react to solve complex system failures. However, more work is needed to examine transference of skills observed in simulators to actual work settings. A competency framework might focus on the individual, but thought should be taken to broaden competency as a collective measure of team performance (collective fluency). Gilbert's (1978, 2007) text *Human Competence* describes Behavior Engineering Methodology (BEM) as a framework for analysis of the sources of behavioral variations seen across these industries and a coherent approach to interventions that increase adaptive behavior by crew members. This methodology identifies approaches to control sources of behavioral variations that threaten operational integrity within the interlocking behavior of multiple workers.

CRM orchestrates cooperation among crew members that have different vantage points on a complex and dynamic process. Combined, these perspectives optimize adaptive behaviors by all members of the team. SOPs are commonly used to guide consistent behavior by crew members and essentially are rules that describe the standard sequence of behaviors and expected results that experts validate as optimal for a given job or task. These rules are antecedent controls and are commonly found to be most effective when consequences (feedback or reinforcement) establish their control of behavior.

Gilbert's (1978, 2007) BEM can be seen as a way to assess crew behavior management in a complex environment. Competency is a critical feature of CRM and in adherence to standardized work where an individual's capabilities must enable them to perform at the level required by the standards. An entry level of proficiency is assumed to be within the repertoire of the oil rig workers (e.g., WSL, Driller, Tool Pusher, Floorman) so that their job aids (tools, instructions, data, etc.) occasion the desired interlocked behaviors under normal operating conditions. A deeper analysis of each of the six domains of CRM leads to assessment of CRM as a chain of behaviors that crew members exhibit as they conduct complex processes, detect and diagnose problems, and adjust operations to maintain procedural integrity. Each of the six competency domains is considered below as building blocks for a comprehensive assessment of CRM competency. For sake of clarity, the six domains are examined arbitrarily as relatively separate response classes. In actuality, the competencies are interwoven as crew members interact with the work context (e.g., the setting, equipment, other personnel, guidance systems, etc.) to complete workflows, detect and diagnose problems, decide on corrective actions, implement solutions, and debrief before the next workflow. Assessments of these competencies by direct observation of behaviors in context (in simulators or at actual worksites) entail assessors measure dimensions of these six competencies during scheduled observation windows. The briefing, operations, and debriefing chronology provides a useful framework in which the observer can view and score behaviors critical in these domains. The competency profile for a given individual would rate observed effectiveness in communication, SA, decision making, teamwork, management of limits of crew members' capacities, and leadership as seen during actual and simulated work events. Competency in the technical domains (e.g., well site engineering) would also be assessed. These six domains are examined below.

Communication

The dynamic nature of HROs necessitates the coordinated behaviors of multiple individuals performing multiple job functions simultaneously to achieve safe and effective results. These results cannot be achieved consistently without effective planning and communication to interlock behaviors. It is important to note that in these dynamic environments, communication is not just top-down, but across levels of a networked workforce. The purpose of targeting communication processes among employees is to break through potential barriers that have been established through hierarchies.

Skinner's analysis of verbal behavior (1957) can be used as a foundation for our understanding of communication. Skinner describes verbal behavior as the behavior of an individual (speaker), which results in the behavior of another individual (listener) interacting with the environment in a manner consistent with the behavior of the first individual (speaker). Reinforcement in such instances is indirect; rather than the direct manipulation of the environment producing reinforcement, the speaker's behavior is reinforced by the listener's direct manipulation of the environment. The speaker and listener roles can fluctuate quite rapidly in everyday life; this is also evident in dynamic, high-risk work environments. With regard to the analysis of communication, a majority of the literature focuses on the topographical characteristics that focus primarily on the verbal behavior of the speaker. In many organizational settings, the dynamic interaction of teams requires our focus on ways by which verbal behavior and its products may affect the listener's behavior. This approach to analysis of language and communication is mainly captured by the functional account of verbal behavior. Relational Frame Theory (Hayes, Barnes-Holmes, & Roche, 2001) provides an empirically supported functional approach to the analysis of language. RFT emphasizes that when we learn to relate events and objects in a certain way, such as comparing them, the function (or meaning/properties) of one event or object transfers to (rubs off on) the other. This transformation of stimulus functions helps to explain why we can say we are happy, for example, when we hear a piece of music that we listened to during a fun winter holiday: the functions of a camp fire, friends, laughter, and food are not only related to the song (i.e., we think about the holiday when we hear the song), but the song has also acquired the enjoyable stimulus function of the holiday (Flaxman, Bond, & Livheim, 2013).

Houmanfar, Rodrigues, and Smith (2009), and Houmanfar and Rodrigues (2012), note that many communications serve to alter the function of stimuli in the workplace, which in turn impacts employee behavior. Rules or statements that change the reinforcing or punishing effectiveness of consequences (in much that same way the establishing operations nonverbally alter the effect of consequences) have been called augmentals (Houmanfar et al., 2009; Maraccini, Houmanfar, & Szarko, 2016; Stewart, Barns-Holmes, Barnes-Holmes, Bond, & Hayes, 2006). Formative augmentals establish a previously neutral stimulus as a reinforcer or punisher. For example, "If we keep costs associated with non-productive time under $100,000 for the month, employees will receive a bonus," will probably result in employees seeking feedback on company expenses, possibly a previously neutral stimulus, and attempting to stay below the specified spending limit. Motivative augmentals, on the other hand, alter the effectiveness of stimuli by altering a consequential function. For example, "Safety is the backbone of our company reputation. If we don't promote safety, we will lose our stature in the industry." This statement takes a stimulus (safety) that already functions as a reinforcer for employees and increases its reinforcing effectiveness.

In high-risk industries, the first instance is the most likely. Some potentially catastrophic change occurs in the environment, and it is up to the crew in that environment to alter their behavior in such a way as to avoid an escalating event. Communication between crew members in such a situation can allow for the generation of motivative augmentals (MOs) that may evoke problem-solving behavior. MOs may be statements that alter the effectiveness of stimuli by altering a consequential function and can be used to increase the importance of team goals while communicating a clear connection between the team actions and goals (Houmanfar et al., 2009)

From a behavior analytic perspective (Houmanfar & Johnson, 2003), team communication can be defined as a psychological event in which team members engage in verbal problem solving under the antecedent and consequential control of an absence of effective rules or presence of heuristic rules. This delineation means that the lack of rules is an antecedent for activity that is itself oriented toward the establishment of such actions (e.g., complete, clear, and accurate specification of organizational contingencies).

As has been discussed conceptually (Houmanfar & Johnson, 2003; Houmanfar et al., 2009) and demonstrated experimentally, no rule and/or implicit rather than explicit (Smith, Houmanfar, & Louis, 2011) and inaccurate rather than accurate (Smith, Houmanfar, & Denny, 2012) rules generate environmental ambiguity. In these studies, environmental ambiguity associated with no rule or ambiguous/ inaccurate ones were found to occasion problem-solving behavior among the verbal participants, which in turn led to reduced performance and the self-generation of inaccurate organizational rules on the part of participants. Conversely, implicit (or heuristic) explicit but accurate rules, which minimize environmental ambiguity, were found to produce greater and longer lasting levels of performance.

With regard to HROs, effective communication involves verbal interactions between crew members from all different levels of a hierarchy. Potential systemic barriers to effective communication must be overcome in order to promote safety of a crew. Such barriers include environmental obstacles such as a loud work environment, or interpersonal obstacles such as rigid adherence to hierarchical structures and perceived status granted by such structures for certain roles. In the airline industry, if copilots notice a potential problem, they need to communicate that to the captain, whose responsibility is to then attend to the communicated information and factor that into decision making.

The traditional approach to leadership consisting of chain of command (top-down) approach has to be revisited in the context of CRM. Instead, leaders have to take into consideration the ever-evolving external environment and verbally evaluate the potential adaptations the organization can make to those possible futures. These relations are based on verbally constructed outcomes that, for the leader at least, bears some connection with the current situation. However, these relations must be communicated effectively to the rest of the people in the team if they are to behave in accordance with said relations.

Moreover, individuals' histories of relational networks have a significant influence on the way by which a collectivity of individuals in given interlocked contingencies respond to organizational information generated by each other through communication networks. This interaction between relational networks and communication networks can be captured through the phenomenon of self-organization that is one of the characteristics of social systems (Houmanfar et al., 2009).

Situational awareness

The second component of CRM is SA. SA is described as the ability to monitor or perceive elements in the environment, the comprehension of their meaning, and the projection of their status into the near future. This definition closely approximates the most commonly utilized definition in SA research within clinical psychology: "SA is the perception of the elements in the environment within a volume of time and space, the comprehension of their meaning, and the projection of their status in the near future" (Endsley, 1995a, 1995b). The majority of SA research to date relies on Endsley's foundational concept. While this model comes from cognitive psychology and posits mental processing of information, it can be interpreted in a more explicit manner from a behavioral perspective.

Killingsworth, Miller, and Alavosius (2016) analyze the three components of SA presented in Endsley's model (1995a) in behavioral terms. A brief summary of their analysis is as follows: (a) *perception* can be thought of in terms of stimulus control, conditional discrimination, and observing responses; (b) *comprehension* involves verbal responses relevant to tacting the observable features and underlying functions of different stimuli, as well as their relation to other stimuli and events; and (c) *projection* can be analyzed similarly to predicting, which involves behaving in certain ways based on one's learning history and how that history is interacting with current contingencies (Skinner, 1974).

A number of assessment protocols have been developed to assess SA but the literature offers few published reports on their validation (Durso, Dattel, & Tremblay, 2004; Salmon, Stanton, Walker, & Green, 2006). Despite the relevance of SA to high-risk industries, relatively little objective research has been conducted in regard to measuring the critical behaviors (Craig, 2012). Killingsworth et al. (2016) provide an account of objective behavioral measures of SA that focus on fluency of crew members' behavior in detecting stimulus changes in the work context, communicating these changes to others, and adapting behaviors to meet prevailing conditions. Their analysis and recommendations for behavioral assessments need not be repeated here and readers are referred to that paper for more detail.

Decision making

In complex, dynamic processes anomalies occur that pose choices by operators at critical points to maintain control of the process. For example, an unexpected pattern of data may reveal malfunction or deviation from the prescribed workflow (e.g., unusual pressure readings from the wellbore indicate loss of well control). These set the occasion for follow-up by crew members to investigate and determine the nature of the problem. The diagnosis of the problem entails technical skill in the critical operations (e.g., engineering of the well) as well as human factors in coordination of input from team members leading to collective identification of the problem and mutually agreed upon remediation plan. On oil rigs, the WSL is the equivalent of the captain of a ship and charged with the authority and responsibility to decide on a course of action. How the leader gathers information from the team is important as their unique vantage points on the problem reveal variables affecting decisions. The leader, in light of the team investigations, takes the choice of action with input from crew members that might involve their considerable effort (e.g., leaving their positions, visually inspecting equipment, conducting tests, etc.). Some leaders may act on preconceived definitions of the problem, impulsively decide on a course of action before diagnosis is complete, or otherwise not engage crew members in the decision-making process. In HROs the complex nature of the multiple sources of anomalies warrants collective participation in the assessment and open discussion of the remediation plan.

Risk discounting is a potential threat to decision making (Sigurdsson, Taylor, & Wirth, 2013) especially in complex process malfunctions. Many variables influence decisions, including time pressure, client expectations, probability of negative outcome, delay of possible consequences, (Green & Myerson, 2004) and various interpersonal and culture variables. How problems are framed and described to decision makers alters their discounting curve (Brown & Alavosius, 2014) indicating that language used to convey choices influences decisions. Both the technical competencies of the leader and crew members to ascertain the technical problem and the human factors involved in describing and selecting the optimal solution among a range of options impact the quality of the decision. Making a wise choice is a function of the process by which the team understands the anomaly and their history in regard to risk discounting experiences with similar problems in the past. Training in simulators to solve problems within the stressors likely to be encountered at work sites can establish a repertoire of problem-solving behaviors that adapt to novel situations.

A number of models for decision making have been developed in aviation (U.S. FAA, 1991) and provide a framework for training and assessing competency. DODAR is an acronym for a decision-making process used within aviation that represents the typical process (Moriarity, 2015). DODAR entails a circular flow of steps by which a leader and team members troubleshoot a problem and arrive at a solution. *Diagnose* is the first step to define the problem and what might be causing it. *Options* is inventorying the choices and timeframes for corrective action. *Decide* is to choose the best option available to the crew. This entails discussion and input from crew members. *Act* or assign is the leader designating appropriate actions to be taken by crew members. *Reviewing* is monitoring the plan and expected outcomes. If the plan is not resolving the problem, DODAR is started again until the solution is reached. An assessor can observe a crew encountering a problem within a simulated workflow and score the speed and accuracy of individual and collective behaviors as the team completes DODAR through resolution of the anomaly.

Teamwork

Teamwork is the coordinated individual and collective behaviors of a crew. One focus of CRM is the breakdown of hierarchical barriers among crew members. This break down allows for more effective coordination of cooperative behaviors as it levels the playing field, so to speak. A core tenet of CRM is that crew members work together toward a common goal (i.e., teamwork). When analyzing the coordinated behaviors of a crew, it is important to distinguish between instances of crew members behaving with respect to outcomes that benefit only themselves versus outcomes that benefit the entire team.

A unit of analysis for teamwork can be found in the metacontingency (Glenn, 1988, 2004; Houmanfar, Rodrigues, & Ward, 2010; Malott & Glenn, 2006; Smith, Houmanfar, & Louis, 2011). Metacontingencies describes selective contingencies that operate on interlocked patterns of behavior between one or more persons or groups of persons. When the behavior of one person (e.g., a crew member at a well site) becomes interlocked with (i.e., dependent upon) the behavior of another, a pattern of behavior emerges, which Glenn (2004) is described as interlocking behavioral contingencies (IBCs). IBCs, when they occur, have a measureable effect on the aggregate outcome (e.g., drilled well). In other words, "metacontingency holds that interlocked behaviors of members constituting a group are selected by the shared environmental consequences they produce for the group members." (Smith et al., 2011). The complexity of the interactions necessitate definitions of the individual and collective behavior classes in context (Bar-Yam, 1997) that combine to form teamwork. The analyses require scaling measures from parts (individuals) to wholes (teams) so that the actions are understood as a coordinated, interlocked behavioral system operating in some organized context.

The role of language is crucial in a metacontingency (Blakely & Schlinger, 1987) but insufficient to understand teamwork, as individual and collective behaviors are coordinated by rules, but members must also track consequences resulting from actions. As teams adapt to changing conditions, the rules that govern their interactions and their learning histories in similar environments are better or worse at enabling adaptive behavior. It is the interlocking contingencies of individual behaviors that account for the metacontingency and its influence on the team outcome.

Management of limits of crew members' capacities

Increasingly complex technology guide operators in HROs often in conjunction with parallel monitoring of multiple data streams; however, even with advanced control systems, safety protocols, and accident mitigation software, human operators are still ultimately responsible for assessment. Unexpected events can be catastrophic in HROs. Prevention focuses investigators to examine condition chains, including interlocked behavior within work flows, how humans fail to sustain vigilance for extended periods, and other threats to operational integrity. Using technology to reduce workload can reduce error and prevent operators from being overwhelmed with data; however, computer-based HCI that reduce variability or error in one domain can set the occasion for new types of human error in others. (Yang et al., 2012). Stress, fatigue, habituation and other factors limit humans' ability to sustain optimal performance. When workflow is paced by automated controls, the demands on humans may impede how they self-manage their performance. The human response to overwhelming demands is unpredictable with reactions like withdrawal, escape, inflexible repetition of ineffective behavior, and avoidance of further stimulation being dysfunctional responses.

Training an adaptive, flexible response can be difficult when operators adhere to standard work instructions but then must detect and respond to novel environmental variations. This is compounded when responses of team members are interlocked to meet demands. Human errors may occur as near misses that increase risk but do not result in negative consequences. Errors, in these cases, may remain below detection and notification threshold and are often unreported. These events are resource intensive to investigate and without detectable consequence (Preischl & Hellmich, 2016) so opportunities to learn prevention is lost. There is value in examination of near misses as they can reveal undetected sources of variation. When design itself is prone to unknown error, operators may repeatedly encounter unpredicted stimuli without contacting a consequence. They may habituate to those stimuli (McSweeney, 2004;

McSweeney & Swindell, 2002) and not respond effectively to important signals. This has been termed "normalization of deviance" (Vaughn, 1996) and is a common feature of suboptimal work behavior learned by workers as they acclimate to the work setting. Habituation can also occur to established alarms as when a worker initially reacts to a warning signal in the environment, but over time the signal no longer occasions a response. A worker may fail to respond to an H^2S alarm despite being trained in the danger and protective action during drills, as there is no consequence for not responding if the alarm is set to blare at low concentrations. If the signal is not paired with a consequence to maintain the discriminative properties that control responses of survival, then stimulus control is lost. This helps explain why there are workers who complete training and understand the risks, but then deviate in the behavior in the field.

Flexibility training can successfully adapt the human response in ways that control room safety technologies cannot. Kim and Byun (2011) studied two licensed crew members of nuclear power operators in simulators. Operators were required to mitigate problems by coordinating team members with personnel outside the control room and expert raters scored their individual and team performance using a selection of measurement tools. Their nontechnical competencies were evaluated as attitudes (questionnaires), individual performance (video recording), and collective performance (video recording and simulator records). Results showed that CRM training increased "coordination, communication and team-spirit" most notable at the level of collective (team) performance. This is interesting as the impact was not significant when examined at the level of each individual. It suggests that all (or most) crew members are to be engaged in CRM training, not just the team leader, for results to be seen.

Carvalho, Benchekroun, and Gomes (2012) identify proactive process as key to the resilience of a nuclear power plant disrupted by variations. SAis maintained and validated through information dissemination occurring during shift changeovers. This is parallel to patient handoffs in the medical field where information exchange during shift changeover reduces error. Danielson, Alvinius, and Larsson (2014) report that SA establishes a common operating picture using values, routines, and rules to set context and prioritize communication. They found that distant proximity and communication barriers can create a disjointed SA while sufficient, timely dissemination of information can expand it. Communicating important information about dynamic environments via briefings and debriefings is critical to effective SA by teams working in complex systems.

Assessment of verbal communications entails measuring the speaker and listeners' behavior. These verbal exchanges can be coded along dimensions of specificity/ambiguity, completeness, accuracy, clarity and other indices of information transfer. Data on communications are taken through logbooks, formal and informal verbal exchanges, information panel walkthroughs, and documented transformation adjustments to scheduled plans. Some of these data streams are collected by the control systems; some are collected by direct observation (live or video) of social interactions. It is instructive to note that competency in a collective situation can be measured at the individual and team level and Kim and Byun (2011) reported the most significant results were seen at the team level where the context of CRM is the team members within a control room.

Crew leadership

As mentioned earlier, CRM necessitates the support of leadership to be effective in that hierarchical leaders are in the position to organize and manage the resources available for a job site. By identifying some key outcome measure (e.g., rates of injury), the safety performance of a leader can be assessed by the performance of a crew. Effective leaders result in effective crew members who produce desired results. Using crew safety as an example, effective crew leaders will design and manage contingencies in a work setting such that there are few, if any, injuries in that particular environment. An effective leader, therefore, facilitates the expected performance of their team (Abernathy, 1996, 2000, 2009; Houmanfar et al., 2009).

According to Houmanfar and Rodrigues (2012), the performance of teams relies on several factors that managers can alter in order to facilitate team success. Performance tends to be better when team members share the same goals and are committed to the same task. Establishing shared goals among team members can be accomplished by laying out a clear vision for the team that is in alignment with the goals and mission of the organization. Specifying clear rewards or outcomes that will arise from team success can also aid in increasing the reinforcer value of the team goals. The team will be more committed to the task if the goals are deemed important and team members believe that they can be achieved. If necessary, augmentals can be used to increase the importance of team goals while laying out a clear connection between the team actions and goals—placing feasible team behaviors in frames of before-after with the team goals—may help increase belief in the possibility of accomplishing the team goals.

It is important to note that leadership in this context is not restricted to organizational leaders; while these individuals are important to the systemic implementation of CRM, any member of a crew can demonstrate leadership. Krapfl and Kruja (2015) identify two key features of leadership: the term itself describes a wide variety of behaviors, and the context in which leadership is observed must be accounted for. A detailed account is given of a "Leadership Behavior Menu," in which behavioral factors of leadership are identified that can be applied in a wide variety of contexts by many different individuals. Some of these leadership behaviors overlap with the most important skills of CRM; therefore, we can see this menu as a list of competencies for leaders. Components of this menu are mapped onto the critical skills of CRM below.

Crew leaders' foci

Collective SA

While not explicitly discussed by Krapfl and Kruja (2015) as a component of leadership, SA can be related to their description of execution skills. Essentially, this describes the ability of crew leaders to make things happen. This does not solely refer to the planning stages of some project or task. Rather, this involves seeing the project or task through to completion by engaging the team throughout the process. Leaders in this regard do not sit back and let others execute the plan for them. Instead, they are involved in each stage of the plan's implementation. It is during this critical stage that SA is essential. The execution of plans will inevitably deviate off course. Effective leaders will perceive, comprehend, and project the changes in a given situation and help guide the team back on course. They create and convey a common picture of the situation so all crew members are aligned. At times, external forces (e.g., demands from clients) may question the integrity of operations and threaten to disrupt teamwork. The effective leader responds to such intrusions and defends the crew members from distractions so that the crew manages the integrity of the process underway.

Leadership of teamwork

Team-building skills and enabling skills (Abernathy, 1996; Houmanfar, Alavosius, Morford, Herbst, & Reimer, 2015; Krapfl & Kruja, 2015) are leadership behaviors that focus on teamwork. Team-building skills involve the selection of effective team members and are therefore necessarily directed toward upper-level leaders in an organizational hierarchy. In CRM the leader is responsible for ensuring that all members of the crew have the competencies necessary to perform their particular task. To do this, they need to utilize the resources that characterize the roles that perform the task and measure the capacity of the team members performing a particular task to ensure that each crewmember is qualified for the role that they fill. This can be explicitly verified during briefing events where the leader confirms that all crew members are present, ready, and able to complete the upcoming tasks. Enabling skills, on the other hand, involve fostering opportunities for team member growth. Many different members of a team can accomplish this. Leaders, in that regard, can come from any level of the organization. Delegation, support, guidance, and feedback are all achievable by each member on a collaborative team. When members of a team work in coordination with a common goal, they create interlocking contingencies that are reinforced at the group level. This interlocked behavior, by definition, puts members of a crew into contact with other members of a crew, which then may create collective contingencies for the tasks being performed.

CRM, leadership, social validity, and HRO culture

Krapfl and Kruja (2015) conclude that the establishment of an organizational culture is "more influenced by the leader than any other single factor." In order to build and sustain a culture of safety, for instance, leaders within HROs must demonstrate the importance of this focus through their own behavior. A leader's emphasis on the importance of CRM, for instance, helps create a safety culture in which organizational members are more likely to adhere to safer behaviors both individually and in team contexts. This is in part due to the nature of CRM as a system of targeting SA, communication, and teamwork at the individual and group level.

Team leaders within HROs have the opportunity to create a work environment in which prosocial behavior is highly valued. Pro-social behavior in these industries can range from ensuring the safety of members of a crew to minimizing or avoiding any detrimental outcomes of work processes on the environment (i.e. a catastrophic oil spill or fatal airplane crash). Recall reports of US Airways flight 1549 being struck by a flock of birds, resulting in the malfunction of both engines. Captain Chesley "Sully" Sullenberger's exemplary leadership resulted in a controlled water landing that saved the lives of all 155 on board the plane. During the ensuing investigations, it was determined through flight simulations that any other alternative course of action would have resulted in mass casualties and destruction of property. The individual and collective behavior of the captain and crew members define exemplary responding of the flight crew in a crisis situation and set performance aims, which might be established in training other flight crew.

Houmanfar et al. (2015) identify three key features of prosocial behavior: "(a) operating in the context of positive reinforcement contingencies for others, (b) minimizing aversive or coercive conditions and contingencies of others while not explicitly operating as *part* of those conditions or contingencies, and (c) aiding others in identifying or achieving optimal levels of choice." On an oil rig, the WSLs, for instance, are in the position to create contingencies supportive of safety behaviors for their team that meet this definition by (a) reinforcing adherence to SOPs during typical working conditions or to acceptable behavior variation leading to beneficial outcomes during a potential crisis event; (b) providing feedback for erred performance in a nonaversive manner, even allowing team members the opportunity to correct mistakes rather than punishing behavior; and (c) providing opportunities for behavioral variation when plausible.

Conclusion

CRM is a systemic intervention that focuses on the reduction of human error through training and behavioral change, while utilizing contextual resources available to assist in these aims. Many different organizations across high-reliability industries have proposed their own account of what skills constitute effective

CRM. We posit that these skills can be grouped together into six broad behavioral classes: communication, SA, decision making, teamwork, managing human capacity, and leadership. Each of these behavioral classes were examined from a behavioral perspective, and relevant analogous research was discussed.

Review of the literature indicates that many HROs are developing expertise in behavior science applications to enhance CRM. The initiatives reveal common directions and areas for cross industry dissemination. Table 1 illustrates the status of key features of CRM in the selected industries reviewed in this paper.

Aviation is the exemplar industry with the most mature CRM processes enabled by high-fidelity simulators and a well-established competency framework to assess crew capability. The nuclear power industry also has an impressive safety record with advanced training and simulators. Medicine is challenged by a culture of under-reporting, likely as a result of malpractice issues, with uncertain metrics on patient safety and medical error. Medicine is pursuing CRM and looks to aviation and military applications for inspiration. Oil field services are initiating formal CRM training and developing a competency framework to gauge the ability of WSLs for CRM, although, rig simulators are relatively low fidelity when compared to those used in aviation.

Effective training and maintenance of these CRM and leadership behavioral classes will help create and maintain an organizational culture with an emphasis on respect and safety. Additionally, the effective implementation of CRM allows organizations to address prosocial behavior in a more effective manner; from keeping their own employees safe to preventing major catastrophes with widescale environmental impact.

The role of leadership in creating and fostering an organizational culture, which effectively utilizes CRM, is essential. From organizational leaders' power to implement change across an entire system down to instances of leadership from a member of a crew in promotion of CRM, the function of leadership is essential to sustaining the shift to (and continued use of) CRM in any given organization. Such a shift is especially critical in high-risk industries, as promising results have been demonstrated by those leading industries implementing CRM: aviation, medicine, and nuclear power. The oil field services industry is poised to follow suit and create work environments that are safer for both their employees and the environment in which they operate. As with other high-risk industries, oil field services span the globe, therefore, the potential impact is quite substantial.

The focus on crew behavior in the context of CRM is a useful approach for behavior analysis. By analyzing communication networks, instructions (e.g., SOPs) and other rules, verbal coordination of behaviors, accuracy and latency of responding, and the interlocked behaviors seen in team dynamics, we can objectively measure skills of CRM. By adding objective measurement elements to CRM skills, behavior analysis is extending the conceptual literature from cognitive psychology. Analyzing key behaviors in their context allows us to develop measures of competency that can be used to inform organizational leaders with respect to training, employee feedback, policy changes, and other pragmatic adjustments to the work environments in HROs.

References

Abernathy, W. B. (1996). *Sin of wages*. Memphis, TN: PerfSys Press.

Abernathy, W. B. (2000). *Managing without supervising: Creating an organization-wide performance system*. Memphis, TN: PerfSys Press.

Abernathy, W. B. (2009). Walden two revisited: Optimizing behavioral systems. *Journal of Organizational Behavior Management, 29,* 175–192. doi:10.1080/01608060902874567

Alavosius, M. P., Houmanfar, R., & Rodriquez, N. J. (2005, November). Unity of Purpose/ Unity of Effort: Private-sector preparedness in times of terror. *Disaster Prevention and Management, 14*(5), 666–680. doi:10.1108/09653560510634098

Bar-Yam, Y. (1997). *Dynamics of complex systems*. Reading, MA: Addison-Wesley.

Binder, C. (1996). Behavioral fluency: Evolution of a new paradigm. *The Behavior Analyst, 19,* 163–197.

Blakely, E., & Schlinger, H. (1987). Rules: Function-altering contingency-specifying stimuli. *The Behavior Analyst, 10*(2), 183–187.

Brown, T. W., & Alavosius, M. P. (2014). Language and discounting behavior (unpublished doctoral dissertation – Alavosius Advisor). University of Nevada Reno, Reno, NV.

Carvalho, P. V. R. D., Benchekroun, T. H., & Gomes, J. O. (2012). Analysis of information exchange activities to actualize and validate situation awareness during shift changeovers in nuclear power plants. *Human Factors and Ergonomics in Manufacturing & Service Industries, 22*(2), 130–144. doi:10.1002/hfm.20201

Chase, P. N., & Bjarnadottir, G. S. (1992). Instructing variability: Some features of a problem-solving repertoire. In S. C. Hayes, & L. J. Hayes (Eds.), *Understanding verbal relations* (pp. 181–193). Reno, NV: Context Press.

Cima, R. R., Kollengode, A., Storsveen, A. S., Weisbrod, C. A., Deschamps, C., Koch, M. B., & Pool, S. R. (2009). A multidisciplinary team approach to retained foreign objects. *Joint Commission Journal on Quality Patient Safety, 35*(3), 123–132. doi:10.1016/S1553-7250(09)35016-3

Craig, C. (2012). Improving flight condition situational awareness through human centered design. *Work, 41,* 4523–4531. doi:10.3233/WOR-2012-0031-4523

Danielsson, E., Alvinius, A., & Larsson, G. (2014). From common operating picture to situational awareness. *International Journal of Emergency Management, 10*(1), 28–47. doi:10.1504/IJEM.2014.061659

Deepwater Horizon Study Group. (2011). *Investigation of the macondo well blowout disaster*. Retrieved from http://ccrm.berkeley.edu/pdfs_papers/bea_pdfs/dhsgfinalreport-march2011-tag.pdf

Dekker, S. W., & Woods, D. W. (2009). The high reliability organization perspective. In E. Salas, & D. Maurino (Eds.), *Human factors in aviation* (2nd ed., pp. 123–146). New York, NY: Wiley.

Durso, F. T., Dattel, A. R., & Tremblay, S. (2004). SPAM: The real-time assessment of SA. *A Cognitive Approach to Situation Awareness: Theory and Application, 1,* 137–154.

Endsley, M. R. (1988, May). *Situation awareness global assessment technique (SAGAT)*. Aerospace and Electronics Conference, 1988. NAECON 1988. Proceedings of the IEEE 1988 National (pp. 789–795). Dayton, OH: IEEE.

Endsley, M. R. (1995a). Toward a theory of situation awareness in dynamic systems. *Human Factors, 37,* 32–64. doi:10.1518/001872095779049543

Endsley, M. R. (1995b). Measurement of situation awareness in dynamic systems. *Human Factors, 37*, 65–84. doi:10.1518/001872095779049499

Epps, H. R., & Levin, P. E. (2015). The TeamSTEPPS approach to safety and quality. *Journal of Pediatric Orthopedics, 35*(5), S30–S33. doi:10.1097/BPO.0000000000000541

Flaxman, P. E., Bond, F. W., & Livheim, F. (2013). *The mindful and effective employee: An Acceptance & Commitment Therapy training manual for improving well-being and performance.* Oakland, CA: New Harbinger Publication, Inc.

Flin, R., & O'Connor, P. (2001). Applying crew resource management in offshore oil platforms. In E. Salas, C. A. Bowers, & E. Edens (Eds.), *Improving teamwork in organizations: Applications of resource management training* (pp. 217–233). Hillsdale, NJ: Erlbaum.

Gaba, D., Howard, S., Fish, K., Smith, B., & Yasser, S. (2001). Simulation-based training in anesthesia crisis resource management (ACRM): A decade of experience. *Simulation & Gaming, 32*(2), 175–193. doi:10.1177/104687810103200206

Gilbert, T. F. (1978, 2007). *Human competence: Engineering worthy performance.* Publication of the International Society for Performance Improvement. San Francisco, CA: Pfeiffer.

Gillespie, B. M., Gwinner, K., Fairweather, N., & Chaboyer, W. (2013). Building shared situational awareness in surgery through distributed dialog. *Journal of Multidisciplinary Healthcare, 6*, 109–118. doi:10.2147/JMDH.S40710

Glenn, S. S. (1988). Contingencies and metacontingencies: Toward a synthesis of behavior analysis and cultural materialism. *The Behavior Analyst, 11*, 161–179.

Glenn, S. S. (2004). Individual behavior, culture, and social change. *The Behavior Analyst, 27*, 133–151.

Green, L., & Myerson, J. (2004). A discounting framework for choice with delayed and probabilistic rewards. *Psychological Bulletin, 130*, 169–792. doi:10.1037/0033-2909.130.5.769

Haig, K., & Sutton, S. (2006). SBAR: A shared mental model for improving communication between clinicians. *Joint Commission Journal on Quality Patient Safety, 32*(167–175). doi:10.1016/S1553-7250(06)32022-3

Hamilton, W. I., Kazem, M. L. N., He, X., & Dumolo, D. (2013). Practical human factors integration in the nuclear industry. *Cognition, Technology & Work, 15*(1), 5–12. doi:10.1007/s10111-012-0213-z

Hayes, S. C., Barnes-Holmes, D., & Roche, B. (2001). *Relational frame theory: A post-Skinnerian account of human language and cognition.* New York, NY: Guilford Press.

Haynes, J., & Strickler, J. (2014). TeamSTEPPS makes strides for better communication. *Nursing, 44*(1), 62–63. doi:10.1097/01.NURSE.0000438725.66087.89

Houmanfar, R., & Johnson, R. (2003). Organizational implications of gossip and rumor. *Journal of Organizational Behavior Management, 23*, 117–138. doi:10.1300/J075v23n02_07

Houmanfar, R. A., Alavosius, M. P., Morford, Z. H., Herbst, S. A., & Reimer, D. (2015). Functions of organizational leaders in cultural change: Financial and social well-being. *Journal of Organizational Behavior Management, 35*, 4–27. doi:10.1080/01608061.2015.1035827

Houmanfar, R. A., & Rodrigues, N. J. (2012). The role of leadership and communication in organizational change. *Journal of Applied Radical Behavior Analysis, N1*, 22–27.

Houmanfar, R. A., Rodrigues, N. J., & Smith, G. S. (2009). Role of communication networks in behavioral systems analysis. *Journal of Organizational Behavior Management, 29*, 257–275. doi:10.1080/01608060903092102

Houmanfar, R. A., Rodrigues, N. J., & Ward, T. A. (2010). Emergence and metacontingency: Points of contact and departure. *Behavior and Social Issues, 19*, 78–103. doi:10.5210/bsi.v19i0.3065

Howard, S., Gaba, D., & Fish, K. (1992). Anesthesia crisis resource management training: Teaching anesthesiologists to handle critical incidents. *Aviation, Space, and Environmental Medicine, 63*(9), 763–770.

IOGP. Report 501. (2014a). *Crew resource management for well operations teams*. Project commissioned by OGP's Safety Committee and the Well Experts Committee to the University of Aberdeen. International Association of Oil & Gas Producers.

IOGP. Report 502. (2014b). *Guidelines for implementing well operations crew resource management training*. Well Experts Committee. Training, Competence & Human Factors Task Force. International Association of Oil & Gas Producers.

Jenkins, J. C., & Gallimore, J. J. (2008). Configural features of helmet-mounted displays to enhance pilot situational awareness. *Aviation, Space, and Environmental Medicine, 79*(4), 397–407. doi:10.3357/ASEM.2195.2008

Kanki, B., Helmreich, R., & Anca, J., & ScienceDirect (Online service). (2010). *Crew resource management* (2nd ed.). Amsterdam, Boston: Academic Press/Elsevier.

Killingsworth, K., Miller, S. A., & Alavosius, M. P. (2016). A Behavioral interpretation of situational awareness: Prospects for organizational behavior management. *Journal of Organizational Behavior Management, 36*(4), 301–321. doi:10.1080/01608061.2016.1236056

Kim, S. K., & Byun, S. N. (2011). Effects of Crew Resource Management training on the team performance of operators in an advanced nuclear power plant. *Journal of Nuclear Science and Technology, 48*(9), 1256–1264. doi:10.1080/18811248.2011.9711814

King, H. B., Battles, J., Baker, D. P., Alonso, A., Salas, E., Webster, J., ... Salisbury, M. (2008). TeamSTEPPS: Team strategies and tools to enhance performance and patient safety. In K. Henricksen, J. B. Battles, M. A. Keyes, & M. L. Grady (Eds.), *Advances in patient safety: New directions and alternative approaches (Volume 3: Performance and Tools)*. Rockville, MD: Agency for Healthcare Research and Quality.

Krapfl, J. E., & Kruja, B. (2015). Leadership and culture. *Journal of Organizational Behavior Management, 35*, 28–43. doi:10.1080/01608061.2015.1031431

Malott, M. M., & Glenn, S. S. (2006). Targets of intervention in cultural and behavioral change. *Behavior and Social Issues, 15*, 31–56. doi:10.5210/bsi.v15i1.344

Mann, S., Marcus, R., & Sachs, B. (2006). Lessons from the cockpit: How team training can reduce errors in L&D. *Contemporary OB/GYN, 51*, 34.

Maraccini, A. M. (2016). *Examining the impact of an interprofessional education training package on communication during handoff performance in medical and nursing students: A Behavior analytic approach to assessment and intervention* (unpublished doctoral dissertation--Houmanfar Advisor). University of Nevada Reno, Reno, NV.

Maraccini, A. M., Houmanfar, R. A., & Szarko, A. (2016). Motivation and complex verbal phenomena: Implications for organizational research and practice. *Journal of Organizational Behavior Management, 36*, 282–300. doi:10.1080/01608061.2016.1211062

McSweeney, F. K. (2004). Dynamic changes in reinforcer effectiveness: Satiation and habituation have different implications for theory and practice. *The Behavior Analyst, 27*(2), 171–188.

McSweeney, F. K., & Swindell, S. (2002). Common processes may contribute to extinction and habituation. *The Journal of General Psychology, 129*, 364–400. doi:10.1080/00221300209602103

Meshkati, N. (1997, April). *Human performance, organizational factors, and safety culture*. NTSB symposium on corporate culture and transportation safety, Washington, DC.

Morey, J. C., Simon, R., Jay, G. D., Wears, R. L., Salisbury, M., Dukes, K. A., & Berns, S. D. (2002). Error reduction and performance improvement in the emergency department through formal teamwork training: Evaluation results of the MedTeams project. *Health Services Research, 37*(6), 1553–1581. doi:10.1111/hesr.2002.37.issue-6

Moriarity, D. (2015). *Practical human factors for pilots*. London, UK: Elsevier.

Naderpour, M., Lu, J., & Zhang, G. (2016). A safety-critical decision support system evaluation using situation awareness and workload measures. *Reliability Engineering & System Safety*, *150*, 147–159. doi:10.1016/j.ress.2016.01.024

Northwest Airlines. (2005). *Flight operations manual (9.5.1)*. Eagan, MN: Northwest Airlines.

Preischl, W., & Hellmich, M. (2016). Human error probabilities from operational experience of German nuclear power plants, Part II. *Reliability Engineering & System Safety*, *148*, 44–56. doi:10.1016/j.ress.2015.11.011

Salmon, P., Stanton, N., Walker, G., & Green, D. (2006). Situation awareness measurement: A review of applicability for C4i environments. *Applied Ergonomics*, *37*(2), 225–238. doi:10.1016/j.apergo.2005.02.00

Savage, I. (2013). Comparing the fatality risks in United States transportation across modes and over time. *Research in Transportation Economics*, *43*(1), 9–22. doi:10.1016/j.retrec.2012.12.011

Sigurdsson, S. O., Taylor, M. A., & Wirth, O. (2013). Discounting the value of safety: Effects of perceived risk and effort. *Journal of Safety Research*, *46*, 127–134. doi:10.1016/j.jsr.2013.04.006

Simon, R., Langford, V., Locke, A., Morey, J. C., Risser, D., & Salisbury, M. (2000). A successful transfer of lessons learned in aviation psychology and flight safety to health care: the MedTeams system. *Patient Safety Initiative*, 45–49.

Skinner, B. F. (1957). *Verbal behavior*. New York, NY: Appleton-Century-Crofts.

Skinner, B. F. (1974). *About behaviorism*. New York, NY: Vintage.

Smith, G. S., Houmanfar, R., & Denny, M. (2012). Impact of rule accuracy on productivity and rumor in an organizational analog. *Journal of Organizational Behavior Management*, *32*, 3–25. doi:10.1080/01608061.2012.646839

Smith, G. S., Houmanfar, R. A., & Louis, S. J. (2011). The participatory role of verbal behavior in an elaborated account of metacontingency: From conceptualization to investigation. *Behavior and Social Issues*, *20*, 122–146.

Stewart, I., Barns-Holmes, D., Barnes-Holmes, Y., Bond, F. W., & Hayes, S. C. (2006). Relational frame theory and industrial/organizational psychology. *Journal of Organizational Behavior Management*, *26*, 55–90. doi:10.1300/J075v26n01_03

Sullenberger, C., & Zaslow, J. (2009). *Highest duty: My search for what really matters*. New York, NY: William Morrow & Company.

Turner, P. (2012). Implementation of TeamSTEPPS in the emergency department. *Critical Care Nursing Quarterly*, *35*(3), 208–212. doi:10.1097/CNQ.0b013e3182542c6c

United States Federal Aviation Administration (FAA). (1991). *Advisory circular: Aeronautical decision making*. AC No: 60-22. US Department of Transportation. Retrieved from http://rgl.faa.gov/Regulatory_and_Guidance_Library/rgAdvisoryCircular.nsf

United States Federal Aviation Administration (FAA). (2004). *Advisory circular: Crew resource management training*. Washington, DC: U.S. Dept. of Transportation, Federal Aviation Administration.

Vaughn, D. (1996). *The Challenger launch decision: Risky technology, culture, and deviance at NASA*. Chicago, IL: University of Chicago Press.

Vidulich, M. A., Stratton, M., Crabtree, M., & Wilson, G. (1994). Performance-based and physiological measures of situational awareness. *Aviation, Space, and Environmental Medicine*, *65*(5), A7–A12.

Waag, W. L. (1994). Tools for assessing situational awareness in an operational fighter environment. *Aviation, Space, and Environmental Medicine*, *65*(5), A13–A19.

Wagener, F., & Ison, D. (2014). Crew resource management in commercial aviation. *Journal of Aviation Technology and Engineering*, *3*(2), 2–13. doi:10.7771/2159-6670.1077

Ward, M., Zhu, X., Lampman, M., & Stewart, G. (2015). TeamSTEPPS implementation in community hospitals. *International Journal of Quality Assurance, 28*(3), 234–244.

Wulfert, E., Greenway, D. E., Farkas, P., Hayes, S. C., & Dougher, S. C. (1994). Correlation between self-reported rigidity and rule-governed insensitivity to operant contingencies. *Journal of Applied Behavior Analysis, 27*(4), 659–671. doi:10.1901/jaba.1994.27-659

Yang, C. W., Yang, L. C., Cheng, T. C., Jou, Y. T., & Chiou, S.-W. (2012). Assessing mental workload and situation awareness in the evaluation of computerized procedures in the main control room. *Nuclear Engineering and Design, 250*, 713–719. doi:10.1016/j.nucengdes.2012.05.038

Zeltser, M. V., & Nash, D. B. (2010). Approaching the evidence basis for aviation-derived teamwork training in medicine. *American Journal of Medical Quality, 25*(1), 13–23. doi:10.1177/1062860609345664

Behavioral Education in the 21st Century

KENT JOHNSON

Behavior analysis significantly impacted education in the 20th century with many procedures for improving behavior, management, and instruction. Today, 21st century education is grappling with other goals that behavior analysis can also address, especially the need to broaden its focus from knowledge acquisition to real-world application, communication, and problem solving. Recent developments in flipped classroom approaches are ripe for behavior analysis technology, as are socially engaged approaches such as project-based learning. I outline a generative instruction approach to application and activity-driven education that improves social interaction, and thinking, reasoning, and problem solving in the classroom. Current interests in broader approaches to improving schools by addressing poverty and economic inequality with interventions that foster nurturing environments and prosociality also provide opportunities for applying behavior analysis, particularly community school experiments. We should hitch a ride on all these fronts to remain relevant and productive members of educational communities in the 21st century.

WHAT WE HAVE ACCOMPLISHED IN K–12 EDUCATION

Behavior analysis has developed many procedures that have been implemented in hundreds of K–12 schools and colleges throughout the United States, Canada, and overseas. Empirically supported methods, tools, and curricula have been developed for changing a wide variety of behavior. Behavioral education has designed classroom procedures to increase academic engaged time, set expectations for learning and performance, systematically praise and ignore behavior, and organize and manage classrooms. Popular procedures include our good behavior game, token economies, and daily report cards. Behavioral education has also developed discipline procedures, including reprimanding, time out from positive reinforcement, response cost, and positive practice (Mayer, Sulzer-Azaroff, & Wallace, 2012). In a large-scale effort, behavior analysts have developed Positive Behavior Interventions and Supports, a school-wide system of positive discipline (Horner, Sugai, & Anderson, 2010; Positive Behavioral Interventions and Supports, 2015). This system thrives in more than 10,000 American schools to date.

Behavior analysis has also developed teaching methods, tools, and specially designed curricula for establishing academic repertoires. Tom Gilbert's mathetics (Markle, 1990) and its offspring, Direct Instruction (Engelmann & Carnine, 1982), involve a four-step, recursive procedure that is widely used in American education today: (a) Model, demonstrate, and show, (b), guide first performance attempts, (c) test or release students to perform on their own, and (d) provide delayed testing to ensure maintenance. Classwide peer tutoring (Delquadri, Greenwood, Whorton, Carta, & Hall, 1986) is another instructional procedure developed by behavior analysts that is popular in American education. Ogden Lindsley's precision teaching (K. Johnson & Street, 2013, 2014a; K. J. Johnson & Street, 2012), the methodology of building newly acquired skills and strategies to fluency with acceleration, helped spawn the requirement that federal dollars in primary education be awarded contingent on using reading programs that emphasize reading fluency (U.S. Department of Education, Reading First, 2014).

A survey of current education-related practices is reflected in the various topics of chapters in two recent edited volumes of behavior analysis research. Madden (2013) includes chapters on intellectual and developmental disabilities, autism, verbal behavior, severe problem behavior, attention-deficit/hyperactivity disorder, and reading. McSweeney and Murphy (2014) include chapters on autism, parenting, education, developmental disabilities, precision teaching, contingency management, and verbal behavior.

WHAT WE HAVE ACCOMPLISHED IN HIGHER EDUCATION

Our behavior analytic 20th-century higher education accomplishments focused on knowledge acquisition. Cognitive behavioral psychologist Benjamin Bloom (1980) developed mastery learning in the 1960s at the same time behavior analysts developed their own procedures for mastery learning. We developed programed instruction (PI; Skinner, 1968/2003), the Personalized System of Instruction (PSI; K. R. Johnson & Ruskin, 1977; Keller, 1968), and a Computer Assisted Personalized System of Instruction (CAPSI;

Pear & Martin, 2004). These methods were enormously popular in college teaching in the 1960s and 1970s. Hundreds of college courses in over 40 different fields of study used programmed instruction, PSI, and CAPSI (K. R. Johnson & Ruskin, 1977). Madden's (2013) edited volume of research also includes a chapter on higher education.

Despite these accomplishments, a glaring problem currently hinders American education's success. A broader application of behavior analysis concepts and principles could provide significant solutions.

SOME CURRENT PROBLEMS IN AMERICAN K–12 EDUCATION

Headlines identify poor academic achievement as the major problem in public education compared with achievement in other countries. Federal programs such as No Child Left Behind (NCLB; U.S. Department of Education, No Child Left Behind, 2015) and Race to the Top (RTTT; U.S. Department of Education, Race To The Top Fund, 2014) and other statewide efforts (State of Washington, Elementary and Secondary Education Act, 2014) focus on student achievement and teacher quality, defined by test score results, as the target behaviors to change. These programs oversimplify the problems with American education by focusing narrowly on student achievement on paper-and-pencil or computer-generated high-stakes tests. Since 2001, states have been diverting hundreds of millions of dollars each year to testing and test preparation. In some districts, 20% of school days are spent on test preparation because their very existence depends on their test scores (Ravitch, 2013).

A large and growing number of educators are proponents of a backlash against high-stakes testing, arguing that other important goals of education are being ignored, such as communicating and engaging with others, developing participatory citizens who have a broad perspective about the nature of a good society and how to propel democracy into the future, inspiring learners to be independent and creative thinkers and problem solvers in their daily lives, and developing character (Ravitch, 2013). These arguments are consistent with the broader view of knowing, understanding, and cognition advocated by B. F. Skinner and other radical behaviorists (e.g., Skinner, 1974). In that account, cognition involves the whole organism in interaction with its environment. The demarcation between thought and action is considered artificial. Knowing is ongoing behavior in interaction with an environment. Comprehensive education involves a full range of activities beyond taking tests that teach the learner to apply initial learning under real-world contingencies. Skinner's vision of educating the whole person to successfully behave under real-world contingencies is detailed in his utopian novel, *Walden Two* (Skinner, 1948).

Recent neuroscientific research in embodied and embedded cognition supports the radical behavioral position. Beilock (2015) describes research demonstrating how critical movement is for understanding. She describes Glenberg's (2004) research showing that third-grade children who solved a word problem by acting it out were two times more likely to get the problem correct than students who did not. Glenberg, Jaworski, Rischal, and Levin's (2007) research in reading comprehension extended these findings by demonstrating that first and second graders assigned to an action reading group who acted out events described in each sentence of a passage with toy objects answered more questions about the passage correctly and remembered at least 50% more details of the story compared to students who read each passage twice. To quote Beilock,

> This new research in embodied learning helps provide a roadmap for how to structure educational activities to best help kids learn. The mind is not an abstract information processor largely divorced from the body and the environment. It is highly influenced by the body and movement. (p. 57)

Other embodied cognitive scientists describe both embodied and environmentally embedded approaches to cognition and explicitly align themselves with radical behaviorism, including Chemero (2009), who recently gave an invited address at the 2010 Association for Behavior Analysis International conference, and Louise Barrett (2011; 2014), who actually wrote a chapter for a comparative evolutionary psychology handbook titled *Why Behaviorism Isn't Satanism* (Barrett, 2014).

APPLICATION ACTIVITY–DRIVEN EDUCATION IN THE FLIPPED CLASSROOM IN GRADES 6–12

Many middle school and high school math, science, and social studies teachers across America are replacing traditional classroom activities—teachers telling, showing, and lecturing for knowledge acquisition—with videos that can be watched at home. Thousands of teachers nationwide are assigning Salman Khan's Internet-based lectures and exercises as homework. The Khan Academy website (The Khan Academy, 2015) is packed with short videos and exercises in logical sequences to learn math, science, finances, and more. Khan also incorporates many behavioral procedures in conjunction with the lecture videos, including pretests, goal setting, progress mapping, time management, badges to earn along the way, and social network formats. In addition, inspired by Khan Academy, thousands of teachers are making their own videos to introduce skills, concepts, and principles and assigning their videos as homework, along with correlated readings and websites. Schools with at-risk learners who do not have the capacity to watch homework videos could use their federal after-school dollars to establish video laboratories.

So what was traditionally classwork is now becoming homework. And what was formerly homework is now becoming classwork. These middle and high school teachers devote class time to exercises, problem sets, and projects that were formerly homework, greatly increasing peer and teacher interaction and focusing on a wide variety of cognitive behaviors. Students are receiving much more ongoing feedback on activities than they could when it was assigned as homework.

Educators call this model the "flipped classroom" (Knewton, 2014). More than 15,000 teachers currently belong to the flipped learning network (www.flippedlearning.org). Because no data exist on the effectiveness of these modern activity-driven shifts in education, behavior analysts should conduct rigorous experimental analyses of Kahn Academy as well as flipped classroom procedures.

Reading the flipped classroom network entries you will see that mastery learning is resurging! With mastery learning, students study and perform on assessments until they reach a mastery criterion. This arrangement requires self-pacing—not every student reaches the mastery criterion at the same time, so time to learn is variable. In typical educational settings, time to learn is a constant: A test is administered, ready or not, on a certain calendar date, or an activity is assigned and then due on a specific date. So learning flips from a constant time frame to a variable time frame. In mastery learning we see another flip: Performance criteria are now constant, not variable. In traditional education when performance is evaluated on a certain calendar date, students perform variably. Some perform in the excellent range, some are good, some are average, and some are poor. In mastery learning, performance criteria are constant: Everyone works until they reach the criteria. They do not vary. So with mastery learning resurging in flipped classrooms we see the double flipped classroom. Not only do home and school activities flip their time slots, but now time to learn flips from a constant to a variable, and performance criteria flip from a variable to a constant.

The October 23, 2013, *New York Times* reported that flipped classroom teachers are also reading behavior analysis procedures. They are reading Bloom's classic 1968 article "Learning for Mastery"; they are reading his 1980 book *All Our Children Learning;* and they are reading Kulik, Kulik, Bangert-Drowns, and Slavin's (1990) meta-analysis of mastery learning, which prominently displays the effects of Keller and Sherman's PSI (Keller, 1968).

APPLICATION ACTIVITY–DRIVEN HIGHER EDUCATION

It is alarming to note that behavior analysis programs in higher education are nearly extinct; it is very hard to locate more than a dozen colleges and universities that still implement PI, PSI, or CAPSI. The dearth of current PI, PSI, and CAPSI applications may reflect higher education's rejection of their narrow focus on test scores and need to focus on embodied and embedded cognitive behavior.

Baker et al. (2015/this issue) from the University of Nevada School of Medicine (UNSOM) and Behavior Analysis Program offer an excellent discussion in "Cultural Change in a Medical School: A Data-Driven Management of Entropy." They describe the contradictions inherent in medical schools, which reward faculty for independent, entrepreneurial research and clinical practice, though the result is a fragmented, nonhierarchical faculty structure and culture. Using an interview-driven approach based on Houmanfar's behavioral systems analysis of UNSOM and objective measurement of implicit attitudes and biases of medical students, Baker and his colleagues describe how a series of curricular innovations to address their problems, monitored by continuous faculty interviewing, and assessment of medical students' biases transformed their culture to one with greater faculty engagement, a collectively designed curriculum sequence, and a focus on "communication, investment, accountability, transparency and partnership."

Using the power of behavioral systems analysis and continuous verbal monitoring, the UNSOM faculty progressed to a collective understanding of the best interests of the larger medical school environment and subordinated their individual worlds to the needs of the larger school environment. The resulting faculty interactivity also unexpectedly moved their curriculum away from lecturing and other passive processes for knowledge acquisition and toward more activity-driven education, focusing on lifelong learning, teamwork competencies, and contemporary problems in health care and healthy living. These changes created a much more satisfied faculty and student body. UNSOM's communication process arrived at a place consistent with a radical behavioral account of education.

Behavior analysts should learn from Houmanfar's UNSOM results and move efforts beyond knowledge acquisition in both K–12 and higher education, consistent with a radical behavioral account of education (Baker et al., 2015). Activity-driven education is where a communicative process may likely lead. An emphasis on application activities provides opportunities for students to learn to apply their learning in real-world contexts while being supported by teacher and peer coaching.

So, if knowledge acquisition occurs outside of class time, enhanced with mastery learning procedures such as PSI, CAPSI, and PI, then class time can be devoted to activities that benefit from active social engagement and peer and teacher coaching. But just what should those activities look like? Behavior analysis can design many models.

GENERATIVITY IN K–12 AND HIGHER EDUCATION

One model takes this opportunity to emphasize *generativity* in the classroom in a 21st-century behavioral approach to progressive education akin to what

John Dewey described at the turn of the 20th century (Dewey, 1902/1976). Let me clarify what I mean by *generativity*. Educators cannot possibly teach everything that needs to be learned in order to become an effective, independent adult. Even full mastery of an entire curriculum would not do the trick. Effective citizens must demonstrate generativity. They must engage in behaviors they have learned in instruction under a vastly wider variety of stimuli and context than those presented in classrooms. They engage in novel untaught blends and recombinations of behavior that they learned in school in the context of new stimuli not presented in previous instruction. Effective citizens must learn how to learn without teachers and instruction. Other ways people talk about generativity include generalization beyond instruction, figuring things out, creative discovery, and so forth.

Some behavior analysts have already started to design and research how to teach students to figure out solutions to problems without directly teaching them. At least six groups of behavior analysts have been studying generativity. This work began with Skinner and Epstein's generativity demonstrations in the Columbian simulation project in the 1970s. About the same time, Israel Goldiamond developed a nonlinear and systemic research and therapy model at the University of Chicago (Goldiamond, 1975; Layng, 2009). Also in the 1970s, Murray Sidman's stimulus equivalence paradigm fostered a research program at Northeastern University in Boston that looked at generative behavior (Sidman, 2009). Johnson and Layng's generative instruction model developed at Morningside Academy in Seattle in the 1980s has been adopted by more than 140 public schools and agencies in the United States, Canada, and Europe to date (K. Johnson & Street, 2014a, 2014b; K. J. Johnson & Street, 2004, 2012). Vicci Tucci's competent learner model, which provides staff development for professionals and paraprofessionals who work with children with autism and developmental disabilities, also focuses on arranging contingencies to promote generative performance (Tucci, Hursh, & Laitinen, 2004). Steve Hayes's relational framework theory model (Fox, 2015) also studies verbally produced generative phenomena.

In the Morningside model of generative instruction (K. Johnson & Street, 2014a, 2014b; K. J. Johnson & Street, 2004, 2012) we have designed procedures for teaching that require students to engage more frequently in figuring out how to do things without being taught and to apply what has been taught without being shown, all based on previous teaching. We make generativity more likely by teaching generative repertoires such as questioning diagramming, thinking through interacting, and organizational repertoires. Teachers across the spectrum from kindergarten to professional education assume their students know how to think, reason, and problem solve, but many do not. Many students do not engage in self-questioning. Many students do not know how to reason a problem to a solution and think by interacting with others. Many are also disorganized and inefficient in their thinking.

GENERATIVITY WITH TALK-ALOUD PROBLEM SOLVING

Let us examine one generative repertoire that an effective adult must demonstrate: reasoning from problem to solution. In a radical behavior analysis of thinking and reasoning, thinking is behavior even if we cannot see it. Deciding what to buy at a grocery store involves reasoning, solving a math word problem involves reasoning, making predictions while reading a mystery involves reasoning. We can apply what we know about observable behavior to events like thinking that we cannot see—that is the radical component of radical behavior analysis. A significant amount of thinking is private verbal behavior: conversing with oneself as a speaker and listener in the same skin, as Skinner put it. At Morningside Academy we explicitly teach effective private dialogue by first teaching overt problem-solving dialogue skills. We apply Arthur Whimbey and Jack Lochhead's (1999) Thinking Aloud Problem Solving (TAPS) method. Research shows that TAPS improves reading comprehension, vocabulary acquisition, writing and editing skills, math performance, direction following, understanding assignments, standardized achievement test scores, and even IQ (Whimbey, Johnson, Williams, & Linden, 1993). Xavier University, an African American college in New Orleans, requires entering students to participate in a 4-week precollege summer program called Project SOAR (Stress on Analytical Reasoning) that teaches TAPS. Students who participate in the summer program gain 2.5 grade levels on the Nelson-Denny reading test and an average of 120 points on their SAT tests. They are twice as likely to pass science and math in the college sequence. More African American students, in fact, are accepted to medical and dental schools from Xavier than from any other U.S. college (Whimbey et al., 1993). The chemical engineering department at McMaster University, a very selective engineering university in Canada—a Canadian Ivy League school, if Canada had an Ivy League—has a specific program devoted to teaching problem-solving processes that uses TAPS as a primary teaching method (McMaster University, The McMaster Problem Solving [MPS] Program, 2015).

Morningside's principal, Joanne Robbins, has designed a teacher training program, *Learn to Reason With TAPS: A Problem Solving Approach* (2014). In her program, TAPS begins as a cooperative learning strategy that engages students initially in content-free exercises such as solving logic problems, puzzles, or brainteasers. Her program teaches our students both speaker and listener repertoires separately—one learner performs out loud as the speaker/actor/problem solver; the other performs as the active listener, continuously providing meaningful feedback. Learners provide overt responses so we can provide reinforcement, corrections, and shaping. When students have mastered both the speaker and listener roles, we provide a variety of problems to solve independently and require them to comment out loud on their own speaking, as a listener would. At this stage, the learner is practicing combining his or her speaker and listener repertoires in the same skin in a controlled intraverbal chain. During this phase of the teaching process, we provide reinforcement, corrections, and shaping, just as we did when we paired students up to engage in each of the roles separately. Finally, each student practices covertizing the speaker and listener routines while maintaining problem-solving fluency. Of course, by encouraging them to covertize the speaker and listener routines, we can see only the outcomes of the private dialogue in a correctly solved problem.

AN EVEN BIGGER PICTURE: CARING SOCIETIES

Anthony Biglan, senior scientist at the Oregon Research Institute in Eugene, Oregon, has identified many social behavior problems of children and youth, including depression, anxiety, smoking, physical inactivity, alcohol and drug abuse, unhealthy diets, antisocial behavior, risky sexual behavior, and early childbearing, that could also have a significant impact on the success of American education (Biglan, 2015). He advocates for evidence-based interventions for these problems and names several successful family-based programs, including the Nurse-Family Partnership, Healthy Start, Family Checkup, Parent Management Training Oregon, the Incredible Years, multisystemic therapy, and Multidimensional Foster Family Care (Biglan, 2014, 2015).

Biglan has also provided a nonlinear analysis—that poverty and economic inequality are the major factors perpetuating these problem behaviors. These problem behaviors thrive in stressful and threatening environments, all of which share a common set of environmental conditions, and require systemic interventions that foster prosociality and nurturing environments. Biglan defines *prosociality* as "a constellation of behaviors, values, and attitudes that involve cooperating with others, working for the wellbeing of others, sacrificing for others, and fostering self-development" (2015, p. 10). He documents prosociality as associated with fewer behavior problems, doing better in school, more and better friends, better health, and more success in business. Systemic interventions that address nonlinear problems also foster *nurturing environments* that minimize toxic biological and psychological conditions, promote and reinforce prosocial behavior, limit opportunities for problem behavior, and promote psychological flexibility. These systemic interventions require broad coalitions of organizations in public health, human services, and business to "create a movement to promote nurturance in families, schools and communities; and to advocate for the policies needed to evolve our societies toward greater nurturance" (Biglan, 2015, p. 131).

Viewing the problems of American K–12 education and the social behavior problems of children and youth from 10,000 feet up, a vision is becoming clear: Behavior analysis in education in the 21st century should provide analyses of the educational and social problems of children and youth, evidence-based interventions for each, nonlinear analyses of poverty and economic inequality, and systemic interventions that supplement and reframe the evidence-based topical interventions accordingly.

Another popular educator, Diane Ravitch, has also written about the problems with NCLB and RTTT legislation and has proposed systemic solutions to the social and academic behavior of children and youth in America. Ravitch is a research professor of education at New York University, was appointed a member of the National Assessment Governing Board by President Bill Clinton, and is a best-selling author and leading authority on U.S. education.

In her most recent book, *Reign of Error,* Ravitch (2013) refutes the claims that test scores are falling and the educational system is broken and obsolete. In fact, according to the only authoritative measure of academic performance, the National Assessment of Educational Progress (NAEP), test scores are at their highest point ever recorded. For example, on fourth-grade reading assessments, 29% scored at the proficient level in 1992; in 2011, 34% were proficient. The proportion of students who are below the basic level has actually declined. Fourth-grade mathematics test results show even more dramatic improvement: 65% of students were at the basic level or above in 2000, but by 2011, 82% were at the basic level or above. There are no stakes attached to performance on the NAEP, and the methodology behind the administration is more rigorous than that of any other state or federal academic assessment procedure in America. The appendix in Ravitch's book provides graphs of all current NAEP data.

Another myth claims that minority populations have made no gains. Examining math scores by demographic reveals that all populations have shown performance increases in since 1992: Yes, Caucasian student performance rose by 29 points—but African American students gained 36 points, Hispanic students gained 29 points, and Asian students gained 31 points. On a cautionary note, however, although the gaps between White and Black student performance were narrower in 2007 than in any previous assessment, White students had scores that averaged 26 points higher than those of Black students in each subject. And the achievement gap between White and Hispanic students did not change significantly between 1990 and 2009. So although all groups have improved significantly, the gaps remain a large and important indicator of inequality in the United States (National Center for Education Statistics, 2014).

On international tests we also see that U.S. test scores are not falling from previous levels. We are not falling behind other nations. And another observation: American students are demonstrating competence in far more difficult topics in math and science than their peers in past decades. Visit the NAEP website and see for yourself: Can you reach the basic level on the eighth-grade math test? Good luck! (National Center for Education Statistics, 2015).

Data on American high school graduation rates and dropout rates are also misleading. Although 78% of high school students are graduating within 4 years, if you examine the rate after 6 years since beginning high school and include general equivalency diploma counts, you will see that 90% of American students are graduating from high school.

Ravitch (2013) not only believes that legislation such as NCLB and RTTT are focused on problems that do not really exist but believes that they have created other serious problems. They have proposed that charter schools are an attractive remedy for our failing public schools. NCLB assumes that if taxpayer dollars are awarded to both public schools and charter schools, competition and choice will improve public education. The increased importance and amount of high-stakes testing and associated consequences promulgated in laws like NCLB and RTTT, along with federal dollars for achievement improvement and advocacy of charter school remedies, has facilitated an emerging market for Wall Street hedge fund managers and other investors. Currently, thousands of tutoring companies and public school reform vendors exist in America to claim a share of taxpayer dollars. Corporate-friendly local and state officials have used test results to justify closing schools in low-income communities of color and transferring control of them to private charter operators. The original charter school idea that began as a series of small, controlled experiments within public school districts to promote innovation in the classroom and share the results with other schools in the district has turned into a means for private charter operators to *compete* with public schools and do business with almost no rules or oversight. One report documented $100 million of taxpayer dollars in waste, fraud, and abuse (Center for Popular Democracy, 2015; Integrity in Education, 2014). Testing, competition, and choice have redefined the original meaning of public school reform: a quest for equal access to education, the development of knowledgeable thinking citizens in a democracy, and other factors in the relation between school and society.

So although we are not fairing as poorly as critics would have you believe, Ravitch believes that the educational system still needs reforms. She discusses the problems of low professional standards for teachers and administrators in some detail and also addresses the problems of stifling regulation. However, unlike the corporate critics who actually assert that they can reform public schools by increasing test scores and ignoring poverty and economic inequality (Ravitch, 2013, pp. 91–92), Ravitch provides a nonlinear analysis with systemic interventions to preserve and further improve American public schools, including prenatal care for every pregnant woman; early childhood education for all children; medical and social services that poor children need to keep up with their advantaged peers, including a nurse, doctor, or health clinic, to ensure that children get regular medical

checkups and prompt treatment for illnesses; summer programs that provide academic maintenance activities and literacy and enrichment activities
in sports and the arts; and parent education to support and intensify the
impact of all of the other interventions. Her arguments for each systemic
intervention as it relates to school achievement are detailed and meticulous.

Community school experiments are a recent phenomenon that aligns
with Biglan and Ravitch's theses. Community school experiments design
concentric circles of ever-widening wraparound school services based on formal assessments of community needs. The Henderson-Hopkins Community
Center in Baltimore, Maryland, is a large-scale example of a community school experiment (Johns Hopkins School of Education, 2015). It is
accessible to the entire community on evenings, weekends, and sum-
mers. Henderson-Hopkins contains an early childhood center with programs
for toddlers, a preschool, a family center with computers, dining facilities, food education programs, a library, and observation rooms so that
community members can see masterful teacher–child interactions to emu-
late. Henderson-Hopkins also contains an elementary and a middle school
that provides personalized learning in classrooms with computer-assisted
instruction—Henderson-Hopkins is a very high-tech place. You will also find
art and music studios, a gymnasium that also serves as an auditorium, and
health suites operated by Johns Hopkins medical school. The Henderson-
Hopkins community school appears to provide solutions to a vast array
of direct problems in a presumably prosocial and nurturing environmental
network.

HITCH A RIDE!

So, "Hitch a ride!" is my theme. Behavior analysis can participate in a
broader vision of the scope of American public schools and their current shift
toward real-world application activity–driven education. Behavior analysis
can develop effective instruction for both the homework and the classwork
domains of the flipped classroom model in K–12, college, and professional
education. For knowledge acquisition, behavior analysts can help teachers
in America develop interactive activities for their lectures and other content,
with immediate confirmation, corrective feedback, and cheerleading along
the way. With our help teachers could incorporate individual learner shaping interventions for errors, performance mastery criteria, practice to fluency
by building performance frequencies with acceleration, continuous ongoing
monitoring of performance while learning, and instant data displays showing growth acceleration and accuracy and frequency of performance during
learning. We can also provide mastery procedures for assessing knowledge
acquisition, like PSI and CAPSI. We can create mobile learning for knowledge
acquisition, on the go, outside the classroom, saved in a cloud!

Behavior analysts can also renew John Dewey's progressive education by developing real-world applications and promoting generative behavior during class time with behavior analytic project-based learning procedures and by teaching teachers how to use TAPS to teach thinking, reasoning, and problem solving.

We also need to hitch a ride by participating in community school models like Henderson-Hopkins. Our 20th-century educational accomplishments would offer valuable components to a community school. Behavior analysts could even launch their own behavioral community school experiment!

ACKNOWLEDGMENTS

Portions of this article were presented at the Special Seminar on Leadership and Cultural Change, May 24, 2014, in Chicago, Illinois.

REFERENCES

Baker, T., Schwenk, T., Piasecki, M., Smith, G. S., Reimer, D., Jacobs, N., ... Houmanfar, R. (2015/this issue). Cultural change in a medical school: A data-driven management of entropy. *Journal of Organizational Behavior Management*.

Barrett, L. (2011). *Beyond the brain: How body and environment shape animal and human minds*. Princeton, NJ: Princeton University Press.

Barrett, L. (2014). Why behaviorism isn't Satanism. In J. Vonk & T. K. Shackelford (Eds.), *The Oxford handbook of comparative evolutionary psychology* (pp. 17–38). Oxford, England: Oxford University Press.

Beilock, S. (2015). *How the body knows its mind*. New York, NY: Simon & Schuster.

Biglan, A. (2014). Nurturing environments. Retrieved from www.nurturingen vironments.org

Biglan, A. (2015). *The nurture effect: How the science of human behavior can improve our lives and our world*. Oakland, CA: New Harbinger.

Bloom, B. S. (1968). Learning for mastery. *Evaluation Comment, 1*(2), 1–12.

Bloom, B. S. (1980). *All our children learning*. New York, NY: McGraw-Hill Education.

Center for Popular Democracy. (2015). Charter school vulnerabilities to waste, fraud, and abuse. Retrieved from www.populardemocracy.org/news/charter-school-vulnerabilities-waste-fraud-and-abuse

Chemero, A. (2009). *Radical embodied cognitive science*. Cambridge, MA: MIT Press.

Delquadri, J., Greenwood, C., Whorton, D., Carta, J., & Hall, V. (1986). Classwide peer tutoring. *Exceptional Children, 52*, 535–542.

Dewey, J. (1976). The child and the curriculum. In J. A. Boydston (Ed.), *John Dewey: The middle works, 1899-1924: Vol. 2. 1902-1903* (pp. 271–291). Carbondale: Southern Illinois University Press. (Original work published 1902)

Engelmann, S., & Carnine, D. (1982). *Theory of instruction: Principles and applications*. New York, NY: Irvington.

Fox, E. (2015). An introduction to relational frame theory. Retrieved from foxylearning.com/tutorials/rft

Glenberg, A. M. (2004). Activity and imagined activity can enhance young children's reading comprehension. *Journal of Educational Psychology, 96*, 424–436.

Glenberg, A. M., Jaworski, B., Rischal, M., & Levin, J. R. (2007). What brains are for: Action, meaning, and reading comprehension. In D. McNamara (Ed.), *Reading comprehension strategies: Theories, interventions and technologies* (pp. 221–240). Mahwah, NJ: Erlbaum.

Goldiamond, I. (1975). A constructional approach to self-control. In A. Schwartz & I. Goldiamond (Eds.), *Social casework: A behavioral approach* (pp. 67–130). New York, NY: Columbia University.

Horner, R. P., Sugai, G., & Anderson, C. M. (2010). Examining the evidence-base for school-wide positive behavior support. *Focus on Exceptional Children, 42*(8), 1–16.

Integrity in Education. (2014). Report: Charter school vulnerabilities to waste, fraud and abuse. Retrieved from www.bit.ly/charterfraud

Johns Hopkins School of Education. (2015). Henderson Hopkins. Retrieved from www.hendersonhopkins.org

Johnson, K., & Street, E. M. (2013). *Response to intervention and precision teaching: Creating synergy in the classroom.* New York, NY: Guilford Press.

Johnson, K., & Street, E. M. (2014a). Precision teaching: The legacy of Ogden Lindsley. In F. K. McSweeney & E. S. Murphy (Eds.), *The Wiley-Blackwell handbook of operant and classical conditioning* (pp. 581–609). Hoboken, NJ: Wiley.

Johnson, K., & Street, E. M. (2014b). The sciences of learning, instruction and assessment as underpinnings of the Morningside model of generative instruction. *Acta de Investigacion Psicologica, 4*, 1772–1792.

Johnson, K. J., & Street, E. M. (2004). *The Morningside model of generative instruction: What it means to leave no child behind.* Concord, MA: Cambridge Center for Behavioral Studies.

Johnson, K. J., & Street, E. M. (2012). From the laboratory to the field and back again: Morningside Academy's 32 years of improving students' academic performance. *The Behavior Analyst Today, 13*, 20–40.

Johnson, K. R., & Ruskin, R. S. (1977). *Behavioral instruction: An evaluative review.* Washington, DC: American Psychological Association.

Keller, F. S. (1968). Good-bye, teacher . . . *Journal of Applied Behavior Analysis, 1*(1), 79–89.

Knewton. (2014). The flipped classroom. Retrieved from www.knewton.com/flippedclassroom/

Kulik, C-L., Kulik, J., Bangert-Drowns, R., & Slavin, R. (1990). Effectiveness of mastery learning programs: A meta-analysis. *Review of Educational Research, 60*(2), 265–299.

Layng, T. V. J. (2009). The search for effective clinical behavior analysis: The nonlinear thinking of Israel Goldiamond. *The Behavior Analyst, 32*, 163–184.

Madden, G. J. (Ed.). (2013). *APA handbook of behavior analysis: Vol. 2. Translating principles into practice.* Washington, DC: American Psychological Association.

Markle, S. M. (1990). *Designs for instructional designers.* Seattle, WA: Morningside Press.

Mayer, G., Sulzer-Azaroff, B., & Wallace, M. (2012). *Behavior analysis for lasting change*. Cornwall-on-Hudson, NY: Sloan.

McMaster University. (2015). The McMaster Problem Solving (MPS) Program. Retrieved from www.chemeng.mcmaster.ca/mcmaster-problem-solving-mps-program

McSweeney, F. K., & Murphy, E. S. (Eds.). (2014). *The Wiley-Blackwell handbook of operant and classical conditioning*. Hoboken, NJ: Wiley.

National Center for Education Statistics. (2014). National Assessment of Educational Progress, Achievement Gaps. Retrieved from www.nces.ed.gov/nationsreportcard/studies/gaps

National Center for Education Statistics. (2015). National Assessment of Educational Progress. Retrieved from www.nces.ed.gov/nationsreportcard

Pear, J. J., & Martin, T. L. (2004). Making the most of PSI with computer technology. In D. J. Moran & R. W. Malott (Eds.), *Evidence-based educational methods* (pp. 223–243). San Diego, CA: Academic Press.

Positive Behavioral Interventions and Supports (2015). http://www.pbis.org

Ravitch, D. (2013). *Reign of error: The hoax of the privatization movement and the danger to America's public schools*. New York, NY: Knopf.

Robbins, J. (2014). *Learn to reason with TAPS: A problem solving approach*. Seattle, WA: Robbins/Layng.

Rosenberg, T. (2013). In 'flipped' classrooms, a method for mastery. *New York Times*, October 23, 2013.

Sidman, M. (2009). Equivalence relations and behavior: An introductory tutorial. *Analysis of Verbal Behavior, 25*, 5–17.

Skinner, B. F. (1948). *Walden two*. New York, NY: Macmillan.

Skinner, B. F. (1974). *About behaviorism*. New York, NY: Knopf.

Skinner, B. F. (2003). *The technology of teaching*. Cambridge, MA: B. F. Skinner Foundation. (Original work published 1968).

State of Washington. (2014). Elementary and Secondary Education Act. Retrieved from www.k12.wa.us/esea

The Flipped Learning Network. (2015). www.flippedlearning.org

The Khan Academy. (2015). www.khanacademy.org

Tucci, V., Hursh, D., & Laitinen, R. (2004). The competent learner model: A merging of applied behavior analysis, direct instruction, and precision teaching. In D. J. Moran & R. W. Malott (Eds.), *Evidence-based educational methods* (pp. 109–123). San Diego, CA: Academic Press.

U.S. Department of Education. (2014). Race To The Top Fund.Retrieved from www2.ed.gov/programs/racetothetop/index.html

U.S. Department of Education. (2014). Reading First. Retrieved from www2.ed.gov/programs/readingfirst/index.html

U.S. Department of Education. (2015). No Child Left Behind. Retrieved from www2.ed.gov/nclb/landing.jhtml

Whimbey, A., Johnson, M., Williams, E., & Linden, M. (1993). *Blueprint for educational change: Improving reasoning, literacies, and science achievement with cooperative learning*. Seattle, WA: Morningside Press.

Whimbey, A., & Lochhead, J. (1999). *Problem solving and comprehension* (6th ed.). Hillsdale, NJ: Erlbaum.

Positive Behavior Interventions and Supports (PBIS)
www.pbis.org
Reading First
http://www2.ed.gov/programs/readingfirst/index.html
No Child Left Behind (NCLB)
http://www2.ed.gov/nclb/landing.jhtml)
Race to the Top (RTTT)
http://www2.ed.gov/programs/racetothetop/index.html
Washington State Federal Guidelines
http://www.k12.wa.us/esea/
The Khan Academy
www.khanacademy.org
The Flipped Classroom
www.knewton.com/flipped-classroom/
The Flipped Learning Network
www.flippedlearning.org
Relational Frame Theory
https://foxylearning.com/tutorials/rft
McMaster University Problem Solving Program
http://chemeng.mcmaster.ca/mcmaster-problem-solving-mps-program
Anthony Biglan
www.nurturingenvironments.org
NAEP White, Black and Hispanic achievement gaps
http://nces.ed.gov/nationsreportcard/studies/gaps/
National Assessment of Educational Progress
http://nces.ed.gov/nationsreportcard
Center for Popular Democracy charter school examples of waste, fraud and
   abuse
http://populardemocracy.org/news/charter-school-vulnerabilities-waste-
fraud-and-abuse, http://bit.ly/charterfraud
Henderson-Hopkins Community School
www.hendersonhopkins.org

Cultural Change in a Medical School: A Data-Driven Management of Entropy

TIMOTHY BAKER, THOMAS SCHWENK, and MELISSA PIASECKI

GREGORY S. SMITH

DANIEL REIMER

NICOLE JACOBS, GWEN SHONKWILER, JENNIFER HAGEN
and RAMONA A. HOUMANFAR

Medical school organizations are incredibly complex entities operating within multifaceted systems that exert multiple environmental pressures on the internal practices of the schools. Moreover, the components of medical schools operate within the contingencies of the medical school as a whole, such as the recent curricular change that occurred at the University of Nevada School of Medicine. That change required organizational and cultural changes in many different areas within the school and at all levels of the school's organizational hierarchy. Three separate studies were conducted during this time of transition to evaluate the practices of major stakeholders within the organization: emerging leader interviews and a Faculty Forward© survey for faculty and the application of the Implicit Relational Assessment Procedure for students. The results are depictive of ways by which behavioral systemic assessments can serve as important tools for guiding comprehensive and empirically based success in complex organizational systems.

The culture of academic medicine in general, and of medical schools in particular, is thought by many to be different than that of other academic units in higher education and other professional schools. Although a common aphorism in academic medicine is the observation that "when you have seen one medical school, you have seen one," implying that each medical school is unique in its structure and function, the differences among medical schools are probably less than those between medical schools and other academic and professional schools. The primary reason for these differences is that medical schools are usually responsible for large clinical operations, and the faculty and staff members in medical schools provide clinical care in addition to teaching and conducting research, unlike, for example, engineering schools, which do not generally run major engineering enterprises, or business schools, which do not run corporations.

The result of this fundamental difference is that medical schools are constantly balancing the individual prerogatives and career development needs of their faculty and staff members with the institutional service needs of providing medical care, engaging and serving the community, and managing a major business enterprise. Faculty members who are selected for their initiative, creativity, innovation, independence, and self-motivation are also expected to function as employees of sometimes multibillion-dollar clinical enterprises that serve thousands patients on an annual basis. The most successful of these enterprises create a culture in which individual faculty career needs can be productively matched and balanced with institutional service needs; integrated models of collaborative biomedical and clinical science teaching can be developed; and team-based science can address complex, interdisciplinary medical issues. The resultant culture influences faculty engagement and behavior, curriculum development and implementation, role modeling, professionalism, and the overall success of the institution in meeting its complex missions.

All of these forces have operated in the past few years at the University of Nevada School of Medicine (UNSOM), exacerbated by significant additional economic and political assaults. The state's severe recession detracted substantially from the school's funding base, with a potential impact on the school's accreditation. The school suffered from political instability regarding whether it was adequately serving a geographically large, highly urbanized state with substantial health care inadequacies and disparities and campuses in Reno and Las Vegas, separated by 450 miles. The school had also experienced frequent and turbulent leadership changes in the school and in its parent university over the preceding 12–15 years. The result was a faculty that was fragmented, disengaged, lacking vision, and distrustful. As described in a common phrase, "The whole was less than the sum of the parts." Any one individual faculty member was probably meeting his or her professional and academic obligations, working hard and meeting performance expectations, but the school as a whole was not meeting its institutional missions.

Many visual metaphors have been used to describe this situation, including the classic "herding cats" and the related image of "pigs on ice." A somewhat more elegant image is that of a symphony orchestra, in which the quality of the orchestra's performance is not simply the cumulative impact of each musician's ability, but the way in which these abilities are woven together to create music that no one musician could make alone. Intrinsic to these images and metaphors is the concept of managing entropy in an organization. This concept is discussed more widely in business organizations but less so in academia because, in general, there is no need to manage entropy in an organization that has relatively less need to meet larger institutional missions. In the case of medical schools, the need to manage entropy is paramount, and it was particularly so in the case of UNSOM. Our ability to meet our organizational missions was significantly compromised, as was our ability to support the very individual faculty career development needs that had become overly dominant.

Entropy is defined in thermodynamics as the tendency for systems to move from a state of higher organization to one of lower organization (Bar Yam, 1997; Brethower, 1999). It is a measure of randomness or chaos. The entropy of a closed system is constantly increasing and never spontaneously moves from a state of higher entropy to one of lower entropy. Phrased in the converse fashion, closed systems never spontaneously move from a level of lower organization to higher organization (Bar Yam, 1997; Brethower, 1999).

The role of leadership of a complex academic, professional, and corporate organization such as a medical school, to a considerable extent, includes the task of managing entropy. Left to its own direction, a group of highly educated faculty and staff members can generate highly productive, appropriate, and useful programs and activities, none of which may relate to the institution's overall mission. This may affect the ability of the institution to meet its clinical service, student teaching, residency and fellowship training, research development, and community engagement objectives. There is a critical need to find the correct balance between individual faculty and staff career development needs and institutional needs. This requires the creation of an expectation of accountability by the institution to its members' career development and by its members to the institution's mission; a high level, quality, and frequency of communication; transparency regarding the institution's missions relative to its resources; and, above all else, data-driven decision making, with the data often coming in the form of behavioral and attitudinal assessments.

In the case of UNSOM, we committed to creating a culture that was at one and the same time more faculty-centered and more driven by institutional missions; more focused on student needs and educational outcomes; more supportive of professional development and scholarship; and more committed to improved clinical, educational, and research operations. Two projects are reported here, one concerning faculty perspectives regarding a major medical student curriculum transformation, and the other a set of student attitudes, bias, and values that influence students' development of appropriate professional behaviors.

INSTITUTIONAL HISTORY AND CULTURE

UNSOM was founded in 1969 as the School of Medical Science, with the first class of 32 medical students matriculating on the campus of the University of Nevada, Reno, in 1971. Philanthropist Howard Hughes's multi-year, multimillion-dollar financial commitment, along with support from the state legislature, provided the necessary resources to provide medical education in Nevada. For the first 7 years, students attended the School of Medical Science for 2 years, then were required to transfer to an out-of-state school to complete clinical training and receive their MD degrees. This model of medical education resulted in few physicians coming back to complete residency programs and eventually practice medicine in Nevada. In 1978, with increased federal funding, the school was able to negotiate affiliation agreements with nine hospitals and multiple outpatient clinics in Reno and Las Vegas. This growth allowed the medical school to expand the curriculum and provide patient care settings for students to complete their clinical education. Beginning in 1981, UNSOM began awarding the Medical Doctor (MD) degree to graduating students.

All students begin their medical education program in Reno for the first 2 years and complete a minimum of two community-based preceptorships with primary care physicians during this phase of their training. During the third year, all students must spend 18–24 weeks on the Las Vegas campus for surgery and obstetrics and gynecology clerkship rotations, and the remainder of their clinical training can be completed on either campus. Currently, two-thirds of all UNSOM students complete their entire third and fourth years of training in southern Nevada. As a community-based medical school, UNSOM does not have an academic medical center associated with the institution. UNSOM is reliant on a relatively small number of full-time faculty members, numerous community-based physician educators, and support from affiliated public and private hospitals to provide clinical sites for medical student training.

UNSOM AND BEHAVIORAL SYSTEMS ANALYSIS

Because the medical school administration team understood the inherent risks of attempting to measure one's own performance, a relationship was established with colleagues in the Behavior Analysis Program (Department of Psychology) at the University of Nevada, Reno. It was decided to adopt a behavior analytic approach when describing, evaluating, and assessing UNSOM as an organization. The first step in adopting a behavioral systems approach was to provide a theoretical foundation for the administrative team at the school of medicine. This culminated in a series of seminars on behavior analytic theory, including an overview of behavioral systems analysis. In addition, descriptive accounts of the organization were developed and discussed based on conceptualizations of the macrosystem (Malott, 2003) and the metacontingency (Glenn, 2004; Houmanfar, Rodrigues, & Ward, 2010; Malott, 2003; Malott & Glenn, 2006; Mawhinney, 1992, 2001, 2009).

The complete results of the organizational assessment are outside the scope of this article. However, the relevant aspects of the macrosystem and metacontingencies are discussed briefly.

UNSOM'S MACROSYSTEMS AND METACONTINGENCIES

UNSOM exists within a macrosystem that is defined by numerous cultural, political, and economic factors. The demographics of the state are unique: Nevada is the 7th largest state as defined by geographic size but ranks 35th in population, making it the 9th least densely populated state in the United States. Almost 75% of the state's population resides in the Las Vegas metropolitan area; however, historically, development began in the northern region of the state where deposits of silver and gold were discovered in the 19th century. Nevada can be described as highly diverse with a single, densely populated urban area and large expanses of sparsely populated mountainous, high-desert areas.

The annual report from the National Education Association in 2014 ranked Nevada 6th in the nation for per capita expenditures on police and fire protection services, 13th in expenditures for corrections, 28th in expenditures for highways, and 50th in expenditures on higher education. State budget appropriations for higher education were reduced by 31% from 2009 to 2013. Because of the state's severe shortage of health care professionals UNSOM was spared a majority of these budget cuts, with medical education budgets reduced by less than 15% during this same time.

Interactions between the numerous groups, faculty, staff, and administrators create an intricate and interwoven metacontingency, the aggregate product of which is a class of graduating medical students. An analysis of the interlocking behavioral contingencies demonstrated a complex system that promoted silo-based decision making. There were spheres of interconnect-edness and influence that needed to change in order to successfully carry out a school-wide curricular change. Figure 1 illustrates the metacontingency of medical education and the place it occupies within an even broader metacontingency of health care using Houmanfar et al.'s (2010) elaborated account of metacontingency. Medical schools produce students and trained specialists who then enter into a larger physician workforce. Physicians practice in the context of communities—where their patients reside and also professional communities with specialty-specific traditions and practices. Each of these levels operates within an even broader context—the cultural milieu composed of history, technology, government rules, resources, and institutions. Though other factors also were influencing the change process, the analysis was limited to the faculty and institutional forces driving changes in the medical student curriculum.

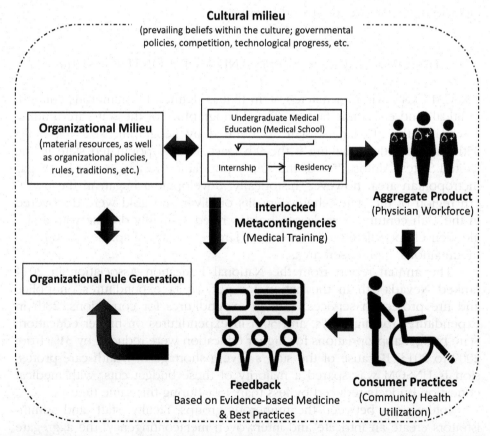

FIGURE 1 The metacontingency of medical education and the broader metacontingency of health care using Houmanfar et al.'s (2010) elaborated account of metacontingency.

Administratively speaking, UNSOM is an academic and budgetary unit of the University of Nevada, Reno, but is heavily influenced by statewide political forces, defined by a historic north versus south regional competition for power, influence, and resources. Between-department interconnectedness was minimal, with little communication occurring across department leadership. This led to a curriculum that was not coordinated by topic or organ system and therefore occasionally contained unintentional redundancies. This system also encouraged competition for class hours, as state dollars were awarded to departments based on the number of classes taught. In addition, there was little incentive to match class content and the knowledge, skills, and abilities required of practicing physicians, as state dollars were not based on content delivered. Basic science faculty and clinical faculty had very little interaction, creating even more silos with minimal feedback loops for organizational self-correction.

MACROSYSTEM AND METACONTINGENCY CHANGES

UNSOM's program for the MD degree is accredited by the Liaison Committee on Medical Education (LCME). Following the most recent site visit by an accreditation team in 2009, officials from the LCME came to Reno and Las Vegas in early 2010 to meet with university officials and the medical school faculty. The primary purpose of this visit was to emphasize a need for institutional change at UNSOM. There were four primary areas of focus by the LCME: (a) turnover in key medical school leadership positions; (b) an outdated approach to curriculum management and teaching methodologies; (c) stability of revenue sources to adequately fund medical education; and (d) a lack of diversity in the population of students, faculty, and staff members.

LCME officials also noted a perceived lack of curricular oversight by a faculty committee, the Medical Education Steering Committee. These observations stemmed from an existing curriculum that had developed based on the aforementioned competition between departments for state dollars, given that state dollars were awarded based on the number of courses. The result of this competition led to department chairs having a large influence on the curriculum structure with potentially less regard for integrated educational practice.

The rapid population growth in the Las Vegas area over the past 25 years resulted in a shift of the political power base from north to south. The impact of this shift, together with the continued shortage of physicians statewide, resulted in pressure to expand medical education opportunities in southern Nevada. It also altered the needs for staff and faculty by location, with an increased need for clinical faculty in southern Nevada.

In addition, the leadership and hierarchical structure of UNSOM was disrupted. There were multiple changes in leadership at all levels. The medical school dean position was held by two interim deans over the course of 3 years. A permanent dean was hired in July 2011, 1.5 years after the start of the planning for the curricular change. In addition, the Office of Medical Education was led by an interim associate dean who had been appointed in late 2009. A permanent associate dean for medical education was appointed by the new dean at the beginning of 2012.

The aforementioned factors influenced the climate of the macrosystem, and added attention from the LCME finally precipitated several important changes at UNSOM. First and foremost was a renewed effort to recruit a new dean and provide stable leadership, which was achieved in 2011. The second priority was to begin a process of curricular reform to create a vertically and horizontally integrated curriculum that would rely less on passive modes of classroom instruction, increase student engagement by adopting more inter-active teaching modalities, and allow more time for student-directed learning. Curricular integration in medical education is defined in two ways: horizontal integration, defined as teaching foundational science content from disciplines such as anatomy, biochemistry, physiology, and pharmacology concurrently based on an organizing principle such as an organ system or patient pre-sentation; and vertical integration, defined as teaching foundational science content within a clinical context during Years 1 and 2 and reempha-sizing foundational science concepts during clinical rotations in Years 3 and 4.

EVALUATION OF CURRICULAR CHANGE: FACULTY ENGAGEMENT

UNSOM administrators recognized the importance of assessment and evaluation of the process of change and requested the formation of a committee specifically to create an evaluation strategy. The committee, called the Curriculum Evaluation Group (CEG), was composed of UNSOM administrators; faculty representatives; and consultants from the University of Nevada, Reno, Behavior Analysis Program. The CEG created a strategy to determine the impact of major curricular change on UNSOM. It included measures of student performance on standardized exams (like the Step 1 exam, a national licensing exam that tests the scientific and clinical content that students are exposed to during Years 1 and 2 in medical school) as well as other performance indicators (such as scores on Standardized Patient [SP] exams). SP encounters are an evaluation and training tool that utilize actors in simulated medical settings. A medical student practices clinical skills, such as taking blood pressure and listening to the heart, on the actor. In addition, the student also must engage the actor appropriately, taking a patient history and interacting with the SP as he or she would with a patient. The SPs are trained to evaluate each student on both his or her clinical skill and interpersonal performance.

The CEG also identified the need to determine the impact of the curricular change on the medical school faculty. Unlike the student population, faculty members were not already engaged in recurrent measures that would provide an assessment or evaluation of the effect of curricular change on the faculty during the change. The CEG recommended that an internal feedback loop be created to allow for faculty members to comment on the change process. It was decided that conducting faculty interviews would provide a good indication of faculty members' interpretations of the change. An additional benefit of the interviews was the opportunity to code and quantify discrete areas that could be used to identify patterns in faculty responding, leading to targeted decision making as the change process progressed.

Faculty Feedback

Following the suggested change by LCME officials, some UNSOM faculty leaders had emerged as champions of the process and were engaged in planning the new curriculum. The new leadership represented faculty from the existing leadership, former course directors, and faculty from clinical departments who had not formerly been involved with teaching students in Years 1 and 2. The CEG determined that this group should be the primary population to select for interviews based on their experience working within UNSOM, their current roles, and their indicated interest in curricular change.

There were three main objectives to these interviews. First, it was important to determine how the faculty members were affected by the change to an integrated, block curriculum. Second, it was important to integrate faculty responses into a descriptive, graphical account and to identify patterns in responding. Third, the descriptive analysis was to be used to provide recommendations in terms of organizational change strategies that promoted faculty engagement and buy-in to other institutions undergoing curricular change.

Method

PARTICIPANTS

The interviews targeted *emerging faculty leaders,* defined as UNSOM faculty members who had demonstrated interest in the curricular change process by attending at least two meetings regarding the curricular change. Attendance logs were used to determine faculty participation at these meetings. Initially, 22 faculty members were identified as emerging faculty leaders for the first phase of interviews. One year later, an additional 17 faculty members were identified for the second phase of interviews. The groups were mutually exclusive, with no overlap. Faculty who were previously identified for the first phase of interviews were removed from the list for the second phase.

During Phase 1, 15 out of 22 UNSOM faculty members responded and were interviewed during the period of August through November 2011. During Phase 2, 10 out of 17 UNSOM faculty members responded and were interviewed during the period of September 2012 through January 2013.

PROCEDURE

UNSOM faculty members who met the criteria were invited through e-mail to participate in the interviews. The e-mail indicated further follow-up by the researchers to solicit their participation and scheduling of the interviews. Included in the e-mail was an information sheet that provided a thorough outline of the study and the interview process. These potential interviewees were then contacted by researchers (via phone and e-mail); were allowed to ask any questions about the research; and, if they agreed to participate, were scheduled for the interview.

The semistructured interviews had a number of preset questions developed by the CEG. However, faculty members were allowed to address related concerns if they came up during the interview process. Participants were informed that the interview would be recorded for the purpose of transcription. In addition, they were asked to give permission for the interviewer to use direct quotes from the interview, if appropriate, and were told that quotes would be used to highlight particular areas and provide examples to UNSOM administration. All direct quotations were anonymized to protect participating faculty.

An audio recording of each interview was then transcribed and compiled using a coding system. The coding system utilized a similar development process to the coding system developed by Smith, Houmanfar, and Denny (2012) to measure social interaction. The system was composed of 12 comment areas: time, effort, money, support, clarity of communication, LCME interaction, administrative interaction, peer interaction, buy-in, student education outcomes, department structure, and faculty development (see Table 1). Each area had an operational definition and was mutually exclusive from all other comment areas. Each comment was also coded as having a positive or negative direction. A positive code meant that the participant mentioned a strength or benefit to the curricular change. A negative code meant that the participant mentioned a weakness or detriment to the curricular change. In combination, each comment was designated both an area (such as money) and a direction (such as positive), for a total of 24 possible coding outcomes.

Results

The results (see Figures 2 and 3) provide a descriptive account of emerging faculty leaders' perspective on curricular change process. The compiled

TABLE 1 Coding Categories Used for the Faculty Interviews

Coding category	Examples of possible positive comments	Examples of possible negative comments
Time	Enough time, more time available	Not enough time, taking up too much time
Effort	Manageable effort, can be done easily	A lot of effort, too difficult to accomplish
Money	Reasonable financial support, could promote financial efficiency	Not enough money, lack of efficient approach to financial management
Support	Reasonable support services, nonteaching faculty involvement	Not enough assistance, support staff or nonteaching faculty
Communication clarity	Reasons for changes made clear, decisions communicated clearly	Reason for changes unclear, decisions not clearly communicated
LCME interaction	LCME was helpful, LCME was supportive	LCME was heavy handed, LCME was not supportive
Administrative interaction	Participation encouraged, discussion of guidelines	Participation discouraged, not encouraged, requirements imposed
Peer interaction	Constructive decision making with others, better knowledge of others' work, promotion of collaborative approach to teaching	Unconstructive or uncooperative conversations with others
Faculty buy-in	Faculty on board, faculty wanted to participate	Faculty not on board, faculty didn't want to participate
Student outcomes	Standardize scores increase, placement positions are more prestigious, easier transition between Years 2 and 3, residencies, fellowships	Standardize scores decrease or stay the same, placement positions are less prestigious, difficult transition between Years 2 and 3, residencies, fellowships
Department structure	Restructuring of departments seems beneficial	Restructuring is not needed or could be detrimental
Faculty development	Between-department collaboration, more multidisciplinary interaction, increased awareness of others' expertise and practices, can promote faculty collaboration	Not helpful, can be distracting, can promote competition

Note. The table provides examples for each category but does not include the full definition of each category. LCME = Liaison Committee on Medical Education.

results were calculated a number of different ways, one of the most useful being the calculation of the percentage of faculty leaders who made at least one comment in each area. These results indicate areas that a large portion of the faculty acknowledged as positive or negative, providing guidance to administrators regarding areas of concern that should be addressed in order

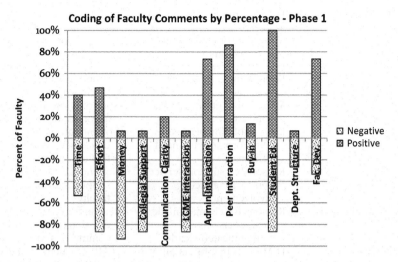

FIGURE 2 The percentage of faculty who made at least one comment in each area during the first phase of the interview process, with positive and negative comments delineated. Faculty members were able to talk about multiple topics in each area, so it is possible that a single faculty member could make at least one positive and at least one negative comment in one area. LCME = Liaison Committee on Medical Education; Admin = administrative; Ed. = education; Dept. = department; Fac. Dev. = faculty development.

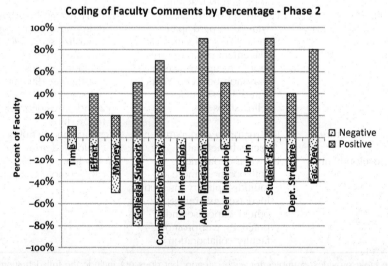

FIGURE 3 The percentage of faculty who made at least one comment in each area during the second phase of the interview process, with positive and negative comments delineated. Faculty members were able to talk about multiple topics in each area, so it is possible that a single faculty member could make at least one positive and at least one negative comment in one area. LCME = Liaison Committee on Medical Education; Admin = administrative; Ed. = education; Dept. = department; Fac. Dev. = faculty development.

to facilitate the change and indicating benefits and positive outcomes that could be emphasized and utilized to increase the effectiveness of change. This approach to data collection and analysis removed the potential bias of a single faculty member making numerous negative comments about one area he or she was concerned about, artificially inflating the results to be skewed.

As shown in Figures 2 and 3, areas of concern that were indicated in the first phase of interviews included, for example, concerns about time, money, effort, and support. The time faculty members were putting into preparing for a major curricular shift was substantial, and the faculty expressed concern that the effort was considerable. Many mentioned that the curricular change was occurring with limited to no funding, meaning that most of the emerging leaders who were interviewed were not receiving compensation for their work at the time of the interview. There was also substantial concern, mainly among the basic science faculty, that clinical faculty would not be involved in the planning and implementation of the new curriculum as much as was required. This concern was mainly due to past difficulty integrating clinical faculty into the old curriculum.

Comparing Figure 2 to Figure 3 reveals a substantial drop in concern about time and effort during the second phase, about 40% and 60%, respectively. Concerns about money also dropped considerably, at about 40%, though about 50% of the faculty members still mentioned money as a concern during the second phase. These changes were most likely due to the Phase 2 group observing and interacting with the group from Phase 1. Phase 2 faculty had, at the time of the interviews, seen 1 year successfully planned and implemented, removing some of the uncertainty about the process, which decreased the concerns about time and effort. Support remained about the same, indicating that faculty did not see an indication that they would receive needed support for the curricular change. Far fewer faculty members expressed negative comments regarding the LCME during the second phase compared to the first, which can be attributed to both the length of time between the phases and the fact that other, positive contingencies were affecting organizational change.

Areas indicated by the interviews as benefits had to do with faculty and students. For example, almost all the faculty (85%) in the first phase (see Figure 2) mentioned that peer interaction was one benefit of the change. Many faculty members did not intermingle frequently with anyone outside their department. The new curriculum change process required interdisciplinary teams, requiring faculty to interact with other departments. Faculty indicated their enjoyment at meeting people who had worked in their building for years but whose names they had never had the chance to learn. Many mentioned that they felt stimulated and excited working with individuals they had never worked with before. In addition, students were a priority for faculty. Every faculty member mentioned at least one positive about student education outcomes. These consisted of comments that were complimentary of the students entering into UNSOM as well as those who had completed UNSOM coursework. Faculty unanimously expressed confidence in the students' ability to succeed, regardless of the curriculum they were exposed to, and said they could see how the new curriculum would help organize the students' learning. There were slightly fewer faculty members who mentioned these benefits during the second phase, though this is mainly attributed to the institutionalization of interdisciplinary work and maintained emphasis on student performance as the highest priority for UNSOM.

APPLICATIONS OF DATA

The results of the interviews were utilized to provide feedback to the administrators at UNSOM in a variety of capacities and have been used to guide organizational changes. The dean was presented with an executive summary of the interview results with detailed analyses too extensive to be addressed here. This included a breakdown of the overall data in multiple different ways as well as an analysis of the change in concern over time. After the first phase, the dean requested that the interview process continue with the second phase of faculty, as presented here. In addition, he requested that the interviews reoccur periodically. The second round of interviews has been completed with the faculty from Phase 1 at this time, though only preliminary results have been calculated.

General results and a brief methodology were presented to UNSOM faculty during a town hall meeting. This presentation was followed up by a lunch with the dean targeting a select few who had been invited to participate in the CEG interviews. This lunch provided a venue for dialogue between the dean and faculty members about the curriculum change. Many of the faculty expressed their satisfaction with the lunch and the chance to interact directly with the dean to discuss their concerns and enjoy their successes. The development of this feedback system demonstrated the utility of communication networks across hierarchical structure in the promotion of a collaborative approach toward the management of a complex social system (Houmanfar, Rodrigues, & Smith, 2009).

A secondary feedback mechanism that provided data on faculty members' satisfaction with their teaching roles, as well as many other areas, was a Faculty Forward© survey administered in the spring of 2013. The Faculty Forward program uses a comprehensive, validated survey instrument that measures levels of satisfaction with 14 domains of faculty professional life, including institutional mission, fairness, relationships, compensation, and global satisfaction. The survey is administered by the Association of American Medical Colleges (AAMC), responses are de-identified and aggregated, and an $N = 5$ rule is used so that individuals' responses are anonymous. The AAMC benchmarked UNSOM's data with other participating schools that had recently completed the survey as well as data from a peer group of schools with similar characteristics to UNSOM. Schools in earlier cohorts have published their findings as well as resulting work in leadership development, promotion, and mentoring (Bunton et al., 2012).

Our administration of the Faculty Forward program in the spring of 2013 resulted in an 83.4% response rate compared to an average response rate of 61.7% in the national cohort. At the outset of UNSOM's Faculty Forward project, the dean appointed a taskforce of academic and administrative faculty to generate participation, analyze the data, and recommend program planning based on our results. Each department chair received his or her department data for discussion with the respective department faculty members. Based on that discussion, each chair was asked to populate a report template that included an action plan. Using the overall school data and the chairs' reports, the taskforce identified key themes with the Faculty Forward data set. Our faculty indicated high degrees of satisfaction with their work and colleagues. Faculty members expressed a desire for improvement in communication, mentoring, clarity of promotion and tenure guidelines, as well as support for part-time and administrative faculty.

The University of Nevada, Reno, Institutional Review Board approved our request to submit the list of faculty members who had participated in the CEG interviews to the AAMC so that we could compare the CEG responses with the Faculty Forward results. Specifically, we sought to compare levels of satisfaction among the CEG participants with the overall faculty responses. Faculty members who participated in the CEG were given the option to opt out of this process, and none chose to do so.

The AAMC provided aggregated data for the CEG faculty members, and the results demonstrated that on almost every question for which there was a significant difference between groups, as demonstrated by the Mann–Whitney U test, the CEG respondents reported less satisfaction than the overall faculty (see Table 2). One interpretation of these results is that self-selected curricular leaders may have higher expectations regarding their own

TABLE 2 Comparison of Faculty Forward© Responses

| Faculty Forward survey question | Satisfaction rating (1 = *least satisfied* to 5 = *most satisfied*) | | |
	CEG subgroup ($N = 23$)	UNSOM total ($N = 229$)	p (95% CI)
The dean's priorities for the medical school are reasonable	3.00 (0.97)	3.67 (0.88)	.0021
My department is successful in retaining racial/ethnic minority faculty members	3.05 (1.19)	3.64 (0.82)	.017
My overall compensation	3.64 (1.14)	2.98 (1.1)	.0131

Note. CEG = Curriculum Evaluation Group; UNSOM = University of Nevada School of Medicine; CI = confidence interval.

career development, as well as those associated with the success of the school of medicine. Moreover, these individuals' engagement with the curricular change process allowed for more direct observation and understanding of the impact of change at the individual and organizational levels.

It is also important to note that the curriculum reform was occurring in the context of increased productivity demands for clinical faculty and increased competitiveness for research dollars for the basic science faculty. Although the dean's office committed significant funds to support the process of curricular development, it was in the context of a need to increase clinical productivity. The aforementioned results correlated with those from the CEG faculty interviews in terms of significant faculty concerns associated with resources, especially pertaining to the commitment of clinical faculty members' time. The overall data collected through CEG interviews and Faculty Forward programs demonstrated a greater sense of urgency for (a) program development to address the concerns of these faculty leaders in education and (b) a better understanding of the importance of clearly communicating what changes are being made directly as a response to their input.

RESULTING ORGANIZATIONAL CHANGE

From 2010 to August 2012, UNSOM administrators working together with faculty members from the basic science and clinical departments in Reno and Las Vegas worked continuously to create new curricular content for the first 2 years of the curriculum. From the start, this restructuring process was a faculty-driven, bottom-up process facilitated by the Office of Medical Education.

The Office of Medical Education provided administrative support and established regular channels of communication with the faculty members on northern and southern campuses for an inclusive restructuring process. All faculty members were invited to participate in the initial statewide teleconference planning sessions during which institutional objectives were revised. Documents were posted and shared on a website to promote transparency during the change process. Participating faculty members were encouraged to contact colleagues at other medical schools and research curricular structures being used in other LCME-accredited schools. After a faulty-wide vote was conducted and a decision made in late 2010 to adopt an organ-based, block structure similar to the model the University of California at Los Angeles (UCLA) had developed and implemented, UNSOM received collegial support from faculty peers at UCLA's David Geffen School of Medicine as a result of outreach efforts by UNSOM faculty.

Beginning in late 2011, a curricular restructuring account was set up for the Office of Medical Education with state dollars that had been redirected from UNSOM departments that had previously administered courses in the old curriculum. This signaled a shift in funding priorities and in curricular control from department chairs to the Office of Medical Education and the Medical Education Steering Committee. Support for faculty efforts in planning and implementing the new integrated curriculum was a frequently discussed topic at faculty meetings, and the dean was proactive in addressing this issue by providing financial support in the form of teaching stipends for those willing to serve as block leaders in the new curriculum.

The dean also changed the administrative infrastructure at UNSOM by creating a new senior-level position designed to provide direct oversight of the medical education program. This included admissions, student affairs, curriculum management, faculty development, and continuing medical education. Previously all of these units had operated independently and reported directly to the dean.

The success of the faculty engagement project prompted further collaboration between UNSOM and the Behavior Analysis Program in another critical area of curricular change, namely, student engagement. In accordance with the curricular redesign required by LCME standards, UNSOM adopted an emerging behavioral assessment technology, the Implicit Relational Assessment Procedure (IRAP; Barnes-Holmes, Barnes-Holmes, Stewart, & Boles, 2010), and produced an online, Web-based version of the assessment, which has been used to assess the implicit attitudes of medical students. To date, first-, second-, and third-year students have been assessed with this tool at various points in their medical education and training as the initial phases of a long-term, longitudinal assessment of multiple classes of students as they progress through medical school and beyond (e.g., entering medical school, after Year 2, after Year 4, after residency). An overview of the development and implementation of this project, including how the data are shaping curricular redesign, is provided in the following sections.

CURRICULAR MANAGEMENT OF IMPLICIT ATTITUDES OF MEDICAL STUDENTS: STUDENT ENGAGEMENT

Medical education is a complex and difficult (often seemingly impossible) task: to take a diverse group of students and, over the course of just 4 years, transform them from laypersons to physicians—physicians responsible for making life-and-death decisions on a daily basis. In total, 18,156 students graduated from U.S. allopathic (i.e., MD-granting) medical schools in 2013 (AAMC, 2013). Although this clearly shows it is not impossible, it is certainly well recognized that it is an incredibly difficult task.

Just making doctors, however, is not sufficient. Society demands, rightfully so, that we make good doctors. A lengthy debate regarding how to operationally define what it means to be a good doctor could occur, but any list of desirable characteristics is likely to include some basic qualities, such as smart, compassionate, empathetic, fair, and socially aware, among many others. In reality, what defines a good doctor rests with the values of the individual patient, as it is in the interaction between the physician and the patient that the social significance of medicine predominantly rests.

It is paradoxical that the process of creating a physician can be destructive to the desired outcome of making a "good" physician. As is universally known, medical school is difficult. It is arguably the most difficult professional school to which one can be accepted and then succeed. Beyond the stress of the 4 years of medical school lies residency training, in which students specialize in fields such as surgery, internal medicine, or pediatrics. Residency training can last from 3 to 7 years, and it is not uncommon for these physicians to work for 24 hr straight (and in recent years, as long as 30 or even 36 hr straight) and upward of 80 hr per week.

Medical education is also unique in that the transition between medical school and residency training is unpredictable, incredibly stressful, and not entirely in the control of the person experiencing it. The National Residency Matching Program pairs graduating students with a residency program using an algorithm to match students and residency programs based on mutual interest in each other. The result can be an added layer of stress to bear at the end of medical school due to uncertainty over where one will be spending the next few years of one's life. When taken together, the processes of applying to, matriculating from, and succeeding in medical school, added to the processes of applying to, being matched in, and succeeding in residency training, lead to a long-standing and substantial amount of stress. What does this amount of stress do to a student?

It is well known that empathy scores tend to decrease over the course of medical school (Neumann et al., 2011). However, it is unclear whether the stress of medical school reduces compassion, empathy, and other traits ascribed to a "good" doctor or whether it merely unmasks a lack of compassion and empathy that was already present in students.

Given the tremendous amount of stress, burnout is a major concern for physicians and those in training. Burnout in the professional setting is characterized by feelings of emotional exhaustion, depersonalization, and a low feeling of personal accomplishment (Maslach & Jackson, 1981). Many factors can contribute to the development of burnout, including the process of becoming a physician. Dyrbye and colleagues (2014) recently assessed burnout among medical students, resident physicians, and early career physicians using a standard tool in the field, the Maslach Burnout Inventory (MBI; Maslach & Jackson, 1981). This tool includes three scales that assess the areas of emotional exhaustion, depersonalization, and sense of personal accomplishment. Dyrbye et al. categorized a person as exhibiting professional burnout if he or she scored high on either the emotional exhaustion or the depersonalization domain. Their results showed that the scores of 55.9% of medical students, 60.3% of residents/fellows, and 51.4% of early career physicians were indicative of clinically significant levels of professional burnout.

Implicit Attitudes

The data from Dyrbye et al. (2014) represent explicit measures of burnout in that they are based on self-report, survey-type responses. Explicit measures are generally characterized by self-report measurement methods, in which the respondent has time to consider the response being provided. As a result, these measures suffer from common challenges associated with self-report, such as inaccurate or falsified responses due to self-presentational strategies on the part of the respondent to conceal certain attitudes.

Explicit measures, in this case of attitudes, are contrasted with implicit measures of attitudes, which have been measured through various computer-based programs designed in part to circumvent the aforementioned concerns with explicit measures. For the present purposes, *attitudes* are defined as verbal judgments or evaluations pertaining to specific stimuli or concepts. Implicit attitudes are described as being brief, immediate (sometimes referred to as *automatic*) verbal reactions to stimuli that people encounter and are considered less susceptible to control by the respondent, especially when they are forced to be emitted very quickly under time pressure (Barnes-Holmes et al., 2010). Implicit assessment tools measure response latencies of respondents to various combinations of stimuli presented onscreen. The response latencies to different pairings of stimuli are calculated into D-scores, which essentially represent a Cohen's *d* effect size of latency differences, which in turn are used to infer a person's implicit attitudes pertaining to the stimuli presented in the implicit assessment (see Barnes-Holmes et al., 2010, for a detailed review).

The IRAP (Barnes-Holmes et al., 2010; Levin, Hayes, & Waltz, 2010) was the implicit assessment tool utilized for assessing implicit attitudes regarding burnout at UNSOM, and it was borne out of a behavior analytic theory of language and cognition known as relational frame theory (RFT; Hayes, Barnes-Holmes, & Roche, 2001). Simply stated, RFT asserts that complex human behavior consists of relational responding between many stimuli (including arbitrary stimuli) and thus forms the basis of language and human cognition. Stimuli, which in the case of language are arbitrary symbols, words, and phrases, are not simply associated with one another independent of any context but rather are related to one another (through the behavior of relating) and nonarbitrary stimuli based on their meaning. The term *meaning* itself can evoke a lengthy discussion, but for the present purposes, it is understood as stimulus function. Stimulus functions of various stimuli are in turn derived from experiences shaped through operant learning. Therefore, the way an individual relationally responds to stimuli is based on the current stimulus functions of those stimuli, which are a product of the sum of the individual's experiences with those stimuli and current contextual influence. Thus, relational responding between two specific stimuli, as is the case in a standard IRAP procedure, is different for different people, with different learning histories, in different contexts.

As an example, consider the Major League Baseball team the Chicago Cubs. Depending on where someone is from (e.g., Chicago vs. St. Louis, the north side of Chicago vs. the south side of Chicago), the stimulus "Chicago Cubs" in all forms (e.g., written words, spoken words, team symbol, and the team of players themselves) may participate in an entirely different relational frame with regard to the concept (or stimulus) of "good" (i.e., the stimulus function). Some people will respond to one stimulus, "Chicago Cubs," in terms of (i.e., relationally to) another stimulus, "good," as though they are similar or equivalent, whereas others will relationally respond to those stimuli as being dissimilar or opposite of each other. Furthermore, the speed with which one emits these relational responses will vary based on his or her history of responding to those stimuli as such. The way a person relationally responds to various stimuli (thus determining his or her stimulus functions) is a product of the person's lifelong experiences (e.g., being raised on the north side vs. the south side of Chicago) and culture.

Applied to medical education, RFT suggests that a group of medical students, diverse in many ways, including demographically, culturally, and educationally, will present a diverse set of implicit attitudes. Those who make the choice to enter the field of medicine come from diverse backgrounds and from a variety of cultures, with a wide range of experiences having shaped their attitudes and the way they interact with the world around them. With few exceptions, an undergraduate degree is a requirement for entrance to medical school, but generally the prerequisite coursework prior to matriculation is not standard from school to school. Furthermore, there is no "correct" undergraduate path or major, so some students may have backgrounds in the sciences, whereas others may have obtained degrees in the humanities. The diversity of educational experience is additive to the demographic diversity and cultural diversity represented in a typical medical school class. Because it is the culmination of a lifetime of experiences, in all aspects of life, that forms the basis of the implicit attitudes of each individual, a diverse group of people, such as that seen in a medical school class, would bring with them a diverse set of attitudes.

The foregoing discussion raises important questions, such as, What are the implicit attitudes medical students bring to the table when they first enter medical school? and, How do these implicit attitudes evolve over the course of medical education and training? These questions represent the primary purpose of the ongoing research program described next, which utilized the IRAP to assess the implicit attitudes of medical students at UNSOM. As noted, this research program is ongoing, with the initial phase (i.e., assessing baseline implicit attitudes of incoming medical students) well under way and the extended phases of assessing longitudinal, within-cohort changes in implicit attitudes—with and without specific intervention—just becoming available for study.

Method

PARTICIPANTS

During their orientation week of medical school, 59 first-year (Year 1) medical students at UNSOM were assessed using the IRAP. In addition, 45 students were assessed during the brief transition course between their second and third years (Year 3) of medical school. The particular IRAP targeted relational responses between the categorical stimuli "I am" and "I am not," which signified an assessment of an attitude toward a personal characteristic students felt about themselves, to eight specific burnout target stimuli, which were "competent," "caring," "enthusiastic," "positive," "callous," "drained," "overwhelmed," and "stressed" (see Figure 4 for a screenshot example of the procedure).

PROCEDURE

During the assessment, students were initially presented with a burnout-related target stimulus, such as "competent," and a categorical stimulus, such as "I am," and were asked for a binary relational response, with the two possible options being "yes" and "no." In certain IRAP preparations, such as the Mixed-Trial IRAP (Levin et al., 2010), an additional stimulus is presented onscreen as an additional contextual cue that allows attitudes toward individual stimuli to be assessed, as opposed to only groups of similar stimuli (see Levin et al., 2010, for a detailed explanation). In the present study, these additional stimuli were "agree" and "disagree" (see Figure 4), such that students were asked to either agree or disagree with respect to their own personal attitudes as they responded to each presentation of certain stimuli.

For example, on an "agree" trial, if the students felt they were competent, they would press the key on the keyboard that corresponded with "yes." On a "disagree" trial, students would necessarily answer the opposite of what they answered on the "agree" trial; thus, if they felt they were competent, they would press the key on the keyboard that corresponded with "no," essentially disagreeing with their explicit attitudes. The converse was also true, whereby if students truly felt they were not competent, they would select "no" during the "agree" trial and "yes" during the "disagree" trial. It should be noted, however, that although a student may not have wanted to admit to feeling incompetent, for example, and would therefore not have answered such on an "agree" trial, the assessment does not rely on an honest response during "agree" trials and thus can handle situations in which students may provide inaccurate/falsified responses in the presence of the "agree" and "disagree" stimuli.

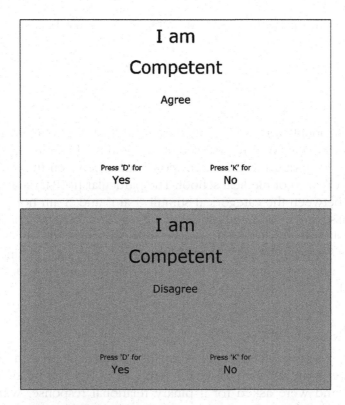

FIGURE 4 Screenshots of Implicit Relational Assessment Procedure (IRAP) computer program used to assess students' implicit attitudes. Burnout IRAP stimuli shown with "agree" stimulus (upper panel) and "disagree" stimulus (lower panel). "Agree" trials were presented with a light green background and "disagree" trials were presented with a light red background to facilitate discriminative properties of the task.

In addition, as is common to virtually all implicit attitude assessment tools, it was important for students to respond to each trial rapidly, within a 3-s time constraint. If a student took too long to respond to the stimuli in a given trial, the program prompted them to "GO FASTER!" by displaying that text onscreen in bold red font.

Results

Group-level analyses of the two classes of students indicated that the Year 1 students generally did not exhibit implicit biases associated with being burned out. However, the Year 3 students exhibited implicit biases that were associated with a greater degree of burnout, relative to the Year 1 students, for the majority of the eight burnout stimuli assessed, with the exceptions of "caring" and "callous" (see Figure 5). Independent-samples *t* tests conducted for each stimulus between the two classes of students indicated that the differences in group-level D-scores were significantly different for the "drained"

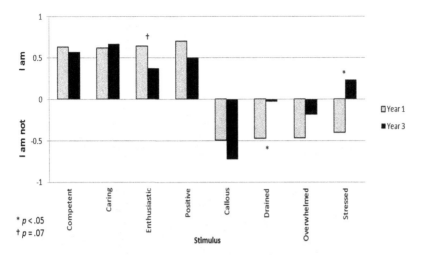

FIGURE 5 Group-level average Implicit Relational Assessment Procedure (IRAP) D-scores for individual burnout stimuli across two classes of medical students. Year 1 students completed the IRAP during the orientation week of medical school entrance, and Year 3 students completed the IRAP during the transition course between Years 2 and 3 of medical school. Statistically significant differences are indicated in the figure.

and "stressed" stimuli and approached statistical significance for the "enthusiastic" stimulus: "drained," $t(1, 56) = -2.18$, $p = .03$; "stressed," $t(1, 66) = -3.14$, $p = .002$; "enthusiastic," $t(1, 94) = 1.84$, $p = .07$.

Figures 6 and 7 depict histograms of students' IRAP results for two individual stimuli ("enthusiastic" and "stressed," respectively), categorized into strong, moderate, weak, or neutral IRAP effects, based on D-scores. It was found that although the majority of Year 1 students demonstrated moderate to strong implicit biases of being enthusiastic, there were some students who displayed opposing implicit biases (i.e., weak to moderate bias of not being enthusiastic). A similar pattern for the Year 1 students was observed for the "stressed" stimulus, in which nearly 40% of Year 1 students exhibited a strong bias of not being stressed, however nearly 25% of students demonstrated an implicit bias of being stressed to at least some extent (i.e., weak, moderate, or strong). With regard to both individual stimuli, it was observed that the Year 3 students generally demonstrated a shift toward being more burned out (i.e., less enthusiastic and more stressed).

APPLICATIONS OF DATA

The data presented here allow medical educators the opportunity to assess baseline attitudes as they are, to document the evolution of these implicit attitudes within classes on a longitudinal basis, and to develop interventions toward preventing decline and promoting improvement. Although we did

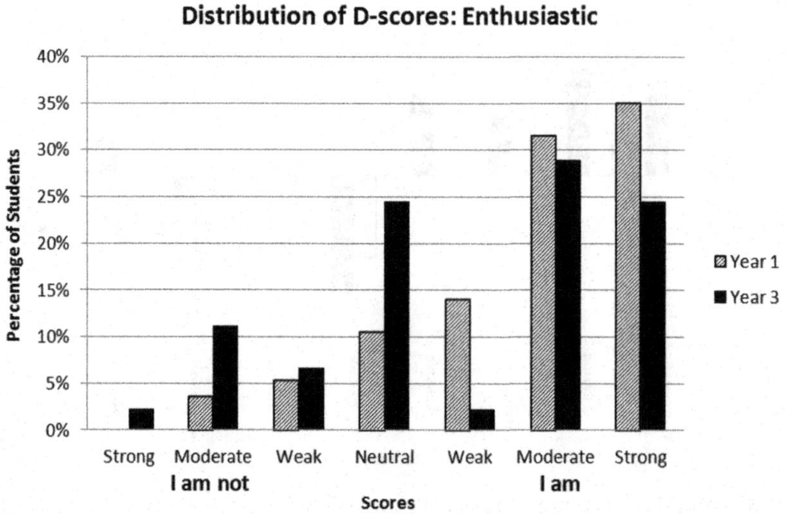

Distribution of D-scores: Enthusiastic

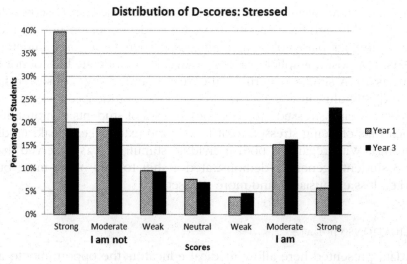

FIGURE 6 Histogram of student D-scores for the "enthusiastic" stimulus across two different classes of students. Year 1 students completed the Implicit Relational Assessment Procedure (IRAP) during the orientation week of medical school entrance, and Year 3 students completed the IRAP during the transition course between Years 2 and 3 of medical school.

not access and evaluate individual student data, the results provided do allow for curricular interventions aimed at an entire class. One major area of focus is based on the concept of self-awareness. One expectation is that

Distribution of D-scores: Stressed

FIGURE 7 Histogram of student D-scores for the "stressed" stimulus across two different classes of students. Year 1 students completed the Implicit Relational Assessment Procedure (IRAP) during the orientation week of medical school entrance, and Year 3 students completed the IRAP during the transition course between Years 2 and 3 of medical school.

merely bringing to the attention of the students the fact that they exhibit these implicit attitudes, and the extent to which they may be completely at odds with students' established explicit attitudes, will be helpful in developing a context for students' ongoing development as physicians. There is some evidence in clinical medicine (Green et al., 2007) to suggest that being aware of an implicit attitude may by itself reduce some of the potential negative impact of implicit biases.

RESULTING ORGANIZATIONAL CHANGE

IRAP data pertaining to a range of target concepts have allowed for the design of specific curricular interventions to address areas such as implicit bias (e.g., implicit bias toward stigmatized groups of patients, such as obese, poor, and transgender patients). Thus far, we have incorporated content on mindfulness, acceptance and commitment training, perspective taking, and values clarification toward numerous targets of implicit attitude assessments beyond just burnout (e.g., obesity). Beyond the curriculum, data such as these inform cocurricular programs at UNSOM as well. The Student Wellness Program aims to combat many of the sources of burnout before they become a problem. Although it is too early to assess the impact this may have on the education of future physicians (i.e., outcome measures), the hope is that it will be a positive one.

As previously noted, the process of educating physicians is a complex and challenging undertaking. Students enter medical school with an incredible diversity of backgrounds, experiences, and abilities, all of which factor into the physician they become. In today's society, there is a tremendous social significance to health care, and people feel the impact of this industry every day. At the center of this social significance is the interaction and relationship between the patient and the physician. It is a relationship that dates back thousands of years and forms the cornerstone of health care. If this relationship can be impacted by the implicit attitudes of physicians, then the more thoroughly these attitudes can be understood, the better this relationship and industry as a whole will be. Utilizing tools such as the IRAP provides an incremental improvement toward this end, in part through the opportunity to affect curricular change in medical school, the goal of which is to continue to improve the quality of education provided to future physicians and to ultimately make better doctors.

GENERAL DISCUSSION

The concurrent interdisciplinary projects described in this article demonstrate the value of bringing behavioral systems and behavior analytic approaches to bear on the complex levels of organizational functioning of a highly unique, incredibly important organization, the aggregate product of which is a steady stream of society's future health care professionals. This value was proactively recognized by the leadership of UNSOM, who reached out to systems and behavior specialists on the same campus in order to optimize the management and effectiveness of large-scale organizational change. By focusing on organization-wide communication across hierarchical levels and horizontally within levels, and through identifying emerging, informal leaders and soliciting their feedback and concerns using multiple methods, such as interviews and surveys, UNSOM and its interdisciplinary partners have been able to facilitate a massive organizational change effort to redesign its curriculum and realign the personal goals of its diverse employees with the primary organizational mission. In conjunction with this effort, the use of emerging assessment technology coupled with contemporary theory on complex human behavior (i.e., RFT) has allowed UNSOM administrators to identify additional targets for curricular change, such as implicit bias. These educational targets are generally either ignored or missed entirely (i.e., the hidden curriculum of medical school) in more traditional medical school curricula, or they are addressed in a manner that has been subjectively and anecdotally regarded as ineffective. However, RFT and various applications of RFT (e.g., acceptance and commitment therapy [Hayes, Strosahl, & Wilson, 1999] and acceptance and commitment training) suggest nontraditional, theory-based approaches to addressing implicit biases that open up new avenues for researching the effects of curricular interventions on implicit bias throughout medical training. More traditional aspects of performance management and behavior analytic practice will also provide objective, performance-based outcome data with which to evaluate the ongoing interdisciplinary efforts at UNSOM. Future evaluation efforts along these lines at UNSOM will highlight important outcome measures, such as students' standardized test scores, graduation rates, success in obtaining residencies, dropout rates, and so on.

Conclusion

Medical school leaders and administrators pay close attention to data. Every year they receive the results of annual student surveys, student scores on national examinations, and the school's results on the residency match. This information is important for internal and external use and helps make adjustments to the curriculum, advising, and other institutional operations.

The collaboration between UNSOM and the Behavior Analysis Program in the Department of Psychology has opened up another portal of data. This interdisciplinary experience has demonstrated that with a behavior scientific vantage point, we have the ability to gain a deeper understanding of attitudes that impact students' approach to patients as well as some of the contingencies that influence faculty engagement and institutional culture.

Understanding these contingencies allows for more thoughtful alignment of faculty rewards with institutional missions.

Leading a large, complex educational institution such as a medical school is ultimately a task of managing and changing culture. As the common saying goes, "Culture trumps strategy," yet changing culture is known to be extraordinarily difficult. Managing entropy is a critical and immediate task for the medical school's leadership team, reducing it to some extent so as to focus faculty and staff energy on institutional missions but not so much as to stifle the creativity and innovation necessary for long-term success. The major institutional changes required are culture driven. Changing organizational practices is most effective when data driven. The multidisciplinary collaboration described in this article along with the use of several other data sources demonstrate the value of behavioral assessment and analysis of the attitudes and behaviors of faculty and staff members and students in driving these decisions. As members of an institution with complex and socially significant missions, we embrace this information as a means of improving our primary product—skilled and compassionate physicians.

ACKNOWLEDGMENTS

Portions of this article were presented at the Special Seminar on Leadership and Cultural Change, May 23, 2014, in Chicago, Illinois.

REFERENCES

Association of American Medical Colleges. (2013). *Graduation fact table, 2013*. Retrieved from https://www.aamc.org/download/321532/data/2013facts table27-2.pdf

Bar-Yam, Y. (1997). *Dynamics of complex systems*. Reading, MA: Addison-Wesley.

Barnes-Holmes, D., Barnes-Holmes, Y., Stewart, I., & Boles, S. (2010). A sketch of the Implicit Relational Assessment Procedure (IRAP) and the relational elaboration and coherence (REC) model. *The Psychological Record*, *60*, 527–542.

Brethower, D. M. (1999). General systems theory and behavioral psychology. In H. D. Stolovitch, & E. J. Keeps (Eds.), *Handbook of human performance technology: Improving individual and organizational performance worldwide* (pp. 67–81). San Francisco, CA: Jossey-Bass Pfeiffer.

Bunton, S. A., Corrice, A., Pollart, S., Novielli, K., Williams, V., Morrison, L., . . . Fox, S. (2012). Predictors of workplace satisfaction for U.S. medical school faculty in an era of change and challenge. *Academic Medicine*, *87*, 574–581.

Dyrbye, L. N., West, C. P., Satele, D., Boone, S., Tan, L., Sloan, J., & Shanafelt, T. D. (2014). Burnout among US medical students, residents, and early career physicians relative to the general US population. *Academic Medicine*, *89*, 443–451.

Glenn, S. S. (2004). Individual behavior, culture, and social change. *The Behavior Analyst*, *27*, 133–151.

Green, A. R., Carney, D. R., Pallin, D. J., Ngo, L. H., Raymond, K. L., Iezzoni, L. I., & Banaji, M. R. (2007). Implicit bias among physicians and its prediction of thrombolysis decisions for Black and White patients. *Journal of General Internal Medicine*, *22*, 1231–1238.

Hayes, S. C., Barnes-Holmes, D., & Roche, B. (2001). *Relational frame theory: A post-Skinnerian account of human language and cognition.* New York, NY: Kluwer/Plenum.

Hayes, S. C., Strosahl, K. D., & Wilson, K. G. (1999). *Acceptance and commitment therapy: An experiential approach to behavior change.* New York, NY: Guilford Press.

Houmanfar, R. A., Rodrigues, N. J., & Smith, G. S. (2009). Role of communication networks in behavioral systems analysis. *Journal of Organizational Behavior Management*, *29*, 257–275.

Houmanfar, R. A., Rodrigues, N. J., & Ward, T. A. (2010). Emergence and metacontingency: Points of contact and departure. *Behavior and Social Issues*, *19*, 78–103.

Levin, M. E., Hayes, S. C., & Waltz, T. (2010). Creating an implicit measure of cognition more suited to applied research: A test of the Mixed-Trial Implicit Relational Assessment Procedure (MT-IRAP). *International Journal of Behavioral and Consultation Therapy*, *6*, 245–261.

Malott, M. E. (2003). *Paradox of organizational change.* Reno, NV: Context Press.

Malott, M. E., & Glenn, S. S. (2006). Complexity and selection: Implications for organizational change. *Behavior and Social Issues*, *13*, 89–106.

Maslach, C., & Jackson, S. E. (1981). The measurement of experienced burnout. *Journal of Occupational Behavior*, *2*, 99–113.

Mawhinney, T. C. (1992). Total quality management and organizational behavior management: An integration for continual improvement. *Journal of Applied Behavior Analysis*, *25*, 524–543.

Mawhinney, T. C. (2001). The organizational behavior management culture: Its origins and future directions. *Journal of Organizational Behavior Management*, *20*(3–4), 1–8.

Mawhinney, T. C. (2009). Identifying and extinguishing dysfunctional and deadly organizational practices. *Journal of Organizational Behavior Management*, *29*, 231–256.

National Educational Association. (2014). Rankings and Estimates: Rankings of the States 2013 and Estimates of School Statistics 2014. Washington, D.C.: NEA Research.

Neumann, M., Edelhauser, F., Tauschel, D., Fischer, M. R., Wirtz, M., Woopen, C., . . . Scheffer, C. (2011). Empathy decline and its reasons: A systematic review of studies with medical students and residents. *Academic Medicine*, *86*, 996–1009.

Smith, G. S., Houmanfar, R., & Denny, M. (2012). Impact of rule accuracy on productivity and rumor in an organizational analog. *Journal of Organizational Behavior Management*, *32*, 3–25.

Enhancing the Behavioral Science Knowledge and Skills of 21st-Century Leaders in Academic Medicine and Science

R. KEVIN GRIGSBY

Contemporary academic medicine and science faces a leadership dilemma. The selection of leaders is based largely on strong records of individual clinical or research accomplishments. Politics, not values, often drives leadership decision making, resulting in a "silo" mentality leading to a poor alignment of resources with goals. Too many leaders are ill-equipped to lead in the current climate, as they are not in possession of the behavioral science knowledge and skills required of leaders to be successful in today's academic health enterprise. A shift in orientation from knowing to doing is a critical leadership competency. This article describes how a specific behavioral protocol is used to enhance leaders' behavioral science knowledge and skills. In turn, these new behaviors allow leaders to enact transformational change in the academic health enterprise.

The North American academic health enterprise comprises more than 150 medical schools and hundreds of teaching hospitals (Association of American Medical Colleges [AAMC], n.d.). These organizations provide unique social value as they educate health professionals, provide patient care, conduct advanced basic and translational research, and enhance the health and well-being of communities. In recent years, the level of complexity of academic health centers has complicated the role of and increased demands on organizational leaders, including academic department chairs.

Ongoing restructuring of health care and insurance markets, driven by economic and policy forces, has resulted in dramatic changes across the entire academic health enterprise. Academic health centers have evolved into complex, adaptive systems and, as such, require reenvisioning of the roles and expectations of leaders, especially those serving as academic department chairs (Blue Ridge Academic Health Group, 2014).

As the organization representing medical school deans, department chairs, and disciplinary chair societies, the AAMC is committed to improving the performance of North American medical schools and teaching hospitals. Over the past 30+ years, the AAMC has offered leadership development programs for deans, department chairs, women in medicine and science, and minority medical school faculty. In order to effect positive change in academic medicine and science, the AAMC helps academic department chairs to acquire the behavioral science knowledge and skills necessary for enacting the type of leadership needed in contemporary academic medicine and science. The desired outcome is a new generation of academic department chairs who successfully meet new institutional expectations by demonstrating mastery of a new set of leadership behaviors. Ultimately, the desired impact is improved organizational performance in fulfilling the missions of academic medicine and science. Kirch et al. (2005) identified eight specific, ubiquitous organizational performance measures: student pass rate for board examinations, percentage of students satisfied with their medical educations, total annual amount of sponsored research, number of patient encounters in the clinical enterprise annual revenues, amount of funding transferred to the medical school from the clinical enterprise, annual clinical enterprise margin, and annual funds raised from philanthropic and other sources.

THE CURRENT LEADERSHIP DILEMMA IN ACADEMIC MEDICINE AND SCIENCE

The academic health enterprise faces a leadership dilemma. Many of the persons who occupy leadership roles at present utilize a leadership style oriented toward the past that emulates a command-and-control approach. Leaders come to their positions expecting to make critical decisions about major organizational issues in medicine and science, only to find their lives driven by the tyranny of the urgent. Just when they think they have conquered the urgent, they find that a conspiracy of interruption has created another set of tasks that must be completed "right now." Too many leaders are ill-equipped to lead in the current climate, as the set of leadership behaviors they have enacted in the past is very limited.

The selection of leaders has typically been based largely on strong records of *individual* clinical or research accomplishments. Demonstration of strong performance as a leader is seldom considered in the selection process. Politics, not values, drives decision making and often results in fragmentation and insularity that leads to poor alignment of resources and goals (Grigsby, Hefner, Souba, & Kirch, 2004). Leadership diversity is limited, as the pool of potential leaders is composed of persons with the strongest records of individual accomplishment. Thus, very few women or underrepresented minorities occupy leadership positions as department chairs or deans (AAMC, 2015).

Leading is viewed through an epistemological lens of *knowing* rather than through an ontological lens of *being and acting* (Erhard, Jensen, & Granger, 2012). Many leaders in academic medicine and science have participated in leadership development programs and, in doing so, have acquired greater knowledge of leadership principles and techniques. However, knowing about leadership is not the same as enacting leadership. Thus, a shift in orientation from knowing to doing is needed in today's academic health enterprise. Effective leadership requires acquiring and enacting new behaviors. Teaching specific behavioral protocols helps leaders in academic medicine and science move beyond an informational approach (knowing) and allows them to embrace a transformational approach (doing) to leading their organizations. Communicating with employees in a manner that guides their behavior toward being more efficient and productive is a critical leadership skill (Houmanfar, Rodrigues, & Smith, 2009), yet many leaders in academic medicine and science, especially those who are new to these positions, are lacking in this and other communication skills (Quillen, Aber, & Grigsby, 2009).

Traditional Leadership Characteristics and Behaviors

Medical school deans have been viewed as the persons primarily responsible for fulfilling the missions of the academic health enterprise. Articulating a compelling vision of the future and creating an organizational culture are implicit in the deans' charge to lead (Schein, 1992). However, the day-to-day heavy lifting required to enact the vision falls to the medical school academic departments and their leaders, the department chairs. Chairs work with and through people and other organizational resources to fulfill the missions of the organization. For decades, most department chairs were selected based on their histories of individual success as scientists, clinicians, and scholars. Their approach to leadership was *laissez faire*, trusting that sufficient resources and hard work on the part of the faculty would result in success—and it usually did. Over the past decade, "someone moved the cheese" (Johnson & Blanchard, 2008), and leading a department became much more difficult. The responsibilities of the chair, the expectations of the chair, and the critical skills required of the chair have changed.

Increased Demands: Same Title, Different Job

One experienced former academic department chair expressed the current situation aptly: "Medicine chairs were once among the scholarly leaders in their medical schools. Now they're 'harried middle managers rather than leaders'" (Kastor, 2013, p. 912). The declining tenure of department chairs may be an indicator of how difficult the job has become. The median tenure of first-time chairs appointed between 1979 and 1983 was 11.5 years for basic science chairs and 9.7 years for clinical chairs. The median tenure declined to 8.4 years for basic science chairs and 7.9 years for clinical department chairs first appointed between 1994 and 1998 (Rayburn, Alexander, Lang, & Scott, 2009).

Department chair turnover has increased in frequency, leading to more frequent appointment of interim department chairs, many of whom are unprepared for the demands of the position (Quillen et al., 2009). Even first-time chairs who have been carefully selected through lengthy search processes "are often insufficiently prepared for the demands of their roles" (Lieff et al., 2013, p. 960). A recent AAMC Advisory Panel on Health Care (2014) report argues that the skills required of future academic department chairs cannot be limited to academic and clinical leadership alone: The ability to lead and manage teams, to lead faculty through dramatic change, and to manage multiple allegiances are core skills required of 21st-century department chairs.

Current department chairs have been described as "beleaguered" by the daunting nature of their jobs. Limiting the scope of the academic department by reducing the responsibilities expected of departments has been offered as one possible solution (Ende, 2013). Others acknowledge the increased demands and urge new chairs to embrace the challenges of the position (Kastor, 2013). Clearly, the increasing complexity of the leadership role requires that new and existing department chairs and other leaders acquire new skills.

New Behavioral Science Knowledge and Skills for Leading Academic Departments in the 21st Century

Contemporary academic department chairs in medicine and science must add new *behavioral science knowledge and skills* to their limited set of leadership skills. An orientation to the anticipated leadership demands of the future, rather than a reliance solely on leadership behaviors that worked in the past, will not lead to success in the present and future. New leadership behaviors include "promoting collaboration, building and supporting a culture of peer accountability, having an institutional orientation, and demonstrating the ability to have frank, face-to-face discussions with faculty members regarding detailed aspects of performance" (Grigsby et al.,

2004, p. 573). In the past, having conflict resolution skills, demonstrating and modeling emotional intelligence, and building and leading teams were not expected of leaders—but they are expected and required for success in the current environment. Incorporating new skills and abilities into one's behavioral repertoire requires making the philosophical shift from the *epistemological* to the *ontological* (i.e., being and acting as a leader). Traditional department chair development programs emphasize learning *about* leadership. Knowing more about leadership is good—but increased knowledge alone is not sufficient. A person can know a lot about leadership and still fail to *enact* it. Equating talking about something with actually doing something about it has been described as a "knowing-doing gap" (Pfeffer & Sutton, 2000). In order to help leaders to move beyond the knowing-doing gap, contemporary leadership development efforts sponsored by the AAMC have emphasized the adoption of new *behavioral science knowledge and skills.*

Undergraduate and graduate medical education now requires medical students and residents to demonstrate specific behavioral competencies. Likewise, leaders in academic medicine and science must demonstrate that they possess the necessary knowledge about leadership and manifest this knowledge through the explicit enactment of leadership behavior. Palmer, Hoffman-Longtin, Walvoord, Bogdewic, and Dankoski (2015) identify six key leadership competencies: leadership and team development, performance and talent management, vision and strategic planning, emotional intelligence, communication skills, and commitment to the tripartite mission. Just as opportunities for practicing the enactment of new behaviors are now fundamental building blocks of student learning in academic medicine and science, the acquisition and demonstration of new behaviors are building blocks for training academic department chairs and other leaders.

Since October 2009, the AAMC Executive Development Seminars for Associate Deans and Department Chairs has trained 65–80 faculty members from member organizations each year, stressing the adoption of enhanced behavioral science knowledge and skills including the foundations of leadership, interpersonal and interorganizational communication, negotiation, financing the missions of academic medicine, and performance management. Since May 2010, the AAMC Executive Development Seminars for Interim and Aspiring Leaders has focused on the same competencies to train 25–45 faculty members each year. Presentations to other AAMC affinity groups (e.g., the Group on Faculty Affairs, Group on Diversity and Inclusion, and Group on Research Education and Training); presentations at AAMC professional development programs (e.g., the Early Career Women Faculty Professional Development Seminar and the Mid-Career Women Faculty Professional Development Seminar); and focused presentations to associations of academic department chairs in family medicine, pediatrics, emergency medicine, psychiatry, and physiology have helped hundreds of leaders each year to learn and adopt a new set of leadership behaviors, including interpersonal and interorganizational communication, negotiation, and performance management. In addition to AAMC-sponsored opportunities, leadership training focused on the acquisition of new leadership behaviors has been presented at more than 30 member organization campuses to audiences ranging from 15 to more than 100 faculty members. As with any innovation, adoption of this enhanced behavioral science knowledge and skills for leaders will take time before it is fully embraced across the academic health enterprise (Rogers, 2003). Acquiring new leadership behaviors can be daunting because of the volume of information and skills to be learned. Trying to learn everything all at once can overwhelm even the most motivated learners. Therefore, teaching about specific behaviors required the use of a *behavioral protocol* specific to each new leadership behavior.

What Is a Behavioral Protocol?

A behavioral protocol comprises a set of heuristic rules to be followed given certain circumstances. These rules can shape the behavior of others by specifying behavioral contingencies under which the behavior of others can be controlled or influenced. Learning the set of rules guides the leader's behavior to move beyond *knowing* about something to actually *doing* something. For example, department chairs often need to make critical comments about the behavior of the persons they lead. But most of them have never learned how to make critical comments that result in changed behavior. Leaders often ignore problematic behavior or avoid confronting it in the hope it will stop without intervention. For the most part, this approach is only successful in postponing the conflict. Too often, problems escalate while leaders ignore or avoid necessary difficult conversations. Acquiring a new set of skills allows department chairs and other leaders in academic medicine to address problem behaviors with the confidence that the behaviors will be eliminated, reduced, or managed.

Critical Comments That Result in Changed Behavior

Using a specific behavioral protocol to make critical comments about the behavior of others increases the likelihood that others will adopt new, more desirable behavior (e.g., "in this situation, doing this will result in this consequence . . ."). Practicing enactment of the new behavior in a controlled environment with targeted coaching on how and when to implement the protocol is a key component of the training experience. The behavior science technology, known as behavioral skills training (Miltenberger, 2015), moves the persons being trained beyond simply knowing to doing—demonstrating mastery of the new skill. Department chairs (and other leaders) have the opportunity to learn and demonstrate mastery of these skills in formal leadership development workshops or in individual leadership coaching sessions.

Often the learning occurs when the leader has the opportunity to implement the protocol in real time, dealing with a specific individual or group of individuals who have engaged in behavior in need of change. Leaders are taught how to create conditions that are most conducive to implementing the protocol before taking action and then to enact the following sequence.

ASK THREE QUESTIONS

The first step in the protocol is to ask and answer three questions: Do you have enough time to complete the conversation? Are you out of the view of the public in a location where you can have a discrete conversation? Are you the right person to make the criticism? If the individual leader can answer all three questions affirmatively, proceeding to the next step is a reasonable course of action. If the answer to one or more of the questions is "no," then working to create the conditions in which the questions can be answered affirmatively makes sense. If those conditions cannot be created, exploring another approach or strategy is warranted.

IT'S ABOUT YOU—START BY SAYING "I," NOT "YOU"

Leaders are taught to frame the issue as related to one's personal response or reaction to other persons' behavior. This step often feels counterintuitive, as the goal is changing the behavior of someone else. However, the most effective approach to the problem is *not* to focus on the other person but to focus on *you* and your response/reaction to the other person's behavior. Keeping the focus on how you feel about the behavior reduces the possibility that the other person will feel blamed or, possibly, shamed. It is not about blame or who is right or who is wrong. It is about changing the behavior of other persons. Starting with "you" often results in other persons feeling identified as "the problem." Remember, the person is almost never the problem—The person's behavior is the problem. Starting with the word "I" reduces other persons' tendency to be defensive. There is no need to apologize for offering the criticism. Starting with "I'm sorry, but . . ." decreases the chance your comments will be taken seriously.

DON'T FOLLOW "I" WITH "ALWAYS" OR "NEVER"

"You *always* interrupt me! You *never* let me finish what I'm saying!" *Always* and *never* are often used to increase drama in exchanges about conflict. Behavior regarded as negative may occur frequently, but it is rarely the case 100% of the time. The use of "always" and "never" exaggerates the problem. Hyperbole of this sort does not add value to the conversation and often increases emotional volatility. The ironic humor in the statement "Never use never and always avoid always" helps learners to remember this point.

OWN YOUR FEELINGS, OR THEY WILL OWN YOU

Remember, the key to engaging with another person is to focus on your response/reaction to the other person's behavior. It is about how the behavior is affecting you: physically, emotionally, and cognitively. Follow "I" with a statement about how you feel or felt about the behavior or about how you are experiencing or experienced the other person's behavior. Are you confused? Angry? Hurt? Baffled? Acknowledging your own feelings improves the chance that others will view you as an authentic and engaging person and, in turn, seriously consider what you are saying.

SAY "WHEN" RATHER THAN "BECAUSE"

Use of the term *when* rather than *because* is very helpful. Use of the term *because* often leads others to become defensive: Persons may feel they have been identified as "the cause." Again, the person is not the problem; the behavior is the problem. Trying to determine the cause can be very time consuming and very complicated and typically is not fruitful.

DESCRIBE THE BEHAVIOR EXPLICITLY

Use terms related to the senses to describe the behavior. What did the person do that you saw, heard, smelled, tasted, or touched? When did it occur? Did it occur once, or has it occurred more than once? If it has occurred more than once, how often?

DESCRIBE IDEAL ALTERNATIVE BEHAVIORS

Describe, from your perspective, alternative or ideal replacement behaviors. Ask whether the person understands what you have described. Ask whether the person has considered alternative behaviors. Engage the other person in brainstorming alternative behaviors the person can enact. Take the time to listen generously—that is, try to turn off your own inner dialog and truly hear what the individual is telling you. Suspend judgment and avoid interpretation as to the meaning of the behavior. Be willing to consider all alternatives. Be willing to compromise.

PUT IT ALL TOGETHER

Finally, put it all together, as in this example: "I was annoyed when you criticized the proposed changes in curriculum and did not offer any alternative or solution. Offering critical comments is important. However, unless solutions are proposed, the process won't move forward. When you offer criticism, please propose a solution."

The Challenge of Demonstrating New Behavior

Although language without action may create a knowing-doing gap (Pfeffer & Sutton, 2000), language remains the bridge between the present and the as-yet-uncreated future. The vocabulary of terms, phrases, and other aspects of language people use to shape the behavior of others is known as a *conversational domain* (Souba, 2010). The conversational domain affords leaders in the academic health enterprise the opportunity to transform organizations. Houmanfar, Rodrigues, and Smith (2009) and Houmanfar, Rodrigues, and Ward (2010) offer behavior analytic accounts of how leadership communication influences the behavior of followers. There is empirical evidence that this occurs through the communication and rule generation of leaders and the subsequent rule following of followers (Smith, Houmanfar, & Louis, 2011). There is little doubt department chairs know about the importance of language and leadership presence, yet they often fail to enact effective leadership. Why? The experience of the AAMC suggests that it is because they do not know how to enact effective leadership behaviors. Moran (2013) has argued that leaders must not only commit to delivering feedback to persons they lead but have proper training on how to do it. Wiseman, Bradwejn, and Westbroek (2014, p. 378) have proposed a new model of leadership for academic medicine in which real value is found in "behavior, behavior, behavior." Grigsby et al. (2009) and others believe the AAMC should play a role in teaching academic department chairs specific behavioral protocols that will allow them to enact new leadership behaviors. Ultimately, leaders should be able to clearly specify which behaviors need to be improved, communicate this information immediately following the enactment of the behaviors, and then positively reward desired behavior when it is demonstrated.

Better Leadership, Better Organizational Performance

Department chairs and other leaders in academic medicine and science need new behavioral science knowledge and skills to be successful in today's academic health enterprise. Teaching them how to implement a specific behavioral protocol helps to shift their orientation to leadership from knowing to doing. Enacting the protocol increases the likelihood that followers will adopt new, more desirable behavior. This shift in orientation is a critical step in the acquisition of new leadership behaviors. Practicing the new behavior in a controlled environment with targeted coaching on how and when to implement the protocol is a key component of training department chairs and other leaders. Adopting specific behavioral protocols is a key component of improving the effectiveness of leadership practices across the missions of academic medicine—teaching, research, patient care, community engagement—and across the organizational settings of academic medicine—classrooms, laboratories, hospitals and clinics, communities.

Health care and insurance markets, driven by economic and policy changes, have been restructured. Unprecedented, dramatic changes are occurring across the entire academic health enterprise. The challenge and complexity of navigating these changes is daunting. These organizations are complex adaptive systems—and those complexities have very real implications for navigating and managing change. The unique social value provided by these organizations is of great consequence to the nation and the health and well-being of its citizens. Leaders in academic medicine and science need tools to help them to move beyond *knowing* about problems and to actually *doing* something about those problems.

The behavioral systems analysis approach offers great potential for creating an interdisciplinary alliance between clinical and basic laboratory science and behavioral science. At the level of training physicians for the future, Baker et al. (2015/this issue) stress the use of behavior analytic tools to better understand the behavioral science knowledge and skills and attributes of what makes a good doctor. At the level of organizational change, applying the behavioral systems analysis approach to organizational leadership practices allows experts to better understand what is needed to manage change occurring in the organizational culture of academic medicine and science. It would be wise to heed Glenn and Malott's (2004) suggestion that even though complexity cannot be eliminated, it can be managed. As leaders adopt and enact new behaviors, change can be better managed, and real transformational change in the academic health enterprise becomes possible.

ACKNOWLEDGMENTS

I have no conflicts of interest to report. I am the sole author of this article. A portion of the information was presented at the Association for Behavior Analysis International 2014 Seminar on Leadership and Cultural Change, Chicago Hyatt Regency McCormick Place, May 23–25, 2014.

REFERENCES

Association of American Medical Colleges. (2015). *The underrepresentation of women in leadership positions in U.S. medical schools* (Analysis in Brief Vol. 15, No. 2). Washington, DC: Author.

Association of American Medical Colleges. (n.d.). *About the AAMC*. Retrieved from https://www.aamc.org/about/

Association of American Medical Colleges Advisory Panel on Health Care. (2014). *Advancing the academic health system for the future*. Washington, DC: Association of American Medical Colleges.

Baker, T., Schwenk, T., Piasecki, M., Smith, G. S., Reimer, D., Jacobs, N., ... Houmanfar, R. (2015/this issue). Cultural change in a medical school:

A data-driven management of entropy. *Journal of Organizational Behavior Management, 35*, 95–122.

Blue Ridge Academic Health Group. (2014). *A call to lead: The case for accelerating academic health center transformation*. Atlanta, GA: Emory University.

Ende, J. (2013). Bigger chairs at smaller tables. *Academic Medicine, 88*, 916–917.

Erhard, W. H., Jensen, M. C., & Granger, K. L. (2012). Creating leaders: An ontological/phenomenological model. In S. Snook, N. Nohria, & R. Khurana (Eds.), *The handbook for teaching leadership: Knowing, doing and being* (pp. 245–262). Thousand Oaks, CA: Sage.

Glenn, S. S., & Malott, M. M. (2004). Complexity and selection: Implications for organizational change. *Behavior & Social Issues, 13*, 89–106.

Grigsby, R. K., Aber, R. C., & Quillen, D. A. (2009). Commentary: Interim leadership of academic departments in AAMC schools. *Academic Medicine, 84*, 1328–1329.

Grigsby, R. K., Hefner, D. S., Souba, W. W., & Kirch, D. G. (2004). The future-oriented department chair. *Academic Medicine, 79*, 571–577.

Houmanfar, R., Rodrigues, N. J., & Smith, G. S. (2009). Role of communication networks in behavioral systems analysis. *Journal of Organizational Behavior Management, 29*, 257–275.

Houmanfar, R., Rodrigues, N. J., & Ward, T. A. (2010). Emergence and metacontingency: Points of contact and departure. *Behavior and Social Issues, 20*, 122–146.

Johnson, S., & Blanchard, K. (2008). *Who moved my cheese?* New York, NY: Putnam.

Kastor, J. A. (2013). Chair of a department of medicine: Now a different job. *Academic Medicine, 88*, 912–913.

Kirch, D. G., Grigsby, R. K., Zolko, W. W., Moskowitz, J., Hefner, D. S., Souba, W. W., . . . Baron, S. D. (2005). Reinventing the academic health center. *Academic Medicine, 80*, 980–989.

Lieff, S., Banack, J. G. P., Baker, L., Martimianakis, M. A., Verma, S., Whiteside, C., & Reeves, S. L. (2013). Understanding the needs of department chairs in academic medicine. *Academic Medicine, 88*, 960–966.

Miltenberger, R. G. (2015). Behavioral skills training procedures. In *Behavior modification: Principles and procedures* (6th ed.) (223–242). Boston, MA: Cengage Learning.

Moran, D. J. (2013, May). How a leader speaks: Using commitment-based leadership to deliver feedback to employees. Proceedings of the 9th International Conference AARBA. Verona, Italy. *Journal of Applied Radical Behavior Analysis*, 9–15. Retrieved from http://www.aarba.eu/public/download/jarba2013/JARBA_2013_1_Public_Lesson_9May.pdf

Palmer, M., Hoffman-Longtin, K., Walvoord, E., Bogdewic, S. P., & Dankoski, M. E. (2015). A competency based approach to recruiting, developing, and giving feedback to department chairs. *Academic Medicine, 90*, 425–430.

Pfeffer, J., & Sutton, R. I. (2000). *The knowing-doing gap*. Boston, MA: Harvard Business Press.

Quillen, D. A., Aber, R. C., & Grigsby, R. K. (2009). Interim chairs in academic medicine. *American Journal of Medicine, 122*, 963–968.

Rayburn, W. R., Alexander, H., Lang, & Scott, J. L. (2009). First time department chairs at US medical schools: A 29 year perspective on recruitment and retention. *Academic Medicine, 84*, 1336–1341.

Rogers, E. M. (2003). *Diffusion of innovations* (5th ed.). New York, NY: Free Press.

Schein, E. H. (1992). *Organizational culture and leadership* (2nd ed.). San Francisco, CA: Jossey-Bass.

Smith, G. S., Houmanfar, R., & Louis, S. J. (2011). The participatory role of verbal behavior in an elaborated account of metacontingency: From conceptualization to investigation. *Behavior and Social Issues, 20*, 122–146.

Souba, W. W. (2010). Perspective: The language of leadership. *Academic Medicine, 85*, 1609–1618.

Wiseman, E., Bradwejn, J., & Westbroek, E. M. (2014). A new leadership curriculum: The multiplication of intelligence. *Academic Medicine, 89*, 376–379.

Behavior Analytic Concepts and Change in a Large Metropolitan Research University: The Graduation Success Initiative

Douglas L. Robertson and Martha Pelaez

ABSTRACT

The Graduation Success Initiative is a complex, organization-wide application of behavior analytic concepts to improving under-graduate student retention and on-time graduation at a large metropolitan research university. The behavior analytic concepts discussed here include culture, supraorganismic phenomena, selecting environments, macrobehaviors, macrocontingencies, interlocking behavioral contingencies, metacontingencies, and rule-governed behavior. We introduce a change template that includes all pertinent agents in the university system and that focuses change efforts specifically on desired behaviors, targeted behaviors, strategic interventions, and reinforcing contingencies for each of the categories of agents. The Graduation Success Initiative produced a 16-point increase in on-time graduation in 4 years.

Undergraduate student success (as defined by variables such as retention and on-time graduation) has become a key indicator of college and university performance and is now typically an important part of performance-based funding and institutional rating systems. Supporting the academic and career success of undergraduates not only is the right thing to do but has also become critical to college and university base budgets, particularly for public institutions. The costs of students not completing their baccalaureate degree programs in 6 years, or not completing them at all, are high for individual students, their families, their colleges and universities, and regional and national economies. Selecting environments have made undergraduate student success a preeminent product of American colleges and universities.

In this article, we discuss from a behavior analytic perspective a national award–winning (http://undergrad.fiu.edu/gsi/gsi-news.html), university-wide set of systemic interventions called the *Graduation Success Initiative* (GSI; http://undergrad.fiu.edu/gsi/advisors.html). The GSI has transformed the administration of the undergraduate curriculum of a large metropolitan

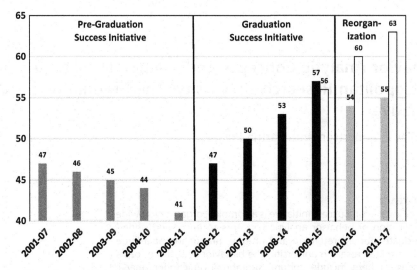

Figure 1. Six-year graduation rate (percentage who graduate on time) for cohorts of first-time-in-college students at FIU: (a) pre-GSI actual rates are dark gray, (b) GSI actual rates are black, (c) post-reorganization projected rates are light gray, and (d) target rates of FIU's *Beyond Possible 2020 Strategic Plan* (approved by the FIU Board of Trustees in March 2015) are white. FIU = Florida International University; GSI = Graduation Success Initiative.

research university and reoriented the university toward undergraduate student success. The GSI's systemic interventions are complex and extensive and produced at Florida International University (FIU) a 16-point increase in on-time graduation in 4 years, a significant turnaround from the institution's historical low to its historical high (see Figure 1).

Our purpose in discussing this case study is twofold: (a) to demonstrate the practical utility of behavior analytic concepts in guiding effective organizational change management, and (b) to describe specific ways to improve undergraduate student success in colleges and universities. Our intended audience includes practitioners, researchers, and theoreticians in the fields of behavior analysis, organizational change management, and higher education. We begin by setting the context and providing the key theoretical perspectives and definitions before diving into the details of the case study, FIU's GSI.

Contexts

The contexts that relate to our topic are myriad, and the perspective of the observer is critical. For example, if we look to improve student success at FIU from the point of view of the Florida State University System's Board of Governors (BOG), we see ourselves as policymakers who are establishing rules and contingencies to shape the behavior of university presidents with the idea that the presidential behavior shaping will trickle down through bureaucratic layers and affect students, economies, and constituents in positive ways.

However, if we are university presidents, the BOG is viewed as a part (albeit a significant part) of our selecting environment. To keep things manageable in our presentation, we adopt the single point of view of analysts and discuss three contexts at three different scales: organizational, state, and national.

Organizational context

FIU

The organization discussed here is large, and it exhibits high degrees of *environmental, component,* and *hierarchical* complexity (Glenn & Malott, 2004). FIU is a public metropolitan research university located in Miami, Florida, with both the *highest research activity* and *engaged* Carnegie designations. FIU's fall enrollment for 2015 was 54,093, of which 45,240 were undergraduates, and it is the fourth largest public university in the United States. Less than 10% of FIU's undergraduates live in campus housing. Moreover, 60% of FIU's newly admitted students are transfer students; 40% are first-time-in-college students (FTICs). Its primary feeder institutions are also large and complex: The Miami Dade County Public School District is the fourth largest in the nation, and Miami Dade College is the largest community college in the country. These three institutions constitute a huge informal urban public education system (Robertson, 1992). FIU is a Hispanic Serving Institution (HSI), and 88% of its students are underrepresented student populations (63% Hispanic). A total of 57% of FIU undergraduates receive a Pell grant, an indicator of student financial need and institutional commitment to access. FIU is first in the nation in awarding bachelor's and master's degrees to Hispanic students. FIU is rated 17th in the nation by *Washington Monthly,* which rates schools based on their contribution to the public good in three broad categories: social mobility (recruiting and graduating low-income students), research (producing significant scholarship and doctorates), and service (encouraging students to give something back to their country). FIU ranks above major national universities such as Princeton, Yale, Cornell, Columbia, Pennsylvania, Johns Hopkins, Ohio State, Texas, Duke, and many other familiar names. FIU produces $133 million a year in sponsored research and awards 159 research doctorates. The goals in FIU's new 5-year strategic plan include both undergraduate student success and research productivity. However, of the 20 strategic goals, 13 focus on undergraduate student success (see Table 1). Notwithstanding this major commitment to access and success, the faculty reward system strongly favors sponsored research and publication in refereed, high-impact journals consistent with other research universities.

Leadership change

In July 2014, the FIU president began a second 5-year term and selected a new provost. In April 2015, under the provost's leadership, the new

Table 1. The 20 Critical Performance Indicator Goals From FIU's *Beyond Possible* 2020 Strategic Plan (http://stratplan.fiu.edu).

2014	Performance indicator	2020
79%	FTIC 2-year retention with GPA above 2.0[a]	90%
53%	FTIC 6-year graduation rate[a]	70%
64%	AA transfer 4-year graduation rate	70%
68%	Percentage of bachelor's degrees without excess hours[a]	80%
77%	Graduates employed full time or in continuing education[a]	80%
46%	Bachelor's degrees in strategic areas[a]	50%
52%	Graduate degrees in strategic areas[a]	60%
$26,000	Average cost per bachelor's degree[a]	$20,000
$36,200	Median wage of bachelor's graduates[a]	$40,000
6,219	Bachelor's degrees awarded to minorities[a]	7,200
1,982	Number of first-generation graduates	2,300
4,737	Number of students participating in internships	6,000
159	Research doctoral degrees per year	200
83	Research staff/postdoctoral Fellows	129
2	Number of patents per year	20
2:8	Number of startups—AUTM:SBDC definitions	5:20
$176 million/ $53 million	Private gifts (total endowment)/private gifts (annual gifts)	$300 million/ $70 million
$197 million/ $20 million	Auxiliary revenue per year/auxiliary operating income	$240 million/ $25 million
$133 million/ $107 million	Research expenditures/S&E expenditures	$200 million/ $165 million
54,000/67:8:25	Total FIU students enrolled/mode of delivery (face to face: hybrid:online)	65,000/30:30:40

Note. FIU = Florida International University; FTIC = first-time-in-college students; GPA = grade point average; AA = associate's degree; BOG = Board of Governors; AUTM = Association of University Technology Managers; SBDC = Small Business Development Center; S&E = Science and Engineering.
[a]These nine performance indicators serve as part of the Florida BOG's 10 metrics that are used to determine performance-based funding allocations for FIU. The 10th BOG metric—university access rate (percentage of undergraduates with a Pell grant)—is not part of FIU's 2020 goals because access is such a central and well-developed part of the university's mission and operation that FIU consistently exceeds the BOG's highest benchmark (30%) by 20 percentage points (e.g., FIU reached 51% in the most recent funding cycle).

administration began significant reorganizations of the university. These rolling reorganizations are changing the organizational context of our discussion considerably, and it is impossible to know their effect as we write this article, although data-based projections are possible (see Figure 1).

State context

Florida state university system

Public postsecondary education in Florida is divided into two sectors: (a) community colleges (which now have some 4-year degrees and are called *colleges*) and (b) universities. The Florida College System includes 28 locally governed public colleges that are coordinated by the Florida Department of Education. Florida's 12 public universities are presided over by the Florida BOG, which plays a significant role in appointing individual university presidents and trustees and establishes State University System policy with the support of a State University System chancellor and staff. Florida's 12 public universities comprise two flagship universities, three large metropolitan research universities (FIU is one of them), four regional universities, one Historically Black College or University, and two specialized universities (a state system honors college and a new polytechnic university).

Beginning two funding cycles ago for fiscal year 2014–2015, the BOG implemented a performance-based funding system that ranks Florida's public universities annually and allocates funding according to performance rank. The system (almost like a token economy system) is complex and evolving. However, in broad strokes, it involves 10 metrics, nine of which focus on undergraduate education (see Table 1). These metrics align with the performance indicators of the BOG's own 2025 Strategic Plan (http://www.flbog.edu).

Originally universities received 0–5 points for each of the 10 metrics, either for *Excellence* (meeting or exceeding set performance benchmarks) or for *Improvement* (meeting or exceeding the university's performance the previous year; see http://www.flbog.edu/about/budget/docs/performance_funding/PBF-Model-Benchmarks-2015–16.pdf). Now universities receive 0–10 points for each of the 10 metrics. Universities are allowed to choose the higher number between Excellence and Improvement, and in this fashion each university arrives at a total performance score initially somewhere between 0 and 50 and now between 0 and 100. For each funding cycle, a certain percentage of all universities' base budgets is taken and added to any new state money to create a reallocation pool based on performance ranking. If a university scores half or less of the total possible points, it loses the funds that were taken from its base budget and does not get that money back. The three lowest scoring universities, regardless of whether their scores are higher than half of the possible points, do not receive additional state funding and must submit and implement an improvement plan in order to get back the money taken for the reallocation pool. The ranking system is intentionally designed to function such that there will always be three institutions that do not get additional funding no matter how good their performance is nor how much it has improved. Roughly simultaneous with the advent of the BOG performance-based funding system came its moratorium on approving tuition increases. So this performance-based funding system with its 10 metrics, nine of which focus on undergraduate education, is the primary source of new funding for Florida's public universities.

Legislature and governor

The legislature and governor in Florida are solidly Republican and largely conservative in terms of political philosophy. Although they are certainly not a monolithic group, their shared belief appears to be that public higher education should primarily focus on high-quality workforce development and economic development. Performance-based funding for Florida's public universities, with its emphasis on timely graduation and postgraduation employment, has the staunch support of both the legislature and governor, who control the final allocation of university funding.

National context

We should note that the emphasis on retention and timely graduation that is evident in Florida is widespread nationally among public and private funding programs for higher education. Funding opportunities are often closely tied to a data-based demonstration of improvement on these and related metrics. These environments are the ones in which FIU competes for additional funding that is critical not only to its development but more fundamentally to its survival.

Key theoretical perspectives and definitions

The work of behavior analysis has overwhelmingly been at the level of the organism. However, the behavior analytic perspective has obvious utility at larger scales, such as those of organizations and cultures, and this usefulness has supported the emergence and development of the field of organizational behavior management. Sigrid Glenn has been working individually and collaboratively for 30 years on developing a language and conceptual structure with which to analyze and discuss group units such as organizations and cultures and essentially extending the work of behavior analysis to a larger systems perspective so as to connect individuals and groups in dynamic relationship within a behavior analytic framework (Glenn, 1986, 1988, 1989, 1991, 2003, 2004, 2010; Glenn & Malagodi, 1991; Glenn & Malott, 2004; Malott & Glenn, 2006).

Some constructive published conversations with Glenn's point of view have emerged (e.g., Glenn, 2010; Houmanfar & Rodrigues, 2006; Houmanfar, Rodrigues, & Ward, 2010), and some useful commentary exists regarding the work yet to be done (e.g., Mattaini, 2004). However, Glenn's work in developing fundamental concepts still prevails and promises usefulness, and we utilize it here to define core concepts used in this analysis.

In addition to presenting selected concepts from Glenn's work (*culture, supraorganismic phenomena, macrobehavior, macrocontingencies, metacontingencies,* and *approaches to change*), we also address the key concepts of *rules* and *rule-governed behavior* (Houmanfar, Rodrigues, & Smith, 2009; Malott, 1992; Pelaez, 2013; Pelaez & Moreno, 1998). We have long worked within a complex dynamical systems perspective in our analysis of human experience (Robertson, 1983, 1984a), organizational development

(Robertson, 1984b), adult development (Robertson, 1988), urban postsecondary education (Robertson, 1991, 1992), college teaching (Robertson, 1996, 1999, 2000, 2001, 2002), behavior analysis of development (Novak & Pelaez, 2004), and rules and rule-governed behavior (Pelaez, 2013; Pelaez & Moreno, 1998), and complex dynamical systems is the overarching perspective that influences our discussion.

Culture and supraorganismic phenomena

This case study includes the intentional change of an organizational culture, and it is useful to begin our discussion with a definition of culture. Glenn (2004) defined *culture* as "patterns of learned behavior transmitted socially, as well as the products of that behavior (objects, technologies, organizations, etc.)" (p. 139). The concept of culture can be applied at various scales, including that of an organization.

When we are interested in organizational culture, we focus on patterns of behavior that are related to but not dependent on the learning history of the individual and that exist supraorganismically. Glenn (2004) explained it as follows:

> Culture begins with the transmission of behavioral content, learned by one organism during its lifetime, to the repertoires of other organisms. Thus, the locus of cultural phenomena is supraorganismic. Unlike learning, which is localized in repeated temporal relations between the actions of a single organism and other empirical events, the locus of cultural things is supraorganismic because it involves repetitions of the interrelated behavior of two or more organisms; one organism's behavior functions as the situation or consequences in the operant contingencies accounting for the behavior of the other. Such transmission requires no new biological trait or behavioral process, but it does initiate a new kind of lineage: a culturo-behavioral lineage. (p. 139)

Although cultural phenomena exist supraorganismically, we must remember that they are interrelated with and dependent on the learning of individuals. Intentional change in an organization such as a university must involve both the cultural and the individual (or behavioral) levels of analysis and intervention. Glenn (1988) expressed this interrelationship nicely:

> Because many individuals in a culture participate in the same cultural practices, it would be tempting to consider their behavior as functionally interchangeable. While that may be so at the cultural level, at the behavioral level it is not. Each individual's behavior must emerge as a function of specific historical, behavioral contingencies. Whatever a change in cultural practices involves at the cultural level of analysis, it also must involve changes in contingencies of reinforcement for the individuals participating in the practice. Sociocultural systems arise from the interrelationships among the contingencies of reinforcement of which individuals' operants are a function.... Obviously the social contingencies are replicated across individuals and generations or there would be no cultural continuity. (p. 167)

Cultural continuity in our university system, therefore, like in other organizational systems, has occurred for many decades. The continuity of our cultural practices becomes evident when one examines the persistent behavior patterns of faculty, students, and administrators, even in the face of major state-level funding changes. We continue here by addressing foundational concepts that we have used in our approach to strategic interventions.

Macrobehaviors

Put simply, a *cultural practice* is a particular behavioral pattern that many people exhibit. In an organization such as a university, an example would be the majority of students in cohort after cohort for decades taking more than 6 years to finish a baccalaureate degree program or not finishing at all. Glenn (2004) referred to cultural practices as *macrobehavior*:

> Much of the behavioral content of individual human repertoires is similar to the content of many other humans. The term *cultural practices* refers to similar patterns of behavioral content, usually resulting from similarities in environments.... The need for a term subsuming a supraorganismic class of behaviors is recognized, [and] we will use the term *macrobehavior* here. (p. 140)

We use the term *macrobehavior* to refer to behavioral patterns that are shared by large proportions of the individuals who occupy the various roles in FIU's organizational systems (e.g., faculty, students, and administrators).

Macrocontingencies

The cumulative effect of macrobehaviors Glenn (2004) called *macrocontingencies*, which she defined as follows:

> ... the relation between a cultural practice and the aggregate sum of consequences of the macrobehavior constituting the practice. ... The recurring behavior of each person has its own effects, and the relation between the behavior and that effect can alter the probability of the recurrence of that individual's behavior.... In addition to those individuated consequences, the combined behavior of all the people (the macrobehavior) has a cumulative effect. This effect cannot function as a behavioral consequence because it is not contingent on the behavior of any individual.... It is contingent on the macrobehavior of the cultural practice. An important feature of macrocontingencies is that their cumulative effects are additive. (pp. 142–143)

So using our example of prolonged undergraduate study at FIU, the macrobehaviors of dropping out or not graduating on time produce the macrocontingency of significant numbers of young adults in South Florida experiencing the double jeopardy of high student loan debt and underemployment.

The extent to which untimely progress to degree had become a cultural practice or macrobehavior at FIU is illustrated by the reaction to a joke the student body president made when speaking at a commencement 5 years ago before the GSI began. A student website had been started that invited completing the stem "You know that you are an FIU student if . . ." (à la comedian Jeff Foxworthy's joke stem "You know that you are a redneck if . . ."). The student body president had selected several entries from the website for her speech, but the one that got the entire arena to laugh the loudest was "You know that you are an FIU student if you are starting your eighth year and still haven't graduated."

Metacontingencies

When making intentional changes in an organization to improve its function, we need to identify the key recurring behavioral patterns at the cultural level that need to be changed. Glenn (2004) called these recurring behavioral elements *metacontingencies*, and they need to be distinguished from mere cumulative consequences such as *macrocontingencies*.

> A clear distinction between the concepts of metacontingencies and macrocontingencies is needed.... The concept of metacontingencies addresses evolution by selection when the lineages that evolve are not the recurring acts of individuals . . ., but rather are recurring interlocking behavioral contingencies (IBCs) that function as an integrated unit and result in an outcome that affects the probability of future recurrences of the IBCs.... The recurring IBCs comprise operant contingencies in which the behavior of two or more people functions as environmental events for the behavior of the others. The outcomes produced by recurrences of the IBCs are not the cumulative effect of the participants behaving individually, but rather the effect of their interrelated behavior.... Metacontingencies, then, are the contingencies of cultural selection. They give rise to the organized collections of behavioral contingencies that constitute increasingly complex cultural-level entities.... Cultural complexity is the outcome of cultural selection that results in nested hierarchies of IBCs. (pp. 144–145)

So if department chairs and their faculty interact in such a way that they are not aware of the courses that their students need in order to progress, frequently the courses are not offered. Those consequences of those interrelated behaviors on the part of the department chair and faculty become part of the environment in which the student attempts to progress in a timely fashion. The interrelated behavioral patterns and contingencies (interlocking behavioral contingencies) recur and so become a metacontingency. Because they recur broadly in the university in many departments, they become a metacontingency at a higher organizational scale. If college deans are not focusing on undergraduate student success metrics, then the departmental metacontingency of not offering courses that allow students to progress in a timely fashion is reinforced, and we have a metacontingency at the college level. If the provost behaves similarly, then we have a university-level meta-contingency. These interrelated metacontingencies illustrate the phenom-enon of the nested hierarchies of recurring interlocking behavioral contingencies that undergo cultural selection. Because of the significance of the BOG's performance-based funding system in FIU's selecting environ-ment, these metacontingencies do not serve the organization's continued development and the survival of all of its parts. Even with poor performance in the funding model, the university would surely persist, but with the ensuing budget cuts not all of its parts would survive.

Approaches to intentional change

The approach to university transformation reported in this article utilizes both changing *macrobehaviors* through changing reinforcement systems at the level of individual learning and changing *metacontingencies* particularly through the manipulation of rules (Glenn & Malott, 2004; Houmanfar et al., 2009; Malott, 1999, 2001, 2003; Malott & Glenn, 2006; Malott & Salas Martinez, 2006; Malott, 1992; Pelaez, 2013). Regarding changing *macrobeha-viors*, again Glenn (2004) put it well:

> Because the macrobehavior of cultural practices is a function of operant contin-gencies that operate independently, but concurrently and similarly, on the behavior of many people, behavior analysts have rightly called for analysis of the contin-gencies that maintain the behavior that constitutes the practice. ... When inter-ventions are designed to alter the cumulative effect of a cultural practice, they must necessarily identify the operant contingencies that account for the behavior of individuals who participate in the practice. The more individuals whose behavior changes, the greater is the impact on the cumulative effect. This method of cultural intervention entails modifying the operant contingencies that are likely to maintain the behavior of large numbers of people. (p. 148)

Regarding the "engineering" of *metacontingencies*, Glenn (2004) had this to say:

> Because much of the operant behavior of modern humans is embedded in orga-nizations that have recurring IBCs [interlocking behavior contingencies], survival of those organizations is, at the very least, important to those humans. The fact that the organizations exist at all, however, suggests that the IBCs were selected by their external environment and, therefore, are an important part of the larger culture, whether or not alternative organizational structures are considered more desirable. Engineering, then, can also occur with respect to the IBCs in metacon-tingencies. (p. 148)

Changing the interlocking behavioral contingencies of metacontingencies can come from two types of interventions: (a) in the environment utilizing selection processes, and (b) directly in the metacontingencies themselves. First, the selecting environment can be changed so that it favors different metacontingencies. In Florida, that is exactly what the BOG has done through its new performance-based funding system that favors undergraduate student success. One can also apply this environmental manipulation at intraorganizational scales, where the selecting environments within the university favor metacontingencies that promote undergraduate student success, such as when student success metrics are included in the evaluation of the president, provost, deans, and chairs.

It is useful to think of metacontingencies in terms of three interrelated phenomena: (a) interlocking behavioral contingencies, (b) an aggregate product, and (c) a receiving system (Glenn & Malott, 2004, p. 100). For FIU metacontingencies that pertain to undergraduate student success, a receiving system would be the Florida BOG, and the desired aggregate product (as defined by the performance-based funding metrics) would be minority students who persist and graduate on time in majors of strategic workforce emphasis without excess hours and who are employed at a high salary or are pursuing further education within 1 year of graduation. The receiving system functions as a selecting environment for the interlocking behavioral contingencies that produce or do not produce the desired aggregate product:

> Analogous to operant reinforcement in individual behavior, the external environments of organizations deliver selecting consequences. Customers "buy" (or don't buy) the organization's products, shareholders buy or sell their stocks, granting agencies award grants or don't, government regulators award passes or levy penalties, and so forth. Most of these consequences are contingently related, however imperfectly, to the products off the interlocking behavioral contingencies. (p. 100)

The second type of intervention is also used by the GSI and involves intentionally changing the interlocking behavioral contingencies of metacontingencies so as to better adapt the university to its selecting environment (e.g., BOG performance-based funding) delivering the desired aggregate product (e.g., employed graduates). This approach is more proactive and gets quicker results. Glenn (2004) described this second approach as follows:

> This tactic entails altering the components of the IBCs [interlocking behavior contingencies] so that they are better adapted to the current selecting environment. Planned variations of the recurring IBCs can be designed to produce outcomes more suitable to the demands of the external environment. Engineering change to enhance the survival of organizations (recurring arrangements of IBCs) requires analyses of current metacontingencies and also analyses of the specific behavioral contingencies that affect the outcome of IBCs. It should be obvious that all of the IBCs and the operant contingencies in complex organizations cannot be analyzed. There must be some way to distinguish between those that can be ignored and those that must be addressed. (p. 148)

As we will see, one of the contributions of the GSI is that it illustrates the use of big data analysis to identify the critical metacontingencies that must be addressed.

The higher education literature includes a number of major works that address the issue of best practices regarding what institutions can do to promote student success (e.g., Astin, 1977, 1985, 1993; Chickering & Reisser, 1993; Kuh, Kinzie, Schuh, & Whitt, 2010; Pascarella & Terenzini, 2005; Tinto, 1994, 2012). However, the clear direction among institutions that have become leaders in these efforts to improve student success is to focus on developing sophisticated algorithms either by their own internal research groups or by vendors, or by both, that analyze extremely large internal data sets with many, many variables to produce actionable results for their decision makers regarding their students. For example, when vendors come into institutions now, they first create a digital footprint, which means that they catalog *every* available data point that is routinely collected digitally, ranging from predictable data points such as performance data entered into course learning management systems to more exotic data points such as swipes in the food court on students' payment cards. The point here is that these ongoing analyses of extremely large data sets are very useful in identifying metacontingencies that are critical to making strategic interventions that lead to the desired change and that they come from an institution's analysis of itself, not from the general literature.

Rules and rule-governed behavior

Manipulating *rules* and thereby shaping *rule-governed behavior* (Houmanfar et al., 2009; R. W. Malott, 1992; Pelaez, 2013; Pelaez & Moreno, 1998) are useful tools for intentionally changing *macrobehaviors* and *metacontingencies*. Skinner drew a distinction between *contingency-shaped behavior*, which is maintained by direct consequences and prompted by discriminative stimuli, and *rule-governed behavior*, which is controlled by verbal behavior and only indirectly controlled by consequences (Skinner, 1953, 1957, 1966, 1969). Skinner (1969) construed *rules* as verbal stimuli that specify behavior and its consequences, either directly or indirectly.

Pelaez's (2013) recent analysis of rules and rule-governed behavior pertains importantly to the GSI interventions. Her analysis of rule following includes the interrelation between the form and function of the rule. For example, each contingency set verbally described in a rule or instruction given to a student involves a mutually dependent relationship between the verbal rules (stimuli) and the individual's selected responses. Pelaez's taxonomy of rules includes at least five dimensions (or continua) that affect their function and effectiveness: (a) *explicit versus implicit*: "Rules can be distinguished based upon the completeness or specificity of the contingencies expressed" (p. 262), (b) *accurate versus inaccurate*: "An *accurate* rule specifies contingencies that, when followed, match certain event-consequence relationships in the environment—they are congruent (that is, they have correspondence with the environmental contingencies experienced by the subject)" (p. 263), (c) *lower versus higher rule complexity*: "The contingencies specified in a rule include at least one relation between the behavior, its antecedent stimuli, and its consequences ... *[R]ule complexity* refers to the number of dimensions of the antecedent stimuli and their relations" (p. 263), (d) *rules provided by others versus self-provided rules*: "In cases of *rules provided by others*, the speaker (rather than the listener) specifies, implicitly or explicitly, the criterion for the listener's behavior. In the case of *self-provided (self-given) rules*, the speaker and the listener are the same individual" (p. 264), and (e) *immediate versus delayed contingencies*: "A rule could specify or imply *immediate* or a *delayed consequence* for following or not following such rule" (pp. 265–266).

In transforming FIU's administration of the undergraduate curriculum to reorient the university toward student success, new rules (or in university parlance, "policy") were developed in order to change individual behavior and organizational metacontingencies to promote student retention, on-time graduation, and vocational launch. The rules were provided by others (e.g., for students by the university, for advisors by their supervisors, and for academic administrators by their supervisors) with the aspiration that they would generate self-provided rules that would be congruent with student success and the goals of the organizational interventions. The strategic new rules were as explicit, accurate, and as simple as possible with as immediate consequences as possible.

The Graduation Success Initiative

The purpose of the GSI is to improve undergraduate student success as defined by specific metrics. When the GSI began in 2011, the emphasis was on improving the 6-year graduation rate of cohorts of FTICs (see Figure 1). With the advent of the Florida State University System's performance-based funding in 2014, the metrics defining undergraduate student success expanded to include nine of the 10 Florida BOG's metrics that focus on undergraduate education. Furthermore, with the university's approval of its new *Beyond Possible* 2020 Strategic Plan in 2015, the list of metrics that define undergraduate student success has expanded to 14: the 13 of 20 strategic plan metrics that relate to undergraduate education plus the BOG's access metric that expresses the percentage of undergraduates receiving Pell grants (see Table 1). These metrics define the *products* that an important element in the university's *selecting environment* (the Florida State University System's BOG) overtly wants from the university.

Immediate results and system building

The GSI has two interrelated goal domains that require simultaneous, not sequential, attention:

- *Immediate results*: Developing data-based practices for rapid improvement in retention and on-time graduation.
- *Sustained, long-term results*: Building a comprehensive, university-wide system that sustains significantly higher levels of retention, on-time graduation, and integration of academics and career development and thereby changes the university culture to one in which on-time graduation and career readiness are the expected norm.

Immediate results

FIU needs to make immediate improvements in its student success metrics (*products*) because of the urgency in the university's *selecting environment* related to the BOG's performance-based funding as well as to selection criteria of other public and private funding sources with similar emphases on timely graduation and workforce development. Critical to making this rapid progress (*product improvement*) is work of the Division of Undergraduate Education's Office of Retention and Graduation Success (ORGS). With the advent of the GSI in 2011, ORGS was created and grown to include four doctorally prepared and one master's-prepared behavioral scientists whose major purpose is to conduct research on FIU's students related to their academic success and to make data-based practice recommendations to appropriate FIU faculty and staff. At universities, offices of institutional research are typically consumed by generating reports that are simple tabulations rather than sophisticated statistical analyses and predictive modeling. The presence of FIU's research group in ORGS is a rare occurrence broadly in American higher education but certainly not uncommon among the colleges and universities that are making significant progress in improving student success. Often this work is outsourced to vendors who call it *predictive analytics* or *data science*. However, the work is simply applied behavioral science all the same, and FIU is fortunate to have this function in house. This granular analysis of FIU's students, not analysis taken from the published research literature that may or may not apply to FIU's students, has proven invaluable in moving the needle quickly on key student success metrics.

For example, prior to each fall, the ORGS research team conducts a simple analysis and identifies all undergraduate students who are well positioned to graduate by the end of that academic year (have a grade point average (GPA) of 2.0 or higher and have at least 100 semester credits). Every undergraduate student at the university has an academic advisor, and these advisors are expected to work their caseloads *proactively* (reaching out to students), not *reactively* (waiting for the students to appear on their doorstep). The ORGS researchers give each advisor the list of his or her well-positioned students so that the advisors can contact these students in order to have a graduation planning session. The supervisors of the advisors and the deans in each college are notified of this process. In addition, the ORGS researchers analyze the remaining courses needed among these well-positioned students and get that information to the pertinent chairs and deans. In an August 2013 survey that sampled from more than 8,700 undergraduate students who were well positioned to graduate, the greatest perceived barrier was overwhelmingly course availability (simply having the required courses offered and with sufficient seats)—63% compared to 31% for financial issues. The Division of Undergraduate Education created GSI Course Availability Grants for departments that lacked resources to fund additional sections and Degree Completion Grants for students who needed just a bit more money (up to $1,200) in order to finish on time. These interventions exemplify changing conditions in order to change *macrobehavior* rapidly within this cadre of undergraduates who were well positioned to graduate.

System building for ongoing improvement

The GSI's evolving set of university-wide interventions to create new rules and new systems and subsystems of *interlocking behavioral contingencies* and *metacontingencies* that generate the desired student success *products* is complex. However, the GSI's fundamental conceptual framework is simple and focuses on the student: (a) help students to discern an appropriate goal (major and career) early, preferably at admission; (b) provide a clear path to that goal; (c) give immediate feedback whether on or off the path; and (d) remove barriers and add supports on the path. The GSI framework is replicable at any institution regardless of size, type, or resource availability. This framework generates specific problems to be solved, such as the following:

- How do you get students to discern an appropriate major (one that fits their preparation, ability, preferences, vocational interests, and goals) when they apply for admission or soon thereafter?
- How do you create a clear semester-by-semester map for all majors of what courses to take in order to get from admission to graduation in 4 years, or at least in 6 years?
- How do you track the progress of more than 45,000 undergraduates, give them immediate feedback on whether they are on track, and guide them in what to do if they are off track?

- How do you identify the common barriers keeping students from progressing as well as the most frequent and consequential supports that are needed by students to persist and advance along their paths?

Building a system that solves problems such as these requires significant change in many *metacontingencies* that involve many agents in the university system and subsystems. An accurate figure that shows the many systemic agents that have been involved with the GSI transformation has been developed and utilized. However, the figure is too complex to be presented here. Table 2 simplifies this list of agents considerably and presents the change template that has been used in the GSI.

In its 4-year history, the GSI has had essentially two phases: (a) Phase I, focusing on *advising* and Points 1–3 in the conceptual framework (identifying an appropriate behavioral goal, providing a clear path to that goal, and giving contingent feedback whether on or off the path); and (b) Phase II, focusing on *teaching* and Point 4 in the conceptual framework (adding supports and removing barriers on the path).

Participation in this work has been extensive throughout the university and has involved integrating efforts both *vertically* (e.g., among faculty and staff with direct service responsibilities for undergraduates and all levels of administrators up to the trustees) and *horizontally* (e.g., academic advising, teaching faculty, predictive analytics, technology, enrollment services, academic departments and colleges). This vertically and horizontally integrated conceptual framework that includes every systemic agent involved with undergraduate student success has produced a simple organizing template that guides the overall institutional change process (see Table 2). It provides a framework for identifying and targeting critical *macrobehaviors* and *metacontingencies*.

The change discipline captured in the template begins by identifying the behaviors that are desired on an agent's part in order to promote student success as defined by the designated metrics that have been discussed previously ("Desired Behavior" in Table 2). Then, the current behavior of the agent is analyzed against the desired behavior ("Targeted Behavior"

Table 2. Simplified University-Wide Change Template.

ELEMENTS	DESIRED BEHAVIOR	TARGETED BEHAVIOR	STRATEGIC INTERVENTIONS	REINFORCING CONTINGENCIES
STUDENTS				
ADVISORS				
ENROLLMENT SERVICES				
FACULTY				
ACADEMIC DEANS				
PROVOST				
PRESIDENT				
TRUSTEES				

in Table 2). These agents may be categories of actors (such as students, advisors, admissions counselors, faculty, chairs, and deans) rather than individuals (such as the president or provost). In the case of categories of actors, the objective is to identify current behavior that is typical of the category (frequently exhibited by individual members of the category) and is problematic with regard to promoting student success as defined by the metrics (i.e., interferes with generating the *product* desired by the *selecting environments*). Next, a "Strategic Intervention" (see Table 2) is developed and implemented that works to change the behavior of the agents from the targeted problematic behavior to the desired behavior. Finally, contingencies are secured in the system that reinforce the desired behavior ("Reinforcing Contingencies" in Table 2). In system building, the focus is on changing metacontingencies, and one useful tool is the strategic manipulation of *rules*. In illustrating the use of this change template, we concentrate on the transformation of the university admission and advising systems (or the GSI's Phase I) because these interventions are the oldest and most mature and therefore are those for which we have the most data.

Transforming the admission system

Desired and targeted behavior

Let us start with students. The GSI conceptual framework begins by clearly stating that the *desired behavior* of students is that they identify their appropriate major at admission to the university or as soon as possible thereafter. An appropriate major is defined as one that fits the student's abilities, preparation, goals, interests, and vocational choices. The FIU data strongly indicate the value of finding an appropriate academic home early. For example, in 2009, prior to the GSI, of the students who were admitted to a major, 77% graduated on time. However, more than 5,900 students (21% of active undergraduates) had earned more than 72 credits (of 120) but were not admitted to a major. A policy (*rule*) existed that students were supposed to be admitted to their major at 60 credits, but the rule was not enforced, largely because the rule observance was devoid of contingencies for anyone at that time—students, faculty, or staff. Notwithstanding the 77% on-time graduation rate of students in majors, overall graduation rates for the university were percentages in the dismal mid-40s and falling. The consequence of academic homelessness appeared to be vulnerability to dropping out: In 2009, among students who dropped out, 75% had never formally declared a major. If students did persist even without a major, usually they were doomed to prolonged study beyond the limits of their financial aid. This situation provides a good example of the ineffectiveness of rules for which the contingencies are not immediate. So with the GSI the *targeted behavior* for students was delayed selection of their appropriate major.

Strategic interventions

An explicit *rule* has been instituted that every student must declare a major at admission. The challenge is to try to make sure that the major is appropriate and not frivolous or fanciful. A *strategic intervention* involved standing the academic progression paradigm on its head. Prior to the GSI, the sequence had been for students to become admitted, then begin receiving academic advising, and later begin career development. With the GSI, academic advising and career development have been integrated and have become a part of the admission process right from the beginning. When students apply for admission to FIU, as part of the admission process they take a 10-min online vocational interest assessment. The assessment instrument is a respected and validated career development tool first introduced in 1938 by Dr. Frederick Kuder (http://www.kuder.com). The Kuder tool has been branded MyMajorMatch for FIU in line with the naming of its suite of GSI tools: MyFIU, MyMajor, MyMajorMatch, My_eAdvisor, and Panther Degree Audit (http://undergrad.fiu.edu/gsi/advisors.html, http://undergrad.fiu.edu/gsi/advi sors-tutorials-training.html). MyMajorMatch provides the applicant with an assessment of his or her vocational interests expressed in terms of the job taxonomy system used by the national Occupational Information Network (O*NET; http://www.onetcenter.org/) under the sponsorship of the U.S. Department of Labor's Employment and Training Administration. The MyMajorMatch taxonomy has 16 job *clusters* that are then divided into 77 job *pathways*. All of FIU's undergraduate majors are mapped onto the 16 clusters and the 77 pathways. From June 2011 through June 2012, applicants received notice of their top five clusters of interest based on their inventory results. After June 2012, applicants were informed of their top five pathways, a much finer grained analysis than clusters.

Essentially, MyMajorMatch is an online learning system that teaches applicants what their top vocational interests are, what their FIU major would be if they wanted to pursue a particular vocation, and what the names of the majors mean defined in terms of what they would actually take. College applicants, particularly first-generation students, frequently do not understand what the names of various majors mean except in the most general terms. A tool was created called *MyMajor*, an easily searchable website describing all of FIU's majors in terms of the following information: (a) a nontechnical, student-friendly program description; (b) admission requirements; (c) career opportunities (for Florida, any specific state, or the United States as a whole); (d) contact information; and (e) semester-by-semester Major Maps (for FTICs and transfer students). These semester-by-semester maps define the major in curricular detail, specifying exactly which courses the student should be taking each semester in order to graduate in 4 years for FTICs and in 2 years for transfer students. The site has a "compare" button that allows students to make side-by-side comparisons of up to three majors. MyMajorMatch links seamlessly to MyMajor. Students take the inventory and receive their top five vocational interests with a handy tab of recommended majors for each one that takes them directly to that major in MyMajor with their defining Major Maps.

The creation of the Major Maps was a collaboration between the faculty responsible for each of FIU's 70 majors and the researchers in the Office of Retention and Graduation Success (ORGS). Using multivariate statistical techniques, the researchers were able to identify not only *critical indicator courses* (courses in which performance correlated significantly with retention and on-time graduation) but also the level of performance that was necessary in those courses. For example, ORGS research found that if journalism majors did not achieve at least a B- in their freshman composition class, then they had only an 18% chance of graduating on time. These research results were given to faculty to apply in creating their Major Maps for students. Not only are the Major Maps crucial for defining the meanings of the names of majors for applicants, but as we see later they constitute a core intervention for Points 2 and 3 of the GSI conceptual framework—providing a clear path to the goal of on-time graduation in an appropriate major and giving immediate feedback whether on or off the path—both of which are the basis for the tracking tool, My_eAdvisor. The Major Maps function as sets of explicit rules regarding what courses to take, when to take them, and what performance threshold pertains.

We should note that the system attempts to *accelerate* the discernment process for selecting an appropriate major, not to *foreclose* it. The data clearly indicate that for FIU students the romantic vision of a 2 + 2 model (2 years of general exploration followed by 2 years of specialization) does not lead to on-time graduation. As we have seen, the FIU data simply do not support the belief that after 2 years of taking disconnected courses in a cafeteria-style general education program students have a Damascus Road experience and know clearly what major and profession they wish to pursue and then do so promptly and successfully. The GSI system—high tech and high touch—attempts in a focused, intentional way to help students to learn quickly what it is they would like to do to earn a living and what they should study to do so.

Reinforcing contingencies

Contingencies have been designed to reinforce the students' behavior of discerning and selecting an appropriate major at admission. Applicants have to declare a major as part of the admission process; it is an explicit *rule*. So one reinforcement is simply being allowed to complete the admission process. "Undecided" and "undeclared" are not options. If an applicant is truly clueless or resistant for some reason to declaring a major, he or she can select one of six exploratory tracks: (a) administration and management, (b) biological and environmental sciences, (c) global and social sciences, (d) humanities and the arts, (e) health sciences, and (f) physical science and engineering. Each exploratory track has a curriculum designed to help the student to discern his or her major quickly. An explicit policy (*rule*) has been created that all exploratory students must have a major before they earn 45 credits. It is interesting that only 2% of entering students declare an exploratory major. Only students' academic advisors can change their majors, and frivolous major changes have been eliminated. Stealth majors, in which a student declares one major (e.g., liberal studies, with few specific requirements) but really pursues another major (e.g., business administration, with a calculus requirement that presents a barrier to many aspiring stealth majors), have been all but eliminated because the tracking tool, My_eAdvisor, lets advisors know immediately whether students are off track for their declared majors. If students want to change their majors, they must have a serious interaction with their academic advisor.

Remember that one of the desired behaviors is *discerning* an appropriate major, not just *declaring* one. Taking MyMajorMatch and going through the learning system that it entails is an important part of this discernment process. Applicants receive a To-Do List on their MyFIU portal as part of the admission process. In addition to listing such things as sending transcripts and payment for admission fees, it also includes taking MyMajorMatch. The clear and intended impression is that completing MyMajorMatch is a required part of the admission process. So being able to remove it from the To-Do List is reinforcing. In fact, neglecting to take the inventory does not stop the admission process, but the applicant does not know that. In addition, after admission, the student's advisor notes immediately that the student has not taken MyMajorMatch and strongly and persistently encourages the student to complete that task. So another reinforcement for the student's discernment behavior is the positive or negative feedback of the advisor regarding completing MyMajorMatch.

Lastly, the empowerment that comes to the student from the MyMajorMatch learning system (i.e., knowing one's professional interests and specifically how those interests can be pursued in this new academic environment) provides another reinforcement, perhaps the most powerful one. If the assessment really works—actually provides useful information that promotes students' success—then its reputation of utility becomes a reinforcement for its completion by succeeding cohorts.

During the 4 years of its use (October 2011–November 2015), 65,640 MyMajorMatch assessments have been completed (Figure 2 displays the top interest clusters). The tool is definitely being used.

Initial research (Trusty, 2014) supports the efficacy of MyMajorMatch as a tool for helping students to identify an appropriate major. A cohort of 12,697

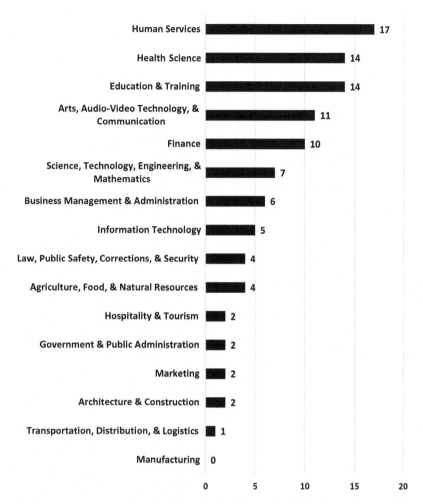

Figure 2. Cumulative percentages (October 2011–November 2015) of top interest clusters for Florida International University applicants and students taking the MyMajorMatch assessment.

students who entered FIU prior to August 6, 2012, and had access to MyMajorMatch constituted the study's sample. Their academic performance was examined for the next three semesters that made up the academic year 2012–2013. These students all had the opportunity to take MyMajorMatch and to accumulate three semesters of coursework. Of the 12,697 students in the sample, 6,506 (51%) students completed MyMajorMatch. Remember that its completion is not actually required to complete the admission process; it only appears that it is required. The study's dependent variable was GPA. There were two independent variables: (a) congruence between the major selected by the student and the majors indicated by MyMajorMatch, and (b) whether the student took MyMajorMatch.

The findings (Trusty, 2014) showed significantly higher GPAs for students who selected a major that was in their top five interest clusters than for those who did not: analysis of variance for the first semester, $F(5, 6500) = 2.335$, $p = .040$; cumulative through second semester, $F(5, 6{,}129) = 2.530$, $p = .001$; cumulative through third semester, $F(5, 4636) = 4.511$, $p < .0005$. The effect was strongest for students who selected a major congruent with their top three interest clusters. This difference in GPAs grew with each succeeding semester, thus indicating a compounding positive effect of selecting an appropriate major as indicated by MyMajorMatch.

For entering freshman (Trusty, 2014), the difference in cumulative three-semester GPAs for students who took MyMajorMatch (61%) and those who did not take MyMajorMatch (38%) was also statistically significant: analysis of variance cumulative through third semester, $F(1, 4373) = 41.661$, $p < .0005$. This finding was true whether or not the students who took MyMajorMatch selected majors congruent with their interest clusters. It is interesting that women were overrepresented among those students who took MyMajorMatch (women = 57%, men = 44%), and men were over-represented among the students who chose not to take MyMajorMatch (women = 43%, men = 56%).

Completing MyMajorMatch does appear to have value for discerning an appropriate academic major early in the student's academic career. This utility reinforces its promotion and use in future cohorts.

Transforming the advising system

The *interlocked behavioral systems* of students and advisors illustrates nicely the way in which the GSI is actually a massive and complicated transformation of *metacontingencies* extending through reporting systems all the way from students to the Board of Trustees.

Desired and targeted behavior

Selecting an appropriate major puts the student on the path to on-time graduation in that appropriate major *if* the student follows that path as prescribed in the semester-by-semester Major Map, which then becomes the *desired behavior*: staying on track. The *targeted behaviors* (such as not consulting the Major Maps at all and choosing courses ignorantly, creating schedules of convenience, or listening a little too closely to the advice of uninformed friends or family) are those behaviors that lead the student not to follow his or her Major Map.

Strategic interventions

Two examples of the GSI's strategic interventions to produce the desired behavior are *high touch* (creating 69 new advisor lines in 5 years and introducing a radically different advising paradigm) and *high tech* (the My_eAdvisor tracking tool).

High touch. Early in the GSI, undergraduate advising was removed from the faculty's set of responsibilities and moved to a professional advisor model. Faculty were encouraged to continue to mentor undergraduates, but the core academic advising was put in the hands of master's-prepared professionals. A career path of six levels was created for advisors with the intent of attracting and retaining professionals who were making academic advising a career, not merely something that one did while finishing a terminal degree, waiting to find a real job, supplementing the family income, and so forth. The GSI moved the university to a caseload advising model. Annual investments over 5 years added 69 advising lines to approach the 400 to 1 ratio of students to advisors that is a best practice established by the National Academic Advising Association. Every student is assigned to a professional advisor at admission.

The new academic advising paradigm is a caseload model that requires advisors to work their caseloads proactively and that involves two new integrations into the explicit, interlocking rules for, and responsibilities of, the academic advisors: (a) integrating lower and upper division advising, and (b) integrating career development with academic advising. Because students select their majors at admission and enter their colleges immediately, the need no longer existed for a university cadre of lower division advisors who advised the general education program and helped students to discover a major in their first 2 years. The course recommendations for the first 2 years are now embedded in the Major Maps, and the advisors now have the responsibility of redirecting students to an appropriate major somewhere in the university if the students need a new dream. In addition, they must advise the upper division major. Moreover, academic advisors are now expected to be knowledgeable of MyMajorMatch and the Occupational Information Network (O*NET) and to help students to connect their academic choices to their career development. Finally, academic advisors are expected to work their caseloads *proactively* (desired behavior) rather than waiting *reactively* for students to contact them (targeted behavior). The advisors are given a significant amount of information through both the behavioral scientists in ORGS and the GSI's advising tools (*strategic interventions*), and they are expected to act on that information to reach out both to students who are identified as succeeding and, especially, to those who are identified as at risk (ORGS behavioral scientists have now developed a statistical model that can predict first-to-second-year retention with 50% accuracy for entering students even before they take their first class). This information is readily available for advisors for their caseloads. Dashboards have been created to monitor the advisors' use of such tools as My_eAdvisor, and merit awards are based on their application of the new proactive advising paradigm (*reinforcing contingencies*).

High tech. Now for the high-tech example of a strategic intervention to achieve the desired behavior of students staying on track. My_eAdvisor is a powerful tracking system that was developed internally by an FIU team and that allows students and advisors to monitor academic progress vis-à-vis the Major Map. The Major Map shows semester-by-semester expectations of what courses need to be taken, what grades need to be earned, and what milestones need to be achieved in order to graduate on time. Both students and advisors have My_eAdvisor dashboards with important summaries and quick access to functionalities.

The student's My_eAdvisor dashboard includes: (a) the interactive Major Map, which displays curricular specifications, performance levels, and milestones necessary for the student to graduate on time; (b) advisor messages in addition to automated alerts at the end of each semester if the student strays from the Major Map; (c) universal advising notes, the accumulated notes from interactions with all advisors, which allow students and any FIU advisor to know what advice the student has received; (d) a scheduler, which allows the student access to interact with the advisor's availability and to make an appointment online; and (e) links to pertinent resources. The interactive Major Map is rich in detailed information for students about what they should be doing and whether they are doing it. The closer to the behavior that feedback occurs, the more likely it is that the feedback will be effective. In the case of My_eAdvisor, feedback is given immediately following each semester, and if students need to register for a course to correct a misstep, they can view the available sections and register for the course seamlessly from My_eAdvisor. This feature was challenging to build because of the link to real-time section availability, and no other tracking tool yet developed has it.

The advisors' My_eAdvisor dashboard includes: (a) all students assigned to that advisor, the roster of the advisor's caseload for whom the advisor is held accountable for monitoring the progress and proactively facilitating students' success in graduating on time in an appropriate major; (b) automated alerts at the end of each semester if their students stray from their Major Map; (c) early alerts during the semester from faculty who are teaching their students; (d) the advisor calendar, used to express advisors' availability and to make appointments online; (e) access to advisor notes for all students; (f) access to sending and receiving messages to and from students; and (g) advisors' profiles, including their basic contact information.

Reinforcing contingencies
Reinforcing contingencies for the students staying on track in terms of taking the correct courses, performing at least adequately in those courses, and meeting milestones include an automated system of praise (for staying on track) and alerts (for straying). At present, the system has many more automated alerts than praise, which is an area of needed improvement for

the system. Wired into the system are both *universal* alerts (e.g., maintaining a GPA of 2.0 or above and earning a certain number of credits at various durations) and *major-specific* alerts (e.g., taking the appropriate prerequisite and required courses for the major at the appropriate time). Alerts are generated at the end of each semester based on the students' performance and sent to both the students and their advisors. The advisors contact their students to resolve the alert. Weekly automated reports show whether individual advisors have acted on their alerts. These same automated reports show whether whole colleges or departments are acting on their alerts. Not acting on alerts has negative consequences, and these automated reports negatively reinforce the desired behavior at every level in the advising system. Acting on alerts avoids aversive outcomes. Ultimately, if students repeatedly ignore both their alerts and advisors, the advisor or the system will place a hold on the students' ability to register for courses. This is a primary terminal contingency in a chain of events and alerts. Then the students must contact their advisor in order to lift the hold (eliminating or escaping it), thereby guaranteeing a conversation with their advisor about possible issues.

Each week, My_eAdvisor usage data for all of its tools (not just alerts) are displayed in automated reports for the university as a whole, by college, and by individual advisors within colleges. Thus, students' and advisors' behavior are being regularly monitored. Advising administrators have access to the performance of individual advisors whom they supervise. Unit deans have access to the performance of their advising administrators and advisors. The provost has access to the performance of the entire system and all of its personnel directly and via the dean of undergraduate education.

Transforming gateway instructional systems

Recalling the GSI's conceptual framework—helping students to discern and choose an appropriate goal, providing a clear path to that goal, giving immediate feedback whether on or off the path, and removing barriers and adding supports along the path—we would like to close with a brief discussion of the GSI's next emphasis, which focuses on Point 4 (removing barriers and adding supports along the path).

The work of the behavioral scientists from ORGS shows that poorly performing gateway courses are a major barrier to student progression, particularly in the vulnerable first year. If students fail a course in their first or second semester, not only do they have to take the course over, but they also suffer consequences such as confirming their suspicion that they are not really suitable for college and increasing the possibility of dropping out. This vulnerability is particularly true for minority, first-generation students, such as many of FIU's students. For example, in FIU's 2012 FTIC cohort, 46% of students who failed Writing and Rhetoric I dropped out in their first year. In the same cohort, students who failed one of three basic mathematics courses also dropped out in their first year at a high rate: (a) Intermediate Algebra, 38%; (b) College Algebra, 26%; and (c) Finite Math, 23%.

With the generous support of two grants from the Bill and Melinda Gates Foundation, administered by the Coalition of Urban Serving Universities and the Association of Public and Land-Grant Universities, the GSI has developed and is implementing a comprehensive, multiyear plan to improve the performance of 17 high-enrollment (>1,600), high-failure (>15%), high-impact (strong predictor of dropping out or delayed graduation) courses. In 2014–2015, the combined enrollment in these 17 courses was 44,773. This strategic intervention in a relatively small number of courses could have an extraordinarily large impact. The GSI's Phase I focused on a transforming the admission and advising systems, and now in Phase II the GSI focuses on transforming pedagogy in 17 critical gateway courses en route to transforming the teaching culture throughout the university (see Table 3).

FIU is one of 13 founding universities in the John N. Gardner Institute's Gateways to Completion Project (http://www.jngi.org/g2c/). That work was integrated into the GSI's Phase II emphasis on gateway courses. In 2013–2014, five low-performing courses (Finite Math, General Biology, General Chemistry, Introduction to Statistics I, and Writing and Rhetoric I) were selected for in-depth study by course-specific workgroups that included the department chair, course coordinator, teaching faculty, director of the ORGS, director of the Center for the Advancement of Teaching, and dean of undergraduate education. These five cross-unit teams produced 15 specific recommendations for improvement as measured by DFWI rates (the percentage of students with grades of D, F, Withdrawal, or Incomplete). These recommendations in many cases had direct application to the larger group of 17 gateway courses and became the basis for workgroups in all 17 courses. Many of the recommendations were integrated into the new FIU *Beyond Possible* 2020 Strategic Plan (approved by the FIU Board of Trustees on March 26, 2015).

The 15 recommendations represent a combination of *desired behavior* and *strategic interventions* related to improving the performance of gateway courses, removing obstacles and adding support to students' academic progression, and ultimately improving overall student success as measured by the aforementioned student success metrics. The 15 recommendations are as follows (in no particular order):

- Convert from adjuncts to full-time instructors in all gateway courses, which will involve strategic institutional investment over multiple years.

Table 3. Seventeen High-Enrollment, High-Failure, High-Impact Gateway Courses Targeted for Improvement in 2014–2015.

Course	Title	Enrollment			DFWI rate		
		2012–2013	2013–2014	2014–2015	2012–2013	2013–2014	2014–2015
MAC 1114	Trigonometry	1,476	1,682	2,022	52%	60%	52%
MAC 1140	Pre-Calculus Algebra	1,708	2,337	2,567	48%	58%	46%
MAC 2311	Calculus I	1,542	1,857	2,120	46%	52%	49%
MGF 1106	Finite Math	2,855	2,765	2,230	41%	49%	36%
ECO 2013	Principles of Macroeconomics	1,906	2,196	2,264	31%	41%	35%
CHM 1045	General Chemistry I	2,021	2,286	2,237	36%	39%	40%
ECO 2023	Principles of Microeconomics	2,205	2,048	2,661	21%	36%	21%
STA 3123	Introduction to Statistics II	1,768	2,079	2,447	22%	36%	31%
MAC 1105	College Algebra	2,007	2,035	1,896	38%	35%	36%
STA 2122	Introduction to Statistics I	2,265	2,216	2,023	31%	34%	33%
BSC 1010	General Biology I	1,987	2,250	2,647	29%	30%	29%
REL 2011	Religion: Analysis and Interpretation	1,915	1,951	1,666	19%	21%	19%
REL 3308	Studies in World Religion	2,360	1,848	1,543	17%	18%	16%
ENC 1102	Writing and Rhetoric II	4,507	4,581	5,081	13%	18%	14%
ENC1101	Writing and Rhetoric I	3,836	3,479	4,587	13%	17%	11%
PSY 2012	Introduction to Psychology	2,282	2,110	2,469	14%	15%	10%
SLS 1501	First Year Experience	4,213	3,837	4,313	8%	10%	8%

Note. DFWI = percentage of students with grades of D, F, Withdrawal, or Incomplete.

- Develop automated early alert systems for all gateway courses, which will include required use of a learning management system by faculty as well as clickers to facilitate automated attendance recording.
- Expand the number and use of learning assistants and create a central office that coordinates learning assistant recruiting, training, and strategic deployment.
- Improve gateway course teaching and learning physical environments (e.g., create discipline-specific gateway course learning resource centers and lounges, increase the number of active learning classrooms).
- Expand gateway course bridge programs both in the form of boot camps and in terms of collaboration with feeder secondary schools and community colleges.
- Develop strategic faculty development and awards programs that incentivize and support exemplary pedagogy in gateway courses.
- Develop dependable technological support and training for the use of instructional technology such as learning management systems and clickers, which are both necessary for automated early alert systems.
- Develop new business models that show the savings produced by improved retention and on-time graduation and thereby provide a data-based figure that is available for upfront investment.

- Develop dashboards that provide stakeholders with performance data related to gateway courses at the section level.
- Regularly disseminate predictive analytics to stakeholders.
- Set up robust and regular communication systems among faculty and administrators for feeding and receiving courses, programs, and institutions that provide a basis for curriculum alignment and assessment.
- Create a teaching initiatives coordinating council that regularly brings together all groups at the institution that are involved in major pedagogical reform.
- Incorporate "becoming a university student" learning objectives (e.g., study skills, reading strategies, writing skills, time management) into gateway courses.
- Guarantee course availability.
- Establish learning metrics that demonstrate that improvements in the performance of gateway courses (e.g., lower DFWI rates) are the result of increased student learning and not merely grade inflation.

The basis for *reinforcing contingencies* is clearly present in recommendations that involve creating data-based performance dashboards and awards programs. Because of the clear, statistical connection between overall student success metrics and gateway course performance, the university's performance on these metrics will serve as significant *reinforcing contingencies* for the *desired behaviors* at all levels to improve gateway course performance.

Conclusion

Our purpose in discussing this case study has been to demonstrate the practical utility of behavior analytic concepts such as interlocking behavioral contingencies, metacontingencies, and rule-governed behavior in guiding effective organizational change management and to describe specific ways to improve undergraduate student success in colleges and universities. The organization being transformed is complex *horizontally* with many different groups of agents and *vertically* with many hierarchical levels, and the interventions have been multitudinous. Even so, the theoretical perspectives and conceptual framework that inform these interventions are few and straightforward. We hope that our intended audiences—practitioners, researchers, and theoreticians in the fields of behavior analysis, organizational change management, and higher education—have found the discussion useful.

Funding

Parts of the Graduation Success Initiative have been supported by grants from the U.S. Department of Education's Title V Program; the Walmart

Foundation Student Success Initiative; the Helios Education Foundation; the Helmsley Charitable Trust's Transforming University STEM Education Initiative; the Kresge Foundation; and the Bill and Melinda Gates Foundation Transformational Planning Grant Program and Transformational Change Collaborative, both administered by the Association of Public and Land-Grant Universities and the Coalition of Urban Serving Universities.

References

Astin, A. W. (1977). *Four critical years*. San Francisco, CA: Jossey-Bass.

Astin, A. W. (1985). *Achieving academic excellence*. San Francisco, CA: Jossey-Bass.

Astin, A. W. (1993). *What matters most: Four critical years revisited*. San Francisco, CA: Jossey-Bass.

Chickering, A. W., & Reisser, L. (1993). *Education and identity* (2nd ed.). San Francisco, CA: Jossey-Bass.

Glenn, S. S. (1986). Metacontingencies in Walden Two. *Behavior Analysis & Social Action, 5*, 2–8.

Glenn, S. S. (1988). Contingencies and metacontingencies: Toward a synthesis of behavior analysis and cultural materialism. *The Behavior Analyst, 11*, 161–179.

Glenn, S. S. (1989). Verbal behavior and cultural practices. *Behavioral Analysis and Social Action, 7*(1–2), 10–15.

Glenn, S. S. (1991). Contingencies and metacontingencies: Relations among behavioral, cultural, and biological evolution. In P. A. Lamal (Ed.), *The behavioral analysis of societies and cultural practices* (pp. 39–73). Washington, DC: Hemisphere.

Glenn, S. S. (2003). Operant contingencies and the origin of cultures. In K. A. Lattal & P. N. Chase (Eds.), *Behavior theory and philosophy* (pp. 223–242). New York, NY: Kluwer Academic/Plenum.

Glenn, S. S. (2004). Individual behavior, culture, and social change. *The Behavior Analyst, 27*, 131–151.

Glenn, S. S. (2010). Metacontingencies, selection and OBM: Comments on "emergence and metacontingency." *Behavior and Social Issues, 19*, 79–85. doi:10.5210/bsi.v19i0.3220

Glenn, S. S., & Malagodi, E. F. (1991). Process and content in behavioral and cultural phenomena. *Behavior and Social Issues, 2*(2), 1–14.

Glenn, S. S., & Malott, M. E. (2004). Complexity and selection: Implications for organizational change. *Behavior and Social Issues, 13*, 89–106. doi:10.5210/bsi.v13i2.378

Houmanfar, R., & Rodrigues, N. J. (2006). The metacontingency and the behavioral contingency: Points of contact and departure. *Behavior and Social Issues, 15*, 13–30. doi:10.5210/bsi.v15i1.342

Houmanfar, R., Rodrigues, N. J., & Smith, G. S. (2009). Role of communication networks in behavioral systems analysis. *Journal of Organizational Behavior Management, 29*, 257–275. doi:10.1080/01608060903092102

Houmanfar, R., Rodrigues, N. J., & Ward, T. A. (2010). Emergence and metacontingencies: Points of contact and departure. *Behavior and Social Issues, 19*, 78–103. doi:10.5210/bsi.v19i0.3065

Kuh, G. D., Kinzie, J., Schuh, J. H., & Whitt, E. J. (2010). *Student success in college: Creating conditions that matter*. San Francisco, CA: Jossey-Bass.

Malott, M. E. (1999). Creating lasting organizational change. *Performance Improvement, 38*(2), 33–36. doi:10.1002/pfi.4140380209

Malott, M. E. (2001). Putting the horse before the cart: Process-driven change. In L. Hayes, R. Fleming, J. Austin, & R. Houmanfar (Eds.), *Organizational change* (pp. 297–320). Reno, NV: Context Press.

Malott, M. E. (2003). *Paradox of organizational change: Engineering organizations with behavioral systems analysis*. Reno, NV: Context Press.

Malott, M. E., & Glenn, S. S. (2006). Targets of intervention in cultural and behavioral change. *Behavior and Social Issues, 15*, 31–56. doi:10.5210/bsi.v15i1.344

Malott, M. E., & Salas Martinez, W. (2006). Addressing organizational complexity: A behavioural systems analysis application to higher education. *International Journal of Psychology, 41*(6), 559–570. doi:10.1080/00207590500492773

Malott, R. W. (1992). A theory of rule-governed behavior and organizational behavior management. *Journal of Organizational Behavior Management, 12*(2), 45–65. doi:10.1300/J075v12n02_03

Mattaini, M. (2004). Systems, metacontingencies, and cultural analysis: Are we there yet? *Behavior and Social Issues, 13*, 124–130. doi:10.5210/bsi.v13i2.20

Novak, G., & Pelaez, M. (2004). *Child and adolescent development: A behavioral systems approach*. Thousand Oaks, CA: Sage.

Pascarella, E. T., & Terenzini, P. (2005). *How college affects students: A third decade of research* (2nd ed.). San Francisco, CA: Jossey-Bass.

Pelaez, M. (2013). Dimensions of rules and their correspondence to rule-governed behavior. *European Journal of Behavior Analysis, 14*(2), 259–270.

Pelaez, M., & Moreno, R. (1998). A taxonomy of rules and their correspondence to rule-governed behavior. *Mexican Journal of Behavior Analysis, 24*, 197–214.

Robertson, D. (1983). Human studies: A perspective about perspective. *Alternative Higher Education, 7*(2), 105–115. doi:10.1007/BF01079411

Robertson, D. (1984a). Human studies: An individualized, interdisciplinary major for adults. In J. W. Fonseca (Ed.), *Higher education for adults: Non-traditional paths* (pp. 25–33). Fairfax, VA: George Mason University.

Robertson, D. (1984b). A theory of development and its application to managing departments for faculty development. *Issues in Higher Education, 13*, 478–492.

Robertson, D. (1988). *Self-directed growth*. Muncie, IN: Accelerated Development.

Robertson, D. (1991). An evolutionary response to adult learners: The urban small college. *Innovative Higher Education, 16*(1), 39–48. doi:10.1007/BF00911557

Robertson, D. (1992). Urban postsecondary systems: Higher education's infrastructure in American cities. *Review of Higher Education, 15*(4), 325–339.

Robertson, D. (1996). Facilitating transformative learning: Attending to the dynamics of the educational helping relationship. *Adult Education Quarterly, 47*(1), 41–53. doi:10.1177/074171369604700104

Robertson, D. (1999). Professors' perspectives on their teaching: A new construct and developmental model. *Innovative Higher Education, 23*(4), 271–294. doi:10.1023/A:1022982907040

Robertson, D. R. (2000). Professors in space and time: Four utilities of a new metaphor and developmental model for professors-as-teachers. *Journal on Excellence in College Teaching, 11*(1), 117–132.

Robertson, D. R. (2001). Beyond learner-centeredness: Close encounters of the systemocentric kind. *Journal of Faculty Development, 18*(1), 7–13.

Robertson, D. R. (2002). Creating and supporting an inclusive scholarship of teaching. *The Eastern Scholar, 1*(1), 46–58.

Skinner, B. F. (1953). *Science and human behavior*. New York, NY: Macmillan.

Skinner, B. F. (1957). *Verbal behavior*. Englewood Cliffs, NJ: Prentice Hall.

Skinner, B. F. (1966). An operant analysis of problem solving. In B. Kleinmuntz (Ed.), *Problem solving: Research, method and theory* (pp. 225–257). New York, NY: Wiley.

Skinner, B. F. (1969). *Contingencies of reinforcement: A theoretical analysis.* New York, NY: Appleton-Century-Crofts.

Tinto, V. (1994). *Leaving college: Rethinking the causes and cures of student attrition* (2nd ed.). Chicago, IL: University of Chicago Press.

Tinto, V. (2012). *Completing college: Rethinking institutional action.* Chicago, IL: University of Chicago Press.

Trusty, J. (2014). *Study of outcomes associated with use of the Kuder Career Search with Person Match at a public research university in greater Miami, Florida.* Retrieved from http://www.kuder.com/wp-content/uploads/2014/07/Outcomes-Associated-with-Use-of-KCS-FL.pdf

A Behavioral Approach to Organizational Change: Reinforcing Those Responsible for Facilitating the Climate and Hence Promoting Diversity

Judith L. Komaki and Michelle L. R. Minnich

ABSTRACT

Despite the passage of the U.S. Civil Rights Act in 1964, cries can still be heard for a more diverse workforce. Among the difficulties are retaining often sought-after women and minorities. In this 2-year demonstration, change agents—the provost, deans, and heads of departments/schools of a large public university—were helped to deliberately and directly change the milieu of their departments and schools so as to encourage faculty to remain. Uniquely suited to organizational change, the behavioral approach identifies constructive actions for change agents and, most importantly, provides proven strategies for motivating them. Fostering a supportive climate was defined in terms of change agents' behaviors. The Building Behaviorally Based Climate Survey was developed and validated. Recognition and feedback were provided in what is typically a feedback desert. This reinforcement model can be used to create and sustain inviting atmospheres, hence enticing all faculty, including women and minority faculty, to stay, hence enabling a diverse workforce.

The U.S. Civil Rights Act outlawing discrimination was passed in 1964. Fifty years later, the lack of diversity in the workforce still remains an issue (Dobbin & Kalev, 2016). Disappointed in the relatively sparse gains at high-tech organizations, members of the Congressional Black Caucus converged on Silicon Valley, insisting that companies hire more African Americans (Guynn, 2015). A hunger strike and protests by students at the University of Missouri forced the resignation of the college president with demands, among others, to increase diversity among faculty (Mrig, 2015). Students continue to make clear the need for change. Micah Oliver, president of the Black Student Association at the University at Buffalo, pointed out, "There's a difference in the learning experience that you have when you're learning from someone you believe you can identify with more closely" (Thompson & Walsh, 2015, para. 8).

Lackluster progress of women and minorities in the workplace

The earnings gap is still alive and well. In 2015, men still made more than women; Whites earned more than Blacks (U.S. Bureau of Labor Statistics, 2015). "For those age 25 and older, median earnings for all major race and ethnicity groups increased with educational attainment. However, Blacks and Hispanics generally had lower earnings than Whites and Asians at nearly all educational attainment levels" (p. 4, Table 17).

At the same time, inequalities exist in the distribution of jobs. Thirty-nine percent of employed Whites "worked in management, professional, and related occupations – the highest paying major occupational category –" as did 51% of Asians, 30% of Blacks, and 21% of Hispanics (US Bureau of Labor Statistics, 2015, p. 4). Dramatic declines occur further up in the hierarchy. Among the total employed as chief executives, 26.3% are women, 4.7% Asian, 4.7% Hispanic, and 3.0% Black.

In universities, a similar pattern occurs. Of full-time faculty at degree-granting postsecondary institutions in 2013, 79% were White (43% White males and 35% White females), 10% were Asian/Pacific Islander, 6% were Black, and 5% were Hispanic. At the highest level of full professor, the numbers drop to 4% for Blacks and 3% for Hispanics (National Center for Education Statistics, 2015).

In short, especially in leadership positions, women and minorities continue to be severely underpaid and underrepresented.

Few if any effective ways of promoting diversity

Despite pledges and commitments over the past 50 years, few strategies have been hailed as the way to make sure that underrepresented groups will indeed be represented and even embraced (Komaki, 2007).

Individual empowerment places much of the burden on women and minorities

A prevalent approach sets up women and minorities to be the primary change agents. Enlisted to change themselves, individuals learn to shore up their negotiating skills, set boundaries, and build satisfying careers. Chief operating officer of Facebook Sheryl Sandberg (2013) reflected on her experience of unintentionally holding herself back in her career. In her book *Lean In* she urged women in particular to change themselves—pressing them ... to increase their self confidence, to get their partners to do more at home, to not hold themselves to impossible standards—in her words, to lean in.

An example of individual empowerment can be seen in a program supporting new faculty, particularly faculty of color at Virginia Tech

(Piercy et al., 2005). The aim was to improve the campus climate so as to support faculty diversity and retention. Directives were given in the form of instructional sessions. "Development breakfasts" were held for new untenured faculty at which they learned about grant writing and tenure and promotion dossiers. "A university-wide faculty retention workshop" was attended by senior administrators ranging from department heads to vice-presidents at which they learned about "the negative impact of a homogeneous workforce and the cumulative disadvantages placed on persons from underrepresented groups" (p. 60). It is interesting that no mention was made about what senior administrators could and would do to enhance the climate. Instead, it was assumed that new faculty would learn from the development breakfasts and go on to thrive. Relying on individual empowerment places the onus of responsibility on women and minorities, often irrespective of the context in which these underrepresented groups operate.

Recruitment works, but only if highly sought-after employees stay

Another widespread approach is the hiring of women and minorities. Relying on that strategy only works if the women and minorities do not leave. For Black executives, the turnover rate is 40% higher than for others (Davidson & Foster-Johnson, n.d.). Furthermore, universities must compete with "the much better paying corporate world" (Flaherty, 2015b, para. 2), which, like universities, is eager to fill its ranks with talented women and minorities.

Recruitment is the predominant strategy

In Silicon Valley, women make up 10% to 30% of the workforce (Harkinson, 2015) and Blacks and Latinos "in most cases, less than 10 percent" (para. 4). Like many leaders in industry, Silicon Valley chief executive officers have pledged to improve the diversity of their workforces, but most of their efforts deal almost exclusively with recruitment. The CEO of Apple, Tim Cook, for instance, has pledged more than $50 million to organizations that strive to increase the number of women, minorities, and veterans working in technology: $40 million to the Thurgood Marshall College Fund, which supports public, historically Black colleges and universities, and about $10 million to the National Center for Women and Information Technology (Lev-Ram, 2015).

Similarly, in universities the emphasis is on recruitment. In a bold move, president of Brown University Christina Paxson pledged "to double its proportion of underrepresented minority faculty by 2025" (Flaherty, 2015a, para. 1). To feed the pipeline, Brown developed high-level initiatives: "a new postdoctoral fellowship program, ... a young scholars program, ... professional development opportunities for underrepresented groups" (Flaherty, 2015a, para. 1). To enhance the climate, however, individual departments were pressed into service. To ensure that "underrepresented minorities [will] ... want to stay at Brown," each department was held responsible for developing its own "diversity action plan" and was held accountable using "new metrics ... look[ing] at ... diverse candidate pools and hires in departments" (Flaherty, 2015a, paras. 4, 5, 7). Although Kimberly Griffin at the University of Maryland at College Park sees the benefit of setting diversity goals, she said, "I worry about narrow strategies that focus on short-term recruitment and hiring" (Flaherty, 2015b, para. 8).

To ensure diversity, recruited minorities and women need to be retained
Experts agree that "any successful diversity plan ... will involve not only bringing more black faculty members to campus, but also address the climate issues that will influence whether they stay there" (Flaherty, 2015b, para. 2).

Retention, the missing ingredient, relies on a supportive climate, but efforts to directly build the climate are rare
Unfortunately, once universities make their hires, relatively little attention is paid to "effectively develop, reward, and retain people of color" (Mrig, 2015. para. 9).

Plentiful evidence showing a correlation between climate and intention to stay
A powerful predictor of employees' intention to stay in or leave an organization is the culture or climate of the organization, as study after study has shown (e.g., Carr, Schmidt, Ford, & DeShon, 2003; Claiborne, Auerbach, Zeitlin, & Lawrence, 2015; Daly & Dee, 2006; Garner & Hunter, 2013; Hemingway & Smith, 1999; Lindell & Brandt, 2000; Schneider & Bowen, 1985; Shim, 2010, 2014; Zeitlin, Augsberger, Auerbach, & McGowan, 2014). Shanker (2014) found an "irrefutable relationship" (p. 381) between employee willingness to continue working and organizational climate, with service employees who "could decide how to best do their jobs" and "supervisors who listened to them and were approachable" (p. 385). Furthermore, several top 100 companies have consistently found relationships between climate surveys; employee satisfaction; and outcomes such as productivity, profitability, client satisfaction, and retention (Johnson, 2004).

Because of data collection difficulties, many studies use employees' intentions rather than actual turnover or retention figures. It is not as simple to measure retention as it might initially seem (Waterfield, 2006). One could assume that all that is needed is the number of employees who remain and the number who leave. Complications can arise when evaluating those who leave. Persons can leave voluntarily (e.g., taking a job elsewhere); or non-voluntarily (e.g., disability, termination, or death); or, in universities, after getting turned down for tenure. Hence, taking into consideration these nonvoluntary reasons, it may be necessary to have access to a variety of databases, or even paper files, to calculate retention. This information may not be accessible, which would result in missing data; incomplete files for persons who left is what Ries et al. (2009) found. As a result, many retention studies, including the present one, use intention to stay as the measure of retention.

Evidence exists showing a significant relationship between the two. Employees' stated quit intentions were found to be one of the best predictors of turnover in a meta-analysis of a large body of turnover research (Griffeth, Hom, & Gaertner, 2000).

Few experiments fostering retention or climate appear in the literature

To date, researchers studying retention and turnover have yet to go the next step and try, based on their findings, to improve the climate. Why employees leave, however, continues to be a source of fascination. Concerned about the number of talented officers who leave the military to work in the private sector, Kane (2011) surveyed 250 West Point graduates of classes ranging from 1989 to 2004. He concluded that money was not the biggest factor. What drove officers away was structural: "The military personnel system.... every aspect of it ... is nearly blind to merit" (para. 7). That can be seen in personnel practices "from officer evaluations to promotions to job assignments" (para. 2). Recommendations were made to modify personnel practices. To date, no experiments have appeared in the literature showing that these changes have resulted in more talented officers staying.

As astute observers of organizational behavior know, it is not uncommon for organizations to change their personnel practices in order to upgrade the climate in their organizations. Questions are often raised, such as "How could a long-lived organization continue to adapt its culture and make much needed changes to remain innovative and effective in a global economy?" (Paul & Fenlason, 2014, p. 569). Rarely, however, do these endeavors appear in the scholarly literature. In their edited book on organizational climate, Schneider and Barbera (2014) tracked down industrial/organizational psychologists involved in making these changes and gathered together their accounts involving organizations including Pepsico, 3M and Mayo Clinic. Each of the six organizational change efforts differed in detail, but they were similar in the way they approached the change process: The endeavor typically began with the CEO setting the tone and direction, broadly based changes were made to many personnel practices, and the evaluation of effectiveness was also broadly based. Industrial/organizational psychologists Karen Paul and Kristofer Fenlason (2014) described how 3M's focus on climate began in 2006, when newly appointed CEO George Buckley decided to radically modernize 3M's culture and make it more innovative, flexible, and resilient. The 6-year intervention altered numerous practices, policies and procedures, pay and benefits, careers and leadership, employment partnership, performance, growth and business development, and strategies and business models. To assess whether the changes made a difference, 3M tracked responses to a "Leadership Survey" assessing a wide range of areas, from "commitment to the organization" to "acceptance of change," as well as financial indicators (p. 581).

Invitation to try and bolster retention at a large research university

The president of a large public university invited the first author to tackle the thorny problem of retaining faculty of all types, particularly minorities and women. Efforts had been made to improve the percentages of women and minorities. Year after year, women and minorities were courted and wooed to come to the university, but over time more left than stayed. The percentage of faculty who stayed remained stubbornly stable.

The president was predisposed to an incentive-based approach based on past experience with incentives. Hence, the president was amenable to setting up a demonstration to try and use an approach involving positive consequences for desired performance.

Though unprecedented, the plan was to increase retention by focusing on improving climate using a behavioral approach

Given the proven relationship between climate and intention to stay, it was decided to focus on the atmosphere in each unit to see whether it could be made more supportive. It was assumed that if the atmosphere could be enhanced so that every faculty member, including women and minorities, could experience a warm, inviting milieu, then they too would be more likely to remain at the university.

The behavioral approach targets change agents responsible for crafting the climate

The behavioral approach to organizational change is well suited because it first identifies the persons or groups whose actions are responsible for creating the atmospheres within their units; in this regard, it is quite specific. In the *Report of the Task Force on Women Faculty* (Harvard, 2005), "the two high-leverage points within the system for changing Harvard's success in the identification, recruitment, and retention of women and underrepresented minority faculty ... [are] search committee chairs and department chairs" (p. 28). Hence, the department chairs and deans under the leadership of the provost were identified as the key change agents.

The behavioral approach emphasizes motivating change agents

But it does no good to target the change agents unless one can encourage them to act in ways that improve the milieus in their units. The motivation of the persons responsible for crafting the atmosphere is key to unlocking the climate conundrum.

The behavioral approach is masterful in invigorating people to alter some-times longstanding patterns of behavior. Employees have been motivated to improve performance in a variety of settings in the public and private sectors (Komaki, Coombs, Redding, & Schepman, 2000; Van Stelle et al., 2012). The familiar three-step process of specifying, measuring, and providing positive consequences was used. In an effort to improve customer service, for exam-ple, desired instances of service were specified and measured at least weekly. Feedback was provided, with resulting increases in service provided to customers.

Hence, the objective of this field demonstration was to use the behavioral approach to help change agents deliberately and directly build the climate so as to entice incumbent faculty, particularly women and minority faculty, to stay at the university.

Method and results

Subjects and setting

The setting was the main campus of a large public university. The research took place over 2 years. There were 964 tenured or tenure-track faculty and administrators (department chairs, deans of colleges) in academic depart-ments, schools, and colleges in Year 1 and 1,000 in Year 2.

To set up the project, the president of the university introduced the first author to the system-wide diversity person as well as the chancellor, provost, and diversity and faculty affairs persons for the campus. To hammer out the scope and aims of the research, the first author met with the campus diversity and faculty affairs persons for a full day. Before proceeding, the first author successfully submitted proposals to the institutional review boards of both her university and the university in which this research was conducted. Thereafter, the first author and research associate visited the campus monthly. During Year 2, the second author was the research associate.

Building behaviorally based climate (BBC) survey

Content

The BBC survey assessed the climate in each department, school, and college as well as faculty members' intention to stay at the university (see Table 1).

Intention to stay was operationally defined in a traditional manner with five evaluative statements (e.g., "It would take a lot to get me to leave the department," "If I had to do it all over again, I would still accept this position").

Climate was measured in two ways. First, we used a traditional assessment consisting of nine evaluative statements (e.g., "I find the atmosphere or climate to be supportive," "I feel left out of things here"). As Appendix A shows, some intention to stay and climate items were borrowed from the scales of our industrial/organizational colleagues.

Second, the elusive concept of fostering a supportive climate was behaviorally defined in terms of actions that change agents could take in building such a climate. Three categories were identified: (a) evenhandedness of evaluation, defined as the fairness and accuracy of appraisal; (b) career advisement or mentoring about goals and timetables; and (c) acknowledgment or recognition of expertise, accomplishment, and progress. Although each category reflects a major personnel practice and would be likely to affect the atmosphere, career advising was selected by the university faculty affairs and diversity persons as a critical component. Based on the first author's operant leadership model (Komaki, 1998), in which she found that monitoring and providing consequences separated effective from marginally effective leaders, evaluation and acknowledgment were chosen.

Each category was behaviorally defined, identifying what key movers could do to ensure that faculty were evaluated, mentored, and recognized. Among the behaviors were: provided evidence that evaluations are free from bias, defined what it means to do high quality research, and indicated that expectations are the same for all faculty regardless of rank for evaluation; helped develop a broader network of people who could assist in achieving tenure and gave personalized feedback for mentoring; and inquired about the status of faculty members' research/creative work, asked to read/see work, and nominated a faculty member for a professional award for recognition.

Questions about gender, rank, and ethnicity/race were included in the survey. Respondents were also invited to write open-ended comments about their intention to stay and the climate in their unit.

Format of survey and scoring

A dichotomous scoring system was used in which respondents simply checked yes or no. For the behaviorally based climate items, respondents

Table 1. Building Behaviorally Based Climate Survey.

1. Evenhandedness of evaluation (related to annual merit increases)

   In the *last* academic year, the evaluation committee/administrators in your department ...? (Check all that apply.)

   - ☐ Evaluated your performance fairly and accurately
   - ☐ Defined what it means to do high quality research
   - ☐ Weighed the number of articles written more heavily than the quality of the work done
   - ☐ Simply counted the number of committees I was on for service
   - ☐ Used only student ratings to assess my teaching
   - ☐ Indicated the same expectations for all faculty in the department regardless of rank
   - ☐ Provided evidence that the evaluation was free from bias
   - ☐ Set up an evaluation system in which it is possible to exaggerate your accomplishments
   - ☐ Explained reasoning behind scores and the criteria on which those scores are based
   - ☐ Described what information you should provide prior to the committee evaluating your work (e.g., the number of pages per article, evidence of progress in completing a book)
   - ☐ Provided you with an opportunity to discuss the evaluation
   - ☐ Backed up or provided examples during feedback you received

2. Advice about career advisement

   In the *last* academic year, a colleague and/or administrator in your department ...?

   - ☐ Gave you personalized feedback
   - ☐ Assessed your career goals or timetable
   - ☐ Helped you revise your goals, timetable, or strategy to better attain your goals
   - ☐ Shared valuable workplace experience and knowledge
   - ☐ Assigned a mentor to you
   - ☐ Neglected career related questions you had
   - ☐ Spoke candidly with you about your career
   - ☐ Helped you develop a broader network of people who could be helpful
   - ☐ Explained the procedures for tenure or promotion thoroughly
   - ☐ Recommended you for an opportunity for which you were qualified
   - ☐ Took specific actions that would purposely limit your career, block promotion or tenure
   - ☐ Showed that he/she actually cares at all about you

3. Acknowledgment of expertise, accomplishment, and progress

   In the *last* academic year, a colleague and/or administrator in your department ...?

   - ☐ Provided encouragement or recognition
   - ☐ Shared positive comments with others about your work
   - ☐ Inquired about the status of your research/creative work
   - ☐ Talked to you about something you have written/created
   - ☐ Asked for your opinion on your area of expertise
   - ☐ Treated you and your work with respect and dignity
   - ☐ Made improper remarks or comments about you or your work
   - ☐ Was argumentative, condescending, and/or rude while discussing your area of research
   - ☐ Indicated that a discussion with you gave him/her a different perspective on the topic
   - ☐ Asked to read/see additional work you had done on a particular subject
   - ☐ Expressed negative comments about your work to others
   - ☐ Took you out to lunch to discuss your work
   - ☐ Nominated you for a professional award

4. Climate of the department or school/college (Check all that apply.)

   - ☐ I find the atmosphere or climate to be supportive.
   - ☐ I feel left out of things here.
   - ☐ People in this department take the time to get to know each other.
   - ☐ I find it difficult to work here because of its poor climate.
   - ☐ People in this department enjoy working together.
   - ☐ My opinions do not matter here.
   - ☐ I fit in with other faculty in this department.
   - ☐ People here are rude to each other.
   - ☐ Morale has improved over the past year.

5. Intention to stay in the department or school/college (Check all that apply.)

   - ☐ I intend to keep working here for at least the next three years.
   - ☐ If I had to do it all over again, I would still accept this position.
   - ☐ It would take a lot to get me to leave the department.
   - ☐ I would be happy to spend the rest of my career in this department.
   - ☐ If I could leave this department right now, I would.

indicated occurrence or nonoccurrence. If the action had occurred, they checked a box; if it had not, they left the box blank. For the general climate and intention to stay items, they were asked to check those statements that applied to them.

One of advantages of the dichotomous format was the ease with which respondents could identify whether an action had happened or not. In contrast, using a Likert scale requires that respondents indicate their agreement or satisfaction on a numerical scale of 1 to 4, 5, or 7. Making these fine-grained judgments takes much longer. In contrast, BBC respondents could quickly complete the 51-item survey; a pilot subject remarked that the survey really could be completed in 10 min or less.

Out of the 51 total survey items, 37 were positively phrased (e.g., "provided encouragement or recognition") and 14 were negatively phrased (e.g., "took specific actions that would purposely limit your career, block promotion or tenure"). To score the survey, each positive item checked received 1 point, and each negative item *not* checked received 1 point. Points were then summed and then divided by the total number of items in a particular category (e.g., career advisement, general climate, intention to stay). Category scores thus could range from 0 to 1. Appendix B shows an example of the scoring for the acknowledgment category. If a respondent checked five positive items and left two negative items blank, that person would receive 5 and 2 points, respectively, for 7 points divided by 13 total items, for a score on acknowledgment of .54.

Mean scores were calculated using a median-split approach. Instead of taking responses from the whole group, we used only responses from the bottom half of the group. What this means is that the mean score for a department reflected only those faculty whose responses were in the lower half. The median-split approach took into account *diversity considerations*. It gave women and minority faculty who have typically rated climate lower than the majority a stronger voice. At the same time, it protected their privacy. The median-split approach had other advantages. It reduced the likelihood of a polarized department, in which some faculty were very satisfied and some very dissatisfied, making the top group. Most important, it enabled, indeed propelled, change agents to focus on everyone in the department in line with the adage "A chain is only as strong as its weakest link."

Scores were calculated for each of the five categories for each respondent, and then an individual total score was calculated by summing the category scores. Unit scores were calculated by averaging the total scores for individuals in the unit, and a campus score was calculated by averaging the total scores of all respondents.

Coding of open-ended comments

Respondents' write-in comments were scored in terms of (a) the valence of the comments, whether positive, negative, or neutral; (b) whether they fell into the categories of climate, evaluation, career advisement, acknowledgment, or intention to remain; and (c) the parties responsible (e.g., chairs/deans, colleagues, upper administration/university). In addition, the following were scored: location, salary, resources, policies/communications, as well as topics (such as diversity and the survey itself). The second author and Carol Ann Winters, a graduate student, independently coded the comments using specific criteria and decision rules. Interrater reliability was calculated,[1] with disagreements discussed until consensus was reached.

Survey administration

Faculty received an e-mail from the provost identifying the aim of the study to retain quality faculty and asking for their input on the climate at the university. They were given a link to the survey, which was available online. Faculty were asked to consent to have any data collected from them used for research purposes; they were told that their participation was voluntary, and no colleague or administrator would know who chose to participate or not.

The university's survey group created the survey Web pages (located on university servers) and handled the data collection. Each respondent was given a randomly assigned numerical code, and survey responses were provided to the investigators using that code.

To help boost the response rate, incentives were offered: For each faculty member who completed the survey, the Office of Faculty Affairs contributed $5 to the graduate school's student travel fund, and the four units with the highest response rates received $250 for their enrichment funds. The provost twice sent reminder e-mails to faculty members who had not completed the survey. Feedback on unit response rates to the survey was provided to each administrator and the chancellor three times—twice during the 3-week data collection period and once after the deadline.

Results of the BBC

Response rates

In Year 1, the response rate was 55%, with 515 faculty out of 964 potential respondents completing the survey. In Year 2, 438 out of 1,000 potential respondents completed the survey for a 44% response rate. Any unit with a

---

[1]For overall climate, including all comments scored as positive, negative, and neutral, the interrater agreement score was 84%. The aspects of climate were at least 70%: evaluation (71%), career advisement (89%), and acknowledgment (71%). The interrater agreement scores for parties responsible were as follows: chair/deans (79%), colleagues (81%), and upper administration (77%). Some of the other topics ranged from 84% (survey) to highs of 90% (diversity), 94% (salary), and 96% (resources).

response rate below 33% was not considered representative, and data were not reported. In Years 1 and 2, 44 and 46 units, respectively, completed the survey.

Validation

In order to assess whether intention to stay was positively related to the climate and the three aspects of climate—evaluation, mentoring, and acknowledgment—we calculated Pearson correlation coefficients. Table 2 presents results for Years 1 and 2 aggregated by unit (department, school, or college).

Climate was significantly related to intention to stay in Years 1 and 2 (rs = .73 and .70, $p < .01$, respectively). When faculty in a given department reported that the climate was supportive, they were also very likely to say that they were going to stay in that department. The atmosphere of the unit accounted for 49% to 53% of the variance in faculty remaining at the university.

Similarly, the relationship between intention to stay and each of the three categories of climate was confirmed in both Years 1 and 2: evenhandedness of evaluation (r = .36, $p < .05$, and r = .59, $p < .01$, respectively), career advisement (r = .36, $p < .05$, and r = .62, $p < .01$), and acknowledgment of expertise, accomplishments, and progress (r = .65 and r = .67, $p < .01$).

It is interesting that given the emphasis on positive consequences in the behavioral approach, almost half of the variance in faculty's intention to stay, with correlations at or above .65, was accounted for by the acknowledgment of their expertise, accomplishments, and progress. Those likely to stay felt that their colleagues and/or administrators had not (a) expressed negative comments about their work to others; (b) made improper remarks or comments about them or their work; or (c) been argumentative, condescending, and/or rude while discussing their research area. Those likely to stay felt that their colleagues and/or administrators had (a) inquired about the status of their research/creative work, (b) talked to them about something they had written/created, (c) asked for their opinion on their area of expertise, and (d) taken them out to lunch to discuss their work.

Table 2. Correlations Between Intention to Stay and Climate and Its Categories.

OVERALL ASPECT and category	Year 1	Year 2
CLIMATE	.73**	.70**
Evaluation	.36*	.59**
Career advisement	.36*	.62[a]**
Acknowledgment	.65**	.67**

Note. Data are aggregated by respondent unit. Unless otherwise specified, N = 44 units for Year 1, and N = 46 units for Year 2.
[a]N = 44.
*$p < .05$. **$p < .01$.

Campus findings

The campus-wide results for the first administration of the survey ranged from a low of .46 for career advisement to a high of .63 for the climate of the unit (see Table 3). The results for intention to remain at the university and climate or atmosphere were moderately positive, with scores of .59 and .63, respectively. What this meant was that the respondents answered affirmatively on approximately six of 10 positive items (e.g., "I would be happy to spend the rest of my career in this department") and left blank approximately six of 10 negatively worded items (e.g., "If I could leave this department right now, I would"). For the aspects of climate—evenhandedness of evaluation, career advisement, and acknowledgment—the scores were .54, .46, and .54, respectively. In a similar fashion, the scores indicated that participants checked the box for positively worded items and left the negatively worded items blank about half the time.

Demographics

As shown in Table 3, the majority of the sample was male (69.4%, n = 497) and White American (85.5%, n = 442). In terms of rank, 26.7% of the faculty who responded were assistant professors, 28.8% associate, and 44.4% full (n = 493). (Different sample sizes are noted because not all of the 515 respondents provided demographic information.)

Table 3 lists the responses of faculty by gender and ethnicity for the campus. To protect the confidentiality of the women and minority faculty, no data are reported by gender or race for any specific academic unit; demographic groupings are presented only for the campus as a whole.

Only results highlighting significant differences are discussed. Male (M = .66) and majority (M = .65) faculty were more likely to see the climate as supportive than female (M = .57) or minority (M = .58) faculty members.

Table 3. Mean Scores on Building Behaviorally Based Climate Survey for the Campus and by Demographic Characteristics of Respondents for Year 1.

OVERALL ASPECT and category	Campus (n = 515)	Assistant (n = 132)	Associate (n = 142)	Full (n = 219)	Female (n = 152)	Male (n = 345)	Minority[a] (n = 64)	Majority[b] (n = 378)
		Rank			Gender		Ethnicity	
CLIMATE	0.63	0.64	0.62	0.65	0.57**	0.66**	0.58*	0.65*
Evaluation	0.54	0.54	0.54	0.55	0.53	0.55	0.54	0.55
Career advisement	0.46[c]	0.55**	0.39**	0.34	0.43	0.40	0.42	0.41
Acknowledgment	0.54	0.57	0.52	0.55	0.52[†]	0.56[†]	0.50*	0.56*
INTENTION TO STAY	0.59	0.61	0.60	0.60	0.56[†]	0.62[†]	0.47**	0.64**

[a]Minority consists of American Indian (n = 3), Asian American (n = 32), Black/African American (n = 10), and Hispanic/Latino American (n = 19); other (n = 46) was not included in the analysis. [b]Majority is White American. [c]N = 296; responses from full professors were removed.
[†]$p < .10$. *$p < .05$. **$p < .01$.

Women were more likely to respond, "I feel left out of things here." Men were more likely to say, "I find the atmosphere or climate to be supportive."

In terms of staying, minority ($M = .47$) faculty members were less likely to report that they would remain at the university than majority ($M = .64$) faculty members. "If I could leave this department right now, I would" and "I find it difficult to work here because of its poor climate" were items more likely to be checked by those in minority groups. The majority faculty, in contrast, were more likely to note "I fit in with other faculty in this department" or "It would take a lot to get me to leave the department."

In sum, women and minority faculty were less likely than majority faculty to find the climate of the university inviting and stay in their positions.

Descriptive data from open-ended comments

Almost half of those who responded (47%) took the time to leave comments, with some containing 300 words or more. Appendix C gives verbatim examples across different categories and aspects and for different tones (i.e., positive, neutral, and negative). Appendix D lists percentages of comments received across the same categories, aspects, and tones.

Fully 80% of the comments discussed climate and/or one of its aspects, indicating the importance of the concept of atmosphere and milieu in faculty decisions to stay or leave the university. Some comments were uniformly positive:

> I came to [the university] ... and I am absolutely delighted with my decision. I have benefited greatly from the supportive environment in my department, college, and institute. I find this to be an environment that is highly conducive to productivity....

Others were predominantly negative, with the parties responsible for the poor climate identified as colleagues (19.8%), upper administration (15.6%), and chairs or deans (12.8%). For instance, "There is a lack of vision at the department and the college level. There is too much focus on status quo, bean-counting rather than quality and providing an atmosphere where faculty can take risks ..." Other statements were a blend:

> The ... [college] is a great place to work, despite abysmal salaries and poor facilities. It is because of the great students and colleagues I work with that I stay, to be blunt. I could make far better money elsewhere ...

Colleagues were often singled out as an extraordinary benefit (21.0%), and some highlighted the chair or dean (6.6%). For example,

> Given the difficult circumstances that the larger university community has faced over the past several years, I am encouraged to still feel that I have found a "home" and supportive colleagues. I credit my colleagues, and the leadership of our Dean for this supportive atmosphere.

Commenters were far more negative than positive when discussing the way in which they were appraised ("Annual merit criteria ... not spelled out for [the] department, i.e., how different things are weighted, etc....") and acknowledged ("I feel that my research expertise is supported and appreciated by a few members of my department, but not enough to make me feel extremely comfortable...."). However, comments about the quality of career advisement were more likely to be positive. For instance, "... great strides have been made to professionalize the department and treat junior faculty better. Our relatively new mentoring program has forged successful bonds."

Other factors that are less under the control of university administrators were also mentioned by commenters: location, salary, and resources. Some complained about the relatively high cost of living where the university is located. Others were thrilled: "My intention to stay is based primarily on how much I love living in [city]." References to salary compression were made with comparisons of the current pay scale to that of faculty in the same discipline at other institutions. Resources—their availability and distribution—as well as the lack of funding opportunities were frequently mentioned. For instance, "The [department] is not the problem; it is the state and the lack of funding for the University...."

Motivating change agents by providing feedback and recognition

To make it more likely that change agents would continue their actions, they were provided with information and acknowledged for their efforts.

Celebrating top-rated units
The provost sent out a campus-wide e-mail complimenting the top 13 scoring units. A chart listing the top units in terms of a combined climate-evaluation–advisement–acknowledgment–intention to stay score is shown in Figure 1. Each of these categories was drawn directly from the BBC survey.

Sharing detailed feedback with individual units
Unit members received comparison information about climate and three aspects of the climate for the unit and intention to stay (see Figure 2); means were provided for the unit and for the campus as a whole. For the sample department shown in Figure 2, the mean score for career advisement (.48) was better than the mean for the campus (.39), whereas the score for evaluation was lower (.40 vs. .47, respectively).

Each unit also received (in Year 1) a list of survey questions with which 60% of faculty agreed (marked the box) and disagreed (did not mark the box; see Figure 3). In one department, for example, 60% or more of the respondents marked the box for such items as "I intend to keep working here for at least the next three years," "People in this department take the time to get to

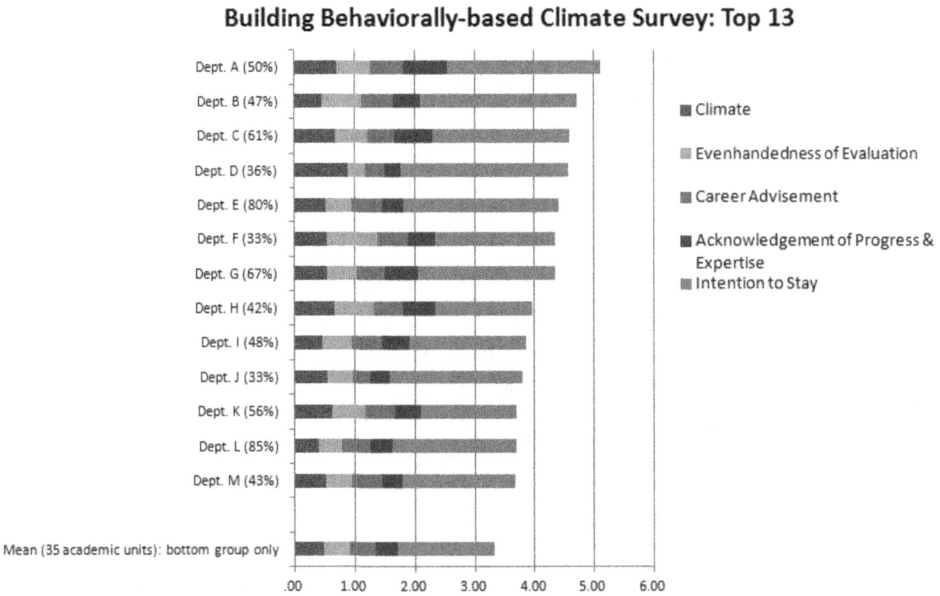

Building Behaviorally-based Climate Survey: Top 13

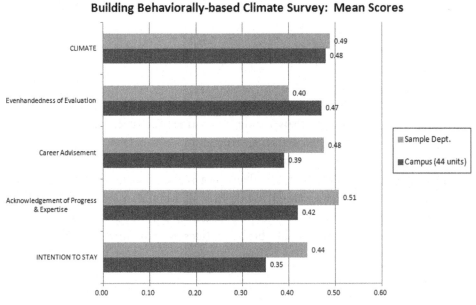

Figure 1. Mock chart distributed to the entire campus about top 13 scoring units on the Building Behaviorally Based Climate Survey. Numbers in parentheses indicate response rates. Overall scores were calculated by adding together the five dimensions; the intention to stay score was multiplied by 4 to bolster its weight. Only scores from the bottom half of the faculty in a given unit were used. Dept. = department.

Building Behaviorally-based Climate Survey: Mean Scores

Figure 2. Feedback chart for a sample unit showing comparisons between mean scores for the unit and for the campus as a whole. For both the unit and campus means, only scores from the bottom half of the faculty were used. Dept. = department.

units did was to schedule or arrange for refreshments at events in which faculty and students participated: weekly coffee klatches, faculty and student performances, monthly off-campus happy hours, and student/faculty performances. One unit head described a front office staff that celebrated every birth and every birthday with photos prominently posted of kindergarten graduations and high school gym meets.

In some cases, the camaraderie was helped by the physical environment (e.g., the lining up of offices with faculty in close proximity who kept their doors open). The fortuitous layout of the department was identified by one chair as contributing to the warmth of the atmosphere: a mailroom large enough to accommodate a large table at which faculty gathered to read their mail and eat their lunch together.

Some of the best practices were more subtle. One unit head preferred meeting face to face rather than relying on e-mail. A back-and-forth procedure for the scheduling of classes, an often-fraught process, was set up by one unit head. Faculty members were invited to come to the office where the entire schedule was posted on the blackboard. The unit head could sometimes manage to change the blackboard schedule, but if not, the unit head would try to negotiate changes with each faculty member to be accomplished the following semester.

Another example of engaging and listening was gleaned from three faculty members in one department who voluntarily spoke with us. Two faculty members stressed the sociability of the department. Another faculty member, a single parent, prized Saturday evenings together with her child. She mentioned her dilemma about the upcoming Saturday evening department party to the chair, who immediately encouraged her to stay home. The faculty member was awestruck at how she had been heard.

Workshop for upper-level administrators to implement best practices

During a workshop for the provost, deans, and associate deans, we identified best practices. A lively discussion occurred in connection with the Friday kudos. One dean mentioned how attempts to get information like that had failed. Another asked whether the dean had tried to solicit the information via e-mail. Another dean talked about how it helped to walk around and speak with faculty. The provost was pleased to see the way in which the deans were focusing on how to execute best practices within their own units.

Discussion

Benjamin Reese, Jr. of Duke University talks about "the challenge of having a diverse leadership and faculty" as being "one of the most important challenges for the academy" (Flaherty, 2015a, para. 39). This demonstration addresses the demanding and rarely researched objective of promoting the diversity of the workforce. The audacious goal was to help change agents—

Behaviorally-based Faculty Climate Survey:
Acknowledgement Category for a Given Department

60% or more of those who responded to the survey **disagreed** with the following:

- ☐ My opinions do not matter here.
- ☐ Indicated the same expectations for all faculty in the department regardless of rank.
- ☐ Took specific actions that would purposely limit your career or block promotion or tenure.
- ☐ Expressed negative comments about your work to others.
- ☐ If I could leave this department right now, I would.

60% or more of those who responded to the survey **agreed** with the following:

- ☐ People in this department take the time to get to know each other.
- ☐ Described what information you should provide prior to the committee evaluation your work.
- ☐ Assessed your career goals or timetable.
- ☐ Inquired about the status of your research/ creative work.
- ☐ I intend to keep working here for at least the next three years.

Figure 3. Feedback for a sample unit, listing survey items with which at least 60% of the faculty in the unit agreed or disagreed.

know each other," and a colleague or administrator "inquired about the status of your research/creative work."

Furthering climate building by describing and cultivating best practices

Top-rated unit heads described best practices

To find out how change agents created a supportive environment, we interviewed the 13 top-rated unit heads. Few unit heads described what they did in terms of evaluating or career advising, but several identified what they did to acknowledge faculty. Friday kudos was how one department chair recognized faculty. Every Friday afternoon, the chair sent a list of fellow faculty who had been quoted in the press; nominated to be on a professional committee; or had books reissued or published, complete with photos of their jacket covers. Another department chair set up a committee responsible for nominating every single faculty person every year for an award at his or her alma mater or in his or her professional organization; a faculty member was charged with getting to know the faculty member to be nominated and writing the nomination.

In a study of tenure-track faculty, one of the most important predictors of intent to leave academia was a lack of a sense of community at one's institution (Barnes, Agago, & Coombs, 1998). What many of the top-ranking the provost, deans, and chairs of departments—to deliberately and directly change the climates of their schools and departments so as to entice faculty, particularly women and minority faculty, to stay. In a striking departure from the norm, the behavioral approach to organizational change was used to try and achieve this objective.

The behavioral approach is unique because it targets the change agents and then identifies what these key movers can do to result in improvements to the bottom line—in this case, faculty retention. It does not stop there though. It facilitates their motivation. To help propel the change agents, it uses the standard three-step process: (a) Specify what change agents should and could do, (b) measure what they do, and (c) provide them with positive consequences.

To specify what the change agents do, we identified three categories—evaluation, career advisement, and acknowledgment—based in part on the first author's operant leadership model (Komaki, 1998). Each category was then behaviorally defined, describing actions that key personnel do to ensure that faculty are well advised, well evaluated, and well acknowledged. Not only was it important to pinpoint what the dean should do (e.g., give personalized feedback), but it was critical that the dean could do the action (e.g., give personalized feedback vs. give an above-average raise). In short, deliberate and direct attempts were made via these actions to identify what change agents should and could do.

To measure these actions, we created the BBC survey (see Table 1). Similar to a behavior checklist, the BBC survey asked respondents to simply check whether a given action (e.g., asking about one's area of expertise) had occurred at least once during the year. Listing the behaviors and using the dichotomous yes/no format enabled the gathering of behaviorally specific information about change agents' actions from hundreds of faculty members on campus, substantially expanding the population typically sampled in many *Journal of Organizational Behavior Management* articles and enabling behaviorally based organizational change endeavors.

The validation of the BBC survey set it apart. It is one thing to say that these behaviors are recommended. It is quite another thing to say that these behaviors are backed up with empirical evidence. Not once but twice it was found that a positive relationship exists between faculty's intention to stay and the behaviors in the categories of evaluation ($r = .36$, $p < .05$, and $r = .59$, $p < .01$, for Years 1 and 2, respectively), career advisement ($r = .36$, $p < .05$, and $r = .62$, $p < .01$, respectively), and acknowledgment ($r = .65$ and $r = .67$, $p < .01$, respectively). What this means is that faculty who were guided well, appraised well, and recognized well were more likely to say that they would be remaining at the university (e.g., "I would be happy to spend the rest of my career in this department"). These figures lent credibility to the behaviors in the BBC survey that no amount of jawboning could provide.

Feedback was provided, enabled by the BBC survey. Unit members were provided with charts showing how the unit compared with the campus average; units members also learned in Year 1 about statements with which 60% or more of the faculty agreed or disagreed. The provost sent a chart identifying the top 13 units along with the names of their leaders and a congratulatory note to all faculty and change agents.

Providing recognition for the quality of climate was no small feat in what is essentially a feedback desert. More than one department chair and dean talked about how years had gone by with nary a word, up or down, about their performance. The BBC survey helped to make visible the invisible, enabling feedback about an elusive concept: climate. The ephemeral nature of climate helps to explain why higher-ups did not know, not being privy to the nuanced day-to-day exchanges among faculty, administrators, and fellow faculty. To illustrate what happens when climate is such an elusive concept, consider this: The provost and faculty affairs and diversity persons were asked in the first year to identify which units were in the top 13. One person guessed that many of the units with bountiful grants and contracts would probably be in the top group; several suggested what turned out to be mid-ranking units. In the end, only four of the top 13 were correctly identified; no one predicted that a small humanities department was in the top group.

Even the unit heads themselves did not know their status. The chair of the small humanities department was stunned, thrilled, and honored to find out that the members of the department had rated their evaluation, career advisement, and acknowledgment so highly. The ephemeral nature of climate attests to the importance of gathering information about it on an instrument like the BBC survey.

Never before had anyone dared to dream that the behavioral approach could be used to foster the climate, which would in turn increase retention, which would ultimately promote diversity in the workforce. Bolstering the climate is not a new idea; experts extol the idea of shoring up the climate in order to keep incumbent women and minorities in the workforce. What is new is a constructive way in which to take the ephemeral but rarely behaviorally defined concept of a supportive climate and facilitate it. Traditionally climate has been measured using statements such as "I feel left out of things" or "The climate is supportive here." Not clear is what the change agent can do in order to foster a supportive climate or to assist in helping faculty feel less left out of things.

What the BBC survey did was to specify what change agents can do. It identified actions that they can take. Specificity, however, is not sufficient. The actions must be under the control of the change agents. Giving personalized feedback is specific, but so is giving higher than average raises. Focusing on actions that change agents can do fosters their motivation. A department chair was pleased with the way in which faculty had rated evaluation and career advisement but disappointed with their ratings of acknowledgment. When viewing the actions that could be taken to shore up recognition, the chair blurted out, "Oh, I could do that"—take a colleague to lunch, read Ramona's work.

It is far too easy to judge the efforts of change agents by the number hired and the number who leave. As the open-ended comments show, faculty stay (or leave) for a variety of reasons, some of which change agents have little if any control over—the location and budget allocation of the university, trailing spouse dissatisfaction, offers from universities with higher ranking departments. What the BBC survey does is to provide evidence of what change agents did to foster the climate so that presidents, chancellors, and provosts, when allocating scarce resources, can consider and daresay give preference to units with more supportive climates.

Using the behavioral approach to promoting diversity entailed a unique set of challenges. Providing feedback by department, often an integral step, had to be adjusted. It was necessary to ensure that women and minority faculty, who have typically rated climate lower than the majority, had a compelling voice. At the same time, it was critical that members of these underrepresented groups not be singled out for their views. Instead of delivering feedback about an entire department, we used a median-split procedure, presenting responses from only the bottom half of the department. What this procedure did was to accentuate the voices of those who had less favorable views about the climate while at the same time protecting the privacy of women and minority faculty in a given department. Another rationale for using this median-split procedure is exemplified in the adage "A chain is only as strong as its weakest link." By focusing on the bottom half, change agents would be encouraged to craft nurturing milieus for each and every member of the department.

In sum, this demonstration shows how change agents now have the means to behaviorally define the often nebulous concept of a supportive climate and to use the BBC survey to assess and motivate department chairs and deans to create warm and inviting atmospheres throughout the organization, which would in turn entice all employees to stay and diversify the workforce.

Acknowledgments

Many thanks to the president, chancellors, provosts, diversity and faculty affairs personnel, deans, and department chairs of the foresighted university, which will remain unnamed, for their support and enthusiasm in our efforts to tackle this challenging yet critical issue. Thanks as well to our colleague Susan Taylor and to Baruch College students Carol Ann Winters and Dan Beckendorf.

References

Barnes, L. L., Agago, M. O., & Coombs, W. T. (1998). Effects of job-related stress on faculty intention to leave academia. *Research in Higher Education, 39*(4), 457–456. doi:10.1023/A:1018741404199

Brand, S., Felner, R., Shim, M., Seitsinger, A., & Dumas, T. (2003). Middle school improvement and reform: Development and validation of a school-level assessment of climate, cultural pluralism, and school safety. *Journal of Educational Psychology*, *95*, 570–588. doi:10.1037/0022-0663.95.3.570

Carr, J. Z., Schmidt, A. M., Ford, J. K., & DeShon, R. P. (2003). Climate perceptions matter: A meta-analytic path analysis relating molar climate, cognitive and affective states, and individual level work outcomes. *Journal of Applied Psychology*, *88*, 605–619. doi:10.1037/0021-9010.88.4.605

Claiborne, N., Auerbach, C., Zeitlin, W., & Lawrence, C. K. (2015). Climate factors related to intention to leave in administrators and clinical professionals. *Children and Youth Services Review*, *51*, 18–25. doi:10.1016/j.childyouth.2015.01.007

Daly, C. J., & Dee, J. R. (2006). Greener pastures: Faculty turnover intent in urban public universities. *Journal of Higher Education*, *77*(5), 776–803. doi:10.1353/jhe.2006.0040

Davidson, M. N., & Foster-Johnson, L. (n.d.). *Keeping color in corporate America: Factors that enhance and diminish organizational commitment for managers*. Retrieved from http://lever agingdifference.com/levdiff/wp-content/uploads/2009/12/LevDIff-Article-KeepingColor.pdf

Delobbe, N., & Vandenberghe, C. (2000). A four-dimensional model of organizational commitment among Belgian employees. *European Journal of Psychological Assessment*, *16*(2), 125–138. doi:10.1027//1015-5759.16.2.125

Dobbin, F., & Kalev, A. (2016, July-August). Why diversity programs fail. *Harvard Business Review*. Retrieved from https://hbr.org/2016/07/why-diversity-programs-fail

Flaherty, C. (2015a, April 6). *Does faculty diversity need targets?* Retrieved from the *Inside Higher Ed* website: https://www.insidehighered.com/news/2015/04/06/brown-u-declares-it-will-double-faculty-diversity-2025

Flaherty, C. (2015b, November 30). *Demanding 10 percent*. Retrieved from the *Inside Higher Ed* website: https://www.insidehighered.com/news/2015/11/30/student-activists-want-more-black-faculty-members-how-realistic-are-some-their-goals

Garner, B. R., & Hunter, B. D. (2013). Examining the temporal relationship between psychological climate, work attitude, and staff turnover. *Journal of Substance Abuse Treatment*, *44*, 193–200. doi:10.1016/j.jsat.2012.05.002

Griffeth, R. W., Hom, P. W., & Gaertner S. (2000). A meta-analysis of antecedents and correlates of employee turnover: Update, moderator tests, and research implications for the next millennium. *Journal of Management*, *26*(3), 463–488. doi:10.1177/014920630002600305

Guynn, J. (2015, August 4). *Black lawmakers call for more diversity in Silicon Valley*. Retrieved from the *USA Today* website: http://www.usatoday.com/story/tech/2015/08/03/congres sional-black-caucus-silicon-valley-tech-diversity/31080247/

Harkinson, J. (2015, June 30). *Jesse Jackson is taking on Silicon Valley's epic diversity problem*. Retrieved from the *Mother Jones* website: http://m.motherjones.com/politics/2015/05/tech-industry-diversity-jesse-jackson

Harvard. (2005, May). *Report of the Task Force on Women Faculty*. Retrieved from http://faculty.harvard.edu/sites/default/files/downloads/Women_Faculty_Full%20Report_0.pdf

Hemingway, M. A., & Smith, C. S. (1999). Organizational climate and occupational stressors as predictors of withdrawal behaviours and injuries in nurses. *Journal of Occupational and Organizational Psychology*, *72*, 285–299. doi:10.1348/096317999166680

Johnson, G. (2004). And the survey says... *Training*, *41*(3), 28–29.

Kane, T. (2011, January/February). *Why our best officers are leaving*. Retrieved from *The Atlantic* website: http://www.theatlantic.com/magazine/archive/2011/01/why-our-best-offi cers-are-leaving/308346/

Komaki, J. L. (1998). *Leadership from an operant perspective*. London, UK: Routledge.

Komaki, J. L. (2007). Daring to dream: Promoting social and economic justice at work. *Applied Psychology: International Review*, *56*, 624–662.

Komaki, J. L., Coombs, T., Redding, T. P., Jr., & Schepman, S. (2000). A rich and rigorous examination of applied behavior analysis research in the world of work. In C. L. Cooper &

I. T. Robertson (Eds.), *International review of industrial and organizational psychology 2000* (pp. 265–367). Sussex, UK: Wiley.

Lev-Ram, M. (2015, March 10). *Apple commits more than $50 million to diversity efforts.* Retrieved from the *Fortune* website: http://fortune.com/2015/03/10/apple-50-million-diversity/

Lindell, M. K., & Brandt, C. J. (2000). Climate quality and climate consensus as mediators of the relationship between organizational antecedents and outcomes. *Journal of Applied Psychology, 85,* 331–348. doi:10.1037/0021-9010.85.3.331

Mrig, A. (2015, November 23). *Improving diversity in higher education - Beyond the moral imperative.* Retrieved from the *Forbes* website: http://www.forbes.com/sites/amitmrig/2015/11/23/improving-diversity-in-higher-education-beyond-the-moral-imperative/

National Center for Education Statistics. (2015). *The condition of education 2015* (NCES 2015-144). Retrieved from http://nces.ed.gov/pubs2015/2015144.pdf

Paul, K. B., & Fenlason, K. J. (2014). Transforming a legacy culture at 3M: Teaching an elephant how to dance. In B. Schneider & K. M. Barbera (Eds.), *The Oxford handbook of organizational climate and culture* (pp. 569–583). Oxford, UK: Oxford University Press.

Piercy, F., Giddings, V., Allen, K., Dixon, B., Meszaros, P., & Joest, K. (2005). Improving campus climate to support faculty diversity and retention: A pilot program for new faculty. *Innovative Higher Education, 30*(1), 53–66. doi:10.1007/s10755-005-3297-z

Reid, L. D., & Radhakrishnan, P. (2003). Race matters: The relation between race and general campus climate. *Cultural Diversity & Ethnic Minority Psychology, 9,* 263–275. doi:10.1037/1099-9809.9.3.263

Ries, A., Wingard, D., Morgan, C., Farrell, E., Letter, S., & Reznik, V. (2009). Retention of junior faculty in academic medicine at the University of California, San Diego. *Academic Medicine, 84*(1), 37–41. doi:10.1097/ACM.0b013e3181901174

Sandberg, S. (2013). *Lean in: Women, work, and the will to lead.* New York, NY: Knopf.

Schneider, B., & Barbera, K. M. (Eds.). (2014). *The Oxford handbook of organizational climate and culture.* Oxford, UK: Oxford University Press.

Schneider, B., & Bowen, D. E. (1985). Employee and customer perceptions of service in banks: Replication and extension. *Journal of Applied Psychology, 70,* 423–433. doi:10.1037/0021-9010.70.3.423

Shanker, M. (2014). A study on organizational climate in relation to employees' intention to stay. *Journal of Psychosocial Research, 9*(2), 381–389.

Shim, M. (2010). Factors influencing child welfare employee's turnover: Focusing on organizational culture and climate. *Children and Youth Services Review, 32,* 847–856. doi:10.1016/j.childyouth.2010.02.004

Shim, M. (2014). Do organisational culture and climate really matter for employee turnover in child welfare agencies? *British Journal of Social Work, 44,* 542–558. doi:10.1093/bjsw/bcs162

Taylor, M. S., Tracy, K. B., Renard, M. K., Harrison, J. K., & Carroll, S. J. (1995). Due process in performance appraisal: A quasi-experiment in procedural justice. *Administrative Science Quarterly, 40,* 495–523. doi:10.2307/2393795

Thompson, C., & Walsh, G. A. (2015, November 15). *Missouri would likely be alone with 10 percent Black faculty.* Retrieved from the Associated Press website: http://bigstory.ap.org/article/f8c454994227483fae71796bcfd4b6fe/missouri-would-likely-be-alone-10-percent-black-faculty

U.S. Bureau of Labor Statistics. (2015, November). *Labor force characteristics by race and ethnicity, 2014* (BLS Reports No. 1057). Retrieved from http://www.bls.gov/opub/reports/cps/labor-force-characteristics-by-race-and-ethnicity-2014.pdf

Van Stelle, S. E., Vicars, S. M., Harr, V., Miguel, C. F., Koerber, J. L., Kazbour, R., & Austin, J. (2012). The publication history of the *Journal of Organizational Behavior Management*: An objective review and analysis: 1998–2009. *Journal of Organizational Behavior Management, 32*(2), 93–123. doi:10.1080/01608061.2012.675864

Waterfield, C. (2006, January). *The challenges of measuring client retention* (Practitioner Learning Program: Putting Client Assessment to Work Technical Note No. 2). Retrieved from http://files.givewell.org/files/MFI/The%20Challenges%20of%20Measuring%20Client%20Retention.pdf

Zeitlin, W., Augsberger, A., Auerbach, C., & McGowan, B. (2014). A mixed-methods study of the impact of organizational culture on workforce retention in child welfare. *Children and Youth Services Review, 38*, 36–43. doi:10.1016/j.childyouth.2014.01.004

Appendix A

Sources of Items in the Building Behaviorally Based Climate Survey

Source	Item
	CLIMATE
Reid & Radhakrishnan (2003)	"I find the atmosphere or climate to be supportive."
	"I feel left out of things here."
	"My opinions do not matter here."
	"I fit in with other faculty in this department."
Brand et al. (2003)	"People in this department take the time to get to know each other."
	"People in this department enjoy working together."
	"People here are rude to each other."
	INTENTION TO STAY
Taylor et al. (1995)	"I intend to keep working here for at least the next three years."
Reid & Radhakrishnan (2003)	"If I had to do it all over again, I would still accept this position."
Delobbe & Vandenberghe (2000)	"I would be happy to spend the rest of my career in this department."

Appendix B

Scoring of Positively and Negatively Phrased Items on the Building Behaviorally Based Climate Survey

Acknowledgment of performance item	Sample response	Points awarded
Positively phrased		
"Provided encouragement or recognition"	☒	1
"Shared positive comments with others about your work"	☒	1
"Inquired about the status of your research/creative work"	☐	0
"Talked to you about something you have written/created"	☐	0
"Asked for your opinion on your area of expertise"	☒	1
"Treated you and your work with respect and dignity"	☒	1
"Indicated … a discussion … gave … a different perspective on the topic"	☐	0
"Asked to read/see additional work you had done on a particular subject"	☒	1
"Took you out to lunch to discuss your work"	☐	0
"Nominated you for a professional award"	☐	0
Negatively phrased		
"Made improper remarks or comments about you or your work"	☒	0
"Was argumentative, condescending, and/or rude while discussing your area of research"	☐	1
"Expressed negative comments about your work to others"	☐	1

Note. Total score: five positive items checked and two negative items unchecked = 7 points out of 13 possible (7/13 = .54).

Appendix C

Examples of Comments Made on Building Behaviorally Based Climate Survey by Category

OVERALL ASPECT, category, and definition	Tone		
	Negative	Neutral	Positive
CLIMATE: atmosphere, environment, or conditions at the university or within the unit	"…At this point I feel that it almost doesn't matter what I do, it won't help, and that nothing short of litigation will ever change the atmosphere here for the better, meaning for the inclusion of people of color and their perspectives." "Problems with the climate in my department are related to a couple of abusive individuals whose demeanor and actions affect everyone else, including graduate students, staff, and faculty. The current tenure system makes it nearly impossible to insist that this abusive behavior cease."	"I think the department and college have flaws and challenges but these have not worsened over the last two years and may be getting better …" "The [department] is not the problem; it is the state and the lack of funding for the University, coupled with a tremendous range of student preparation and interest in their studies."	"I find the climate in the College … to be quite supportive. Given the difficult circumstances that the larger university community has faced over the past several years, I am encouraged to still feel that I have found a 'home' and supportive colleagues. I credit my colleagues, and the leadership of our Dean for this supportive atmosphere." "This department is one of the most collegial and open that I have ever been in. I appreciate the attitude that we may 'agree to disagree', but do not hate each other for differences of opinion." "The climate has improved dramatically since I have been here. Expectations are higher, but they are applied more evenly across the board …"
Evaluation: appraisal or what criteria used (student ratings)	"The department … has serious problems. The main aims—what it means to do high quality research and teaching—is not clear or in previous years at least not stated by 'those' who are running the department. This year there seems to be some changes.… This negative situation started with the previous chair who created a very unpleasant atmosphere. The feeling others and I have is that there are a few people who are political allies and that these people really direct the [department]. The department has an unpleasant political feel and nature … too much to express in a short survey. Evaluations were not done objectively. I think the current Chair wishes to change things, in principle but seems to need or want 'the approval of those few who seem to in charge …'"	None coded	

(Continued)

Appendix C
(Continued).

OVERALL ASPECT, category, and definition	Tone		
	Negative	Neutral	Positive
Career advisement: actions to promote/limit career, feedback or lack thereof, discussions on tenure/promotion process	"…I am continually advised to complete my book and feel continually inadequate about not having done so. It would have helped me to have had some intermediate goals articulated, as well as thoughtful strategies and motivations. Suggestions are given, to be sure, but they're always the same and always monolithic."	None coded	"… Great strides have been made to professionalize the department and treat junior faculty better. Our relatively new mentoring program has forged successful bonds among faculty. Our department is so much more productive than in the past. People get along relatively well and work well together …"
Acknowledgment: recognition or how recognition occurs within the unit (e.g, sharing work, requesting opinions, feeling valued/respected)	"… Faculty do not share what they are doing in their own research or inquire about others …"	"I believe that there is an open dialogue in the College … which is encouraged by the Dean …"	"…I would say that some of colleagues are supportive and others are not, that some discuss their work with each other and others do not … In my department, I find that there are key individuals who are extremely helpful and supportive … These individuals are vital to the positive aspects of my experience here."
Parties responsible:			
Colleagues	"While some of my colleagues are supportive and helpful, most seem to be highly competitive, motivated, independent workers who show little interest in what I do …"	None coded	"I have made a small number of very good friends and they are the number one reason working here is a positive experience. ____ [chair], ____, ____, and ____, all are top notch researchers and very supportive of my work and interested in seeing me succeed here."
Chairs/deans	"The lack of strong intellectual leadership in our department for the past six years has eroded the intellectual coherence and drive of the department …"	None coded	"We have a very supportive and thoughtful dean in ____. He is responsive and willing to listen."
Upper administration (e.g., provost, chancellor, university in general)	"…Furthermore, why has our President never once visited the people who make this university work, the faculty in general and specifically, in my department?"	None coded	None coded

(Continued)

309

Appendix C
(Continued).

OVERALL ASPECT, category, and definition	Tone		
	Negative	Neutral	Positive
Other (e.g., stakeholders)	"I have always found the climate within the University supportive and encouraging. The main frustration relates to negativity that gets directed at ___ from outside sources (e.g., legislature, reporters)."	None coded	"The College … is a great place to work, despite abysmal salaries and poor facilities. It is because of the great students and colleagues I work with that I stay, to be blunt. I could make far better money elsewhere …"
Other reasons for evaluation:			
Location: geographic location, political climate (e.g., liberal, conservative)	"Really the only downside to being at [University] is the current political climate vis-à-vis the University and the State of [state]."	None coded	"My intention to stay is based primarily on how much I love living in [city]. I am inadequately paid (even relative to the low pay scale for our department compared to other math departments), and our department is not given anywhere near sufficient resources or autonomy to do its job well."
Salary: pay, raises	"I have reservations staying at ___ long-term because my pay continues to remain low. I have consistently been ranked as 'exceeding' or 'far exceeding' expectations in my research and teaching, but my pay is over 14 percent below Association of American Universities averages for assistant professors in my field."	None coded	"I applied for other jobs last year. I stayed because I finally got a decent raise. I think it is sad that the only way to get a good raise is to threaten to leave."

(Continued)

Appendix C

(Continued).

OVERALL ASPECT, category, and definition	Tone		
	Negative	Neutral	Positive
Diversity issues: race, age, gender	"It is an extremely hostile not so much because of individuals, but because the complexity of minority issues is taboo. There are long-time colleagues who have acted as a group to qualify their collective advantages in ways that have blocked the depth of creating an open intellectual or mindful exchange of ideas. Over the years this has created personnel and other committees that fail to take into consideration the voices of all those who would dissent in opinion from them. Minorities are included when they are seen as a 'good fit' or being 'like' them in experience and value. As a result many of the [department] committees have failed to act independently or to speak up against wrongful, and discriminatory acts. Faculty is rewarded for silence rather than discussion. Situations are created by the hostile climate to make any dissenting voice not only invisible but collectively to attempt to destroy their validity as human beings and productive members of society ..."	"... It is difficult for me to comment on the climate in my department since I am actually rostered in two departments and the general climate in each differs quite a lot—I am far more ambivalent about one than the other. The department that I feel more positively about is itself going through some faculty turnover at this point and depending on the response to this going forward—especially as regards the retention of junior to mid-level faculty of color—my responses might be much more or less enthusiastic in a year."	"I think our college does an above average job of considering and supporting diversity in a variety of ways, but my sense of the campus is that there is much room for improvement on the climate issue and that this should be handled at some degree in [university public relations and in Freshman orientation—SENDING A STRONG MESSAGE PERSISTENTLY AND EARLY ON of inclusive tolerance and proper academic behavior—over and above 'anything goes' or 'free speech is good.'"

(Continued)

311

Appendix C

(Continued).

	Tone		
OVERALL ASPECT, category, and definition	Negative	Neutral	Positive
Resources: opportunities to pursue other than salary (e.g., graduate funding)	"There are 2 important factors that I find less than ideal at [university], and that would influence my intention to stay here for the long haul … space—there is very limited space in terms of lab space and grad student office space in my department, and we somehow manage to get along being civil, but not everybody is. This often makes it hard to function."	None coded	"I think morale is basically good because most of the faculty are funded and some who are not make valued contributions that earn respect …" "Departmental efforts in research and curricular development are having very noticeable effects on the departmental environment (physical and intellectual) and on student interest and satisfaction with our undergraduate and graduate programs. There have been measurable increases in extramural funding and student enrollment in all of our programs. Things are quite exciting at this time."
Policies/ communications: decisions applied campus wide by administrators	"The most significant barriers to staying here are financial: our salaries are significantly lower than our peers, and then stagnate unless we actively seek outside offers. We shouldn't be encouraged to look elsewhere for a job—the university should be actively trying to retain us. One shouldn't need an outside offer to prove that one's work is valuable …"	None coded	None coded
Media: information reported in the news	"…What can we do to correct the tabloid coverage of this institution in the local and national media, not to mention among various politicians in the statehouse? Things have degenerated to a deplorable degree, and I know that trend is not limited to ____."	None coded	None coded

(Continued)

Appendix C
(Continued).

OVERALL ASPECT, category, and definition	Tone		
	Negative	Neutral	Positive
Miscellaneous Survey: direct comments on Building Behaviorally Based Climate Survey (not surveys in general; e.g., content, format)	"The problem is more complex than your <u>survey can capture</u> ..."	"I was unable to answer several blocks of questions at all simply because some sentences were true for one level of [department]/college but untrue for the other ..."	None coded
Other	"... However, morale is in decline due to discouraging conditions—salaries and unfilled faculty positions—which seem to have no improvement in sight. We have recently (past two years) lost five excellent faculty members, three tenured and two tenure-track. So far, only two have been replaced with regular, tenure-track appointments. Four of these losses were women, two of them minorities. One of the losses was a retirement, the other four resigned to take a position elsewhere."	None coded	"Of three major ... departments (each of which is a world leader in various arena) in which I have participated, this is far and away the most integrated, supportive, healthy (socially) and innovative. The <u>research is world class; the teaching is highly valued</u> and, given the constraints of our institution, remarkably successful; the community is productive and supportive."

Note. Underlining indicates the portion of the comment to which the code was attributed.

Appendix D

Percentages of Comments Made on the Building Behaviorally Based Climate Survey by Coding Category and Tone

OVERALL ASPECT and category	All	Tone		
		Negative	Neutral	Positive
CLIMATE	60.1	40.7	2.9	30.9
Categories of climate				
Evaluation	12.8	11.5	0.0	2.5
Career advisement	7.0	2.9	0.0	4.5
Acknowledgment	18.1	16.9	0.4	2.9
Subtotal	79.8	60.5	3.3	37.4
Parties responsible				
Colleagues	32.9	19.8	0.0	21.0
Chairs/deans	18.1	12.8	0.0	6.6
Upper administration	15.6	15.6	0.0	0.0
Other (e.g., students)	4.5	3.7	0.0	0.8
None indicated	34.6	21.4	2.5	15.2
Other reasons for evaluation				
Location	15.2	11.9	0.0	4.9
Salary	14.4	14.4	0.0	0.4
Diversity issues	11.9	11.5	0.4	0.8
Resources	10.3	9.9	0.0	0.8
Policies/communications	6.6	6.6	0.0	0.0
Media	2.5	2.5	0.0	0.0
Newsworthy Event 1	3.7	3.7	0.0	0.0
Newsworthy Event 2	2.5	2.5	0.0	0.0
Other	19.8	18.9	0.0	1.6
Miscellaneous				
Survey	11.5	9.5	2.1	0.0
Other	9.1	2.5	5.8	0.8
Gave explicit reasons to				
Stay	7.0			
Leave	16.0			
Total		74.9	9.5	46.9

Note. Data represent the mean percentages of commenters who discussed each category or subcategory (number discussing category/number of commenters [*N* = 243]).

Index

Note: Page numbers in *italic* type refer to figures
Page numbers in **bold** type refer to tables